Photoshop®
Astronomy

R. Scott Ireland

Includes Full Res Tutorial Images on DVD

Willmann-Bell, Inc.
T.M.

P. O. Box 35025 • Richmond, VA 23235 • Toll free 1 (800) 825-7827 • (804) 320-7016 • Fax (804) 272-5920

www.willbell.com

Published by Willmann-Bell, Inc.
P.O. Box 35025, Richmond, Virginia 23235

Second Printing

Library of Congress Cataloging in Publication Data
Ireland, R. Scott.
 Photoshop astronomy / R/ Scott Ireland.
   p. cm.
 Includes index
 ISBN 0-943396-85-9
  1. Astronomy photography--Handbooks, mannuals, etc. 2. Adobe
Photoshop--Handbooks, manuals, etc. 3. Imaging systems in astronomy--Handbooks,
manuals, etc. 4. Image processing--Digital techniques--Handbooks, manuals, etc. I. Title.

QB121.I74 2005
522'.63--dc22

                                        2005055867

Photoshop® is a registered trade mark of Adobe Systems Incorporated

Acknowledgements

The concept for this book came about in February, 2003, based upon lectures I presented during a three-day image-processing workshop at the annual Winter Star Party in the Florida Keys. I must thank my publisher and editor, Perry Remaklus and his wife Patricia, who, after participating in that workshop, enthusiastically encouraged me to embark on this project. As Perry pointed out at the time, referring to the thirty-page notebook handed out to workshop attendees, "most of your work is already done — it's here in these pages — you just need to flesh out the details". Well, after more than two years, thousands of hours in front of a computer screen and almost three hundred (condensed) pages of text and illustrations, the details have finally been "fleshed out"!

My lovely wife Lou, who has suffered the fate of a "writer's widow" for a long time now, deserves my heartfelt thanks. Without her love, support and boundless positive energy, I simply could not have done it. This is as much a labor of her love as of mine.

Thanks are also due my family and friends for their cheerful understanding of my plight. There were many promised trips to New York to visit my daughter Colby that never took place. And my best pal for over two decades, Tippy D'Auria, has had to smoke far too many cigars alone the past couple of years. I have also missed the company of my friends at star parties, from which I have been too long absent.

Without the generous contribution of photographs, this book would not have been possible. I want to especially thank my long-time friends Dr. Don Parker, Tim Khan, Herm Perez, Tippy D'Auria, Dr. Lester Shalloway and Monte Wilson. I freely appropriated their images to use as both illustrations and tutorials for the book. Don Parker's guidance on planetary processing and sharpening was, needless to say, invaluable. I always enjoy and appreciate the excited phone calls from Don when he creates or otherwise discovers a new technique. His generosity and unbridled enthusiasm are infectious and have spurred me on to become a better image processor.

Enthusiasm and generosity have also been bestowed by friends who have acted as instructors in the image-processing workshops that I organize each year. In addition to the names already cited above, my thanks go out to Tony Hallas, Bill Williams and Jack Newton, all of whom volunteered their images and talents for the book, and Jim Burnell and Richard Berry for their ongoing participation, encouragement and support.

As I was nearing my writing deadline, it became apparent that I did not have the shots I needed for the chapter on composites and mosaics and that I would not have the time to go out and take them. My frantic plea for help was answered by Robert Reeves and Rick Krejci, who swiftly sent me their images, which were perfect for the tutorials in that chapter. Many, many thanks to Robert and Rick for bailing me out!

Thanks too must go to my "home base", the Southern Cross Astronomical Society (SCAS). SCAS has allowed me to organize the Winter Star Party image-processing workshops since the first one in 2003. That has given rise to this book, as well as speaking engagements around the country. I have had a wonderful time traveling and presenting these workshops, meeting old friends and making many new ones. I also want to thank my friends Sheldon Faworski, Terry Mann, Rick Weiss, Jim Burnell and Alan Traino for all of their help and support with my "traveling workshops".

And a special word of thanks to my friend Barbara Yager, whose tireless devotion to SCAS has made it the wonderful organization it is today. Barb is simply the best public relations person I have ever been fortunate enough to have looking out for me. Her flattering words in print have done much to foster my "astronomical career".

I also wish to express my appreciation to John Koester and David Black for their careful reading of the manuscript and their valuable comments.

Finally, I want to thank all of my workshop participants and the many others who have generously volunteered their time, images, and kind words, including Lucille and Fred Heinrich, Ashley Stevens, Mike Smith, Lou Cox, Les Bildy and Fred Durant.

R. Scott Ireland
Miami, Florida

Table of Content

Chapter 1
Introduction — The Digital Darkroom

The camera is an instrument that teaches people how to see without a camera.

Dorothea Lange

Today is the greatest time to be a photographer since the invention of photography in the early nineteenth century. Current technologies have elevated the photographic art to a potential level of communication and expression undreamed of a mere decade ago. And this accelerated progression of technology continues apace, with no end in sight. I am referring, of course, to the digitization of photography. Digital imaging has completely changed the way we create and use photographs by providing us with a powerful set of new tools, techniques and procedures.

Most of us remember the way things were before. Image capture was the primary focus of our attention. In order to optimize our images, or create photographic prints, we relied upon others — photo labs, color-correction specialists, even the local drug store photo kiosk. How many of you suffered through the process of trying to get a lab technician to print your astrophotographs without a dull green sky background? Some of you regained a measure of control over your images by setting up your own chemical darkrooms. But these were typically limited to black and white printing. Color darkrooms were a very complicated and expensive proposition. Those of us who bravely tried color printing were only marginally successful, although we did not realize it at the time! The very best Cibachrome prints I ever made would hit the trash can without a second thought, compared to the prints I routinely create today with my inkjet printer.

Digital imaging has democratized photography. Complete control of the process is now in the hands of the individual photographer. From conception to creation, optimization and ultimate output, the photographer is now King. He is, finally, the master of his domain.

But all of this power is not free. It comes with a cost. We are faced with a dizzying and constantly changing array of computer hardware, software, monitors, scanners, printers, profiles, papers, inks, calibration devices, digital cameras, CCD cameras and a plethora of related accessories. It is not the cost to acquire these things to which I refer, significant though that may be. Nor is it the equipment, time and expertise required to go out into the field and capture your nascent astrophotographs. I need not remind any of you of the extraordinary challenges involved in that process. Rather, the real cost of digital imaging lies in having to learn a new language.

I remember when I attended my first one-day class on how to use Photoshop. This was in 1997, although it now seems a lifetime ago. While making the long drive home after class, I was very excited. My mind was filled with the possibilities of what I had seen, and what this program could do for my photography. Over the subsequent weeks, as I began work on my own images at the computer, I had great difficulty implementing what I had "learned". I had diligently scribbled notes during the entire class (much to the detriment of my left wrist), and yet, when faced with the power and complexity of the program, I hardly knew where to begin. Photoshop was speaking a language, indeed it *was* a language; one that I had not yet learned.

Over the months and years that followed I gradually learned the language of digital image processing, and I continue to learn more each day. As with any language, one learns best by using it, not just by attending classes and reading, although these things are important too. In hindsight, what would have been most useful to me in the beginning would have been a primer that outlined, step by step, the things I needed to do in Photoshop to optimize my images and why I needed to do them — a primer that did not cut corners and assume that, as a beginner, I did not need to understand the big picture, complex techniques or why things worked. Such a text would have significantly shortened my learning curve.

I have written *Photoshop Astronomy* with this in mind. As you work through the tutorial examples in this book, you will find each Photoshop step described in great detail. A beginner should have no difficulties. But make no mistake; this is not a "Photoshop for Dummies". I have not excluded complex material or procedures. Quite to the contrary, I have included difficult, extended image-processing tasks along with the simpler ones. I trust there are many things within these pages that even seasoned digital imagers will find challenging and useful. I have also included explanations of *how* and *why* things work. "Do this" and "Do that" are not sufficient. It is my firm belief that to speak the language of image processing you must understand the meaning of its "words" and their syntax.

By combining detailed step-by-step descriptions along with explanations and theory, I may sometimes tax the reader's patience. There is also much repetition. If and when you find this tedious — good — it means you are learning.

Vision is a personal experience. Each of us creates our own visual abstraction of reality. Photographs are a further abstraction, and an expression of that individual vision. As the renowned depression era photo-journalist, Dorothea Lange, insightfully realized many years ago, this process flows in both directions. Photographs also teach us to see.

This is the real prize that digital image processing offers. By learning to speak this new and wonderful language, we learn new things about light, color and tone. Things we did not know before. We learn how to see in new ways.

It is my earnest hope that this book will, in some small measure, help you find your own eloquence with this new language, enabling you to create and share your unique visions of the world and the universe beyond.

The Digital Darkroom

The nexus of digital image processes is the digital darkroom. The term "darkroom" is of course a nod to the past. It is no longer necessary to work in the dark when processing photographs, as it was in the days of chemical darkroom work. Although the idea has merit when trying to evaluate color on your monitor screen! The digital darkroom consists of the computer hardware, software and peripheral devices necessary to process an image after capture and then convert the processed image into some form of usable output. In the following sections, we will examine some of the

options and considerations to keep in mind when setting up a digital darkroom, as well as the file structures, workflow and lexicon of digital image processing.

The Computer

In choosing a computer, the first consideration is which platform to use, Windows or Mac? Most graphic arts and imaging professionals still prefer to work in the Apple environment. In truth, either platform may be used today with equal success. It is more important to decide what software you will be using and which platform provides the best support. Many currently popular astronomical software packages are written only for the Windows environment. It is possible to run Windows programs on a Mac, so ultimately this decision is a personal one. All of the examples given in this book assume a Windows orientation, although the keystroke differences are minimal, and I trust that readers using a Mac may easily make the necessary translations. Photoshop works almost identically in both platforms. I apologize for any inconvenience this may cause, but it was necessary for the sake of brevity. I have enjoyed working with both Mac and Windows machines and equally recommend them both.

The rate of change in computer technology is so great that any specific recommendations given here will likely be superseded in a matter of months. But here are some of the things to keep in mind when choosing a machine:

- **Processor speed** More is better. Digital image file sizes continue to grow as technology improves, and a faster processor helps. The tradeoff is cost. As of this writing, Pentium 4 processors are available approaching a 4 GHz speed. When purchasing a new system, my advice is to get the fastest and most up-to-date processor you can afford. This will best support the most recent version of the operating system and other software (including Photoshop), and will extend the useful life of your machine.

- **RAM Memory** This is not the place to save a few dollars. Photoshop is a very RAM-hungry program, and this is a relatively inexpensive way to greatly speed up processing time. Today, I would recommend 1 GB of RAM as a minimum, maybe even 2 GB. There are so many opinions on this subject that you could spend the better part of a week scouring the World Wide Web (web) and still walk away confused. Here's a broad rule of thumb: multiply the file size of the largest images you generally work with by 4, add 500 MB and round up to determine the amount of RAM to buy. For example, if

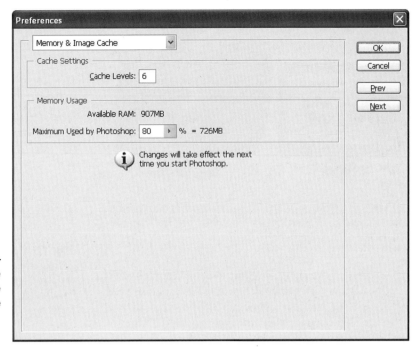

Fig. 1.1 The *Edit|Preferences|Memory & Image Cache* dialog box. With Photoshop, the more RAM you have available the better. Be sure to set Photoshop's Memory Usage in the range of 70% to 80%, but not higher.

you regularly work with medium format scans of 300 MB, get at least 2 GB (300 MB X 4 = 1.2 GB + 500 MB = 1.7 GB). Don't get less than 1 GB under any circumstances. Photoshop file sizes increase rapidly when using multiple layers and alpha channels, no matter what you start with. You must also tell Photoshop how much RAM it can use. This is handled in the *Edit| Preferences|Memory & Image Cache* menu (**Figure 1.1**). Set the "Maximum Used by Photoshop" parameter in the range of 70% to 80%. In general, it is best not to exceed 80%, since this can slow down your operating system considerably or even cause it to crash. If your budget demands some tradeoffs, get a slightly less-fast processor and more RAM.

- **Internal Hard Drives** Saving digital files "offline" on CDs or DVDs sounds good in theory, and indeed it is an essential part of an archival workflow (discussed later), but accessing your files only in this way will quickly become tedious. Set up your computer with a large internal hard drive; better yet, set it up with two large drives. Use one drive for your images and the other for everything else. Or, devote areas of both drives to storing images and employ a portion of the second drive to back up your operating system and other important files. I would recommend drives that are at least 100 GB each and preferably larger. 7200 rpm (or faster) drives are recommended for video image capture when working with webcams and other video sources. Hard disk prices have come down so much that high ca-

pacity/high performance drives should not be an obstacle. Believe me, you can never have too much storage capacity when working with digital images.

- **Optical Drives** A recordable optical drive is a necessary ingredient in any system. Regardless of how much hard disk space you have, you will need to burn disks for offline storage. Invest in a recordable DVD device. These are now inexpensive and will record on various types of media, including many flavors of DVD, CD-R and CD-RW discs.

- **Video Cards** This is another subject area that can give you a large headache while researching what to get for your system. I believe the answer depends upon what other things you are planning to do with your computer. If you play a lot of computer games, or work with 3-D CADD modeling, then a fast card with plenty of on-board video memory is important. Photoshop, however, benefits far more from additional system RAM than additional on-board video memory. I have had good results for several years using Matrox video cards that support the use of dual monitors. With flat panel monitors now becoming standard, you gain a lot of screen real estate on your desk, and a dual monitor system may be something to consider. You can place your image on one screen and the Photoshop Toolbox and Palettes on the other, which can be a big time-saver.

- **Other Considerations** You will need plenty of USB connections, so a powered, external USB port expander (hub) is worthwhile for easy access. A Firewire (IEEE 1394) card is also useful to connect

Fig. 1.2 Eizo ColorEdge LCD flat panel monitors offer professional quality color reproduction, but they are not inexpensive. Models start at around $2,000.

certain peripheral devices, including digital video sources (DV camcorders, etc.). You will also need a SCSI card if you are using SCSI devices, such as a film scanner. Plan on buying a good UPS (uninterruptible power supply) to isolate your computer, monitor and other devices from power dropouts and surges.

Monitors

The monitor is arguably the most important component of the digital darkroom. You will spend a great deal of time viewing your images on it, and it must be able to provide a clear, sharp, accurate and consistent rendition in order to assure quality results. Until recently, CRT (cathode ray tube) monitors were the only choice for professional quality color-calibrated results. While many professionals still adhere to this philosophy, the relentless progress of technology will eventually force all of us to change to LCD (liquid crystal diode) flat panel displays. It is becoming increasingly difficult to find a selection of CRT monitors as more and more manufacturers discontinue their production in favor of the more popular LCD displays. As with RAM memory, your monitor is not the place to cut corners to meet your budget, especially if you decide on an LCD display. You will be better served acquiring a slower processor and putting the extra dollars into a high quality monitor. Unfortunately, they are not cheap. Professional-quality LCD monitors, such as the Eizo ColorEdge series (**Figure 1.2**), are designed for highly accurate color reproduction and calibration, but carry a price tag near $2,000 for the 19-inch LCD monitor, and $3,000 for the 21-inch version. Top-of-the-line models exceed $6,000. Also popular among many graphics professionals is the Apple Cinema Display (usable with either

Fig. 1.3 The Sony Artisan Color Reference System is a professional caliber, self-calibrating CRT system (it comes with its own calibration puck) that retailed for around $1,700. Unfortunately, Sony discontinued production, so it may be hard to find.

Apple or Windows machines), which is an LCD flat panel monitor currently available in 20-, 23- and 30-inch versions. Prices on this monitor have come down. The 20-inch carries a current street price of around $800; the 23-inch is around $1,500, and the 30-inch is around $3,000. These are the two manufacturers that I would currently consider if I needed to replace my beloved Sony Artisan CRT with a new LCD monitor.

If you are "old school" and still prefer a CRT monitor for your color work (you will be in good company), some manufacturers currently popular among photographers include LaCie, Sony, Iiyama and Viewsonic. I am currently using the Sony Artisan Color Reference System (**Figure 1.3**), which is a self-calibrating monitor of very high quality that retailed for around $1,700. However, it was recently discontinued by Sony, so its availability is problematic. The LaCie Electron Blue IV 22-inch is a good bargain at a current street price of under $800 (**Figure 1.4**) and well worth your consideration. This is probably the monitor I would choose if I were to buy another CRT.

I strongly suggest that you spend time researching these and other monitors for yourself before making a selection. There are many online resources and reviews available and the technology changes rapidly, so it is important to stay current.

Color Calibration Systems

The best monitor in the world won't do you much good if it is not calibrated. We will discuss color manage-

Fig. 1.4 The LaCie Electron Blue is a quality 22-inch CRT monitor that can be had at a street price of under $800.

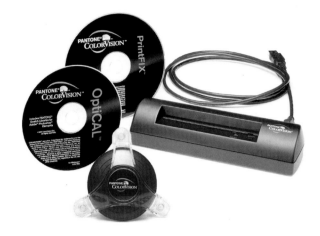

Fig. 1.5 A monitor calibration system is an essential part of any digital darkroom. The ColorVision Spyder (colorimeter) and OptiCal software calibration system is shown here. ColorVision also offers the PrintFIX system for printer color calibration.

ment, calibration and profiles in the next chapter, but in the meantime, add a monitor calibration system to your shopping list, and put it near the top. It is possible to use the Adobe Gamma utility (described in detail in the next chapter) to adjust your monitor "by eye", and this is better than no calibration, but any system that relies on you and your eyes to make color decisions is prone to error. You need a hardware/software system that does not have a brain that interprets what it sees.

A monitor calibration system includes a hardware device (either a colorimeter or spectrophotometer) commonly called a "puck" or "spyder". This is positioned directly over your display and feeds back information to your computer through a USB connection. The other part of the system is the calibration software. The software runs through a series of graytones and color swatches that are optically read by the puck. At the end of this process, a digital file known as a monitor profile is generated and is used to correct your monitor display and make the proper color management translations between your display and all of the other elements of your digital darkroom.

The good news is that there are now several excellent monitor calibration systems available at very reasonable prices, and they are easy to use. Colorimeter systems in the $200 to $350 range include the ColorVision Spyder 2 (**Figure 1.5**), MonacoEZColor with OPTIX-XR and Profile Mechanic — Monitor by Digital Light and Color (the same company that makes Picture Window Pro image-processing software). More so-

phisticated spectrophotometer systems include the popular Gretag Macbeth Eye One Photo, a system highly regarded among professionals for several years now, Colorvision's Spectro Suite and the new X-Rite Pulse Color Elite System. If only the best will do, these systems will set you back between $1,000 and $1,300.

There are color calibration systems available for profiling printers, scanners, digital cameras (**Figure 1.6**) and other devices, including options to expand some of the systems listed above. Some of these are quite good, some aren't. This is an area that requires a considerable amount of investigation and a working knowledge of color management that is beyond the scope of this book to address. That said, to my mind, the holy grail of color management is having all of your fine art prints match your screen exactly, so that "what you see is what you get" is a true statement. As your digital darkroom knowledge progresses, I encourage you to learn as much as possible about color management and the many tools available to achieve a successful, color-managed workflow. (I highly recommend Bruce Fraser's book *Real World Color Management* as being worth your time investment). In the meantime, you must start somewhere and the place to start is your monitor.

At the risk of being annoying, I am going to repeat myself — get a monitor calibration system. Do not trust the many web pages that show you grayscale step wedges and all kinds of color pictures and tell you to adjust your monitor until this or that is this way or that way. You can't color calibrate on the cheap; you need

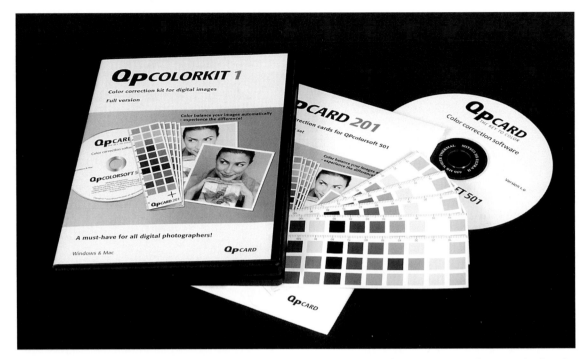

Fig. 1.6 Color calibration systems are also available for digital cameras. Color swatches photographed under different light sources are read by the software to generate individual profiles.

the right equipment. Then, when the next guy complains that your images look too dark or too magenta, you'll know that it's his problem, not yours.

External Drives

As I've already said, you cannot have too much storage capacity when working with digital image files. It is now possible to obtain large capacity (200 GB +) external drives that are small, easy to use and inexpensive (about $1.00 per gigabyte as of this writing). USB or Firewire connections are used to attach these drives to your computer, and they appear in your file manager as another disk drive. Files are copied back and forth easily, just like using your internal hard drives. When the external disk fills up, just plug in a new one. You may also protect your image archive by removing these drives from the computer (just un-plug it) to avoid power surges, viruses and any other ills that might befall your system. You will quickly come to appreciate the time saved by having your image archive online, and not having to find and load a CD or DVD every time you want to access your files.

Other Hardware Accessories

Most of you are already using, or soon will be using, digital cameras. Invest in a card reader ($20 to $30) that handles the type of compact flash cards or microdrives

Fig. 1.7 Compact flash and microdrive card readers are an inexpensive and very useful accessory. Models are available that read a variety of formats. They plug into a USB connection, and when a card is inserted, it appears as a drive on your system.

that you use with your cameras (**Figure 1.7**). While it is possible to transfer files directly from the camera, this is not recommended. It is a better (and easier) workflow procedure to take the card out of the camera and access it with the card reader. When a card is inserted, it will appear as a drive in your file manager,

Fig. 1.8 A graphics tablet expands the capability of many Photoshop tools, and offers a level of precision and control not available when using only a mouse. A Wacom 6 x 8 inch tablet is shown in use here.

and files may be drag-and-drop copied, just like any other drive. But remember to reformat your cards in the camera.

As your Photoshop skills grow, a wonderful accessory that you may want to consider is a graphics tablet. Also called digitizing tablets or drawing tablets, these devices consist of two parts — a flat drawing surface and a specialized digital "pen" that works on the drawing surface. Basically, the system is a mouse on steroids. As you move the pen around just above the tablet, the mouse cursor moves around the image. When you apply the pen to the surface, functions are performed similar to using a normal mouse, but with a lot more precision and a whole lot more options. The system is pressure-sensitive — adjusting the pen pressure as you draw continuously varies things like brush size, transparency, "ink" flow and color. Several Photoshop tools are designed to interact with a graphics tablet, providing new functionality not available any other way. The tablets also work in conjunction with a standard mouse; many of them provide a cordless mouse that works on the tablet surface. Wacom is the big name in graphics tablets (**Figure 1.8**). They offer sizes ranging from 4 x 5 inches up to 12 x 18 inches. Don't get the smallest size, go for the 6 x 8 model (or larger if you've got a lot of desk space you don't know what to do with). This will cost around $300. Once you've used a graphics tablet to create ultra-fine masks for a meteor composite, you will never want to be without one again.

Photo Printers and Accessories

While it is very exciting to create beautiful images on-screen, you will inevitably want to make prints for conventional display in an album or on the wall. The bad news is that print output technology is just as complicated in the digital domain as it is with chemical darkrooms, probably more so. The good news is that desktop photo inkjet printers have become so good and so cheap that it is possible to create archival, museum quality fine-art prints yourself. And this quality is possible without too much hardship. You will need to spend some time understanding the various ink and paper choices available for your printer; how to obtain or create (color management) profiles for your printer when using particular ink/paper sets, and how to set up Photoshop and your printer to play together nicely (color management again). We will cover the basics in the next chapter.

There are so many printer models to choose from, and they change almost daily, that it would be fruitless for me to make specific recommendations. You will not go astray if you stick with the major manufacturers like Epson and Hewlett-Packard. These companies basically invented desktop photo printing and have invested heavily and continuously in improving the technology. I have been using Epson photo printers since the first Epson Photo EX model came out in 1998. This machine was a milestone — for the first time large (11 x 17 inch) images could be printed that looked like real photographs. I am currently using an Epson Stylus Photo 2200 (cost around $650) to make prints up to 13 x 19 inches for display and sale. Epson is replacing this model with the recently announced Stylus Photo R2400 (estimated street price of $850). These types of printers employ pigment-based inks that provide archival longevity, producing color or black and white prints that can last between 75 and 200 years, depending upon the particular papers used and display conditions. There are many other less expensive models from Epson, Hewlett-Packard and other manufacturers that can produce lovely prints. I have seen beautiful small prints from printers costing under $100. I recommend that you do some online investigation when deciding on a printer. There are many resources and discussion groups that will give you a good idea of what is available and the pros and cons of the then-current models. Do not get too hung up on the manufacturers' "dpi" (dots-per-inch) specifications, since these numbers can be misleading. Ever-higher numbers are

R. Scott Ireland

used to try to out-market the other guy, but the highest numbers do not always equate to the best results. How ink droplets behave on paper, and how this relates to the pixels in your image is a lot more complicated than a simple dpi specification can describe.

Experimenting with different fine-art printing papers is a lot of fun. There are many great choices available. About the time you fall in love with one paper, you try another one and fall in love all over again. In addition to those offered by your printer manufacturer, other companies such as Somerset, Moab, Hahnemuhle, Arches, Illuminata, Crane, Lumijet, Lyson, Luminos, Kodak and Ilford, as well as many others, offer an incredible array of papers and surfaces (matte, glossy, semi-gloss) to choose from. If you wish, you may also try third-party inks designed to work with your specific printer. The creative possibilities are endless. Start with your manufacturer's inkset and papers, then try some other papers (make sure you get good profiles). I would not recommend trying other inksets until you become quite proficient.

Unequivocally, the most important accessory for your printer is a good set of color management profiles. Canned manufacturers' profiles must be designed to work with *all* of the printers that roll off the assembly line, not the specific one sitting on your desk. Custom profiling services are available to create profiles for your printer using specific ink/paper combinations. When you settle on the papers you like, you may want to consider this option. You may also purchase devices and software to create your own printer/paper/ink profiles, as I mentioned earlier. Some of these work better than others; since I am not using any of them at the moment, I cannot make a recommendation. Direct your inquiries (online or otherwise) to someone who has used a particular system before making a purchase.

Perhaps the ultimate printer accessory is a raster image processor (RIP). A RIP is a device (firmware, hardware or software) that acts as a sort of special translator between your printer and the rest of your digital darkroom. RIPs have traditionally been used to convert vector graphics, such as Postscript files, into high-resolution raster (bitmapped) images. But RIPs are now available that are designed specifically to optimize the quality of color and black and white prints from certain inkjet printers. A RIP takes over the function normally performed by the printer driver software that comes with the printer. Think of it this way — it's like dropping a Ferrari engine into your Chevy Cava-

lier. I am currently using ImagePrint, (ColorByte software) a software RIP that comes with a huge selection of profiles (available to users from ColorByte's online library) covering just about any ink/paper combination available. The "lite" version of this program (no Postscript capability) is available for several Epson desktop photo printers and retails for $495 (**Figure 1.9**). Other versions for larger format printers start at $1,000 and go up from there. There is some learning curve involved, and setup is not always easy, so consider this an "advanced user option". Other popular RIPs include StudioPrint by Ergosoft, which supports many different printer models and ColorBurst Pro for larger format printers. The differences when using a RIP can be dramatic, as these programs are designed to get the most out of a particular printer model. But it is also possible to get good results using standard printer drivers and very high-quality results using custom (purchased or self-created) profiles. Chromix (see Appendix) is one of the best-known companies that will, for a fee, create custom printer profiles for you remotely. Opinions about the efficacy of RIPs vary widely. In my experience, using a RIP has produced superior results. When you get to the point where you want to perfect the quality of your prints, then it's time to consider RIPs and custom profiles.

Finally, a standardized light source is invaluable for critical evaluation of print colors. An easy and relatively inexpensive solution is the Solux lamp. These are available in different styles and use bulbs of standard color temperatures with very high color rendering indexes (CRI). They are now in use at many museums throughout the world. I use a Solux with 4700 degree Kelvin bulbs to replicate a daylight color temperature when evaluating prints.

Film Scanners and Software

It seems as if film-based photography is headed toward becoming a fringe market, if not altogether obsolete. While I hope that film will still be with us for some time to come (I shoot both film and digital captures, depending upon the subject matter and format), we must all accept that one of the consequences of the digital revolution is the inevitable decline of this medium. Nevertheless, most of us have used film for years and have a large library of slides and negatives. So what do we do with all of these images?

An excellent solution is to incorporate them into your digital workflow. Film scanners are hardware de-

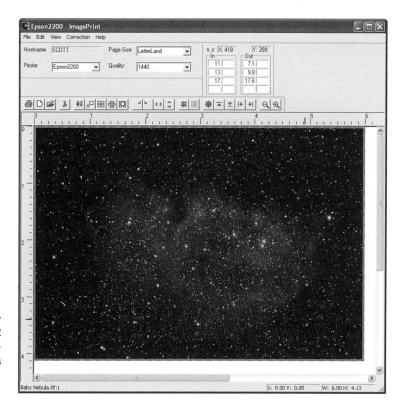

Fig. 1.9 Software raster image processors ("RIPs") are designed to get the best performance possible from desktop photo printers. Shown here is ColorByte's ImagePrint software.

vices designed specifically for this purpose. Traditionally, in order to obtain a high-quality scan of a negative or slide, it was necessary to send your image to a service bureau and have them scan it with a drum scanner. While this is still an option, at $30 or more per scan, it quickly becomes prohibitively expensive.

In 1993, when Nikon introduced its first Coolscan desktop film scanner, high-quality film scans became both portable and affordable. Prices for desktop film scanners have come down steadily over the years; it is now possible to purchase a quality 4000 dpi scanner that can handle both 35mm and medium format films for around $1,500. Quality 35mm scanners can be had for between $500 and $600. While drum scans are still the best available, desktop scanners can produce excellent results. With good software and a modicum of skill, the difference between what you can achieve with a desktop scanner and a professional drum scan is minimal. It only takes a handful of scans for a desktop film scanner to pay for itself, compared to the cost of drum scans.

There are several models for both 35mm and 35mm/medium format films currently available in the Nikon Coolscan series and the Microtek ArtixScan series of film scanners. I have used both Nikon and Polaroid scanners (the Polaroid Sprintscan 120 that I still use was re-released as the Microtek ArtixScan 120tf

when Polaroid went out of the business) and have gotten excellent results from both.

For more control over the process, I advise you to consider using third-party scanning software, rather than the manufacturer's software that comes with the scanner. Two of the best packages available are Silverfast, by LaserSoft Imaging (**Figure 1.10**); and VueScan, by Ed Hamrick (see Appendix). An important feature included as an option in both of these software packages (and few others) is the ability to use IT-8 calibration targets to produce a color management profile for your scanner. Be sure you include this option if you purchase either package. Both Silverfast and VueScan are available for a wide range of scanners, both current and discontinued models. Silverfast is pricey ($400 or more), while VueScan is quite a bargain ($90 for the "pro" version including IT-8 capability). Sometimes you can find Silverfast bundled free when you purchase a scanner, which is also quite a bargain. I use both packages, and highly recommend them.

Optical Storage Media and the Image Archive

We have already discussed internal and external hard disks, but are these alone sufficient for storing your image files? What happens if a hard disk fails? Or a virus infects your system? Or your computer gets hit with

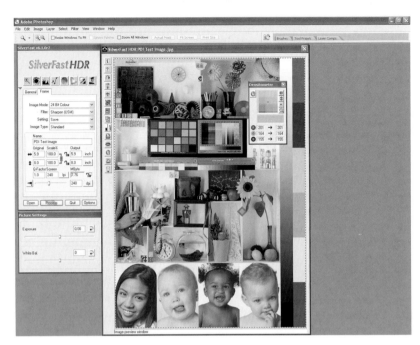

Fig. 1.10 Third-party film scanning software, such as Silverfast and VueScan offers precise control over the scanning process and produces high-quality scans.

lightning?

Like it or not, the task of storing and maintaining your digital image files requires a good bit of thought, time and resources. With film images, we have the comfort and security of knowing that the original slide or negative can always be re-scanned and processed again if necessary. But with digital captures, this is not the case. If the original file is lost, it's gone forever. More care must be taken to assure that duplicate copies are created and stored in a manner that minimizes this possibility. We need an effective strategy for archiving our images.

When film scans comprised the bulk of my digital image collection, my archiving strategy was as follows:

1. Burn a disc containing the original scans and processed image files using the best quality media available — at that time Kodak Gold CD-R discs (no longer available).

2. Duplicate the original disc using the same Kodak Gold CD-R media.

3. Catalog one of the duplicate discs on my main computer system using IMatch image management software and assign image thumbnails to category hierarchies (Astrophotos, Volcanoes, Birds, Landscapes, and so forth, with subcategories below these).

4. Record additional image information using a dBase format software package.

5. Store one CD-R at my workstation and the other at a different geographical location, to minimize the possibility of loss from fire or other calamity.

6. Place both sets of CD-R discs in air-conditioned dark storage using archival quality, acid-free sleeves, notebooks and slipcases.

7. Store the original negatives and slides in air-conditioned dark storage using archival quality, acid-free sleeves, notebooks and slipcases.

Using this system, I did not retain copies of image files on my hard disk, or on an external hard disk. Whenever I wanted to retrieve a particular image, I would locate the thumbnail in IMatch, and the information stored there would tell me which CD-R the image was on (I just number the disks sequentially as I create them "Photos #1", "Photos #2" and so forth). Then I would take the CD from my archival storage album and load the image from the computer's CD drive.

As the proportion of digital captures in my library has grown, I have modified these procedures slightly, as follows:

1. Steps 1 through 7 above are identical, except that I now use both CD-R and DVD-R discs; Mitsui (MAM-A) Gold CD-R; Delkin eFilm Archival Gold CD-R and Mitsui (MAM-A) DVD-R.

2. I add a third redundant copy by keeping all images online, either on the computer's internal hard disks or on Maxtor 300GB external hard disks.

3. I prepare additional IMatch databases as neces-

sary for each internal or external hard disk.

This may seem like a lot of work, and it is. Perhaps I am just an overcautious type of person, but I have not yet lost a single image file. I also carry two FlashTrax portable hard drive devices to make redundant copies of digital camera RAW files when I am shooting in the field. The only time I have one copy of an image is while shooting with the camera. When a compact flash card fills up, I immediately make two copies — one on each FlashTrax unit. That way, if one unit fails, I always have the other one as backup. Some people use laptop computers in the field to download their images and then burn CDs or DVDs for redundancy. At any rate, you must decide for yourself where your comfort zone is and how much trouble and expense you will accept to protect your images. Because I like to photograph transient things like volcanic eruptions, I am very careful, since I can never replicate those images.

I have been using the term *archival* and this warrants some explanation. Basically, it means nothing more than preserving your images for as long as possible, whether they exist as a file on disc, as a piece of film or as a print. Ironically, photographs in any form can be damaged by light (UV light in particular) and are best stored in the dark. Cold dark storage is even better. And there are a host of other things that can damage your images. Suffice it to say that image preservation is a complicated subject, but there are products available that are specifically designed with this goal in mind. For many years now, I have purchased almost all of my storage materials from Light Impressions (see Appendix). This company specializes in archival storage materials and offers a wide selection of products to serve almost any need. I use their library style notebooks with slipcases and specialized CD/DVD storage sleeves to store discs. The same style notebooks are used with other sleeves designed to handle negatives and slides. They also have a wonderful array of products for preparing, matting, framing, displaying and storing prints.

Another consideration is how long will a CD or DVD last? This is a complicated subject, and you will find many varying opinions and experiences. Some of these will shock you, such as those describing images lost after only two years. In general, it seems that CD-Rs are more reliable than CD-RWs, so it is advisable to use the former for archival storage. DVD formats always seem to be in a state of flux, and there are a lot of varying opinions about how long images burned on them will last. Nonetheless, you will end up using DVDs for some of your storage needs since they hold considerably more information than a CD. Some very large files may only be stored on disc this way (video files, for instance). And don't stick labels on your discs. Write on them only as necessary, and use acid-free pens designed specifically for this purpose.

Here's the bottom line. Whatever media you choose only has to last until the next generation of media comes along that replaces it. When that happens, you're going to have to re-copy your entire archive to the newer media anyway. While it's comforting to think that you have CDs that can last 300 years (Delkin Gold and MAM-A Gold CDs), the format will probably be obsolete in 10 years. What you *really* need is to know that your images will remain intact for 15 or 20 years, allowing plenty of time to get you to the next technology. That said, the way I gain this assurance is to just bite the bullet and use the absolute best media I can find. This costs more, but to me it is worth it. I buy CD-Rs that use a gold reflective layer (actual gold, not gold-colored), and special dyes that make them more reliable than traditional CD-Rs. The ones I am currently using are available from MAM-A (formerly Mitsui) and Delkin. I also use MAM-A DVD-Rs, as these are rated highest in quality along with Taiyo-Yuden discs. If these discs last 300 years, that's great, but I don't really care. I just need to know they will last 20 years, so I spend the money to get the comfort of a 10x + margin for error. As this book goes to press MAM-A has announced a gold layer DVD-R product for archival storage, which I would recommend.

Image Management (Cataloging) Software and Image Browsers

To my mind, cataloging software and browsers are two entirely different categories, although many software packages try to do both. I like to use a browser to quickly access and load images into Photoshop and other programs, without the necessity of calling up my entire image archive. Since version 7, Photoshop has come with a built-in file browser, and these browsers have improved with each new release. With the advent of Photoshop CS2 (version 9), Adobe has separated the browser into a standalone program called Bridge (**Figure 1.11**). Since this program is accessible separately from Photoshop, it fills all my needs for a file browser. It is feature-rich and seamlessly integrates with the Adobe Camera RAW utility. Double-clicking on a dig-

Fig. 1.11 File browsers have been integrated into Photoshop since version 7. Shown here is Adobe Bridge, a standalone browser bundled with Photoshop CS2. It is an excellent program that will serve most needs. A powerful feature is the seamless integration with digital camera RAW files. When a RAW file is opened with Bridge, the Adobe Camera RAW interface is activated, providing total control over RAW file conversions.

ital camera RAW file in Bridge opens Camera RAW, providing many sophisticated options for converting the RAW file into a bitmapped image. Adobe offers good online support by frequently updating the utility to handle newly released digital camera RAW formats.

There many other file viewers and browsers available, including the very popular freeware program IrfanView (see Appendix). Some commercially available programs that I have tried include ThumbsPlus, by Cerious Software and ACDSee (see Appendix). I still use ThumbsPlus occasionally, but ACDSee did not behave well on my machines. Frankly, with Adobe Bridge I have no need for any other file browser, but you should look at some of these programs for yourself and decide what features best suit your needs and workflow.

Image management software, also known as cataloging software, is essential in my opinion. You will quickly become inundated with digital images, and most of them will end up with unintelligible file names. No matter how carefully you think you have set up a naming and directory structure scheme, trust me, you will become lost in short order. It is highly desirable to have a system that allows you to create your own custom category structure, conveniently display that category structure, assign an image to multiple categories (date, subject matter, location, etc.), provide a thumbnail view of both the online and offline images with key information shown, and indicate where a particular file is located — pointing you to the specific internal or

external hard disk, CD or DVD that contains the image.

I am currently using IMatch (see Appendix) image management software, a powerful program and a bargain at $60 (**Figure 1.12**). Some of the other programs I would consider include Extensis Portfolio ($200) and Canto Cumulus ($100). Whatever package you choose, be sure that it supports the various file formats you regularly use, such as the RAW files from your digital camera(s). Most good software packages keep their programs up-to-date in this regard, and allow registered users to access these updates free of charge.

Digital Image File Formats

The following is a summary of the principal digital image file formats that you will be working with, along with my comments and suggestions:

TIFF ("Tagged Image File Format"; common file extension *.tif) The TIFF format has long been a universal standard bitmap format in the graphic arts and photo publishing industries. This makes it a good choice for archiving your images, since it is likely to stay around for quite awhile. The format is supported by just about all image-processing applications, and files can be written in RGB, CMYK, Lab, Indexed Color and Grayscale modes. Photoshop supports 8-bit and 16-bit TIFF files; Photoshop CS2 even has limited 32-bit support. TIFF is a lossless format, meaning that image detail and color information is not lost when a file is saved and re-saved. Always choose the "uncom-

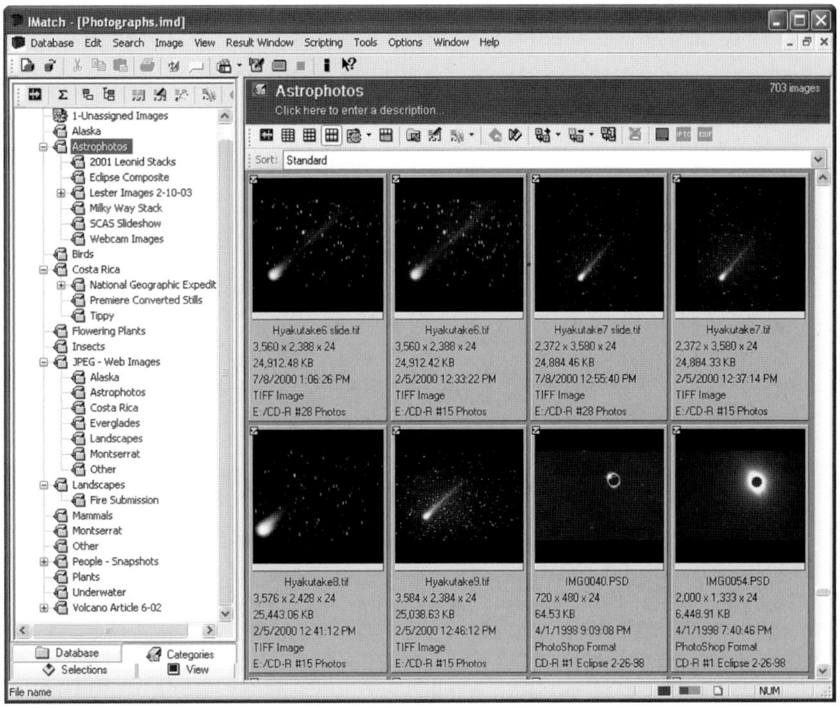

Fig. 1.12 Image management software is essential for managing large libraries of digital images. Both online and offline images are stored as thumbnails in the database along with the location of the image and additional information. The user may create a custom category hierarchy and assign images to multiple categories. The IMatch program is shown here.

pressed" option if given a choice when saving a TIFF file and tag the file with your editing color space. I recommend using TIFF as your main working file format, and also your archiving format, for all "flat" files (no Photoshop layers or alpha channels are saved). Save your archived file (TIFF or PSD) in its highest native resolution — in other words, do not alter the pixel dimensions of your original. If your CCD camera, film scanner or digital camera produces (at its highest resolution) an image with pixel dimensions of, say, 3000 x 2000 pixels, this is what you should archive — do not resample the image. Also, retain the file at its highest bit depth (16-bits), if possible. Then use this archived TIFF to create new files for specific output purposes. For example, when you need an image for web display, you may "downsample" the archived TIFF file to create a smaller JPEG file. To create a large print, "upsample" the archived TIFF for output to your printer.

A word of caution. Never apply overall unsharp masking to your archived TIFF or PSD files. When you resample an image (change its pixel dimensions), you eliminate the unsharp masking halos and soften the image. This means you will have to once again sharpen it, creating unnecessary additional processing that can degrade the image. Save your archived files unsharpened. When you open your unsharpened TIFF (or PSD) archive file and resize/resample it for a specific output, then apply unsharp masking as the final step in the process. An exception to this rule is sharpening planetary images, where complex sharpening procedures are an integral part of creating the basic image.

PSD ("Photoshop Document"; common file extension *.psd) This is the Photoshop format (lossless) and is one of only a few that supports most of Photoshop's features. What does this mean? It means that after you have invested a lot of hours working on an image and creating many layers, adjustment layers, masks and alpha channels, you will want to save a file that keeps all of these things intact, so that you may go back later and continue work where you left off. No matter how great you think the image looks, you will often find that you make more tweaks later. For complex files with many layers, masks and stored selections, save one version of the file in PSD format, then flatten it and save another version as a TIFF to use as your working file. Archive both and don't apply sharpening to either one!

JPEG ("Joint Photographic Experts Group"; common file extension *.jpg) JPEG is the ideal format to use when you need a small file size to display your image on a web page or send it by email. JPEG is a "lossy" format, meaning that something is lost when you save the file — it uses a compression algorithm to alter the image pixels. For this reason, JPEG is not recommended as an archival format. Use your archived TIFF or PSD file to create a JPEG when you need it.

R. Scott Ireland

Fig. 1.13 Create JPEG files from your archived original TIFF or PSD files when you need a smaller file size for the web or to send by email. Photoshop allows you to preview the effect of JPEG compression on the image, and shows the new file size. Never re-save JPEG files, since it is a "lossy" format.

JPEG is principally an 8-bit format. There are 16-bit JPEGs, but the idea is to compress the image to make a smaller file. Why would you want to start out with a 16-bit file that is twice the size of an 8-bit file? It doesn't make sense. You will first need to convert your 16-bit file to 8-bits in Photoshop (*Image|Mode|8 bits/ Channel*), then select *File| Save As* and choose the JPEG format. You will be presented with a screen that allows you to select the amount of compression (**Figure 1.13**). This dialog also shows you the new file size and allows you to preview the effect of compression in the main image window. Generally, it is advisable to choose at least a "Medium" to "High" setting. The higher the quality, the bigger the file, so you will have to decide where the best trade-off occurs. You must never re-save JPEG files, since they are compressed each time, creating more and more image degradation. JPEGs are a one-shot deal.

In some cases, your original files may be in the JPEG format, such as with certain digital cameras. This is a situation where you should retain and archive the original file (the JPEG), but also immediately re-save it as a TIFF and archive this file as well. Use the TIFF as your working file for image processing, so that you may re-save it with no loss of quality.

RAW Files (various file extensions, depending upon the camera manufacturer) Those of you using digital SLR cameras are likely familiar with the RAW file format. Typical file extensions are *crw for Canon and *.nef for Nikon. RAW files contain, for the most part, the uncompressed, unprocessed data captured by the camera's imaging sensor with little or no in-camera processing applied (hence the appellation "raw"). They are not even image files in the conventional sense — RAW files require conversion to a standard bitmapped format, such as TIFF or JPEG, using a conversion utility program like Adobe Camera RAW. RAW files are roughly analogous to the latent image that resides on a piece of exposed film. All of the image information is there, but the image is not visible until the film is developed, and different image renditions can be obtained depending upon how the film is processed. RAW files are lossless (mostly), and provide the maximum amount of image information and processing flexibility that a digital camera has to offer. RAW is therefore the format of choice and should be used whenever you want the best quality captures from your digital camera. Always convert RAW files into 16-bit images and save the RAW files in your archive, along with their converted TIFF and/or PSD counterparts.

DNG (Adobe "Digital Negative"; common file extension *.dng) A big potential problem with RAW files is obsolescence. RAW formats are proprietary — they vary by camera manufacturer and even camera model, and the specifications are not necessarily available to the public. You will encounter this problem as you use different types of software to view and process RAW files. It is often necessary to download updates to accommodate the RAW file specifications used in newer camera models, and it is problematic as to whether or not older camera formats will be supported indefinitely. In some cases, software will simply not read a particular RAW format, even today when RAW is relatively new. So make sure that any software or accessories that you intend to acquire are compatible with the RAW files from your particular camera. But what about accessing these files years from now? How do you know that you will still be able to read them with future software and operating systems? To their credit, Adobe (the company that produces Photoshop) has tried to address the problem of RAW obsolescence by creating the DNG ("digital negative") format. DNG provides an open public standard for use in archiving RAW data files. A freeware DNG Converter program is available on the Adobe website that will convert your RAW files to the DNG format (**Figure 1.14**). Hopefully, DNG, or something like it, will catch on and become a universal stan-

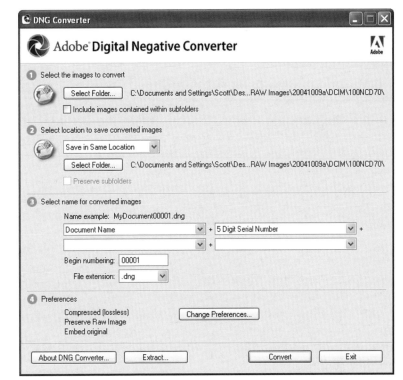

Fig. 1.14 The Adobe DNG ("digital negative") offers the promise of a "universal" RAW file format that will eliminate obsolescence concerns. Unfortunately, it is uncertain at this time whether or not it will be embraced as such by users and manufacturers. The safest bet is to save your RAW files in both their original form, and as a DNG. The freeware Adobe DNG Converter shown here provides an option to embed your original RAW file within the converted DNG file.

dard RAW format. Unfortunately, it is very new, and we have no assurance of that right now. The safest procedure today may be to save your files both in their native RAW format, and as a DNG. The DNG Converter program allows you to embed your original RAW file within the converted DNG file, which is very convenient, although the file sizes are larger.

FITS ("Flexible Image Transport System"; common file extension *.fit) FITS was developed in the 1970s as an archive and exchange medium for astronomical data and has become a standardized file format for transmission of scientific data, in addition to images. FITS is used as a native output format for CCD cameras. You should therefore consider these files as "originals" and archive them along with any converted and processed files that you create in Photoshop or other programs. There is an excellent freeware program available from NASA and the European Space Agency called Photoshop FITS Liberator (see Appendix). This Photoshop plug-in will automatically open when you load a FITS file into Photoshop. It offers a large preview window and histogram, and offers several sophisticated options for adjusting the gamma conversion (see **Chapter 2**) and compressing/stretching the image tonal range. I highly recommend it for working with FITS files in Photoshop.

BMP (Microsoft Windows Bitmap Format; common file extension *.bmp) BMP is a lossless format but it is limited to an 8-bit bit depth. For this reason, I do not recommend it as a primary archival format. However, you may encounter it when working with certain programs (such as video stacking programs). If you have a choice, save the original work in TIFF format. If not, archive the original BMP and make a TIFF working copy.

AVI ("AudioVideo Interleave"; common file extension *.avi) AVI is the most common format for handling video/audio information in a Microsoft Windows environment. With the advent of webcams, specialized astronomical video cameras, DV cameras and similar devices, video capture has become quite popular as a means to create astronomical images. The AVI files produced by these devices can be quite large, and may require the use of fast (7200 rpm +) hard drives in order to avoid dropped video frames. If you have been blessed with a night of good seeing that allows you to capture a high quality video sequence, then by all means you should archive the original AVI files. Yes, the files are huge (think gigabytes, not megabytes) and it is tempting to just retain the stacked, final image. But here again, as your image-processing skills and aesthetic sensibilities change over time, you may wish that you had the original video files for reprocessing. Use DVD-R discs to archive AVI files, and shoot in short sequences (60–90 seconds) to keep the file sizes manageable and minimize planet rotation issues.

Image-processing Workflow

The following workflow steps are just guidelines. They are not cast in stone. Each imaging task presents it own special challenges and may require different steps or a different order. Note too that the Chapters in this book are not arranged in the sequence shown below. The reasons for this are explained in the next section. With those caveats, here then is my suggested workflow.

1. **Begin with a calibrated set of images and perform an initial touch-up.** When working with digital captures, apply any dark, bias and flat-field frames to the images as a first step. Remove obvious scratches, dust motes and large artifacts that remain (this goes for all captures, including film scans). Re-align the color channels of planetary images to correct prismatic dispersion. Correct any elongated stars. Perform any other gross corrections to the image(s). Work on a copy of your image and keep your original captures intact. Work with 16-bit files whenever possible.

2. **Stack.** Stacking is the second line of defense against noise (after calibration) and should be performed early in the workflow. If the frames to be stacked contain dissimilar vignetting or luminance/color gradients, then it may be necessary to perform anti-vignetting and/or color correction on the individual frames before stacking. When stacking FITS files in Photoshop, it might be desirable to perform some gamma correction/ stretching beforehand, but take care to apply these adjustments uniformly to all frames. A tool like FITS Liberator is invaluable in this regard. Always stack images at a 16-bit bit depth, if possible. With webcam images, stacking will likely be your first step, using programs like Registax and K3CCDTools that are specialized for stacking hundreds of individual video frames.

3. **Balance uneven illumination ("Anti-Vignetting" or "A/V").** Apply A/V techniques to the stacked image sets (or individual frames, if necessary) to remove uneven field illumination, luminance gradients and color gradients.

4. **Set the black and white points.** Use Levels or Curves to set the numeric values for black and white, then define each of these points in the image. This will adjust overall contrast by stretching the image tonal range to fit the full tonal scale. The process also performs an initial color correction, and will remove most color casts.

5. **Build the LRGB.** If using separate luminance and color information, combine the high-resolution luminance stack with the underlying color stack to create an LRGB, LLRGB, HaRGB or one of the other luminance layer variants. Sometimes it may be easier to construct the LRGB before establishing the black and white points.

6. **Adjust color and local contrast.** Use Curves and other tools to make fine color corrections and selective color adjustments. Make any saturation adjustments (Hue/Saturation). Also use Curves to make local contrast adjustments to bring out details in a particular tonal range. Employ layering and masking techniques to selectively apply these adjustments.

7. **Apply creative adjustments and special techniques.** Apply any special techniques, such as creating star halos, star shaping, star shrinking, star softening and planetary sharpening techniques.

8. **Apply additional noise reduction.** Smooth background grain; eliminate fine dust spots and scratches, dark speckles and colored pixels; apply median filter techniques and "combine all" layers with Gaussian blur.

9. **Archive your work.** Save your source files (FITS, RAW, AVI, film scans) along with your working files (TIFF, PSD). Do not sharpen your archive files (except for planets). Embed color space and information in your working files; also embed any special processing information.

10. **Size your image for output.** Use your working file to resize or resample the image for printing, publication, Web display or other output.

11. **Apply unsharp masking.** Always apply overall sharpening as the final step after the working file has been resized/resampled for the intended output.

12. **Work in layers whenever possible.** Many of the above steps can be handled by incorporating all of them into a single Photoshop layer stack (the composite and mosaic tutorials are a good illustration of this principle). Develop your "3-D layer thinking" and work with layers rather than performing processing steps in a linear fashion. Streamline processing and perform non-destructive edits

whenever possible using layers. Remember that the most information you will ever have is in your original image capture. All subsequent image processing reduces this information — the more processing steps you apply, the more chance you have of degrading your image. Use the minimal amount of processing necessary to get the job done. Use layers in creative ways to aid this process by trying different layer arrangements and techniques.

How to Use this Book

The Chapters in this book are organized by major image-processing themes, and there is logic to the order of presentation. Some concepts, such as color theory, histograms, tonal scale, channels, layers and so forth, need to be understood in order to more effectively manage and appreciate the tasks presented in later Chapters. For this reason, I recommend that you proceed, in order, through the first four Chapters. From Chapter Five on, the order is not as critical, and you may wish to skip to particular topics of interest. Be aware, however, that there are many basic Photoshop skills that are introduced and then gradually expanded upon as the Chapters unfold. If you encounter difficulty with a particular concept or technique, it may behoove you to "back up" and cover the earlier material. Nevertheless, I have tried to be as complete as possible in describing each processing step and its underlying logic, so that the later Chapters can, for the most part, stand on their own. This necessarily creates a considerable amount of repetition, but as I stated earlier, I believe repetition is important to build technique and solidify understanding.

After the first two introductory Chapters, this book becomes a workbook. Everything is based upon specific tutorial exercises. I encourage you to embrace this concept and diligently work through each example at your computer. To learn Photoshop, you must work in Photoshop. It is just that simple. There is almost a *tactile* quality to the program. Layer masking is but one example. After you have created and worked with many masks, you will be stunned by how simple the process is. You will wonder how something so simple could seem so confusing when first approached. Reading alone, albeit appealing, is insufficient to master Photoshop. You must "get your hands dirty" by working through problems. That said, I have tried to provide sufficient illustrations to allow the reader to work through many of the exercises mentally, and use the book when a computer is not at hand. Such mental exercises will become easier as your Photoshop skills improve.

Finally, I must say a word about "pretty pictures". I believe in them! Photoshop, with all of its complexity, is just a tool. It is no different than the cameras, lenses, telescopes, computers, printers and other tools we use to craft images. It is a means to an end. The real purpose, and reward, is to elicit a gasp from the viewer who is stunned by the beauty and profundity of your image. Real mastery comes when the tools fall away to second nature and become transparent to the process of realizing your photographic vision.

R. Scott Ireland

Chapter 2
The Digital Environment and Color Management

Pixels, Bits and Color Channels

The digital photographs that we create are examples of bitmapped graphics, also known as raster graphics. The fundamental unit of a bitmapped image is the picture element, or pixel. A pixel is an irreducible "light dot" (a square) that is defined by a number in a digital image file. A bitmapped image is composed of a series of pixels arranged in a two-dimensional grid (the bitmap), typically described as so many pixels wide by so many pixels high (the pixel dimensions of the image). Bitmapped images are the principal type of images we work with in Photoshop and other image-processing programs. See **Figure 2.1**. They are commonly used for photographs because they are capable of representing very subtle gradations of tone and color.

The other principal type of digital image is the vector graphic. Rather than being defined by a matrix of pixels, a vector graphic is a sequence of mathematical statements that describes how lines, colors and shapes are constructed. These are the type of image files generally created when using graphics software programs such as Adobe Illustrator and CorelDraw.

Vector images are resolution independent; since they are defined by mathematical formulae, they may be scaled to any size without a loss of image quality or detail. Bitmapped images are resolution dependent; rescaling a fixed grid of pixels may result in a loss of image detail. We will discuss the problem of resizing bitmapped images for printing and Web display in **Chapter 11**

Each pixel in a bitmapped image is stored as a number in a digital file, and it takes a certain number of bits to store that number. The number of bits used to store information about each pixel in an image is known as the *bit depth*. A bit depth of 1 (a "1-bit image") would only display two levels of tonal information per pixel — "on" or "off" — 1 or 0 — black or white. An 8-bit image is capable of displaying 256 (2 to the 8th power) discrete tonal values — black, white

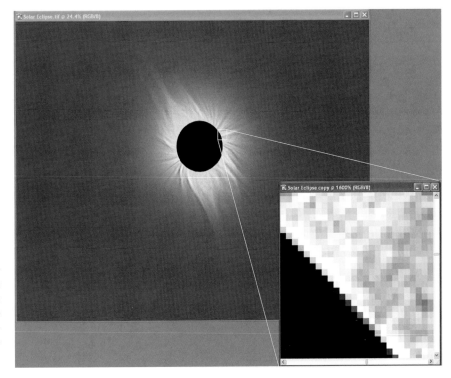

Fig. 2.1 Bitmapped images are composed of pixels — individual squares that contain the tonal information of an image. When resolution reaches 150 to 200 pixels-per-inch, the human eye perceives a smooth, continuous-tone image.

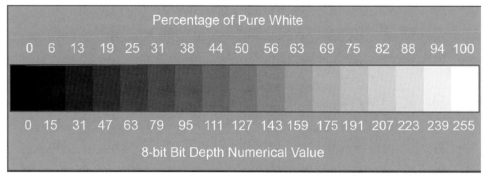

Fig. 2.2 A Grayscale, or Step-Wedge, displaying increments of tonal values in an 8-bit bit depth image. 0 is pure black. 255 is pure white. 127 is middle-gray.

and 254 shades of gray in between. A 16-bit image displays 65,536 grayscale levels (2 to the 16th power). The higher the bit depth, the more shades of gray that can be displayed. A 16-bit digital image file is twice as large as an 8-bit file. Even though the number of grayscale levels available in the 16-bit image grew exponentially when compared to the 8-bit image, the file size only doubled (thankfully!).

8-bit files are the current standard in the graphics and photo industries, although 16-bit files are likely to become the new standard soon. As astrophotographers, we will be interested in working with greater bit depth 16-bit files whenever possible.

Figure 2.2 is a series of gray tones, ranging from pure black to pure white in approximately 6% increments, or 17 steps. This type of graphic is commonly known as a *grayscale* or *step-wedge*, and is helpful when adjusting your computer monitor to the correct brightness and contrast settings. Notice the percentage amounts shown across the top; 0% representing pure black ranging through 100% representing pure white. The numbers below the step-wedge are the numerical values for each luminance level in an 8-bit bit depth file. The numbers range from 0 for pure black to 255 for pure white. A middle-toned gray value is 127, halfway between black and white (with allowance for fractional percentages and rounding). We could, of course, create a step-wedge that displays all of the luminance values available in an 8-bit image by creating 256 separate boxes from left to right, each box increasing by a numerical value of 1.

This step-wedge is included on the tutorial disk. Let's open that file, Grayscale Step-Wedge.tif, in Photoshop (*File|Open*). Make sure that Photoshop's Info Palette and Tools Palette are displayed (*Window|Info and Window|Tools*), and select the Eyedropper Tool

from the Tools Palette (keyboard shortcut — press the letter "I"). Now set the Info Palette Options (a drop-down menu is displayed when you click on the small triangle at the top-right of the Palette, **Figure 2.3**) to RGB Color Mode for the First Color Readout and Grayscale Mode for the Second Color Readout. Move the Eyedropper Tool across the different tonal values in the step-wedge and notice what happens in the Info Palette. The numbers across the bottom of the step-wedge are displayed next to the letters R, G and B (red, green and blue) at the top-left of the Info Palette. Each of the RGB values is the same for any given location on the step-wedge. A second window at the top-right of the Info Palette displays the letter "K" (for black) with percentages of black shown. This number subtracted from 100% gives the percentages of white displayed in the step-wedge.

Now open the Channels Palette (*Window|Channels*) **Figure 2.4**. In Photoshop, channels contain the information that makes up an image. Notice that there are four channels displayed — RGB, Red, Green and Blue. The RGB "channel" is for convenience only, it does not contain any image information. Clicking on it is just a convenient way to display all of the other color channels at once. The image information is contained in the individual Red, Green and Blue color channels. Click on each channel to select it (the selected channel will be highlighted in blue in the Channels Palette) or click on RGB to select them all. Notice that the step-wedge image does not change as you select the individual color channels. Each color channel contains the exact same information, which is why the image appears in shades of gray, and not in color. The Red, Green and Blue ("RGB") luminance values are the same for each pixel in the step-wedge image. A pixel that has a value of 19 in the blue channel also has a value of 19 in the red and green channels. A pixel that has a value of 255 in the green channel will also have a value of 255 in the blue and red chan-

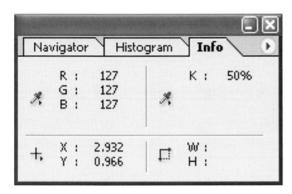

Fig. 2.3 Photoshop's Info Palette displays numerical information about an image. Here we have placed the Eyedropper Tool on the middle square of the step-wedge, halfway between black and white.

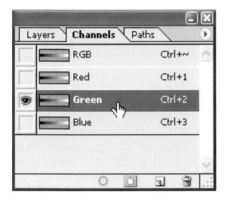

Fig. 2.4 Channels contain the image information. Color images are created by combining the different grayscale tonal values contained in each of the color channels. Here the green channel is selected in Photoshop's Channels Palette. The eye icon to the left indicates visibility of the channel.

nels, and so forth. In an 8-bit RGB color model (more about color models shortly), white (255) displays 100% of a color and black (0) displays 0% of a color. Gray values in between black and white display more or less of a color, depending upon the density of gray.

Color is created by combining the different grayscale values contained in each of the color channels in an image. In an 8-bit bit depth image, each color channel contains integer grayscale values ranging from 0 through 255. Therefore, an RGB image contains 8 bits of data for each of the red, green and blue color channels, or 24 bits of total information. Don't be confused by the terms "8-bit" and "24-bit", they are often used interchangeably and mean the same thing. A 24-bit image (8-bits per channel × 3 channels) is capable of displaying 16,777,216 different colors (2 to the 24th power). Similarly, a 16-bit bit depth image contains 16

bits of information for each of the red, green and blue channels, or 48 bits of total information. "16-bit" and "48-bit" are also terms that are used interchangeably. A 48-bit image (16-bits per channel × 3 channels) can display 2.8 times 10 to the 14th power different colors (2 to the 48th power), far more than the human eye-brain system can discern.

Let's look at an example. From the tutorial disk, open the file Color Channels.tif (*File|Open*). Make sure that the Info Palette and Channels Palette are displayed (*Window|Info* and *Window|Channels*). Notice that the image contains four boxes, each with a numbered point near the middle. These are Color Sampler points and the RGB values for each one are displayed in the Info Palette. The top left box displays as pure red with RGB pixel values of (255, 0, 0) — white in the red channel and black in both the green and blue channels. From the Channels Palette, click on each of the color channels in turn to confirm this. The top right box is pure green (0, 255, 0) — white in the green channel and black in both the red and blue channels. Similarly, the bottom left box is pure blue — 100% (white) blue channel with 0% (black) red and green channels, with an RGB value of (0, 0, 255). Again, click through the individual Color Channels. The bottom right box is pure black (0, 0, 0) — 0% luminosity in all color channels. If you move the cursor onto the background area surrounding the boxes you will see (at the top left of the Info Palette) that it is pure white (255, 255, 255).

Now for the fun part. Let's mix some channels together and see what happens. In the Channels Palette, click on the Red Channel to select it. Notice that an "eye" icon appears in a box at the left of the channel. This indicates that the channel is visible. Now click on the same box in the Green Channel to display the eye icon and make it visible along with the red channel. Be sure that the blue channel is not visible. The background turns to yellow. With all channels visible, the background is white (255, 255, 255). But when we only display red + green, and turn off blue, we get pure yellow (255, 255, 0). Now turn off the Visibility of the Green Channel and turn on the Blue Channel. The background changes to pure magenta (255, 0, 255); red + blue with no green. Now turn off the Visibility of the Red Channel and turn on the Green Channel again. The background changes to pure cyan (0, 255, 255); green + blue with no red. Which brings us to our next subject — color models.

R. Scott Ireland

Color Models

Color models and color spaces are mathematical representations of a human sensory experience. They specify how color information is created, visualized and presented. Ideally, they create a uniform system of color classification in order to establish consistency when dealing with color reproduction and color matching. Color models are frequently referred to as "color spaces", but since working color spaces are also usually called just "color spaces", I thought it best to maintain a distinction in terms. There are several different color models, but the following four are the ones you most need to be acquainted with.

RGB

As we have already seen, RGB is an acronym for Red, Green and Blue, the *additive primary colors*. Colors are created by adding together various proportions of red, green and blue light values. Notice that I said *light* values and not ink or pigment values. The RGB color model is closely associated with *transmissive* light source devices, such as computer monitors and television sets. It is the most commonly used color model in astronomical image processing; you will use it for virtually all your color image-processing tasks. The RGB model is device-dependent, meaning (among other things) that a particular color on your computer screen may not look the same on someone else's computer screen, even though the RGB numbers are the same.

CMYK

CMYK is an acronym for cyan, magenta, yellow and black. Cyan, magenta and yellow are the *subtractive primary colors*. Subtract red from white light and you are left with cyan (green + blue with no red). Subtract green from white and you are left with magenta (red + blue with no green). Subtracting blue from white creates yellow (red + green with no blue). Ring any bells? These are the exact colors we obtained by mixing R, G and B channels in our tutorial example. So, in reality CMY and RGB are related — they are just two sides of the same coin. Two RGB colors are added, or one is subtracted, to create each of the CMY colors. Cyan, magenta and yellow are also sometimes referred to as *secondary colors*.

The CMYK color model is closely associated with *reflective* light sources, such as the printed page and color photographic prints. The pigments in these objects absorb (e.g. subtract) certain wavelengths of white light and reflect the rest. So where does the K (black) come from? In the printing industry, a pure black ink is needed to bolster the cyan, magenta and yellow inks to give good blacks and grays. In theory, equal parts of cyan, magenta and yellow ink create pure black, but in reality you get a yucky dark brown color. Therefore the need for a separate black ink. By the way, your desktop inkjet printer works exactly the same way. Even though it is an RGB device (it is designed to receive RGB information), it actually prints with CMYK inks. The printer software does the conversion from RGB to CMYK.

CMYK is also a device-dependent color model — colors will vary depending upon the particular printer, ink and paper characteristics. You will utilize the CMYK color model from time-to-time to satisfy special image-processing requirements.

HSB

People generally find the HSB color model the most intuitive. This model defines values for Hue, Saturation and Brightness (or lightness). The hue is given as an angular measurement — a position around a color wheel. Saturation relates to intensity — 0% saturation is no color, or gray, 100% is the full, pure hue. Brightness (also lightness or luminosity) ranges from 0% (black) to 100% (white). The brightest, most intense color in the HSB model occurs at a 50% brightness level — halfway between white and black. You will likely not use the HSB color model very much, but it is important to understand the relationship between hue, saturation and luminosity.

Lab

Lab, also known as CIELab, is one of a group of device-independent color models. These models are based upon a structure of imaginary primary colors (X, Y and Z) that can be combined to produce all the colors visible to the human eye. CIE color models form the basis for all color management systems. Because of their device-independence, CIE models are used to translate and convert color data between different device color spaces.

Lab color consists of a lightness (luminance) channel (L) and two color range channels (a and b). The a channel represents colors ranging from green to magenta, and the b channel represents colors from blue to yellow.

You may have occasion to use the Lab color model. It can be useful to separate the color and luminance information in an image.

Grayscale

A grayscale image (commonly known as a "black and white" image) may be displayed in one of the color models. For instance, we have seen that when R, G and B values are the same, white, black or a shade of gray is represented in the RGB model. Grayscale images may also be displayed in Photoshop in grayscale mode (*Image\Mode\Grayscale*). A grayscale mode file is only about one-third the size of a grayscale RGB image, since it only has one channel instead of three.

Color Spaces and Gamuts

The human retina has three different types of color-sensitive cone cells. Each of these responds differently to light depending upon its frequency (color). Therefore, only three numerical values are required to specify any color. So you might think that a red, green and blue value in the RGB color model, for example, should be enough information to unambiguously identify a color. Unfortunately, in the real world, the light frequencies that are "red", "green" and "blue" have many different definitions. Computer monitors, television sets, photographic film, film scanners, film recorders, printers, digital cameras and a myriad of other color-related devices all render and define color in their own unique ways. They each have their own "color space." These device color spaces describe the colors that a given device is capable of rendering. They are device-dependent by definition. Device color spaces are subsets of color models — your computer monitor is an RGB device — color negative film is CMY material, and so forth.

A working color space, also known as an editing color space is device-independent. Working color spaces allow you to perform image processing in a standardized and consistent manner. They are gray-balanced, meaning that colors with equal amounts of red, green and blue will appear neutral gray. They are also perceptually uniform — a change in hue, saturation or luminosity will apply equally to all colors. Working color spaces are subsets of color models — there are RGB color spaces, CMYK color spaces and so on.

Gamut is the universe of colors that a color space or color model can represent. A color space (or model) that has a *wider gamut* than another color space means

that it is capable of displaying a greater range of hue, saturation and brightness. It will contain both more colors, and brighter, more saturated colors. A *narrower gamut* color space displays fewer colors. The Lab color model has a wider gamut than the RGB color model. The RGB color model has a wider gamut than the CMYK color model. The two RGB working color spaces that we will concern ourselves with are the *Adobe RGB (1998)* color space and the *sRGB* color space. sRGB has a narrower gamut than Adobe RGB (1998).

Adobe RGB (1998)

This will be your main RGB working color space. It is "universal" in that it is widely used and understood by professionals in the photographic, graphics design and publishing industries.

Adobe RGB (1998) is a medium to medium-large gamut color space. It is a reasonable choice for an everyday working color space, since it encompasses most of the colors that can be reproduced by today's printers and other output devices. While it has a narrower gamut than the range of human vision, Adobe RGB (1998) has a wider gamut than sRGB and CMYK. Lab color has a wider gamut than Adobe RGB (1998); however, it is difficult to do color corrections in the Lab model. Small changes to the a or b channels can rapidly create unwanted color shifts.

There are some very wide gamut color spaces, such as ProPhoto RGB. While a wide gamut working color space might seem to be the best choice, problems can arise. For example, if processing an 8-bit file (0 to 256 luminosity levels per channel) the greater number of colors in the wide gamut space are "spread" across the same numeric range as a narrower gamut space. This can result in posterization (banding and lack of smooth color transitions) in the image if several image-processing steps are applied. A very wide gamut color space may also contain imperceptible ("imaginary") colors that can give unintended results as the image is processed.

Adobe RGB (1998) is a good choice to use as your main working space, for archiving images and for creating prints.

sRGB

sRGB is the second principal working color space that you will use. It has a narrower color gamut than Adobe RGB (1998), so why do we want to use it? Because it represents the range of colors that is visible on a "typi-

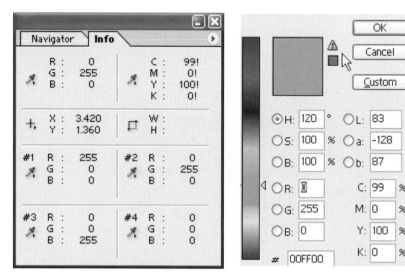

Fig. 2.5 Photoshop's Out-of-Gamut Warning symbols. Exclamation points adjacent to CMYK values (left) indicate colors that cannot be displayed in CMYK. The Color Picker dialog box (right) shows an exclamation point inside a triangle when a color is out-of-gamut. Clicking on it will render Photoshop's best guess as to what the closest "in-gamut" color will look like.

cal" (read inexpensive) computer monitor. The sRGB specification was developed by Hewlett-Packard and Microsoft so that color images would look good, or at least acceptable, on most computer monitors. If you are working in Adobe RGB (1998), and your image is destined for the Web, it makes sense to first convert it into the sRGB color space. Colors, saturation and brightness available in the Adobe RGB (1998) space cannot be fully represented in sRGB, so unless we instruct Photoshop to "remap" the colors to the narrower gamut space, our image may not look its best when viewed on the Web. As a general rule, you want to use a color space that is as large as practical, but that is also appropriate to the intended output destination, or use of the image.

Color Management

So, we have seen that color is a pretty complicated topic. Input devices (such as digital cameras and film scanners) and output devices (such as monitors, printers, film recorders and printing presses) each render color in their own unique ways — they each have their own color space. And although we have only looked at a couple of RGB working color spaces, there are a myriad of others, not to mention CMYK color spaces, and so on. How do we work our way through all of this in order to create the best color images and prints that we can? By using color management techniques and being aware of color space issues as we capture, save and work on our images.

Color management is the process and technology by which we calibrate the color rendered by our computer and all of its input and output devices. It ensures that color information is handled in a uniform and predictable way so that colors will look the same regardless of the hardware used to capture, view or print them. Let's begin this process by setting up Photoshop's color management settings.

Setting up Photoshop for Color Management

1. With Photoshop running, select *Edit|Color Settings* and check Advanced Mode. You should see a dialog box something like that shown in **Figure 2.6**.

2. Take a look at the Working Spaces section at the top of the dialog. I'll wager that your RGB working space is set to sRGB (most times that is the case). Click on the down-arrow next to RGB and examine the drop-down selection box that appears. Wow! There are a lot of RGB working color spaces that Photoshop offers up to us. Select Adobe RGB (1998) as your RGB working space.

3. Now look at the selection of CMYK color spaces. Choose U.S. Web Coated (SWOP) v2.

4. Set the Gray working space to Gray Gamma 2.2 if you are working in Windows on a PC, or Gray Gamma 1.8 if you are working on an Apple Mac-

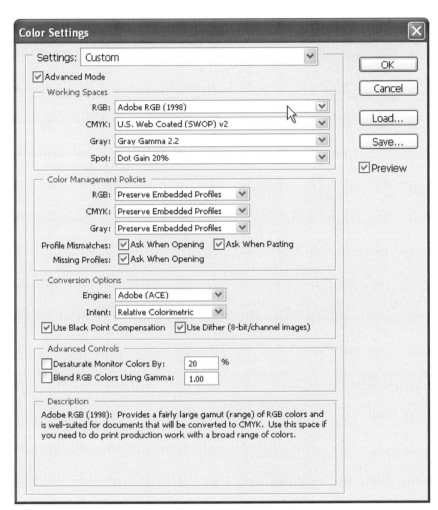

Fig. 2.6 Photoshop's Color Settings dialog (Edit|Color Settings). This is "command central" for color management with Photoshop. Creating a color-managed image-processing workflow starts here. Use the settings shown as your defaults.

intosh.

5. Set Spot to Dot Gain 20%.

6. Color Management Policies tell Photoshop what to do when it encounters a profile embedded within an image, or an image that has no profile embedded. Set these policies to Preserve Embedded Profiles for all working spaces, and check the Ask When Opening and Ask When Pasting boxes. This way, Photoshop will ask you what to do when it encounters a file with no profile, or one with an embedded profile that does not match your working color space.

7. Conversion Options tell Photoshop the methods to use when it translates color information from one color space to another. Set the Engine to Adobe (ACE). Set the Intent to Relative Colorimetric. You may want to use a Perceptual rendering intent for certain images, but for now, leave Relative Colorimetric as your default setting. Check the

boxes next to Use Black Point Compensation and Use Dither.

8. Leave the Advanced Controls boxes unchecked.

9. Click OK to accept your new default color settings. These settings will be retained whenever you open Photoshop unless you change them again.

Now we have Photoshop set up to work in Adobe RGB (1998), to alert us whenever an image file that we open was created in a different color space or has no color space information embedded, and what method to use when converting images from one color space to another. But, as we have seen, every input and output device in our digital darkroom has its own color space. What do we do about those? We use profiles for these devices whenever possible.

Profiles are computer files that describe a device's color space. These files will have the extensions *.icc ("International Color Consortium") or *.icm ("Im-

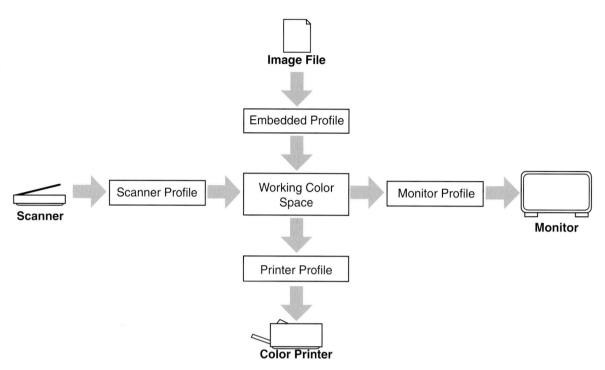

Fig. 2.7 ICC/ICM profiles define the color characteristics of input and output devices. Embedded image profiles tell us the color space in which the image was created.

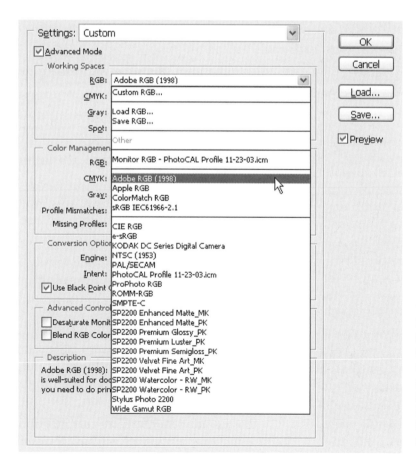

Fig. 2.8 The list of working RGB color spaces available to Photoshop in the author's system. Note that device-specific monitor (PhotoCAL) and printer (Stylus Photo 2200 and SP2200) color profiles are also listed. Photoshop offers maximum flexibility in allowing you to choose how to color-manage your images.

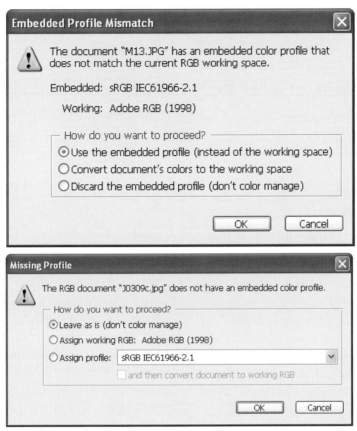

Fig. 2.9 In a color-managed workflow, it is important to keep track of the working color space used for an image by saving embedded profiles. Photoshop alerts us to missing and mis-matched profiles. We are given a choice as to how to manage color in these situations.

age Color Management"). Profiles are found in the following folders:

Windows 98, ME: C:\windows\system\color

Windows 2000: C:\winNT\system32\spool\drivers\color

Windows XP: C:\windows\system32\spool\drivers\color

Mac OSX: \Library\ColorSync\Profiles

Device profiles may be obtained from various sources. Monitor and printer profiles are typically provided by the manufacturer, and may reside somewhere on the installation disks received with these devices. The manufacturers' websites are also a good source for obtaining profiles. Other online resources are also available — a Web search should generate several options for obtaining custom profiles, either free or for a price. Finally, you may create your own profiles using specialized hardware devices (as discussed in **Chapter 1**), software such as Adobe Gamma, or even create a printer profile in Photoshop by using Curves and test prints.

Embedded profiles are saved with an image and describe the working color space that the image was created in or converted to. Whenever we open a file that has no embedded profile, or contains an embedded profile that does not match our working color space (since we have instructed Photoshop to alert us to these circumstances) we will be presented with a Missing Profile or Embedded Profile Mismatch dialog box, like the ones shown in **Figure 2.9**. Photoshop can display images on the screen in different color spaces at the same time, which is a very nice feature and can be quite useful when evaluating and preparing images for printing.

Colors are translated or "mapped" between different devices and color spaces using a color matching module, commonly known as a *color engine*. Apple systems employ the ColorSync engine, while Windows systems currently use ICM2.0. Gamut mapping algorithms, known as *rendering intents*, are employed when the source and destination color gamuts differ. Of the four rendering intents — Perceptual, Relative Colorimetric, Absolute Colorimetric and Saturation — we will use Relative Colorimetric and Perceptual for our work, since these are the ones primarily used for photographs. With Relative Colorimetric, only out-of-gamut colors in the source color space will be "remapped" to the destination color space. This is most useful when the source and destination gamuts do not differ widely. Perceptual remaps all colors in the source to the destination gamut. Perceptual may give better results when there are a lot of out-of-gamut colors in the source color space. We have already instructed Photoshop to employ Relative Colorimetric as our default rendering intent.

Calibrating Your Monitor

An essential ingredient for color management is a calibrated monitor. Without this, all hope of a color-managed workflow is lost, since the colors and tonalities that appear on your screen do not accurately represent the data in an image file. All of us have seen images on the Web that contain horrible color casts. Typically, the photographer is at a loss to explain why the image has a strong magenta or red cast when it looked so perfect on his screen. The answer is that his monitor was not calibrated. Without calibration, "What you see is *not* what you get."

There are basically three choices for monitor calibration. First, we can obtain and use a profile already created for the monitor, typically available from the manufacturer. Second, we can use the Adobe Gamma program (Apple Display Calibrator Assistant is the equivalent for Macs), a software utility provided free with Photoshop, and perform the calibration steps ourselves to create a monitor profile. Third, we may acquire third-party software and hardware specifically designed to calibrate and profile monitors.

Using a manufacturer's profile, while better than nothing, is the least preferable method. Every monitor has unique display characteristics. Two different units from the same manufacturer, and even the same model, will display differently. Furthermore, monitors change as they age. So a "canned" profile is, at best, a compromise based upon how an "average" monitor of that model type should behave.

Creating our own monitor profile is the best method. For those starting out in color management, Adobe Gamma offers an excellent way to begin, and it's free. The downside is that adjustments are made "by eye" on the screen and are therefore somewhat subjective. The ultimate is to use third-party hardware/software packages. Such packages are available from ColorVision, Gretag Macbeth, Monaco Systems and others as de-

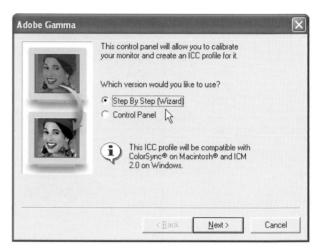

Fig. 2.10 Opening screen of the Adobe Gamma monitor profiling utility.

scribed in **Chapter 1**. These systems use a hardware device, known as a colorimeter (or spectrophotometer), that attaches to your monitor screen. This device "reads" luminosity and color swatches that are projected on the screen by the calibration software and generates a custom monitor profile. Profiles generated in this way are the most accurate, but these packages range in price from a few hundred to several thousand dollars.

Monitor Calibration Using Adobe Gamma

The following is a step-by-step procedure for calibrating your monitor using Adobe Gamma.

1. First, be sure that your monitor has been turned on for at least 30 minutes, so that it has had adequate time to warm up.

2. Lower any ambient light sources. Preferably, work in a darkened room.

3. Start the Adobe Gamma utility. This is found in the Windows Control Panel. You should see an opening screen that looks like **Figure 2.10**. Choose Step by Step (Wizard).

4. Load a profile which Adobe Gamma will use as a starting point. Use your manufacturer's profile if you have one. If not, sRGB will also work fine (**Figure 2.11**). Now type in a descriptive name that includes the date.

5. Adjust your monitor contrast to its maximum setting and then adjust the monitor's brightness control until the inner gray square is just visible inside the surrounding black square (**Figure 2.12**). It sometimes helps to defocus your eyes and/or squint when making this adjustment.

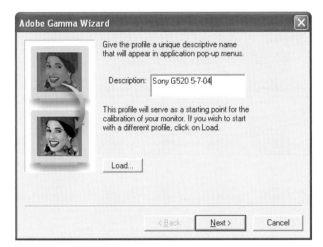

Fig. 2.11

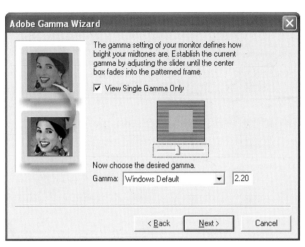

Fig. 2.14

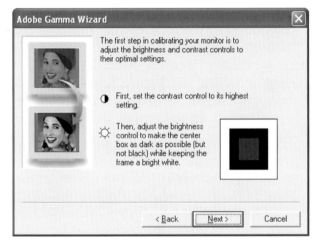

Fig. 2.12

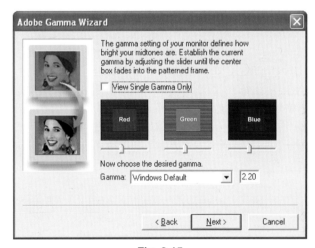

Fig. 2.15

Fig. 2.13

6. The next screen (**Figure 2.13**) will probably display Custom if you started with a manufacturer's profile. If so, leave this setting and go to the next

screen. If not, choose Trinitron if you have a Trinitron monitor or P22-EBU for everything else.

7. In the next screen (**Figure 2.14**) start by checking the View Single Gamma Only box. Adjust the slider until the inner square blends into the outer square. Then uncheck the View Single Gamma Only box to display red, green and blue adjustment windows (**Figure 2.15**). Individually adjust the red, green and blue sliders until the inner color squares match the outer color squares. You may find it helpful to slightly defocus your eyes and/or squint when making these adjustments. Set the Gamma to the Windows Default of 2.20 if using a Windows system; 1.80 if using a Macintosh. By the way, "gamma" is a number that reconciles the non-linear brightness response of your computer monitor with the numbers contained in an image file, according to the following formula: Monitor

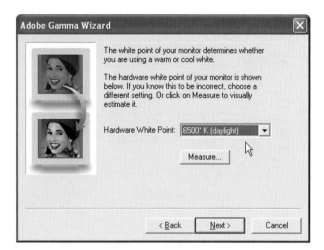

Fig. 2.16

Fig. 2.18

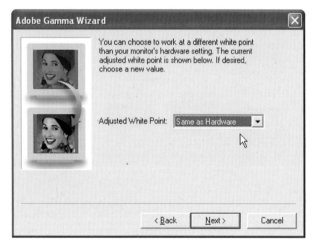

Fig. 2.17

luminance = pixel value^gamma (raised to the gamma power) + black level.

8. Next, using the settings buttons on your monitor, choose a White Point, or Color Temperature of 6500 degrees K (daylight). Then set the Adobe Gamma Hardware White Point to the same setting (**Figure 2.16**).

9. In the next screen (**Figure 2.17**), set the Adjusted White Point to Same as Hardware.

10. In the final screen (**Figure 2.18**), click on the Before and After buttons and examine the result on your screen. If you are satisfied with your profile click Finish and Save the profile with a descriptive name that includes the date. The new profile will be found, along with other color profiles, in the system folder listed earlier.

11. Now we will adjust our screen display settings to

use the profile we created as our default monitor profile. From the Windows desktop, right-click and select Properties. Then select the Settings tab in the Display Properties dialog box. This should look something like **Figure 2.19**. While in this window, be sure that you have set your Color quality to its highest setting, typically "Highest (32 bit)."

12. Next, click on the Advanced button and then the Color Management tab. You should see a dialog box similar to **Figure 2.20**. Click on the Add tab and add the profile you created with Adobe Gamma. Then set this as the default monitor profile. Your monitor is now calibrated.

Unfortunately, Photoshop has no direct way of indicating what monitor profile it is using. However, we can check this indirectly. Open Photoshop, and once again go to the Color Settings dialog box (*Edit\Color Settings*). Click on the drop-down box next to RGB Working Spaces. Among the profiles listed should be one called Monitor RGB and the monitor profile you created and set as your default should be shown here (see **Figure 2.21**). If it is, all is OK. Photoshop is using your profile for color management. Be sure that you don't reset your RGB working color space to your monitor profile. It should be set to Adobe RGB (1998). We are merely checking here to be sure that Photoshop knows your monitor display characteristics *vis a vis* the monitor profile.

A word of caution. If you use a third-party profile or profiling software and a colorimeter or spectrophotometer to profile your monitor, be careful not to "double-profile." Adobe Gamma Loader is installed when

Fig. 2.19 Left Windows Display Properties. Click on the Advanced tab to access Windows color management settings (See **Figure 2.20**).

Fig. 2.20 Right Windows Color Management. Add the profile you created with Adobe Gamma and set it as the default monitor profile. In the above instance, I am using a custom monitor profile created with the ColorVision monitor Spyder (colorimeter) and PhotoCAL software.

you install Photoshop and will run automatically from your Startup menu. Be sure to either remove it (In Windows XP, it is located in \Program Files\Common Files\Adobe\Calibration) or disable it from running at startup using msconfig.exe or a similar utility.

Printer Color Management and Softproofing

It is amazing to think about what has happened to photography in the past few years. Inkjet printing technology, available for a modest price and in a size that easily fits on your desk, has improved to the point where it has become the print making method of choice for many photographers. Unprecedented creative control over the final print is now in the hands of the photographer. To get predictable results from your photo inkjet printer, though, it must be profiled as part of your ICC color managed workflow.

We want to create fine prints that match what we see on our screen, but that goal is difficult. A monitor, just like looking at a slide on a light table, projects (transmits) light, while a print reflects light. Colors in a transmissive system will be far more vivid and have a range of brightness and saturation that is not obtainable with reflective media. A more realistic goal is to match what we see on our screen as closely as we can, being aware of these inherent limitations

Inkjet printers use CMKY inks, even though they are designed to receive RGB input. We know that CMYK has a much narrower gamut than Adobe RGB (1998). We also know that we can see a greater range of colors and brightness on our monitors (sRGB) than can be reproduced in print. So why do we care about using a wider gamut working space if we can't reproduce the colors on paper anyway?

The answer is that color space and gamut issues are just not that simple. In reality, while a printer's CMYK inks are narrower gamut in some ways, they may be "wider" gamut in others. A printer gamut that falls mostly inside the boundaries of another color space may still render some colors that lie completely outside of the "larger" gamut space. Today's photo inkjet printers can produce colors that lie outside of the sRGB gamut and monitor color spaces, even though there are also many sRGB colors that cannot be replicated by the printer. We want to use Adobe RGB (1998) since its gamut exceeds sRGB and includes almost all of the colors your printer can produce. Furthermore, even though some of these colors may not be visible on-screen, by having them fall inside the working space gamut, the final print is more likely to have smoother and subtler tonal gradations. The data exist in the image file, whether or not your monitor can reproduce it, and that gives you more image-processing

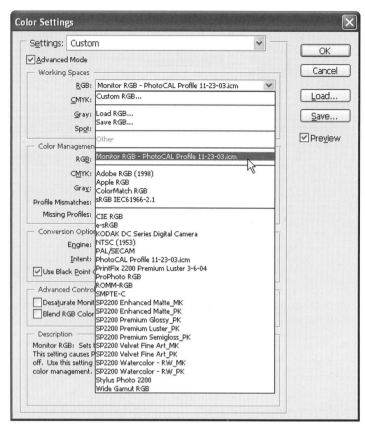

Fig. 2.21 Use Photoshop's Color Settings to be sure your monitor profile is being used for color management. The profile you created should appear next to Monitor RGB.

"headroom." You will be able to perform more image-processing steps without creating posterization or other artifacts in your print.

There is another topic you should be aware of. Metamerism is the characteristic whereby pigment ink colors may change their appearance somewhat depending upon the ambient (viewing) light source. Blue colors in a print viewed under fluorescent light or in daylight may take on a magenta cast when viewed under warm tungsten light. Similarly, black and white images may take on a green cast under certain lighting conditions. You should be aware of these types of peculiarities with the inks and papers you are using, and adjust your print proofing and profiling methods accordingly. A 4700 degree Kelvin viewing lamp, such as the Solux Lamp, can help minimize these issues and is recommended for evaluating prints.

Printer profiles are available from many sources. The manufacturer is a good starting point. Profiles are generally included somewhere on the installation disk that comes with the printer. In addition, check the manufacturer's website for updated profiles (and drivers).

Don't be surprised to find several different profiles, specifying different ink and paper combinations — if these are available you will definitely want to use them (**Figure 2.22**). Different inks and papers produce vastly different results, and such targeted profiles are superior to using a "generic" printer profile. Custom third-party profiles are also available. Some are free for downloading, others are available at a price. There are even services available that will generate a custom profile for your printer, ink and paper combo. Finally, you may create your own printer profiles using third-party hardware/software, such as the ColorVision PrintFix system. As a general rule, the more specific a printer profile is, the better. Some good online resources are listed in the Appendix.

You have three print color management methods to choose from:

- **Method One** Do not use any ICC color management profiles, and create your own custom printer settings using the printer software interface and/or Photoshop.

- **Method Two** Use a "canned" profile from the

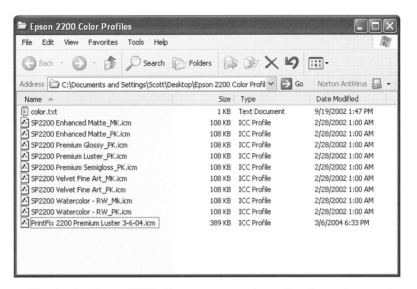

Fig. 2.22 Various printer profiles for the Epson 2200. There are separate profiles for each paper type. Even using the Epson Ultrachrome inkset, there are different profiles for matte black (MK) and photo black (PK) inks. The PrintFix profile at the bottom was created using ColorVision software and a hardware "patch reader" — a test target is printed out and read back into the computer to develop the profile.

manufacturer or a custom profile and let the printer interface handle the color management (ICC/ICM setting).

- **Method Three** Use a canned or custom profile and let Photoshop handle the color management.

Whatever you do, *be sure that you do not "double-profile" by setting both Photoshop and the printer interface to handle color management.* This is a common mistake and it creates a lot of printer woes.

Method One is the "rough and tumble" way to basically create your own profile through trial and error. You use the printer interface to directly alter the various ink colors until what appears in your print closely approximates what is on your monitor. Then you save these settings as your "profile." You may also do this by varying Photoshop's settings, instead of the printer settings. Essentially, you create a custom curve that you apply to the image just before printing it. The curve is created the same way — by looking at a lot of proof prints and making adjustments to the curve through trial and error until the print looks like the monitor image *before* you apply the custom curve. You then save this curve as your printer "profile", and load it into subsequent images as the last step before printing. There are several problems with these methods, and I do not recommend them if you have a good set of printer profiles. By not using a profile, neither Photoshop nor your printer software "knows" your printer's color space

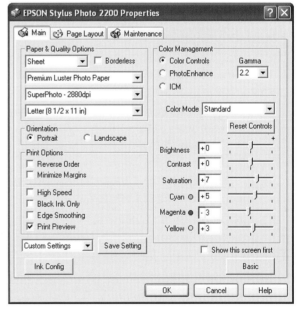

Fig. 2.23 Method One — No color management is used. You adjust the printer CMY and saturation sliders by trial and error to create your own custom print settings. In the Photoshop Print With Preview dialog, the Print Space Profile should be set to "Same as Source", which tells Photoshop not to perform any color management.

characteristics. There is no conversion from your working color space to the printer color space. In other words, you are not performing any color management at all. While this method may work surprisingly well some of the time, in the long run you will likely frus-

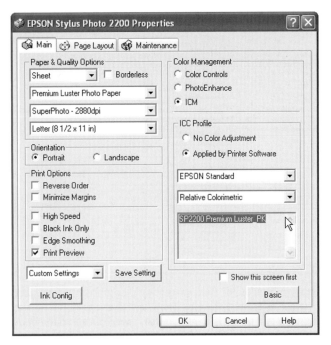

Fig. 2.24 Method Two — The printer software is used for color management. Note the "ICM" and "Applied by Printer Software" settings and the use of a specific paper/ink profile. Photoshop must be configured correctly, as shown in **Figure 2.25**, to avoid "double profiling."

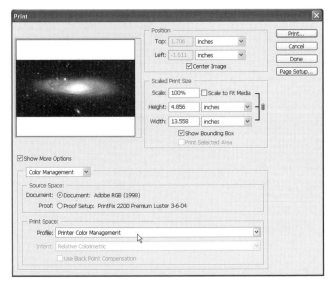

Fig. 2.25 Method Two — Photoshop's Print With Preview dialog color management settings. "Printer Color Management" directs Photoshop to send the embedded Adobe RGB (1998) working space information to the printer, maintaining a fully color-managed workflow. The printer software will handle conversion to the printer's color space based upon the profile used.

trate yourself and waste a lot of ink and paper as "re-profiling" will frequently be necessary. If you do adopt this method, using the printer software (or a combination of printer software settings and a custom Photoshop curve) is probably better in most cases, since you are directly controlling how the inks are applied to paper. **Figure 2.23** shows the Epson 2200 printer software configured for Method One.

The choice between Methods Two and Three is a matter of personal preference. Both use ICM profiles and maintain a color-managed workflow. I prefer to let Photoshop handle all color translations (Method Three), rather than having the printer software perform these tasks. But if you are more comfortable using Method Two, and get the results you want, by all means use it. Either method can work well.

Figure 2.24 shows the Method Two printer software settings for an Epson 2200 printer. These settings will result in color management being handled by the printer software. ICM ("Image Color Management") has been selected. Under the ICC Profile section, "Applied by Printer Software" has been chosen. Based upon the paper selected, the appropriate printer profile appears. The rendering intent shown is Relative Colorimetric, but perceptual may also be chosen if the im-

age warrants its use. Different printers will of course have different settings, but the important point is to direct the printer software to handle color management with an ICC profile.

Figure 2.25 shows how Photoshop should be set up when using Method Two. With Photoshop open, and any image file selected, choose *File|Print with Preview*. Check the box labeled Show More Options to access the print color management settings. Under Source Space choose Document: your Adobe RGB (1998) working space should be shown. Under Print Space Profile: choose Printer Color Management. This maintains a color management link between Photoshop and the printer, and it directs Photoshop to send the embedded Adobe RGB (1998) working space information to the printer software. The printer software will use this information to handle the color translation to the printer color space using the selected printer profile. Note that a setting of "Same as Source" should not be used — this tells Photoshop not to perform any color management; the working space would not be communicated to the printer. Same as Source should only be used for Method One.

Figure 2.26 shows the Method Three printer software settings for an Epson 2200 printer. These settings leave color management to Photoshop. ICM (Image

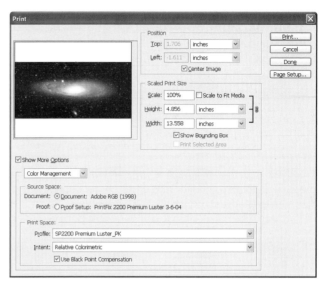

Fig. 2.26 Method Three — Photoshop will be used for print color management. The printer software is set to make no color adjustments to the input it receives.

Fig. 2.27 Method Three — Photoshop's Print with Preview dialog is configured to handle all color management. Photoshop will make the conversion from the working color space to the printer color space, using the specified profile and rendering intent.

Color Management) has been selected, but under the ICC Profile section, No Color Adjustment is chosen. The rendering intent and printer profile settings will be made in Photoshop. For other printers, use settings that result in no printer color control.

Figure 2.27 shows the Method Three setup for Photoshop. With Photoshop open, and any image file selected, choose *File\Print with Preview*. Check the box labeled Show More Options to access the printer color management settings. Under Source Space choose Document: your Adobe RGB (1998) working space should be shown. Under Print Space Profile: choose your specific printer/paper/ink profile. Set Intent to either Relative Colorimetric or Perceptual and check the Use Black Point Compensation box. Photoshop is now set to handle all print color management tasks.

Setting up Photoshop for Softproofing

Photoshop provides a way to get a "sneak preview" of what your image will look like when you print it, using a process called "softproofing." Given a specific printer/paper/ink profile, Photoshop renders an on-screen approximation of how the final print will look. In addition, Photoshop will highlight areas of the image that

have colors outside of the printer's color gamut. This is a very useful feature that can save quite a bit of ink and paper. By knowing the out-of-gamut colors in an image, you may make *subtle* contrast and saturation adjustments to accommodate your printer's color space. Use a delicate touch — large adjustments can result in artifacts and an unnatural appearance.

Softproofing also helps you decide which rendering intent to use, by giving you an on-screen preview of the results. As a general rule, try a Perceptual rendering intent if softproofing shows a lot of image data that fall outside of the printer's color gamut. If most of the colors are in-gamut, try Relative Colorimetric.

Let's set up Photoshop for softproofing. If you have a profile for your printer, use it. If not, just follow along to see how it's done.

1. Start Photoshop, but do not open an image file.

2. Choose *View\Proof Setup\Custom*. A dialog box appears like the one in **Figure 2.28**.

3. Select the specific printer/ink/paper profile that you use most often. If this profile is located in your system color management folder, it should appear in the Profile drop-down selection list. Otherwise, Load it from its file location.

4. Leave the Preserve Color Numbers box unchecked.

5. Check the Use Black Point Compensation box.

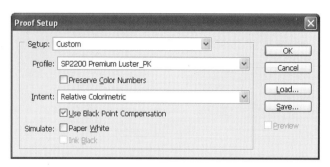

Fig. 2.28 Accurate softproofing with Photoshop requires a properly calibrated monitor and good printer/paper/ink profiles. Setup is accessed with *View | Proof Setup | Custom.*

6. Choose Relative Colorimetric as the (rendering) Intent.

7. Leave the Simulate: Paper White and Ink Black boxes unchecked, if these are shown. The options available depend upon the specific profile chosen.

8. Click OK and exit Photoshop. These settings will be retained as your default softproofing setup. Settings may be changed "on-the-fly" when viewing your image files, but those settings will not be retained when you exit Photoshop. To change the default settings, repeat these steps without an image file open.

To use softproofing, select *View | Proof Colors* (keyboard shortcut Ctrl+Y) with an image file open. Photoshop will then alter the screen view (not the image itself!) to reflect an approximation of how your print will turn out. Experiment with the Paper White and Ink Black settings, and compare your softproof to an actual print (hard proof), to determine the best settings to use for your particular print setup. Paper White takes into account the fact that the paper itself may be a dull white or "off-white" when compared to a brilliant screen white. Ink Black may help if your printer is not capable of a true, dark black. It is also helpful to compare the softproof side-by-side with the unaltered image. Simply duplicate your image file (*Image | Duplicate*) and apply the softproof to the duplicate for such an on-screen comparison.

A screen mask appears over the colors that lie outside your printer's color gamut when you select *View | Gamut Warning* (keyboard shortcut Shift+Ctrl+Y) (see **Figure 2.29**). To enhance visibility, the color of this mask may be changed in the *Edit | Preferences | Transparency and Gamut* dialog box.

Use softproofing to learn how your printer, and particular papers and inks, will render your images.

Eventually, you will be able to "see" the bright, saturated colors that are out-of-gamut and adjust your processing steps accordingly. Softproofing also makes it easy to determine if a different rendering intent will work better for a particular image — simply change the settings and check the result on-screen. Make changes to your images only when necessary to get the best printed results, but be careful not to overwrite your original files. Work with an on-screen duplicate.

Calibrating other Devices

Digital cameras have overtaken film as the most popular method for image capture. Just like any other device in the digital darkroom, digital cameras and digital SLR's can be made more "color accurate" by using ICC profiles. There are many resources available to obtain profiles for digital cameras, and new ones appear daily. There are also ways to create your own profiles, using a standard color chart and Photoshop, or using custom calibration software. An online search should yield a plethora of information on the subject, particularly if you are using a well-known digital SLR.

Be aware of how your digital camera is handling color management (or if it is handling color management at all). Refer to its documentation and check out online resources. Some cameras have sRGB and Adobe RGB (1998) camera settings that only assign these profiles, and perform no color space identification or adjustment. When creating your own profiles, remember that a profile is only accurate depending upon the color temperature of the light and other lighting conditions present when the profile was created. As with printer inks and papers, a set of digital camera profiles needs to be created for all of the various lighting conditions you work in.

If using a digital SLR, consider working in RAW mode to obtain the highest quality images. RAW files contain the unprocessed "raw" data from the image sensor. As such, RAW files have no color space, in fact they have no color at all. The RAW conversion software builds the color information from the raw data, and even allows the user to determine color balance and color temperature. With the advent of CS, Photoshop has a built-in RAW file converter. Whatever method you ultimately use to profile and/or process your digital camera files, let Photoshop convert these files to your working color space. With the default color settings we made earlier in this chapter, Photoshop will present you with an embedded profile mismatch or missing profile

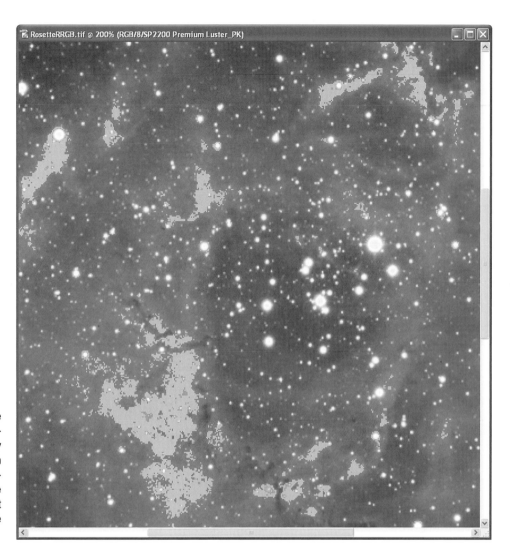

RosetteRRGB.tif @ 200% (RGB/8/SP2200 Premium Luster_PK)

Fig. 2.29 Image colors that lie outside of the printer color gamut are masked in gray (or any other color you choose) when *View|Gamut Warning* is selected. The printer/paper/ink profile used for softproofing and gamut warning is shown in the image title bar.

dialog box when you open the file. If the file has an embedded profile, let Photoshop convert the file to your Adobe RGB (1998) working color space. If the file has no embedded profile, let Photoshop assign your working space profile. If the file has no embedded profile, but you are confident that it was created in a particular color space other than your working space, assign that color space when you open the file *and then* convert the image to your working space after the file is opened. Finally, be sure to embed your working space profile in the processed image file when you save it to maintain a color-managed workflow.

Film scanners should also be profiled, if possible. Here again, investigate the options available for your scanner model. I particularly like working with Silverfast, a third-party program made by LaserSoft (see Appendix) and available for many popular scanners. Silverfast is a professional level program, offering

many powerful prescan options. The program incorporates complete color management into its interface (**Figure 2.30**) and provides for creating a custom scanner profile using a standardized IT-8 color calibration target. With my particular scanner, the difference between using the manufacturer's interface (and profile), and using Silverfast with the custom profile that I generate is like night and day. The custom profile results in far more accurate color. If you do acquire Silverfast, be sure to select the IT-8 calibration module option.

Photoshop's Assign Profile and Convert to Profile Commands

These Photoshop commands are frequently a source of confusion. *Image|Mode|Assign Profile (Edit|Assign Profile* in Photoshop CS2*)* does not do anything other than ascribe a color space profile to the image (**Figure 2.31**). No color space translation is made — no image

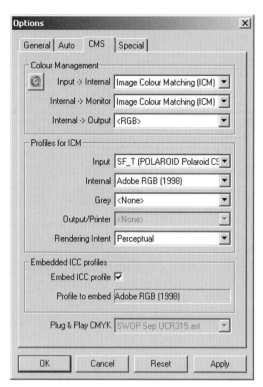

Fig. 2.30 Professional scanning software packages like Silverfast maintain a completely color-managed workflow. In this case, Silverfast was used to generate a custom IT-8 profile for my Polaroid medium format film scanner.

numbers are changed. Photoshop will give you a screen preview of how the unchanged file will look in the chosen color space, but it does not alter the file. For example, this would be useful if you have digital camera files that do not contain embedded profiles, but you know from your camera's documentation that the files are created in the sRGB color space. You would want to assign this profile to the images so that Photoshop "knows" what the colors are, how to display them on-screen and how to handle color management tasks going forward. Once the files were tagged with the sRGB profile, you could then use *Image\Mode\Convert to*

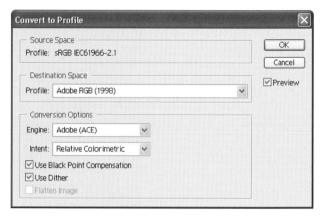

Fig. 2.32 Convert to Profile performs a numerical translation between the Source and the Destination Color Spaces using the rendering intent and other settings that you specify.

Profile (*Edit\Convert to Profile* in CS2) to covert them into your Adobe RGB (1998) working color space (**Figure 2.32**) if you choose. Convert to Profile translates colors from the source color space to the destination color space — the image numbers are changed — using the rendering intent, color engine and other settings that you specify.

Some Final Thoughts and Tips

1. Work from wider gamut color spaces to narrower gamut spaces (with some exceptions). For example, converting a file from sRGB to Adobe RGB (1998) accomplishes nothing. Once colors are gone, they're gone. You can't get them back by changing color spaces. When you need images for the Web, start with your archived files, created in and tagged with your Adobe RGB (1998) working color space, convert those files into sRGB for the Web, and then discard the sRGB files or save them under a unique name (xxxxx-web.jpg). Work from "larger" to "smaller."

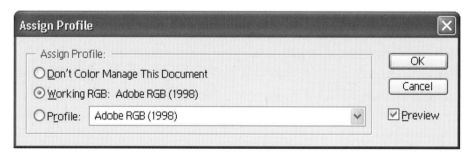

Fig. 2.31 Assign Profile merely "tags" (or "untags") a file with a particular color space profile. No color space translations are performed.

2. Work from "more" information to "less" whenever possible. In reality, the original unprocessed image contains the most information. Everything we do to that image from then on involves selecting, altering and "whittling" down the original information. Try to obtain the largest amount of original information possible (higher pixel dimensions), and the best quality (higher signal-to-noise ratio).

3. Maintain a color-managed workflow wherever possible. Profile your monitor and printer, at a minimum. If you don't have separate calibration devices, find and use the best profiles you can get your hands on. Understand the color settings in Photoshop and those in your other devices. Be sure of what is happening with color management in your system at all times. Be careful not to "double profile."

4. Embed profiles in all your files and set Photoshop to query you on all file profile conversions.

5. Use your printer profiles for softproofing with Photoshop.

6. Work in 16-bits whenever possible. You will need the additional processing "headroom" with astrophotos. Photoshop CS and CS2 make life much easier. They support layering and adjustment layers with 16-bit files.

7. Use on-screen image duplicates to preview and compare color space changes, softproofing, and other changes to the original image.

R. Scott Ireland

Chapter 3
The Histogram and Levels —
Defining Tonal Range

The Histogram

Histograms are one of the most useful tools available to the digital photographer. Any type of digital image, whether from scanned film, a digital camera, webcam, CCD or other device, will benefit from the judicious use of the histogram when performing image processing. Digital camera users have the added benefit of being able to view a histogram on their camera's LCD screen, allowing them to judge and refine their exposures in "real time". Film scans benefit greatly when the scanner software contains a good histogram display that allows the user to fine-tune scans to obtain the maximum amount of information from the film.

A histogram is a graphic representation of the tonal values contained within an image (the tonal range). It is a bar chart — a graph that shows the frequency distribution of luminance (brightness) values. The horizontal axis (x-axis) displays the full range of luminance values available for a given bit depth image file (the tonal scale). In an 8-bit file, the tonal scale (x-axis) would range from 0 at the left to 255 at the right. In a 16-bit file, it would range from 0 to 65,535. The vertical axis (y-axis) graphically displays the pixel count for each luminance value ("level"). **See Figure 3.1**.

Be aware that Photoshop may display 16-bit files using the same 0–255 scale that is used for 8-bit files. The histogram will only show a 255 maximum value, even though the file data are 16-bit. While this may be confusing, it does not affect the image itself, nor does it diminish the benefit of using the higher bit-depth information. The full 16-bit tonal scale is available — only the number range has been modified. In Photoshop CS and later the Info Palette may be set to show 16-bit values.

Notice also in **Figure 3.1** that the sky background peak at the left (dark) end of the scale looks like it has a flat plateau on top. This is merely the limit of the display window; the actual pixel count is not identical for all of those brightness levels — the "mountain peak"

would continue upwards if the display window were larger. The actual count for each level is given below — in this example, there are approximately 298,000 pixels in the image with a luminance level of 30.

Clipping

Histograms make tonal range problems easy to spot — they are immediately apparent. The most common problem is "clipping" — discarding image information at either end, or both ends, of the tonal scale.

Figure 3.2 shows an example of clipped shadow tones. The histogram appears "chopped off" on the left side. The darkest shadow values in an image, known as the black point, should fall above the bottom limit of the tonal scale. Here we see that image data run all the way down to the RGB value of (0, 0, 0) and it is obvious that more information should appear to the left of this value. Some shadow tones have been irretrievably lost. This is a very common problem with astrophotographs, since they contain a lot of dark tonal values (the sky background). But the sky background is not an absolute, featureless black. Its value should be something

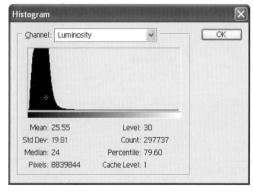

Fig. 3.1 A histogram shows the distribution of luminance values in an image or image channel. Black (0) is at the left; white (255) is at the right; grayscale values are in between. In this example there is a wide peak at the dark end of the scale, typical for the sky background in an astrophotograph.

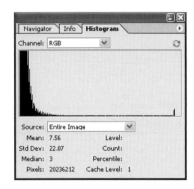

Fig. 3.2 The sky background in this image is too dark. The histogram presses up against the left side (black point; 0 level) and is "chopped off", indicative of shadow clipping. Some of the dark tones in the original image have been lost and cannot be recovered.

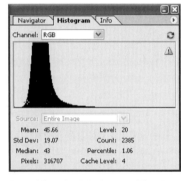

Fig. 3.3 No clipping is evident in this image. The histogram starts to "rise" near a luminance value of 20, an acceptable level for the sky background. All shadow and highlight information is retained. Notice the slight vignetting in this image. We will address how to handle this problem in a later chapter. Do not raise the black point to eliminate vignetting.

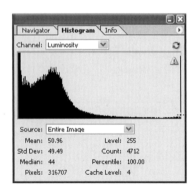

Fig. 3.4 Both shadows and highlights are clipped. Notice the sharp peak at the extreme right of the tonal scale (255, 255, 255). Both the left and right edges of the histogram have been "chopped off." Shadow and highlight information have been irretrievably lost. The image is overly "harsh" and contrasty. Vignetting is exaggerated.

above (0, 0, 0). Compare the clipped shadow tones of the histogram in **Figure 3.2** to **Figures 3.1 and 3.3**, in which the sky backgrounds lie inside the tonal scale — no image information has been lost.

Clipped shadow tones will make the image appear too harsh and contrasty. Faint stars are lost in the back-ground. Subtle tonal information at the dark end of the scale is missing and the sky background will appear unnatural and "non-photographic". A similar result occurs in a daylight photograph that is underexposed, driving all of the tonal values down to a point where shadow details are lost.

Shadow clipping can be caused by a number of things. Underexposed images may not contain enough information to start with. Even with images properly exposed to the sky background limit, clipping can occur if the film scan is not handled carefully to retain all of the tonal information in the original. Poor image-processing techniques, such as using the Brightness and Contrast controls (a typical beginner's mistake) instead of Levels and Curves to adjust the image tonal range, can also result in clipping. Even when using the proper tools (Levels and Curves), care must be taken not to "stretch" the image too far, remapping the image values over too narrow a tonal range.

At the other end of the scale, the brightest highlight values in an image, known as the white point, should fall slightly below the upper limit of the tonal scale. **Figure 3.4** shows an example of clipped highlights and clipped shadows. At the right (highlights) side of the histogram, there is a sharp peak at the maximum RGB value of (255, 255, 255). The histogram "presses" against the right — image highlights have been chopped off and are missing. Highlight details and the subtle color halos surrounding stars have been lost or distorted.

As with shadow clipping, highlight clipping results in too much image contrast and a "harsh" appearance. Noise, graininess, edge effects, vignetting and other problems and artifacts are greatly exaggerated when highlights are clipped or the white point is set too low. The image looses its smoothness and natural photographic appearance, even more so than with clipped shadows.

Highlight clipping can result from overexposure (highlights are "burned out" to a pure, featureless white), poor scanning technique and over-stretching the image tonal range in processing.

It may seem that the white point is a superfluous concept when dealing with astrophotos. With a proper exposure, the brighter stars will appear as a pure white (255, 255, 255) anyway. But we will see shortly the benefit of adjusting the tonal range of our images to place these values a little lower — just inside the maximum value — to something around (245, 245, 245).

"Combed" or "Gapped" Histograms

Figure 3.5 is an example of a "combed" or "gapped" histogram. Image information is missing — the pixel count is 0 at each of gaps. Consequently, smooth tonal

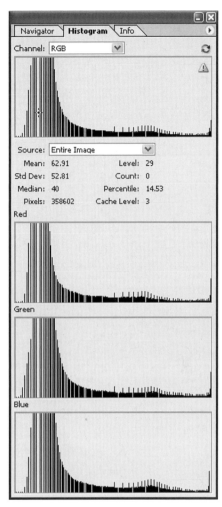

Fig. 3.5 An example of a "combed," or "gapped" histogram. Image information is completely missing in the gaps. Notice the 0 pixel count at a luminosity value of 29. Spikes are also beginning to appear in the midtones and highlights where image data have been "clumped" together from over-processing. This image will exhibit posterization — abrupt and unnatural transitions between tonal values. Smooth tonal gradations have been lost. Using 16-bit image data will help to avoid this problem. Notice also that the highlights are clipped in this example.

transitions are lost and the image will appear "blotchy", harsh and unnatural. Because there are too many abrupt changes between tones, the image looses its continuous tone photographic quality. It is analogous to clipping — combing "throws away", or clips, image data that exist in between the black and white points.

Images with badly combed histograms will exhibit posterization, or banding, which results from the sudden shifts in color and luminosity. Take a look at **Figure 3.6**. Here we see the same 17-step grayscale

R. Scott Ireland

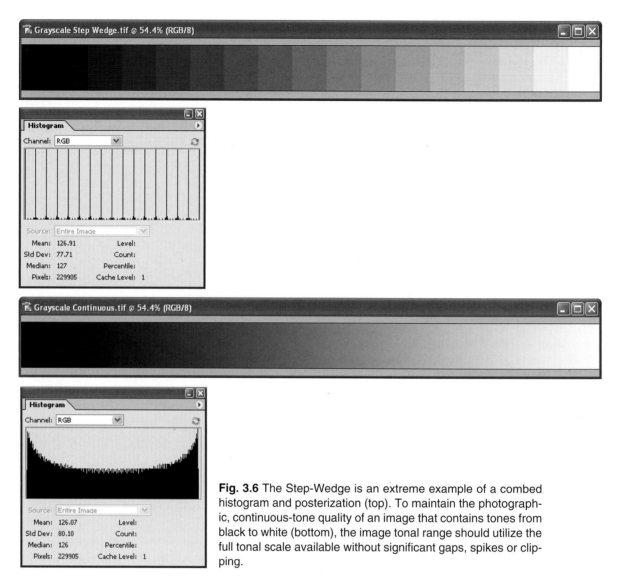

Fig. 3.6 The Step-Wedge is an extreme example of a combed histogram and posterization (top). To maintain the photographic, continuous-tone quality of an image that contains tones from black to white (bottom), the image tonal range should utilize the full tonal scale available without significant gaps, spikes or clipping.

that we examined in **Figure 2.2**, along with its histogram. This shows an extreme case of combing — there are only 17 discrete tonal values in the image. Below it is another step-wedge that is continuous in tone — all 256 tonal scale values (8-bit) are represented (a 256-step grayscale). This histogram shows no gaps. The tonal transitions are smooth and continuous, since all values within the tonal scale are represented by pixels in the image.

Histograms that display very jagged peaks or spikes in the data are analogous to combing, and are also indicative of unnatural image contrast, sharp tonal transitions and posterization.

Our goal, then, is to strive for smooth histograms, without large gaps or spikes, and with image information extending over the entire tonal scale (but not clipped!).

Tonal Scale —16-bit Versus 8-bit Images

The chief cause of combing and "spiky" data is too much image processing applied to an 8-bit image file. We must remember that our starting point — the source image — contains the most information that we will ever have about that image. Each processing step that we apply reduces this original image information by altering pixel values. Our processed image may look better (let's hope so!), but it contains less "true" image information than the original. It looks better because we have selectively and purposefully altered and enhanced the original to show off what we want to show off.

This is why it is preferable to capture the highest quality original image and work with 16-bit image data whenever possible. By starting with more information, and mapping that information over a wider tonal scale (16-bit vs. 8-bit), we can perform more processing steps without creating the types of problems we have just examined. With only 256 discrete tonal values, 8-bit data are susceptible to combing and spiking. Each image-processing step changes numbers, so it is easy to see how only 256 tonal values can become "bunched up" or quantized, creating gaps and spikes. A 16-bit tonal scale, with 65,536 different levels, gives us a lot more image-processing "headroom" to work with by employing a higher sampling frequency — more numbers are used to describe the same range of subject brightness. The same image information is just "chopped up" into smaller pieces. The "in-between" number values that result from pixel manipulations are therefore easier to retain. 16-bit files rarely exhibit gaps, spikes, posterization, pixelation or quantization errors; they can handle a lot more number-crunching than 8-bit files.

Converting an 8-bit image to 16-bits does not accomplish any more than converting an sRGB file to Adobe RGB (1998). Once the image information is rendered into a smaller domain (either bit depth or color space) it cannot be recaptured through conversion. Convert your 16-bit image data to 8-bits only when absolutely necessary, and at the last possible moment in your image-processing workflow.

Dynamic range is a term that you will hear often, and it is used to mean many different things. Basically, it means a range of light, or brightness. The dynamic range of film describes the range of light it is capable of recording, from featureless black to featureless white. This may be listed in terms of "stops" (color transparency film has a dynamic range of about 5 stops; color negative film has a dynamic range of 7 stops; and so forth) or in terms of image density on film, which is described using a logarithmic scale ranging between 0 and 4 ("the film has a Dmin of 0.3 and a Dmax of 3.4"). Scanner specifications are often listed this way ("the scanner has a dynamic range of 3.6"), which ostensibly describes the ability of the scanner to record a range of brightness. You will also hear dynamic range used to describe bit-depth ("16-bit images have a wider dynamic range than 8-bit images"), which is not necessarily accurate. Dynamic range also involves the subject brightness and the ability of the capture device to render that brightness. At any rate, to avoid this type of confusion, I have adopted a convention of describing the total available bit-depth as the tonal scale, and the brightness range of the image as the image tonal range.

Levels–Setting the Black and White Points of an Image

We have just learned that for images containing a full range of brightness values, from nearly black to nearly white (most astrophotographs fall into this category), it is desirable to have the image tonal range extend over the full tonal scale. So how do we accomplish this? By re-defining the black and white points to make the image tonal range fit the tonal scale. Identifying what is "black" (the darkest set of RGB values) and what is "white" (the lightest set of RGB values) in the image causes the other tonal values to "stretch" over the full tonal scale. This process is known as contrast stretching or just stretching. We will use Photoshop's Levels adjustment to accomplish this.

Let's start Photoshop and work through an example.

1. From the Tutorial Disk, open the file Grayscale Step-Wedge.tif (*File|Open*). This is the same file we worked with in Chapter Two.

2. Make sure the Info Palette is visible (*Window|Info; keyboard shortcut F8*).

3. Select the Eyedropper Tool from the Tools Palette. The Tools Palette is typically located at the left side of your screen. If you don't see it there, select *Window|Tools* to make it visible.

4. In the Options Bar at the top of the screen, you will see a Sample Size option for the Eyedropper Tool. Set this to 3 by 3 Average. As a general rule, you do not want to use a Point Sample to make color and luminosity measurements and adjustments. It is too easy to hit a stray pixel that is not representative of the area you are working on.

5. Now let's use the Eyedropper Tool to set some Color Sampler points. While holding down the Shift key, move the cursor over the first box at the left of the grayscale (pure black; grayscale luminosity level 0) and click once. A Color Sampler point appears. If you need to move the point, hold down the Control (Ctrl) key — a dark arrow appears — left-click-hold and drag the point to where you want it, then release the mouse. Notice that a #1 appears in the Info Palette, along with an eyedropper icon and the RGB values for this Color Sampler point.

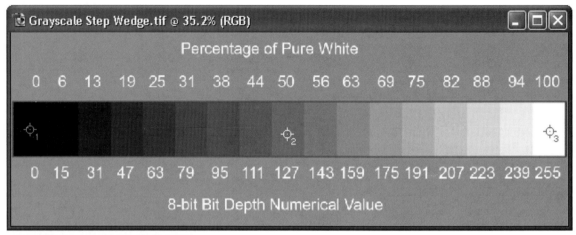

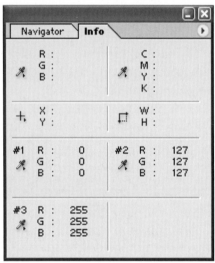

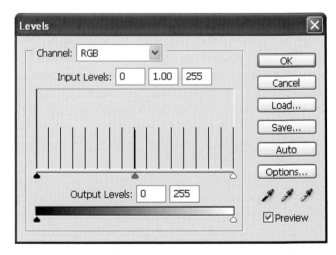

Fig. 3.7 Up to four Color Sampler points may be set in Photoshop using the Eyedropper Tool or the Color Sampler Tool. Establishing shadow and highlight reference points in the image is very useful when using Levels and Curves to set the black and white points (contrast stretching) and color balance an image.

6. Repeat step 5 and set additional Color Samplers at the middle-gray tone box (level 127) and the pure white box (level 255). You should now have 3 Color Sampler points and your Step-Wedge and Info Palette should look something like **Figure 3.7**.

7. Open the Levels dialog box with *Image|Adjustments|Levels* (**Figure 3.8**). Notice the three shaded triangular sliders located directly below the histogram (not the two sliders located below the Output Levels grayscale). These are the Input Levels sliders, and their numerical values are shown in the three boxes above the histogram. The left slider adjusts the black (shadow) point; the right slider adjusts the white (highlight) point. The middle slider (midtones) adjusts the tones between black and white.

8. Make sure the Preview box is checked. This will cause the image to change to show the effect of the

Fig. 3.8 Levels is the adjustment tool to use for setting the black and white points. Unlike Curves, Levels displays a histogram that aids the process. Three adjustment points are available to alter the image tonal range (shadows, midtones and highlights), represented by shaded triangles under the histogram and the shaded eyedropper icons at the lower right.

adjustments you make. Don't worry, though. This is just a "sneak preview". The settings will not actually be applied to your image until you click on "OK" to accept them. Click-hold and drag the shadow (black point) Input Levels slider to the right. You can release the mouse, and then click-hold and move the slider again as many times as you like. Look at what happens to the tones in the step-wedge. As you move the shadow slider to the right, the black point (RGB value of 0, 0, 0) is set at progressively higher levels, the image darkens and contrast increases. The new pixel value of the black point is shown numerically in the left Input Levels box above the histogram. You may also set the black point pixel value by typing a number into this box. Every tone in the image that lies at or to the left of the new black point turns black. If you move the shadow slider all the way to the right, you are left with only the original white box (255, 255, 255) and all of the other boxes have been "driven" to black (0, 0, 0). Notice that as you drag the shadow slider, the midtone slider automatically moves along to the right. It stays halfway between the black and white points. All of the grayscale values above the black point (except the white point which remains at 255, 255, 255) have been lowered in tonal value. Check this by comparing the original tonal values to the new values in the Info Palette. Photoshop's Info Palette has a very nice feature. While working in an adjustment dialog, it shows you both the before and after pixel values, separated by a forward slash mark ("/").

9. Next, experiment with the highlight (white point) slider. Now everything happens in reverse. The higher tonal values are progressively driven towards pure white as you move the slider to the left, and the lower tonal values (except the black point) are all raised in value, since the midtone slider also moves to the left to remain halfway between black and white. The image brightens and again the contrast increases. If you move the white point all the way to the left, all tones in the image, other than the black point, have been driven to pure white. White point pixel values are shown numerically in the right Input Levels box above the histogram. The white point pixel value may also be set by typing a number into this box.

10. Now, put the shadow and highlight sliders back to their original endpoints (or just cancel the Levels dialog and re-open it) and move the midtone ("gamma") slider around. As you move the midtone slider, the black and white points remain fixed, but all of the other tonal values in between are lightened as you move the slider left, and darkened as you move it to the right. The middle box in the Input Levels above the histogram shows a number that changes as you move the slider. But this number does not reflect a single value like the black and white points. Rather, it is a gamma value that represents a set of tonal values. It defines a curve of all pixel values between black and white. This number starts at 1.00 and increases up to around 10.00 as you move the midtone slider to the left, brightening all of the pixels between black and white (raising the curve). When you move the slider to the right, it decreases to a low value of around 0.10, darkening all of the pixel values between black and white (lowering the curve).

11. Once again, put all of the sliders back to their initial positions or just cancel and re-open the Levels dialog. If you've accidentally hit "OK" to accept the Levels changes, then just re-open the file. Now let's take a look at the Output Levels. There are two numerical data entry boxes. The one on the left is for the black point and the one on the right is for the white point. Below these boxes is a small grayscale, and below that are the black and white point sliders. Values may be changed either by typing numbers into the boxes or by moving the sliders. Move the black and white point Output Levels sliders around and see what happens. As you move the black point slider to the right, the whole image lightens and the contrast decreases. The tonal value on the grayscale that lies above the slider is the new definition of what "black" is. As you move the white point slider to the left, the image darkens and contrast also decreases. The grayscale value above the slider is the new definition of "white".

Setting the Input black and white points determines which pixel values *in the image* are defined as black (darkest) and white (lightest). The tonal values in between are remapped, or stretched, to fit these new points. *The tonal range* (dynamic range) of the image is re-defined.

Output levels are used to re-define *the tonal scale* by assigning specific grayscale values to the black and white points, regardless of how and where those points are set in the image (using Input).

R. Scott Ireland

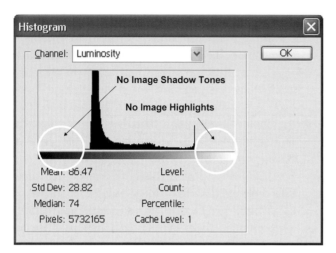

Fig. 3.9 A very low contrast image. The image tonal range only occupies about half the tonal scale. The darkest tones in the image are too light and the lightest tones are too dark. The image black and white points need to be reset to close the gaps on both sides of the histogram.

Levels is one of the main tools to use for adjusting brightness, contrast and color balance. It permits changing the black point, white point and midtones independently of one another, providing control over the process. This is the reason why you never want to use the Brightness/Contrast adjustments in Photoshop. Brightness/Contrast does not provide independent control over the black and white points. Consequently, it is very easy to clip the shadows and highlights, discarding valuable image information. Use only Levels and Curves to make brightness and contrast adjustments.

Setting the Black and White Points using the Levels Sliders — Introduction to Adjustment Layers

1. From the Tutorial Disk, open the file Andromeda Levels Example1.tif (*File|Open*). One of the first things you notice about the image is its lack of contrast. It looks "washed out". The original photograph is a CCD Mosaic that was taken by Tim Khan and the author. That 16-bit file has been converted to 8-bits and the contrast significantly lowered for purposes of this tutorial.

2. Open the Histogram with *Image|Histogram* (*Window|Histogram* if you are using Photoshop CS and later). The histogram should look similar to **Figure 3.9**. Ah, now we see the problem! The image tonal range only comprises half the tonal scale.

There is no image data in the areas circled. The darkest

image pixels have a luminosity level of around 65, and the brightest pixels are around 200. The tonal scale range between 0 and 65, and also the range between 200 and 255, are both virtually empty. We need to move the black point "in" from the left and the white point "in" from the right to close up the gaps.

3. Make sure that the Layers Palette is visible (*Window|Layers*). In our first Tutorial example (Grayscale Step Wedge.tif), we accessed the Levels dialog box through the *Image|Adjustments|Levels* menu command. If we had decided to accept the Levels settings that we made, they would have immediately been applied to the image when we clicked on "OK". The only way we could have gone back and made changes to those settings would have been to use the "Undo" command or Photoshop's History Palette. This is known as a destructive edit — the actual image pixels (the "Background") are changed as you work. But there is another more flexible way to work — by using adjustment layers.

4. Create a Levels adjustment layer by selecting *Layer|New Adjustment Layer|Levels* and click OK when the New Layer selection box appears. We are presented with the same Levels dialog box that we have seen before. But something else has happened too. In the Layers Palette, a new layer ("Levels 1") has appeared directly above the Background Layer (**Figure 3.10**). You can tell that this is an adjustment layer because it has a circular half dark/half light icon (the adjustment layer icon) rather than an image thumbnail like the Background layer.

5. Next, click-hold and drag the Levels Input shadow slider until it lies where data just begin to appear at the left side of the histogram. Then move the highlight slider to where data just begin to appear at the right side of the histogram. Leave the sliders very close to, but just "outside" of, where the image data begin. Clipping will be the result if we "crowd" the data too closely. With the Preview box checked, you see the effect of adjustments immediately in the image. Your Levels dialog box should now look like **Figure 3.11**. The image looks much better. It isn't "washed out" any more. We have adjusted the contrast by stretching the image tonal range to better match the tonal scale. Put another way, we have modified the image to utilize more of the available tonal values. Click

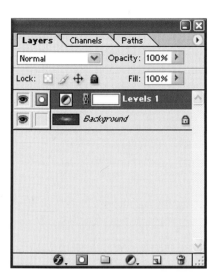

Fig. 3.10 Adjustment Layers do not contain image information, but rather a set of image-processing instructions. They "ride on top" of image layers and allow us to see how the image will look if the adjustments are permanently applied (by flattening the image). Adjustment Layers may be saved with the image file to retain their settings from one editing session to the next.

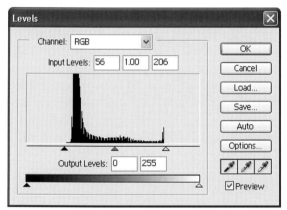

Fig. 3.11 The image black and white points have been modified by moving the shadow and highlight sliders. Normal image contrast is established, since the tonal range has been extended over most of the tonal scale. In order to avoid clipping, it is best to place the black and white points "just outside of" the image data.

OK to accept the settings.

6. But there is a better way to do this. Notice in **Figure 3.11** that the Channel we worked on is "RGB". Using RGB as the "channel" (it is not a true channel, but rather a convenient combination of the other 3 color channels), our adjustments are applied equally to all of the color channels. However, we can get a more accurate result if we examine and adjust the color channels individually. Color casts in the image can be corrected this way. The beauty of adjust-

ment layers is that we can easily go back and modify what we've already done without losing all of our work. Make the Levels 1 layer active (it will be highlighted in blue) and re-open the Levels dialog box by double-clicking on the little half black/ half white circle. The Levels dialog box re-appears with the previous settings intact. In the RGB Channel, move the shadow and highlight Input sliders back "out" to their starting positions (0 and 255). The image reverts to its original low contrast state. Now select the Red Channel from the Channel drop-down selection box (keyboard shortcut Ctrl+1). Move the shadow and highlight Input sliders to just outside the image data endpoints, just like we did with the RGB sliders. If you still have Preview checked, the image colors will get pretty strange. Don't worry — it only happens because we have not yet adjusted the other color channels.

7. Now adjust the shadow and highlight Input sliders of the Green Channel (keyboard shortcut Ctrl+2) and the Blue Channel (shortcut Ctrl+3). Set these in the same manner — put the sliders just outside the points where data begin. Click OK to accept the settings. Once again, the image looks better, with a normal contrast level restored. With this particular image, the difference between setting the individual color channels, and just using RGB to set them all the same way, is very subtle. However, with images having a pronounced color cast, following this simple procedure can go a long way towards fixing the color balance.

8. Let's now use Photoshop's History Palette to examine how much difference setting the individual color channels has made vs. setting all of them together. Make sure the History Palette is visible (*Window|History*). It should look like **Figure 3.12**. The History Palette lets us "go back in time", step-by-step, to an earlier "state" of the image. Each processing step that you apply is recorded as a new image state, so by selecting an earlier one, we temporarily restore the image to that point and eliminate the effect of later processing steps. If you begin new work on an image starting from an earlier history state, the later states are lost. In our example, the image should have 3 history states: "Open", "Levels 1 Layer" and "Modify Levels Layer". Click on "Open" and the image appears as it was when the file was opened. Now click back and forth between "Levels 1 Layer" and "Modify

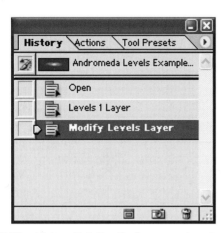

Fig. 3.12 The History Palette. Each processing step creates a new history "state" below the previous one. Photoshop retains 20 history states in its default configuration. You may increase this number by changing the default setting with *Edit\Preferences\General*. The author sets Photoshop to retain somewhere between 50 and 90 history states.

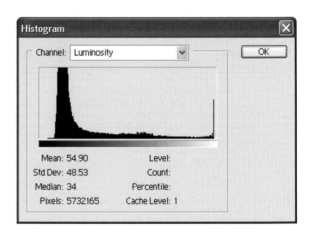

Fig. 3.13 The image histogram after setting the black and white points using Levels. Compare this to the original in **Figure 3.9**. The tonal range has been stretched over the (almost) full tonal scale, building image contrast.

Levels Layer" and you will see the difference between setting the black and white points with RGB or by using each color channel. There is a very subtle difference between the two — using the color channels changes the color balance of the galaxy slightly to make it cooler (more blue). When you are finished with your comparison, be sure to restore the image to its final history state by clicking on "Modify Levels Layer". Just as with layers, the active history state is highlighted in blue. Also make sure we are back in the image layer, instead of the Levels adjustment layer. If necessary, click once on the Background layer to make it active.

9. Finally, let's take a look at the image histogram to see the result of our work. We can't do this using the Levels adjustment layer, because the histogram doesn't change as we make adjustments. It remains the same as it was when we first set up the adjustment layer. So, open a separate histogram with *Window\Histogram* or *Image\Histogram*. It should look pretty much like the one in **Figure 3.13**. Now the image data stretch almost completely across the tonal scale. There is no shadow or highlight clipping — the spike at the right of the histogram (the "burned out" core of the galaxy) was in the original image. But now take a look at the histogram for each of the individual color-channels (select them from the Channel: drop-down box or use the keyboard shortcuts men-

tioned earlier). The histograms are starting to show gapping and a rough profile. This is because the image is 8-bit, not 16-bit, and we had to apply a pretty big adjustment with Levels. This is why it is so important to try to capture a good (full tonal scale) original image and stay in 16-bits as long as possible. The more processing you have to do, the more important this is. But there is a tradeoff. Only with the advent of Photoshop CS (version 8) can you process 16-bit files using adjustment layers. Earlier versions of Photoshop require the file to be converted to 8-bit before adjustment layers may be used. In that circumstance, and as you gain more experience, you may wish to apply Levels and Curves using the *Image\Adjustments* menu commands (destructive edits) while keeping the image in 16-bit mode.

Setting the Black and White Points "By the Numbers" using Target Values in the Image

In the previous example, we stretched the tonal range and improved contrast in the image by setting the black and white points using the Levels Input sliders. Leaving a little space to the left of the shadow data in effect set the darkest image data to a black point higher than 0 in each color channel — to around 20 or so. Similarly, leaving some space to the right of the brightest highlight data established a white point of around 250; less than the 255 maximum available. We did not quite use all of the available tonal scale; rather, we placed the tonal range inside the minimum and maximum values. This is generally (though not always) a good practice to follow.

However, there is a more precise way to establish the black and white points, assuming we know what we want the RGB values of those points to be. We merely specify RGB target values for the black and white points, and then select which points in the image will represent those values. Photoshop handles the rest by stretching the "in-between" tonal values just as in our previous example. Again, we will use the Levels command to accomplish this.

It is easy to determine where the black and white points should be in an average astrophotograph. The sky background represents the darkest tones (black point) and the middle of a bright star represents the brightest (white point). Most astrophotographs have these two features. We do not use the middle-tone ("gamma") Levels adjustment as often, since astrophotos do not usually contain middle-toned gray objects (128, 128, 128) on which to base tonal adjustments. Conversely, with "normal" daylight photographs, there may not be pure black and white points, and it is sometimes more productive to adjust tonality and color by referring to neutral gray objects in the image. A standard grayscale may even be placed in the scene being photographed in order to facilitate such adjustments.

So what RGB values should we use for the sky background (black point) and the center of a bright star (white point) in our images? For stars, the answer is easy. The centers of the brightest stars will appear as pure white. We want to set a target white point between (245, 245, 245) and (248, 248, 248). Why not pure white (255, 255, 255)? Because we want to retain a hint of detail in these areas. Absolute pure white (255, 255, 255) will be completely featureless, without texture of any kind. It is not ideal for making prints, since the white point will be represented by the paper base without any ink. You want to have a set of values that will drive the printer to set down ink at all points from black to white.

The sky background target value is more subjective. I do not wish to spark debate over what a "proper" or "true" sky background color should be. Suffice it to say that it is not pure black — there is always some level of background brightness (unless your image was taken from orbit). Perhaps it should be rendered as a very dark gray (10, 10, 10). Or a very dark blue (10, 10, 15). Maybe it should be a little lighter (20, 20, 20) or (20, 20, 25). Who knows? It's really up to you. My recommendation is that you choose sky background target values that complement your image subjects and are

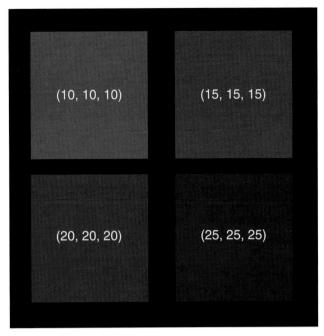

Fig. 3.14 Some typical RGB settings for a neutral gray sky background. Many astrophotographers like to add a touch of blue to their sky backgrounds–try settings such as (10, 10, 15); (15, 15, 20) or (20, 20, 25).

aesthetically pleasing to you.

The tutorial disk contains a file that illustrates what some of these sky backgrounds look like compared to pure black. Let's take a quick look at it.

1. Open the file "Black Point — Sky Backgrounds.psd" (*File|Open*) from the tutorial disk. The image will appear small on the screen since it is only 144 pixels square, so next we'll enlarge it.

2. Make sure that the Toolbox is displayed (*Window|Tools*). Select the Zoom Tool by clicking once on the little magnifying glass icon in the Toolbox (keyboard shortcut — press the letter "Z"). Notice the Tool Options Bar near the top of the window. The options shown here change depending upon which Tool you are using. Click once on the button labeled "Fit on Screen". If your screen is properly adjusted, you should now be able to see four separate dark boxes set against a black background similar to those in **Figure 3.14**.

3. Make sure that the Info Palette is visible (*Window|Info*) and Move the cursor into the image. The RGB values under the cursor are displayed in the Info Palette. Notice the values for each of the boxes. The top left box is dark gray with an RGB value of (10, 10, 10). The top right box is lighter,

but still neutral at (20, 20, 20). The bottom left box is dark blue (10, 10, 15) and the bottom right box is a lighter blue (20, 20, 25). Use these RGB values as a guide when setting the black points (sky backgrounds) in your own images.

4. While still in the image and with the Zoom Tool selected, notice that you can enlarge the screen view by repeatedly left-clicking with the mouse when the Zoom Tool shows a + ("plus") sign. Hold down the Alt key and the tool shows a – ("minus") sign, allowing you to zoom out. Release the Alt key and the + sign returns. If the image is larger than the window, hold down the spacebar and a little white glove appears (the Move Tool). Click-hold and drag to move the image around inside the window.

Let's now proceed with a new technique to set the black and white points using target values. We will work with the same image as in our previous Levels example:

1. Once again, open the file Andromeda Levels Example1.tif (*File|Open*).

2. Make sure that the Layers Palette is visible (*Window|Layers*). As in our prior example, we will create a Levels adjustment layer — but this time we will use a shortcut. Notice that there are several icons at the bottom of the Layers Palette, one of which is a half black/half white circle. Left-click on this icon and an adjustment layer selection box appears. Move the cursor to highlight Levels and click once to select it. A Levels dialog box opens and a Levels 1 adjustment layer appears in the Layers Palette.

3. Now let's determine where the darkest and lightest values in the image are. With the Levels dialog box open, hold down the Alt key and click-hold and drag the Input highlight slider all the way to the left. Don't let go! While still holding down the left-mouse and Alt keys, slowly drag the highlight slider back toward the right. The darkest areas of the image will be the first to appear against the white background. Now move the highlight slider back to its original position. Do the same thing (in reverse) with the shadow Input slider to find the brightest areas. Hold down the Alt key and click-hold and drag the Input shadow slider all the way to the right (the image goes black), then slowly move it back to the left. The lightest areas of the

image will be the first ones to appear against the black background. Put the shadow and highlight sliders back to their original positions and click OK to finish creating the Levels adjustment layer. We have just used the Threshold mode in Levels to find the darkest and brightest areas in the image. The Threshold command converts a normal color image into a very high-contrast black-and-white image. It is handy to use this technique (temporarily, of course!) when seeking candidate black and white points in the image.

4. Perhaps the easiest way to use Threshold is to set up a temporary adjustment layer. From the Layers Palette, use the adjustment layer icon (half black/half white circle) and create a Threshold adjustment layer. Make sure the Preview box is checked. Your screen and Layers Palette should resemble **Figure 3.15**. Move the Threshold slider to the right to find the brightest highlights (the Galaxy core). Now set a Color Sampler point here — move the cursor over that point in the image, hold down Shift and click once. There is already a Color Sampler point placed here (#1) to help you be certain you are in the right place! Similarly, move the Threshold slider to the left side of the displayed histogram to find where the darkest areas are. Set another Color Sampler point in this area — #2 is already there to guide you. There should now be four Color Sampler points — my two (#1 and #2) and your two (#3 and #4). Confirm this by inspecting the Info Palette. We can only have four total Color Sampler points.

5. Click Cancel to not create the Threshold adjustment layer. The Color Sampler points you set will remain; we do not actually need to create the adjustment layer. After identifying the black and white points, we have no further use for it. If you had already created it by clicking OK, then click-hold and drag it to the trash can icon at the bottom of the Layers Palette to discard it.

6. Now that we have established where our black and white points are going to be, we need to set the desired target RGB values and then identify these points using Levels. First, select the Eyedropper Tool (keyboard shortcut — "I") from the Toolbox. In the Tool Options Bar, make sure Sample Size is set to 3 by 3 Average. This way, a representative sample area (3 pixels square) is assured. You do not want to accidentally select a single un-

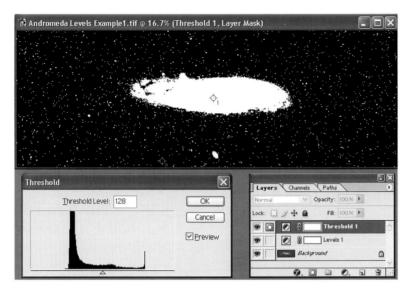

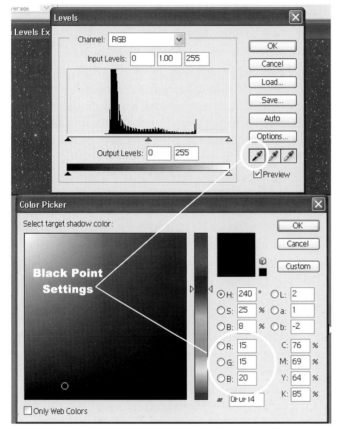

Fig. 3.15 Setting black and white points using target RGB values requires selecting representative shadow and highlight areas in the image. Threshold is a useful tool for this purpose. Here Color Sampler points have already been placed for the black and white points.

Fig. 3.16 (Left) Double-click on the Shadow eyedropper in Levels to set the black point RGB values. Here a dark blue sky background value of (15, 15, 20) is selected.

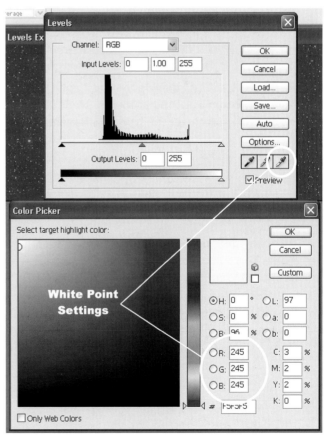

Fig. 3.17 (Right) The white point is set slightly below maximum value in order to retain some detail and texture in the highlights. This will cause a printer to lay down ink in these areas, rather than default to the pure white paper base. In this case, the white point is set to (245, 245, 245).

usual pixel value by using "Point Sample"; this could skew your results significantly.

7. Re-open the Levels adjustment layer dialog box (double-click on the half black/half white icon in the Levels 1 layer). If you did not retain the Levels adjustment layer (steps 2 and 3), just set up a new one.

8. Notice the three eyedropper icons at the bottom right of the Levels dialog box. The left one is used to set the black point, the right one sets the white point and the center one sets any neutral tones. Double-click on the left (black point) eyedropper. A Color Picker dialog box appears. Enter the RGB values (15, 15, 20) into the appropriate numerical boxes in the Color Picker and click OK. Your target black point value has been set (see **Figure 3.16**.

9. Now double-click on the right (white point) eyedropper. Another Color Picker dialog box appears. This time enter the RGB values (245, 245, 245) and click OK. This sets your target white point value (**Figure 3.17**).

10. Click OK to close the Levels dialog box and save the newly selected target colors. Another dialog box will likely appear — "Save the new target colors as defaults?". Click Yes.

11. Select the Zoom Tool (shortcut — "Z"). Zoom well into the area containing the black point Color Sampler. Zoom in to around 400% screen enlargement. The percentage of screen enlargement is shown at the top of the image window next to the file name. Make sure that the Color Sampler sits on a good, representative area of sky background, an area that contains no stars or other features. If you need to move the Sampler point, select the Eyedropper Tool (shortcut — "I"), hold down the Shift key and move the cursor over the Sampler Point. The cursor icon changes into a dark arrow. While continuing to hold down the Shift key, Left-click-hold and drag the Color Sampler to reposition it. Try this now, just to get the hang of it. To remove a Color Sampler point, hold down the Shift+Alt keys. The cursor changes to a small scissors icon when it is over a Sampler point. Left-click once to discard the point.

12. Re-open the Levels dialog box from the adjustment layer (double-click on the half black/half white icon near the left side of the adjustment lay-

er in the Layers Palette). Click once on the Shadow Eyedropper to select it. Now move the cursor into the image and place it over the black point Color Sampler (either the one you set or the one I set; it doesn't matter). If the cursor icon appears as a little eyedropper, you may want to change it to "precise" mode to get a better indication of exactly where it is in the image. Press the Caps Lock key once to turn on the precise cursor mode. When the cursor is lined up (fairly close is good enough) over the black point Color Sampler, left-click once. The black point is now set based on the target RGB values of (15, 15, 20). Notice that the histogram displayed in the Levels dialog box has shifted to the left.

13. With the Levels dialog box still open and with the cursor in the image window, hold down the Shift key and the cursor changes into a small white glove. We have temporarily selected the Move Tool. While holding down the Shift key, left-click-hold and drag with the mouse to move the Zoomed-in image around inside the image window. Move the image to position the white point Color Samplers (bright center of the galaxy) in the center of the window. If you have difficulty getting the image to the right place (Photoshop CS or CS2 sometimes act glitchy in this regard), merely click OK to close the Levels dialog, Zoom back out and Zoom in again on the white point Color Samplers, then re-open the Levels dialog box.

14. Click once on the Highlight Eyedropper to select it. Move the cursor into the image and place it over the white point Color Sampler (either one). Left-click once. The white point is now set based on the target RGB values of (245, 245, 245). The histogram now stretches over most of the tonal scale. Some gapping may appear, since we are working with an 8-bit file and the image requires considerable stretching. Click OK to accept these new black and white point settings and close the Levels dialog box.

15. Make the Info Palette is visible (*Window|Info*). Examine the RGB values shown for the black and white Color Samplers. It is likely that the black point was shifted from its target value when you set the white point. When we make global adjustments to an image, such as setting the black and white points, we must remember that all RGB values are affected by the steps we employ. Setting

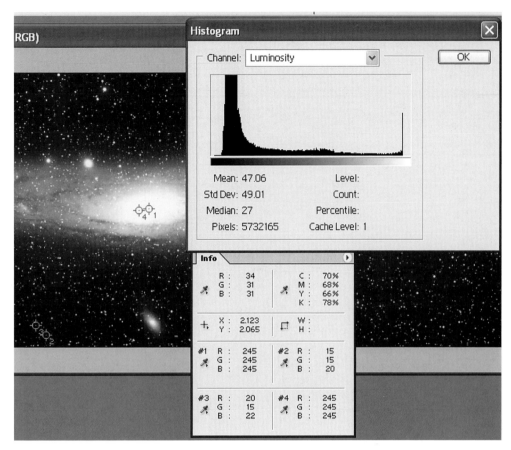

Fig. 3.18 The final result using targeted RGB values to set the black and white points. The white point (Color Sampler point #1) has been set at (245, 245, 245), while the black point (Color Sampler point #2) has been set to the chosen sky background value of (15, 15, 20). The Histogram reflects a tonal range that has been stretched over most of the tonal scale.

the white point affects the black point and vice versa.

16. If necessary, repeat steps 12 through 14 while refining the RGB values in the Info Palette until the desired target values are close to the established black point (15, 15, 20) and the white point (245, 245, 245). Since we are working with a Levels adjustment layer, we are not actually modifying the underlying image pixels with each of these steps. We are merely refining the black and white point settings in the Levels adjustment layer and "witnessing" what effect these settings will have on the image if and when we actually apply them by flattening the image ("Flatten Image" in the Layers Palette menu). This is one of the great advantages of adjustment layers. Had we set the black and white points using the menu command *Image\Adjustments\Levels*, each time we clicked OK to accept a Levels setting we would have changed the actual image pixels (a destructive edit). As a general rule of image-processing workflow, we want to minimize the number of times we alter the

original image pixels (destructive edits), while still achieving our desired final result. Adjustment layers are a powerful tool in this regard.

17. Finally, Double-click on the Move Tool icon (the little white glove) in the Toolbox. This is a shortcut that causes the image to fit on the screen. It does the same thing as the "Fit on Screen" button in the Zoom tool options. Examine the overall image and the RGB values. Turn the visibility of the Levels adjustment layer on and off (click the "eyeball" icon at the far left of the layer on and off) and notice the "before" and "after" Color Sampler values. Also examine the Histogram (*Image\Histogram*). The image, Info Palette and Histogram should look similar to **Figure 3.18**.

Now that we understand the methods to identify and set the endpoints of our tonal scale, what about all of the tones between those extremes? How do we handle those? In our next chapter, we will examine Photoshop's most powerful and elegant tool for making tonal and color adjustments — Curves.

R. Scott Ireland

Chapter 4
Adjusting Color and Local Contrast —
Introduction to Masking Techniques

We saw in Chapter Three how the Levels command, with its "built-in" histogram, is a very convenient tool to use when setting the black and white points in an image. We also observed how setting target black and white points may automatically correct, or at least minimize, an image color cast. Moving the individual Levels sliders in each color channel is another way to modify the color balance of an image — you will remember the example wherein we obtained unusual color shifts until the black and white point sliders were set in all of the color channels.

The problem arises when we try to use Levels to make more subtle color corrections and contrast adjustments. Levels only offers us 3 adjustment points to work with (black point, gamma and white point). It becomes difficult and unwieldy to use when we need to make more precise adjustments to the tonal values between the black and white points.

Fortunately, Photoshop offers us various tools and options for making color and contrast adjustments. One of the great strengths of the program is its broad, open structure. You will find that in most cases, Photoshop allows you to solve an image-processing task in several different ways. In the course of this and subsequent chapters, we will explore how to use many of these color adjustment and color selection tools. But first, let us look at the most important and powerful of these tools.

Curves

If I were going to be stranded on a desert island and I was given my choice of one, and only one, Photoshop tool to take along (presumably whoever banished me to the island would disable everything else in my copy of Photoshop), the choice is simple — Curves.

Curves offers us the most complete control over tone and color of any tool available. With it we may set or alter the white and black points, just as with Levels, but we may also adjust all of the other tonalities with

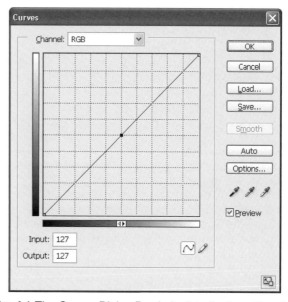

Fig. 4.1 The Curves Dialog Box in its "starting" position, before any adjustments have been made. All input and output tonal values are equal — the Curve is a straight line between the black point (bottom left) and the white point (top right). An adjustment point (also called a control point) has been manually placed at the middle-gray value of 127. Raising the Curve brightens tonal values; lowering it darkens them. Increasing the slope (steepness) of the Curve increases contrast; decreasing the slope lowers contrast. Adjustments are made by moving the Curve or by entering numbers directly into the input and output boxes.

far more precision. Curves allows us to set 16 adjustment points (also called control points) — 14 that we determine for ourselves, plus black and white — compared to only 3 adjustment points in Levels. Becoming adept with Curves takes a bit of work, but the more your image-processing skills advance, the more you will come to rely upon it.

Take a look at **Figures 4.1** and **4.2**. Here we see the Curves dialog box before any adjustments have been applied. Curves is an equal opportunity tool — no matter what your starting image looks like, every Curve starts out as a straight, diagonal line running

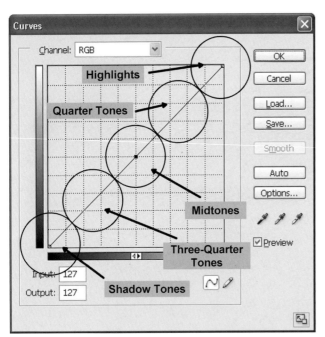

Fig. 4.2 The tonal regions represented by different areas of the Curve. In Grayscale mode, the direction is reversed, with the white point at the bottom left and the black point at the top right. To change the grid display between 4 x 4 and 10 x 10, hold down the Alt key and left-click anywhere inside the grid area. To make the entire dialog box bigger or smaller, click on the size icon at the bottom right.

from the bottom left to the top right. This straight line represents "no change" between the input (horizontal axis) and output (vertical axis) tonal values. For RGB images, black is typically at the bottom left (tonal value of 0) and white is at the upper right (tonal value of 255). A middle-toned value of 127 is located dead center. You may reverse the scale by clicking on the small black and white arrows at the bottom-center of the horizontal axis, but for our purposes leave black at the lower left and white at the upper right (**Figure 4.2**).

One works with Curves by placing points along the line and moving the Curve up or down. Moving a point up (or left) brightens it and moving it down (or right) darkens it. We may move the black and white points also, but this alters our tonal range and changes the shadows and highlights of a normal histogram. Increasing the slope of the Curve increases contrast; decreasing it lowers contrast. One of the reasons Curves is such a powerful tool is that it enables us to leave the black and white points anchored while changing the brightness of the other in-between tones. In other words, *Curves allows us to modify color and contrast without altering the tonal range of the image.*

Let's examine this concept further. **Figures 4.3**, **4.4** and **4.5** graphically illustrate what happens with Curves when the Brightness/Contrast control (*Image\Adjustments\Brightness/Contrast*) is used to alter image brightness and contrast. In **Figure 4.3**, we see a Curve that has been moved up without changing its slope. Overall image brightness has been increased without changing contrast. But the black and white points have been moved, resulting in highlight clipping and a large gap between the tonal range and the tonal scale at the shadow end. **Figure 4.4** reflects the Curves analog to darkening an image with Brightness/Contrast. Here the shadows have been severely clipped and the tonal range/tonal scale gap appears on the highlight side. Finally, in **Figure 4.5**, we see the effect of using Brightness/Contrast to increase the image contrast. The slope of the Curve has been increased (steepened) by moving the black and white points. Contrast is increased, but both ends of the tonal range are now clipped. So, how would we create a Curve representing decreased contrast using Brightness/Contrast? I will leave this to you as an exercise, but I'll give you one hint. The Curve will have 2 gaps at each end of the tonal scale, rather than the 2 flat areas (clipped areas) of **Figure 4.5**.

It should be clear from these examples why *Brightness/Contrast should never be used to make brightness and contrast adjustments!* It is easy to see graphically on the Curve what is happening to the image histogram. When brightness is changed, the Curve is raised or lowered at one end and flattened at the other end. The flat areas correspond to clipped data and the blank areas represent gaps in the tonal range. Increasing contrast results in flat areas on both ends of the Curve — clipping has occurred at both ends of the tonal range.

Now examine **Figure 4.6**. By leaving the black and white endpoints anchored and adjusting only the Curve between these points, image brightness and contrast have been successfully altered to accentuate the nebula. The histogram remains intact, without clipping, and the full tonal scale has been utilized. No other Photoshop tool offers this functionality. Only Curves allows us to adjust the *local contrast* — selectively modifying the brightness of different tonal scale values between the endpoints — without modifying the black and white points we have so carefully set.

Figure 4.6 reflects a type of Curve known as an "S" Curve. An "S" Curve increases contrast by bright-

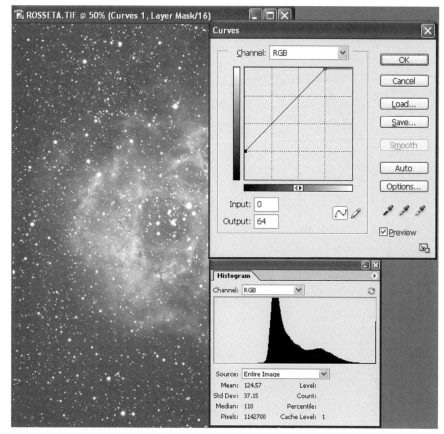

Fig. 4.3 This is the Curves equivalent of increasing image brightness with the Brightness/Contrast command. All tonal levels on the Curve have been raised (brightened) without changing the slope of the Curve (contrast). The black and white points have been changed, the tonal range no longer matches the tonal scale (there is a large gap on the shadow side) and the highlights have been clipped.

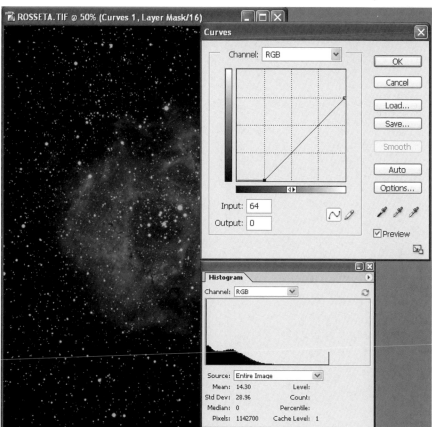

Fig. 4.4 The Curve for decreasing brightness using Brightness/Contrast. Shadows are severely clipped and there is a gap at the highlight end of the tonal scale.

R. Scott Ireland

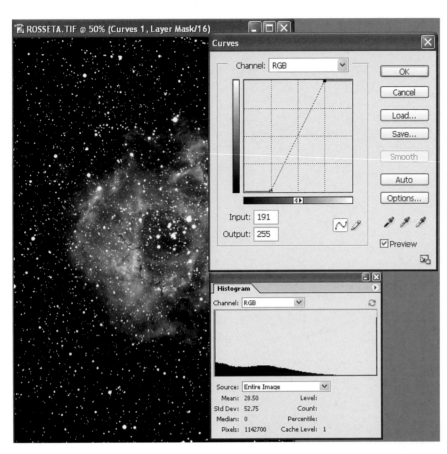

Fig. 4.5 The Curves equivalent of increasing contrast using Brightness/Contrast. The slope of the Curve has been steepened, increasing contrast. But now, both the shadows and highlights are clipped. These areas are graphically represented by the flat areas at each end the Curve.

Fig. 4.6 The correct way to increase image brightness and contrast. An "S" Curve has been created to increase the brightness of the midtones and highlights without changing the black and white points. The slope of the Curve between the three-quarter tones and midtones has been steepened for increased contrast. The histogram reflects no additional clipping (beyond that in the original) and the full tonal scale has been utilized.This fine image of the Rosette Nebula is by Herm Perez.

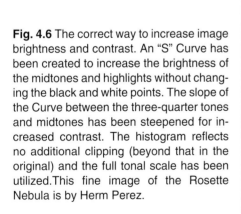

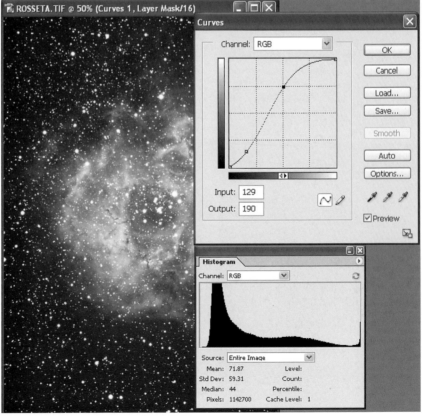

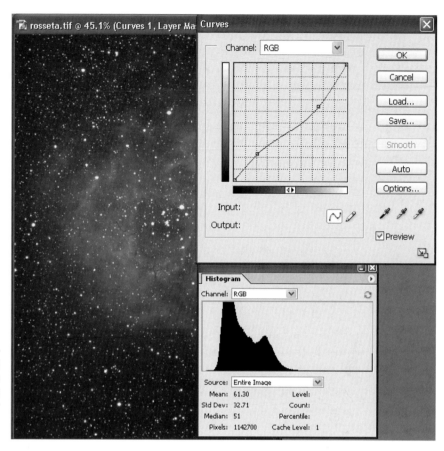

Fig. 4.7 The inverse of an "S" Curve. Overall contrast is reduced by flattening the Curve in the middle — the brightness of the highlights/quarter-tones has been lowered while the shadows/three-quarter tones have been raised.

ening the highlights and quarter-tones and darkening the shadows and three-quarter tones. By raising the "top" of the curve and lowering the "bottom", the slope of the Curve between these areas is steepened, increasing contrast.

If we reverse this procedure, we end up with a Curve that is flattened in the middle, reducing contrast. In **Figure 4.7**, the quarter-tones have been lowered in value, while the three-quarter tones have been raised, resulting in lower contrast between the three-quarter tones and quarter tones.

Using Curves to Adjust Color Balance and Contrast

With the unprecedented number of adjustment points (also known as "control points") available to the user, it should be apparent that Curves is the tool of choice to selectively modify image brightness and contrast. But notice too that the Curves dialog box has a Channel selection at the top. This allows us to adjust the individual red, green and blue color channels in addition to the overall RGB "channel" (which adjusts all the color channels equally). We may place up to 14 adjustment points, plus the black and white points, on *each* of these

Curves, giving us a total of 64 different adjustment points. With that much control available, it is easy to see why Curves is also the tool of choice for making image color corrections.

Let's work through an example:

1. From the tutorial disk, open the file Rosette1.psd (*File|Open*). This is an image of the Rosette Nebula taken by Herm Perez. If you have properly set your working color space to Adobe RGB (1998), you will immediately be presented with an Embedded Profile Mismatch dialog box. Select "Use the embedded profile" and click OK. This instructs Photoshop to display the image in the color space embedded with the image, which is presumably the same space in which it was created, in this case sRGB. Remember, there is no point converting an image created in a smaller gamut color space to a larger gamut space. Once information is gone, you can't recover it by using the larger gamut space. So there is no reason to convert this image to Adobe RGB (1998).

2. Double-click on the Hand Tool icon (little white glove) in the Toolbox to adjust the screen display

R. Scott Ireland

to make the image larger and fit on the screen. This does not alter the actual image pixels. Using the Zoom Tool (the small magnifying glass icon in the Toolbox) merely enlarges (or reduces) the display on the screen.

3. Now take a close look at the image. It is lovely just as it is; do we really need to make any further adjustments to it? Open the histogram with *Image|Histogram* (Photoshop CS and CS2 — *Window|Histogram*). Cycle through the histograms for luminosity and the individual color channels using the Channel drop-down box or these keyboard shortcuts:

   > Ctrl+ ~ (the "tilde" key) for luminosity
   >
   > Ctrl+1 for the red channel
   >
   > Ctrl+2 for the green channel
   >
   > Ctrl+3 for the blue channel

The histograms look pretty good; the blue channel seems to be shifted to the left a little compared to the others, but there are no obvious problems. Close the histogram dialog box by clicking on OK.

4. Next, make the Info Palette visible with *Window|Info* and notice that there are 4 Color Sampler points in the image; point #1 is the white point, located in the center of a bright star; points #2, #3 and #4 are sky background points (black point) placed in different areas of the image (see **Figure 4.8**). Notice that the blue channel values are somewhat lower than the red and green values at each of these points. Select the Eyedropper Tool (keyboard shortcut "I") and make sure that the Sample Size is set to 3 x 3 Average. Now move around to other areas of the image and examine the RGB values. The blue values are lower throughout the image. Even in the areas of red nebulosity (we expect high red values here of course), blue values are lower than green values. The image has a slight yellow color cast (remember the complementary nature of the RGB and CMYK color models; yellow is a combination of red and green without any blue, it is, in essence, minus blue).

Did you see this color cast? Don't feel badly if you didn't, most people would have missed it, even with a color-calibrated monitor. The human eye/brain system is a very wonderful and *adaptable* system. Our brains "know" what most things are supposed to look like and will modify our perceptions accordingly. You have surely seen daylight color-balanced film photographs

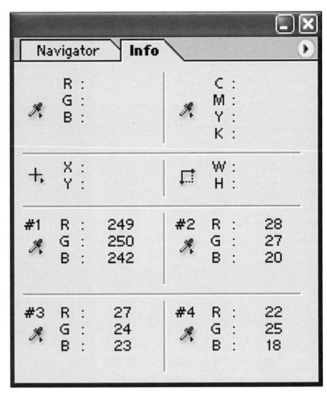

Fig. 4.8 The Info Palette with 4 Color Sampler points. The RGB values are for Rosette1.psd prior to any adjustments. Point #1 is the white point; points #2 through #4 are placed in different background (black point) locations. The image has a slight yellow cast — notice the low blue values at each point.

taken indoors under incandescent light — everything appears with a strong red/orange color cast. But when you relax indoors at night or read under your incandescent lamp, you do not see that same light as red. It looks fairly normal and white or yellow-white. Your brain knows what white, black and the other colors in-between are supposed to look like and it makes corrections on-the-fly. It is the ultimate color correction device.

The quickest way to spot color casts is to compare different versions of the same image side-by-side, each with a different color balance. Color biases will immediately "pop out" at you this way. You may be quite surprised at how easy it is to spot color differences in this manner, and how difficult it is with no comparison image(s). As you do more color correction work, you will become more adept at judging color, both visually and numerically.

One final point. Never underestimate the power of numbers! Learn to evaluate color by reference to RGB pixel values in addition to visual inspection. Make color corrections using numbers, not just "by eye". This

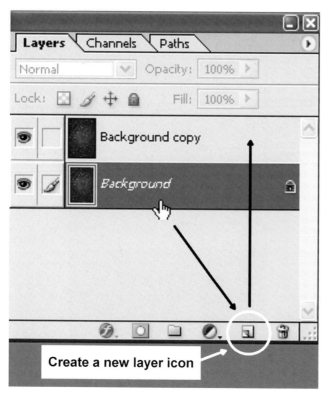

Fig. 4.9 To copy a layer (in this case, the Background layer), click-hold and drag it on top of the "Create a new layer" icon at the bottom of the Layers Palette, then release the mouse. The Background copy layer will appear above the Background. To discard a layer, drag the layer to the trash can icon just to the right of the Create a new layer icon.

will also help to overcome other factors, such as an improperly calibrated monitor. So, let's push on and use Curves to color correct this image "by the numbers".

5. Next, duplicate the image with *Image|Duplicate* and click OK. This leaves the original file alone and gives us an on-screen duplicate with which to make visual comparisons. One could also use the Photoshop Variations command (*Image|Adjustments|Variations*) to see comparison images. However, I find the small image windows unsatisfactory for critical work. Resize the image copy to fit the screen and position it to the right of the original image.

6. With Rosette1 copy the active image (click on it to make it active, if necessary), make the Layers Palette visible (*Window|Layers*). Then duplicate the Background layer — click-hold and drag it to the "Create a new layer" icon at the bottom-right of the Layers Palette (see **Figure 4.9**) then release the mouse. A new layer appears — Background

copy — above the original Background layer. It is identical to the Background layer (the original image). Why duplicate the Background? So that we may retain the original pixels intact on the base layer. Get into the habit of "working vertically" with Photoshop's layers. Perform each significant processing operation on its own layer, avoiding destructive edits. This workflow discipline will allow you to make additional revisions and corrections later without having to start over from the beginning.

7. Rename the Background copy layer to "Global Color Correction" by double-clicking on the layer name, typing in the new name and pressing the Enter key.

8. Add a Curves adjustment layer with *Layer|New Adjustment Layer|Curves* or by using the "Create a new fill or adjustment layer" icon (half black/half white circle) at the bottom of the Layers Palette. Make sure that the adjustment layer is located above the Global Color Correction layer. Layers work on a "top-down" basis. An adjustment made at the top of the layer stack will affect all of the layers beneath it, unless you selectively alter its visibility with masking or by other means. If you need to relocate the position of a layer up or down, just click-hold and drag the layer to relocate it to a new position in the layer stack. Adjust the size and position of the Curves dialog box so that you can clearly see the Rosette1 copy image. You may make the entire Curves dialog box bigger or smaller by clicking on the icon at the bottom right of the dialog box.

9. With the Curves dialog box still open, move the cursor into the image (Rosette1 copy should be the active image), click and hold down the left mouse button and observe what happens to the Curve as you move around in the image. A small open circle moves up and down the Curve corresponding to the mouse movements in the image. This circle shows the position on the Curve for the pixel(s) located under the cursor. To place an adjustment point on the Curve from the image cursor position, release the mouse, hold down the Ctrl key and click once. An adjustment point may also be placed on the Curve by clicking directly on the Curve itself. To remove an adjustment point, click-hold and drag the point outside of the grid area, then release the mouse. You may also delete

R. Scott Ireland

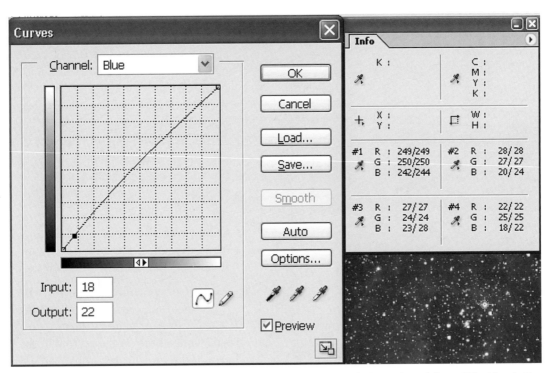

Fig. 4.10 Our first Curves adjustment has improved the overall color balance by adding a little blue to the shadow tones. Curves is a very subtle tool — small adjustments are the order of the day. Changing one tonal area generally affects other areas also, so one must work in steps and keep going back and forth between color channels, making small adjustments to achieve good results.

a point by holding down the Ctrl key and clicking on the point in the Curve.

10. Select the blue channel in the Curves dialog from the drop-down selection box, or with Ctrl+3. Place an adjustment point on the Curve with an Input value of 18. Click on the Curve to place the point and then move it until the Input value reads 18, or better yet just type 18 into the Input box. Don't worry about the Output value, we'll deal with that next.

An adjustment point must be "active" in order to change it. The active point is a dark circle; the inactive points are light circles. You may activate a point by clicking on it, but this can be tricky as it is very easy to nudge the point away from its previous Input and Output values. Instead, use keyboard shortcuts to select an active point. Ctrl+Tab cycles through points up the Curve; Ctrl+Shift+Tab cycles through points down the Curve. Use the up and down arrow keys to change Input and Output values or type in the values.

11. With the point you placed still active (Input value = 18), type 22 into the Output box. Observe the before and after pixel values in the Info Palette. Color Sampler #3 is going to end up a little too

blue, but the other points look better (**Figure 4.10**). We are not finished, but the image color balance has already improved quite a bit. Compare this to the original image (reposition the Curves dialog box if necessary). Now do you see the yellow cast?

12. Place another adjustment point (also known as a control point) on the blue channel Curve at Input value 240 and set the Output to 245. We also want the highlights and quarter-tones to have a bit more blue.

13. Press Ctrl+2 to switch to the green channel Curve. Place an adjustment point with Input-Output values of 25–22. Place another point with Input-Output values of 250–246. Ooops! This last adjustment point has caused the quarter-tones, midtones and three-quarter tones to lose too much green, and the image takes on a magenta cast. We need to "lockdown" that last adjustment point by placing another point (a "lockdown point") close to it and raising the Curve to restore green in the lower tonalities. Place another point on the Curve with Input-Output values of 242–238 (**Figure 4.11**).

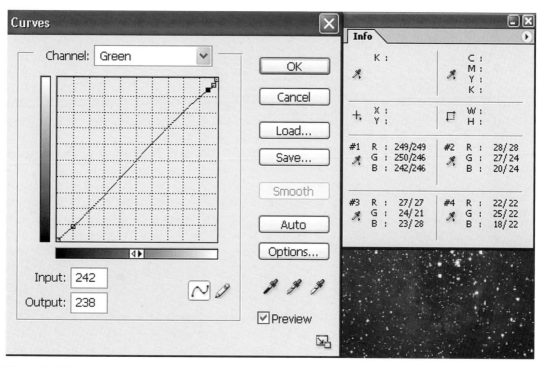

Fig. 4.11 Adjustment point 242–238 is a "lockdown" point. Reducing green in the highlights with the point 250–246 caused the Curve to dip too low in the quarter-tones, midtones and three-quarter tones, giving the image a magenta cast. Lockdown points serve to isolate changes to one area of the Curve.

Working with Curves is an art. You must make small adjustments, patiently and gradually moving toward your goal. Every adjustment may (and usually does) affect other tones and colors, so it becomes necessary to keep "tweaking" the Curve to gradually approach the desired RGB values. There are no knockout punches with Curves.

14. Next we turn our attention to the red values, which are now a bit high in the white and black points. Press Ctrl+1 to switch to the red channel. Starting with the value in Color Sampler #2, let's take a little red out of the shadows/three-quarter tones. Place a point with Input-Output values of 28–24. Color Sampler #4 has too little red. Place another point with Input-Output values of 19–21. Ooops! The Curve above the three-quarter tones has now fallen too low, dropping red out of the nebula and highlights. Place another point with Input-Output values of 42–40. This point serves as one of two lockdown points to maintain the tonal values between the three-quarter tones and quarter-tones. We will place a second lockdown point after we adjust the highlights. Color Sampler #1 shows that our last adjustment has again put too much red into the highlights — the white point now shows

a red value of 249. Place another point with Input-Output values of 249–246. Finally, place the second lockdown point with Input-Output values of 240–234. The red channel curve and Info Palette should now look similar to **Figure 4.12**. Don't worry if your RGB numbers are not exactly the same as the illustrations. They may vary somewhat depending upon the Sample Size setting used for the Eyedropper Tool.

15. Now press Ctrl+~ (the "tilde" key) to switch to the RGB channel. This "channel" adjusts all of the color channels equally. We will now adjust the image contrast locally — modifying selected areas of the tonal range without shifting our histogram endpoints. Our goal is to increase contrast to accentuate the nebula. The way we do this is to create an "S" Curve, since the nebula lies primarily in the midtones and three-quarter tones. We want to increase the slope of the RGB Curve in those specific areas. Place 3 adjustment points on the RGB Curve with Input-Output values of 33–24, 173–219 and 220–232. The adjusted RGB Curve and Info Palette are shown in **Figure 4.13**. Click on OK to close the Curves dialog box.

16. Do you see the yellow cast in the original image

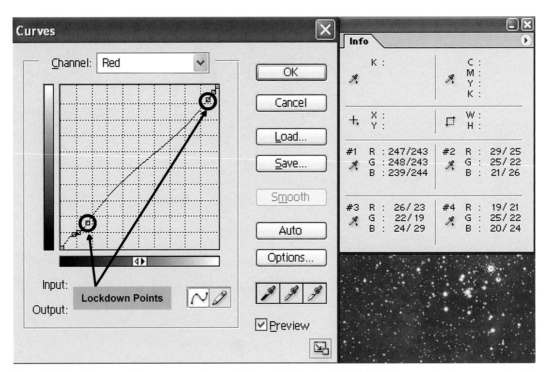

Fig. 4.12 The Curves adjustments to the red channel, affecting the highlights and shadows, required 2 lockdown points to maintain the other tonalities.

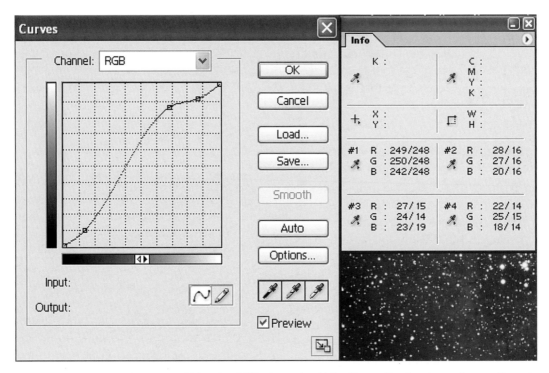

Fig. 4.13 Adjusting local contrast. Using the RGB channel, which affects all color channels equally, nebula contrast has been increased with an "S" Curve. The slope of the Curve has been increased between the three-quarter tones and quarter-tones. Note the RGB values after making color channel corrections. The white and black points are now mostly neutral in tone.

now? Another useful visual aid (particularly if you do not have a side-by-side comparison image) is to "blink" the image-processing changes on and off. With proper workflow technique, your Background layer will always be the original, unmodified image. In the Layers Palette you may turn off the visibility of all the other layers by holding down the Alt key and clicking on the small "eyeball" icon (this indicates a layer's visibility) at the left side of the Background layer. A second click (still holding down the Alt key) turns all of the other layers back on again.

17. Make sure all the layers are visible and Select the Eyedropper Tool from the Toolbox (keyboard shortcut "I"). The Sample Size (in the Tool Options Bar at the top of the window) should be set to 3 by 3 Average. Move throughout the image and examine the RGB values of various sky background points. A careful examination indicates that we have too much blue in some shadow areas and not in others, even though 2 of our shadow Color Sampler points look good. Point #3 is biased toward blue, and other locations in the image vary. What's going on here? Well, be patient! We will find out in our next tutorial exercise.

18. Save this file on your hard drive, keeping all of the layers intact. *File|Save As|Rosette1copy* and in the Format drop-down box select the Photoshop (PSD, PDD) format. Be sure the Save: Layers box is checked and that the Color: ICC Profile box is checked to embed the sRGB profile with the file. Click on Save. Learn to save your work with all adjustment layers, selections and masks intact by using the Photoshop *.PSD file format.

Applying Curves to a Selection — Introduction to Masking and Layer Masking

In our previous tutorial example, we performed an initial color balance on Herm Perez's image of the Rosette Nebula using Curves in each color channel. One thing needs to be clarified. The set of adjustment points that we used is not unique. There is no one set of points that "solves" the color balance of a given image. Any number of alternate sets of points may have worked equally well, or perhaps even better. You build your Curves gradually, by setting points, making small adjustments while referring to Color Sampler points, and then re-adjusting points until you have the results you want. The same or similar result may be achieved through many different sets of points. As an exercise, I encourage you to go back to the previous example and perform the initial color balance by creating your own set of Curves, without reference to the listed adjustment points.

When we concluded our last tutorial it was apparent that our initial color balancing efforts had not been entirely successful. The yellow color cast was removed and the overall contrast improved, but a new problem appeared. Some areas had the proper amount of blue, but other areas had too much blue. By fixing one problem, another problem becomes apparent. This is quite common. An image is a complete, integral structure of tones and colors — changes may resonate throughout an image in unexpected ways. The trick is to be aware of this and use it to your advantage.

Let's get back to work on the Rosette image:

1. Open the file you saved in the previous tutorial — *File|Open* and select Rosette1copy.psd. Click OK to accept the embedded sRGB color profile. If you did not save this file previously, open Rosette1.psd. Create a Curves adjustment layer (*Layer|New Adjustment Layer|Curves*) and select "Load" in the Curves dialog box. From the tutorial disk, load the Curves file Rosette1Curves.acv. Curves may be saved separately in their own files (*.acv). In this case, I saved the color correction Curves from the previous tutorial; you may re-create Rosette1 copy.psd by merely loading those Curves into the original image (Rosette1.psd).

2. Set up a side-by-side on-screen comparison image with (*Image|Duplicate*) and name the duplicate Rosette2copy. This will be our working file. Put Rosette2 copy on the right and size both images to fit on the screen (*Window|Fit on Screen*). Make Rosette2copy the active file by clicking on it once.

3. We know that our problem was uneven blue channel values. So how do we approach solving this issue? We can't place any more Color Sampler points (we've used all 4). How do we tell where to make adjustments? It is frequently helpful to exaggerate image features temporarily, such as contrast, colors or brightness, in order to more easily see subtle aspects of the image. In this case, let's add a Levels adjustment layer above our Curves adjustment layer — *Layer|New Adjustment Layer|Levels* and click on OK, or use the half black/half white circle icon at the bottom of the Layers Palette. In the RGB Channel, move the midtone

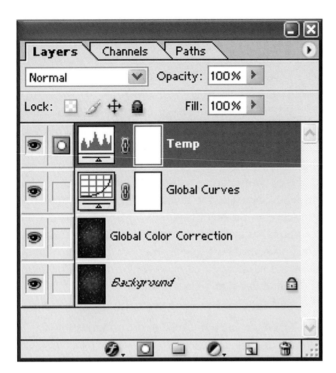

Fig. 4.15 The Quick Mask mode icons in the Toolbox. Clicking on the right square enters Quick Mask mode; clicking on the left square returns to normal editing mode. The keyboard shortcut "Q" enters and exits Quick Mask mode.

Fig. 4.14 Assigning descriptive layer names helps to organize image-processing tasks. Here we have added a temporary Levels adjustment layer to strongly exaggerate image color and brightness differences. This layer will be discarded after we have used it to build a selection mask.

(gamma) slider a good bit to the left to exaggerate brightness. Voila! Our problem immediately becomes apparent. The image contains a brightness/color gradient, or vignette. The edges of the image are not the same color and brightness as the central part. You can see that our 3 shadow Color Samplers lie in the darker edge areas. This is understandable, since the darkest tones in the image were identified in order to establish a black point. Click OK to close the dialog and accept this exaggerated Levels adjustment layer.

4. For good order's sake, let's rename some of our layers. Double-click on the Levels 1 layer name and rename it to "Temp". Rename the Curves 1 layer to "Global Curves". Your Layers Palette should now look like **Figure 4.14**.

5. Don't worry about the fact that the picture does not look good. First of all, the histogram is a little "ragged", since we are working with an 8-bit file. Second, we will discard the exaggerated Levels layer shortly. But first, we are going to use it to help us construct a layer mask.

So, what is a layer mask? For that matter, what is

a mask!? A mask is a grayscale image that is used as a selection device. It operates as a visual filter, allowing an image-processing task to be applied to certain areas of the image and blocking it from other areas. It may also be used to allow certain areas of an image layer to show through into the final image and other areas not to show through. Masks appear in the Channels Palette. They are Alpha Channels — channels that contain information other than image information. A layer mask is used to selectively apply portions of a layer (either an image layer or an adjustment layer) to the overall image.

6. Now we will make a mask that separates the darker edge areas of the image from the central area, in order to apply additional color corrections to the central area without affecting the edges. Enter Quick Mask mode by clicking once on the "Edit in Quick Mask Mode" icon in the Toolbox (**Figure 4.15**). You may also enter (and exit) Quick Mask mode by pressing the letter "Q" on your keyboard. Nothing happens to the image. But notice that the Foreground and Background colors in the Toolbox have changed to black and white, and the file description area at the top of the image window indicates that you are in Quick Mask mode. Double-click on the Edit in Quick Mask mode Toolbox icon to bring up the Quick Mask Options dialog box. You may change the mask color to suite your taste, but generally it is set to

red for easy visibility. When working on red objects, such as nebulae, you may wish to change the color to make the mask easier to see. For this exercise, red will work fine. Make sure that the opacity is set to around 50%, and that the color indicates the masked areas. Click OK and select the Brush Tool (keyboard shortcut "B"). In the Tool Options at the top of the Photoshop window, click once on the Brush icon to bring up the Brush Preset picker. Select a soft-edged brush or use the slider settings to select a brush of around 120 pixels with 0% hardness. Make sure that Mode is set to Normal, and both Opacity and Flow are set to 100%.

7. Set the Foreground Color to Black (the keyboard shortcut "X" will toggle the foreground and background colors back and forth; you may also click on the little double-arrow at the top-right of the foreground/background colors in the Toolbox). Double-check to be sure you are still in Quick Mask mode, and then use the Brush Tool to "paint" over the darker edge areas of the image. If you wish to change the size of your brush, get into the habit of using the left and right bracket keys on your keyboard. This is much faster than using the Tool Options to select a different preset. The right bracket key increases brush size; the left bracket decreases it. Don't worry about being precise as you "paint" your mask. One of the wonderful things about masks is that they are easy to change and refine. Paint your mask until it looks something like **Figure 4.16**. If you make a mistake, switch your foreground color to white (press "X" to toggle colors) and "paint out" the mask. Switch between adding to the mask by painting with black and removing from the mask by painting with white until you are satisfied.

8. Press "Q" to exit Quick Mask mode. The mask changes into a selection border (a line of "marching ants").

With a selection active, anything that you do to the image will be restricted to the area within the selection border.

In this case, we defined the selection border by a reverse procedure — we created a mask over the areas that we did not want to be affected (we "masked out" those areas). Upon leaving Quick Mask mode, the selection border appears around the unmasked areas — in this case, the central portion of the image. With this se-

Fig. 4.16 A soft-edged brush has been used in Quick Mask mode to "paint" a mask over the darker edges of the image. The semi-transparent area in light gray shows the masked area. This typically appears in a red, rubylith style. Remember, "black conceals and white reveals." Masked areas (black) conceal image areas or prevent changes from being applied to those areas. White areas of a mask allow the image to "show through" or permit changes to be applied to those areas. Gray areas partially conceal and partially reveal.

lection active, only that central portion will be affected by any changes or adjustments.

Repeatedly switching into and out of Quick Mask mode can be helpful to visualize and refine your mask/selection. Save the selection you created using Quick Mask with *Select\Save Selection*. Leave the Channel set to New, type in the Name "Edge Mask" and click OK.

9. At this point, save your file (*File\Save As* Rosette2copy.psd). Be sure to leave the boxes checked for Save: Alpha Channels and Layers. This way you can always revert back to this point and not lose your work. Clear the selection border with *Select\Deselect* (keyboard shortcut Ctrl+D).

10. From the Layers Palette, click once on the Global Curves layer to make it the active layer (the active

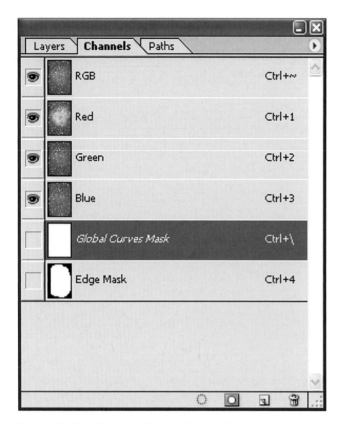

Fig. 4.17 The Channels Palette for the Global Curves layer. The selection we created with Quick Mask, and then saved, appears as an alpha channel ("Edge Mask"). This mask channel will appear regardless of which layer is currently active. The Global Curves Mask is an adjustment layer mask, and is displayed only when the Global Curves layer is active. "Painting" in an adjustment layer mask with black or gray limits the location and amount of the adjustment.

layer is highlighted in blue). Now open the Channels Palette (*Window|Channels*). Your Channels Palette should look like **Figure 4.17**. The selection we saved ("Edge Mask") is shown here as an alpha channel. Click the Edge Mask channel visibility icon (the little "eyeball" at the left) on and off. The mask appears and disappears in the image window. With the Edge Mask visibility turned on, turn off the visibility of the image channels by clicking once on the RGB channel "eyeball" icon. Your mask now appears in the image window. As a shortcut, if you are not in the mask channel, and it is not visible, you may display it in the image window and turn off all of the other channels by holding down the Alt key and clicking on the mask channel. You may edit your masks directly in the mask channel (with or without the image visible). If you now painted white, black or gray

in the image window, you would directly alter your mask. Go ahead and try it. Try painting with a gray tone also. When you are finished, merely delete the brush strokes using the History Palette (select and drag them to the trash can icon), or just close the file without saving, and then re-open it.

"Black conceals and white reveals". Painting a mask with black hides that image area from the layer stack or protects it from adjustment. White "opens up" that area of the image to show through into the layer stack or allow adjustments. Painting with shades of gray partially reveals and partially conceals the area — different shades of gray alter the opacity of the mask.

Masks and selections are different sides of the same coin. A selection is a mask that has been "activated". A mask is a selection that has been "stored" as an alpha channel.

11. While still in the Channels Palette, click-hold and drag the Edge Mask channel onto the "Load channel as selection" icon (a small dotted circle) at the bottom left of the Channels Palette, then release the mouse. Restore the visibility of the image (make the RGB "eyeball" visible) and turn off the visibility of the Edge Mask. Your image should now appear in the window with a selection border active.

12. Make the Layers Palette visible (*Window|Layers* or F7). Make the Temp layer the active layer by clicking on it. Now add a new Curves adjustment layer to the top of the layer stack using the "Create a new fill or adjustment layer" icon (half black/half white circle) at the bottom of the Layers Palette. A Curves dialog box appears. For now, just click OK without making any adjustments. Rename this new Curves layer "Targeted Curves" (double-click on the layer name and type in the new name).

Notice what has happened. The selection border disappeared. Photoshop has converted the selection into a layer mask for the new Curves adjustment layer. When an adjustment layer is created, Photoshop automatically converts an active selection into a mask for that adjustment layer. The thumbnail on the right side of the Targeted Curves layer is the icon for the layer mask (**Figure 4.18**). Notice too that the Temp and Global Curves adjustment layers also have layer mask thumbnails. But, since there were no selections active when we created these layers, Photoshop merely filled

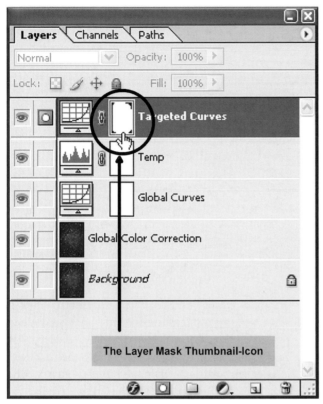

Fig. 4.18 Photoshop automatically adds a mask to an adjustment layer when it is created. If a selection is active, it will define the layer mask. If no selection is active, a completely white mask will be added ("reveal all") that permits application of the adjustment to the entire image (as in the Temp and Global Curves layer masks above). Layer masks may be edited, added or deleted at any point during image processing. To load a layer mask into the image window, hold down the Alt key and click on the layer mask thumbnail.

the masks with white to "reveal all" — adjustments in these layers will apply to the entire image.

13. Next we will soften our mask to smooth it out and make the edge transitions less harsh and obvious. Hold down the Alt key and click on the Targeted Curves layer mask thumbnail (the one to the right). The mask appears in the image window. Select *Filter|Blur|Gaussian Blur*, set the Radius to 40 pixels and click OK. The mask is smoothed considerably (see **Figure 4.19**). Click on the Global Color Correction layer to bring the image back into the window. Blurring a mask is analogous to "feathering" a selection. However, blurring a mask offers more control. You do not have to actually load the mask into the image window to work on it. Merely click once on the layer mask thumbnail to make it active. The image will still

appear in the window but the Gaussian blur (or any other filter or adjustment) will be applied only to the mask. This way you may preview the mask's smoothing effect on the image as you try different blur radius settings.

Even though a mask does not contain image information, it is a grayscale image. You may apply the same adjustment tools and filters to a mask that you apply to an image.

14. Now we will use our layer mask to selectively apply Curves corrections only to the central (non-vignetted) area of the image. Make sure that the visibility of the Temp layer is turned off (no "eyeball" icon visible at the left side of the Layers Palette). Re-open the Targeted Curves dialog box by double-clicking on the Curves thumbnail (the left one) in the Targeted Curves layer. Select the Blue channel (Ctrl+3) and place the following control points: 32–22, 44–33 (a lockdown point to prevent the midtones and highlights from being affected) and 20–21 (also a lockdown point). Click OK to close the Curves dialog box. This set of points slightly lowers the blue values in a narrow segment of the shadow/three-quarter tones. The mask restricts the adjustment to the central image area. I made a few adjustments to the mask I originally created (I painted with white and gray in the bottom left corner to open up this area to more of the targeted adjustment). When I finished finetuning the mask, the color balance of the entire image was fairly neutral. The effect is very subtle and not at all obvious to the eye. The proof of the pudding is in the RGB numbers shown in the Info Palette. This point bears repeating: learn to judge color by numbers as well as by eye.

15. I encourage you to experiment with your mask. Try using gray tones and different Brush flow settings. If you stray too far, merely delete the edits you don't want using the History Palette to restore an earlier History State (click and hold on the first edit you don't want, and drag it to the trash can icon. Be careful, though! Every edit performed after that point will also be deleted). Refine the Curves layers if necessary. Use the Eyedropper Tool and move the Color Sampler points around (hold down the Shift key) until you are satisfied that the yellow color cast has been removed throughout the image while keeping the background blue values neutral. But don't expect ev-

R. Scott Ireland

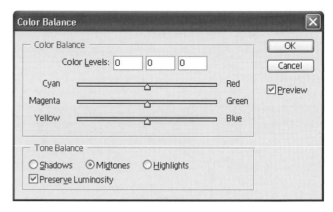

Fig. 4.20 The Color Balance dialog box. Shadows, Midtones and Highlights may be adjusted separately. Moving a slider right adds an RGB color. Moving left subtracts an RGB color (adds a complementary CMY color). "Preserve Luminosity" attempts to alter colors without shifting tonal values.

ery black point you check to be perfectly neutral. That would be unnatural-looking anyway. When you are done refining your mask, discard the Temp layer (click-hold and drag it to the trash can icon at the bottom right of the Layers Palette). The exaggerated Levels setting has done its job by highlighting the gradient problem and offering us an initial guide for creating the mask.

16. Save your final changes to the Rosette2 copy.psd file (*File\Save*). We will use this file again in our next tutorial.

Other Tools for Adjusting Color

Photoshop offers many ways to work with color. While Curves is the ultimate color correction tool, other tools can also be quite useful. Some offer unique settings unavailable with any other tool.

The Color Balance Command

First let's consider the Color Balance command (*Image\Adjustments\Color Balance*). Color Balance is also available as an adjustment layer. (*Layer\New Adjustment Layer\Color Balance*). Refer to **Figure 4.20**, and notice the three color sliders. Each slider has a subtractive primary color (CMY) on one side and its complementary additive primary color (RGB) on the other side. So, for example, by adding Red, we are subtracting Cyan and vice-versa. Adding Magenta is the same thing as subtracting Green. Subtract Yellow by adding Blue. And so forth. Three color level boxes appear at the top of the dialog box. The left box is Cyan-Red, the middle

Fig. 4.19 The original mask (top) has been smoothed using the Gaussian Blur filter with a 40 pixel radius (bottom). This method of smoothing transitions is preferable to feathering a selection. With a mask you have more control over the final result and may preview the effect upon the image while the filter is being applied.

is Magenta-Green and the right is Yellow-Blue. If you move a slider to the right, more of the RGB color on the right is added and the number in the box is positive. Move a slider to the left and the number is negative. You are "subtracting" some of the RGB color. Or, you are adding some of the CMY color on the left. It's the same thing. You say tomato, I say tomahto . . . .

The Color Balance command allows for separate adjustment of shadows, midtones and highlights, similar to Levels. But unlike Levels and Curves, Color Balance has a checkbox called "Preserve Luminosity". By leaving this checked, you are instructing Photoshop to alter the colors but keep the tonal values (luminance values) the same, which is a nice feature. When one channel is lightened, the other two channels are reduced in brightness to compensate. Photoshop will try its best to leave luminance alone, with more or less success depending upon the particular image and how much adjustment is applied.

So, you may wonder, why did we not use Color Balance to color balance our last example (similar to our not using the Brightness/Contrast command to adjust brightness and contrast)? First of all, Color Balance has no Eyedroppers to establish the black point, white point and midtone values. Both Levels and Curves have these. Second, Curves offers us far more control over the color correction process by allowing for so many adjustment points. The Color Balance command is easy to use and understand, and in the right circumstances it can do a good job. It is very effective for removing large, distinct color casts. But subtle corrections are more difficult. When you make adjustments to one area of the tonal scale, values in the other areas will shift also. The Color Balance sliders can be frustrating — you think you've got the shadows right and then the highlights shift. Fix the highlights and the shadows and midtones shift again, and so on. With Curves, you can isolate and lock down your adjustment points and "zero-in" on the desired color values.

As a starting point to adjust obvious color casts, by all means employ the Color Balance command. But make your final, detailed adjustments using Curves.

The Selective Color Command and Color Range

Selective Color (*Image\Adjustments\Selective Color*) is used to make color adjustments to a specific range of colors, without affecting the other colors in an image. Selective Color is also available as an adjustment layer (*Layer\New Adjustment Layer\Selective Color*).

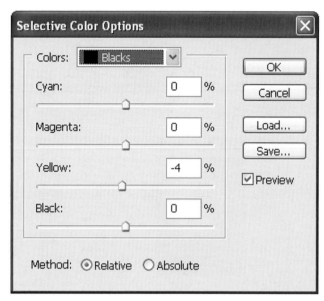

Fig. 4.21 Selective Color adjusts a single range of colors — cyan, magenta, yellow (CMY); red, green, blue (RGB); white, neutral (gray) and black. Color adjustments are made to the selected color range using the subtractive primaries — cyan, magenta, yellow and black (CMYK). The above adjustment to the black tones (sky background) applied to Rosette1.psd does a decent job of removing the yellow cast.

The Selective Color dialog box is shown in **Figure 4.21**. Notice the "Colors" drop-down selection box at the top of the dialog. Here is where you select the color range that you wish to adjust. The choices are (not in this order) the additive primaries — red, green and blue; the subtractive primaries — cyan, magenta and yellow; and whites, neutrals (grays) and blacks. Adjustments are applied to the selected color range using the subtractive primaries and black (CMYK). Here again, if you wish to add red to the selected range, just reduce the percentage of cyan; to remove blue, add some yellow; to add green, remove some magenta, and so on.

Selective Color adjustments are applied as percentages, with a "Method" of either Relative, or Absolute. "Absolute" adds or subtracts the specified percentage value directly to the original value (20% original value +10% adjustment = 30% new value). "Relative" adds or subtracts the specified percentage of the original value (20% original value +10% adjustment = 22% new value).

One problem with using selective color is that color casts are not generally limited to a specific color.

As a general rule, perform overall image corrections first, then work on the specifics (areas, color

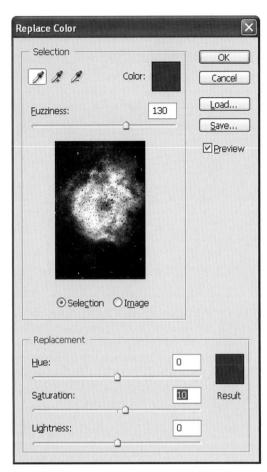

Fig. 4.22 The Replace Color command. A mask is created based on the color chosen with the Eyedroppers, and is expanded or contracted using the Fuzziness slider. The mask is used to selectively apply hue, saturation or lightness adjustments. Replace Color is limited in that it is not available as an adjustment layer, and the slider adjustments (other than saturation) are quite coarse.

ranges, etc.). Work globally first, then locally. This reduces the number of image-processing steps necessary and maximizes image quality.

In practice, Selective Color is generally most useful when working on the extremes of the tonal scale — whites and blacks, and sometimes neutrals. For astrophotographs, Selective Color can be helpful to adjust the sky background by selecting "Blacks". As an independent exercise, try this out using the Rosette1.psd tutorial example. Select "Blacks" as the Color and apply a Relative –4% (minus 4%) adjustment to Yellow. This does a pretty good job of removing the yellow color cast in the image. OK! OK! Don't get mad at me! Yes, this was a lot easier than making all of those Curves adjustments that we struggled through earlier. But make no mistake. Curves is the precision tool; the tool of

choice. If you learn nothing else except how to work with Curves, you will be able to solve almost any color problem. That said, a painter does not use only one brush. The more Photoshop tools and commands that you master, the more proficient, and efficient, you will become. Have as many tools and skills in your image-processing arsenal as possible.

Another, and more powerful, way to make selective color adjustments is to first use the Color Range selection tool (*Select|Color Range*) to create a selection based upon color, and then apply any type of image adjustment to that selection. The selection may also be inverted, feathered, saved as an alpha channel, turned into a mask and so forth. This provides the user much more control over the process. We will examine the use of Color Range selections in some detail in our next tutorial example, and we will meet this most useful tool again in subsequent chapters.

The Replace Color Command

Replace Color (*Image|Adjustments|Replace Color*) is perhaps the least useful of the color adjustment tools when working with astrophotographs. First, and most importantly, it is a destructive edit — Replace Color is not available as an adjustment layer. Once you hit "OK", that's it. You can't go back and fine-tune it except by deleting history states. Second, the same type of adjustment, with far more control, is available by combining a Color Range selection with the Hue/Saturation command, which we will examine shortly. Third, the mask you create with Replace Color cannot be saved or otherwise utilized. It is internal to the command and is "gone" after you apply your corrections. Lastly, I find the hue and lightness adjustments to be quite coarse and difficult to manage well, although the same may also be said of the Hue/Saturation command.

The Replace Color dialog box (**Figure 4.22**) is quite similar to the Color Range dialog box. Both employ color selection Eyedroppers. With Replace Color, the Eyedroppers are used to define a mask; with Color Range they are used to define a selection. Both offer a preview display of the mask/selection in the dialog box, and a Fuzziness slider to adjust the range of colors selected. The left-most Eyedropper is used to select a starting point color by clicking once on a color in the image window. The Eyedropper with a "+" (plus sign) adds colors to the mask/selection; the "–" (minus sign) Eyedropper deletes colors from the mask/selection. The selected areas are shown in white in the mask pre-

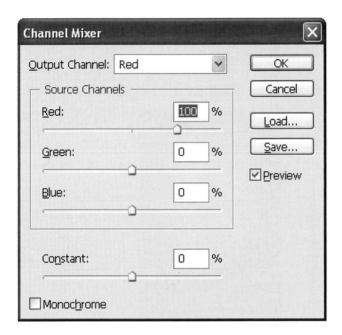

Fig. 4.23 Channel Mixer is the tool of choice for constructing a grayscale image, blending different percentages of the three color channels to bring out the most detail. It may also be used to make color adjustments by "re-mixing" the tonalities in the individual color channels.

view window; masked areas are black; and partially selected/partially masked areas are in gray tones. Hue, saturation and lightness adjustments are then made selectively, based on the mask, by using the sliders at the bottom of the dialog box.

The Channel Mixer Command

The Channel Mixer (*Image|Adjustments|Channel Mixer*) is a powerful and wonderful tool! (**Figure 4.23**). Thankfully, it is also available as an adjustment layer (*Layer|New Adjustment Layer|Channel Mixer*). We will examine the use of Channel Mixer in detail in **Chapter 9** on LRGB and channel mixing. It is without peer in converting a color image to grayscale. By checking the "monochrome" box at the bottom of the dialog box, and then blending selected amounts of each color channel, a black and white image with a maximum amount of tonal information and detail may be created. This works far better than converting the entire image to grayscale (*Image|Mode|Grayscale*), or using the Desaturate command (*Image|Adjustments|Desaturate*).

Channel Mixer may also be used to "re-mix" the tonalities of the color channels, and thereby make some very complex color adjustments. Rather than simply adding or subtracting color, Channel Mixer modifies

the mixture of grayscale tonalities from each color channel (red, green and blue) and directs the result to the selected Output color channel. This can sometimes be useful to "bolster" a weak color channel, without creating an artificial appearance. In other situations, such as when photographing planets using individual color filters, an entire color channel may be artificially constructed using the other two channels, with surprisingly good results. More on this later!

The Hue/Saturation Command

I've saved the best for last. If I could choose a second tool to take with me to my desert island, in addition to Curves, it would be the Hue/Saturation command (*Image|Adjustments|Hue/Saturation*). Why? Because it is the only tool that permits adjusting the amount of a color or colors (saturation), independent of hue and brightness. Hue/Saturation is also available as an adjustment layer (*Layer|New Adjustment Layer|Hue/Saturation*).

First, let me say right now that one should be subjected to a test and licensed before being allowed to use the Hue/Saturation command! It is a very powerful tool, one that is often misused, and it can wreak havoc on an image if not employed with care and finesse. The Hue and Lightness sliders are extremely sensitive — seemingly small adjustments result in big effects on the image. Frankly, I never use the Lightness slider and recommend the same to you. Having worked hard to establish a proper tonal range using Levels and Curves, why use a ham-fisted bludgeon of a tool to screw it up? I rarely use the Hue slider to alter colors either, for the same reason. The real magic of Hue/Saturation lies in the Saturation slider and using the available color range selection tools to target the effect.

Refer to the Hue/Saturation dialog box shown in **Figure 4.24**. In the "Edit" drop-down selection box at the top of the dialog, one chooses either "Master", which applies adjustments to all colors, or a particular additive or subtractive primary color range: Red, Green, Blue, Cyan, Magenta or Yellow. When editing a color range, the bottom of the dialog box shows the now familiar Eyedropper tools. These may be used to select a color from the image itself and add to it using the "+" Eyedropper, or subtract from it with the "–" Eyedropper. The color range shown in the Edit box will automatically change depending upon the image colors selected with the Eyedroppers. The spectrum of colors appearing at the bottom of the dialog box encompasses

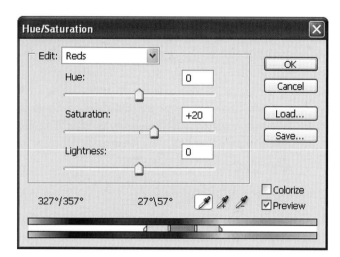

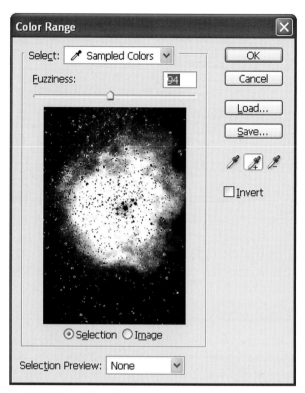

Fig. 4.24 Only the Hue/Saturation command allows for independently modifying saturation — the intensity of a color or color range — without altering the colors themselves (hue) or their brightness levels (lightness). Using the Eyedropper color selectors and the color wheel sliders at the bottom of the dialog allows for precise control over the color range affected.

Fig. 4.25 The Color Range command creates a selection based upon color. Eyedroppers are used to identify target colors within the image. The Fuzziness slider expands or contracts the range of colors selected.

all of the colors in a color wheel, laid out linearly. The top color "line" shows the color wheel before adjustment, the bottom line shows the colors after adjustment. The two white vertical bars in between the color lines define the color range to be adjusted; they may be moved manually by click-holding and dragging either one in or out to contract or expand the affected color range. They will move automatically when colors are selected with the Eyedroppers. Outside of the vertical sliders, on either side, are white triangular sliders. These are the "fall-off" sliders. Think of them as being used to "feather", taper or smooth out the Hue/Saturation adjustments. They define a range of colors, on either side of the adjustment range, across which the adjustments will gradually taper off to zero. Each of the triangular sliders may be moved independently by click-holding and dragging. To move the entire set of adjustment bars and triangles, click-hold and drag the dark gray area between the two vertical bars. To move either the left or right triangle and vertical bar simultaneously, click-hold and drag on the light gray area between the triangle and vertical bar.

Let's work through an example.

1. Open the file Rosette2 copy.psd (*File|Open*). This is the file you saved at the end of the previous tutorial. If you did not save this file, don't worry about it. Open Rosette1.psd from the tutorial disk instead.

2. Next, we will use the Color Range selection tool

to create a selection border around the nebula. Choose *Select|Color Range*. A dialog box like that shown in **Figure 4.25** appears. Be sure that "Sampled Colors" is chosen in the Select drop-down box, "None" is chosen in the Selection Preview drop-down box and that the "Selection" button is chosen under the preview window. Choose the left Eyedropper and click once on a bright red portion of the nebula in the image window. A mask appears in the preview window with the selected color shown in white and everything else in black. Sample additional parts of the nebula using the + (plus) Eyedropper. As a shortcut, just hold down the Shift key while using the initial selection Eyedropper (the left one). If you select too much, for instance the sky background area, then use the – (minus) Eyedropper (or hold down the Alt key while using the left Eyedropper) to remove colors from your selection. Use the Fuzziness slider in conjunction with the Eyedroppers to fine-tune your selection of the nebula. The idea is to make the white, non-masked area in the preview window cover the entire nebula, including the faint outer portions. Adjust the mask until it appears similar to the one in **Figure 4.25**, then click OK.

3. A selection border ("marching ants") now appears in your image window. We will now create a Hue/Saturation adjustment layer with a mask that will apply the adjustments we make only to the nebula. From the Layers Palette, select the top-most layer (so that we will be adding the new adjustment layer to the top of the layer stack). Create a Hue/Saturation adjustment layer (*Layer|New Adjustment Layer|Hue/Saturation* and click OK; or click on the half black/half white circle icon at the bottom of the Layers Palette and choose Hue/Saturation). The Hue/Saturation adjustment layer now appears at the top of the layer stack, along with a layer mask based on the selection we made with Color Range. Remember, an active selection will automatically be turned into a layer mask when an adjustment layer is created. Click on "OK" in the Hue/Saturation dialog box to close it for now.

4. Your Layers Palette should now resemble **Figure 4.26**. Bring the new Hue/Saturation layer mask into the image window by holding down the Alt key and clicking once on the layer mask window. We will now blur the mask slightly so that our saturation adjustments are applied smoothly. Select *Filter|Blur|Gaussian Blur*, set the Radius to 20 pixels and click OK. This also helps to eliminate any star halos inadvertently selected when Color Range was applied. Your layer mask should now resemble **Figure 4.27**.

5. Bring the image back into the image window by clicking once on the Background layer. Re-open the Hue/Saturation dialog box by double-clicking on its icon at the left side of the Hue/Saturation adjustment layer. Set "Edit" to the "Master" channel. We need not worry about selecting a particular color channel, since we have already selected the nebula itself (all red) using Color Range. Increase the Saturation slider to +20 and click OK to close the dialog box. Now examine your results by clicking the visibility of the Hue/Saturation adjustment layer on and off (click on the little "eyeball" icon at the left side of the layer). The effect should be subtle, not overpowering, giving the nebula a little more emphasis. Zoom into the image and move around to examine the nebula. Be sure that there are no unnatural-

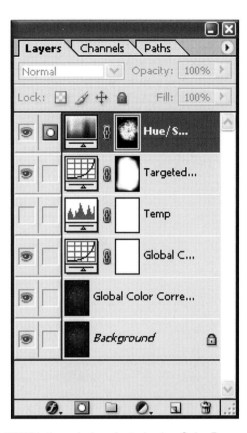

Fig. 4.26 With the nebula selected using Color Range, a layer mask is automatically created when the Hue/Saturation adjustment layer is added (top of the layer stack). Saturation adjustments made with this layer will be applied only to the nebula.

looking areas and that the star colors are unchanged. If necessary, you may refine your layer mask by painting with black, white or gray. You may also vary the saturation settings or the opacity of the entire layer. When you are satisfied, I invite you to open the original image (Rosette1.psd) and compare the two images side-by-side. You will be astounded at the difference.

Now let's try selectively adding saturation a different way.

6. Delete the Hue/Saturation adjustment layer and layer mask we just created by click-holding and dragging it to the trash can icon at the bottom-right of the Layers Palette. If you prefer to keep this version of the image to experiment with later, then save it first (*File|Save As*), giving it a different file name.

7. Add a new Hue/Saturation adjustment layer to the top of the layer stack, just as we did in step #3 above. This time, the layer mask will be blank

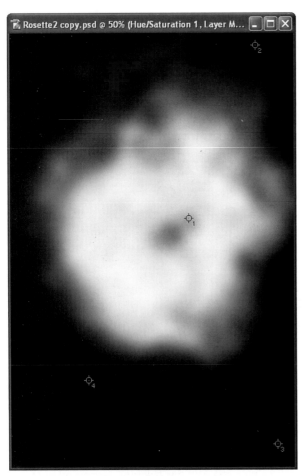

Fig. 4.27 The Hue/Saturation layer mask after applying a 20 pixel Gaussian Blur. Adjustments will be applied smoothly, giving the image a more realistic appearance with less chance of posterization or other processing artifacts.

since there is no selection active.

8. With the Hue/Saturation dialog box open, select "Reds" (shortcut Ctrl+1) in the Edit drop-down selection box. Be sure that the Preview box is checked.

9. Click once on the left Eyedropper (this is the initial color selector). Move into the image window and click once on a bright red portion of the nebula. Ring any bells? This is the same procedure we used within the Color Range dialog box in step #2. This time, we are working directly within the Hue/ Saturation dialog to define the range of colors to adjust. Instead of "physically" isolating the nebula

with a selection/mask, we are isolating the nebula colors.

10. Sample several additional areas of the nebula using the "+" (plus) Eyedropper (or hold down the Shift key while using the left Eyedropper). The white vertical sliders at the bottom of the dialog may move apart slightly as more nebula colors are selected. The area between the two vertical bars defines the range of "reds" to be adjusted.

11. Move the fall-off sliders — the white triangles on either side of the vertical sliders — inward so that they are just outside of the selected color range. Since we are not limiting our working area with a selection or mask, we want a fairly sharp fall-off. We do not want to alter magenta or orange/yellow tones, only the red nebula.

12. Set the Saturation slider to +20 and click OK to close the Hue/Saturation dialog. Here again, examine the results carefully to be sure that there are no unnatural artifacts created and that the star colors remain intact. If necessary, re-open the Hue/ Saturation dialog box and make adjustments (love those adjustment layers!).

Both of these methods targeted the Saturation adjustment to the nebula only. In some cases, you may find it beneficial to combine multiple selection methods. For instance, a layer mask may be used to isolate an image area, and then a particular color range within that area may be further targeted from within the Hue/ Saturation dialog.

A common problem when increasing image saturation is *posterization*, which manifests itself as a "clumping together" of colors and a loss of detail in the saturated areas. This occurs because increasing saturation drives more of the pixels toward their purest colors. *In general, avoid saturation increases of more than +20*, and be careful even at that setting. Apply your saturation adjustments selectively, as we did above. Examine results carefully and back off if artifacts appear. Saturation is an incredibly useful tool to emphasize (or de-emphasize) color, but it must be used with care. Subtle adjustments are the order of the day.

Chapter 5
Stacking

One of the first things someone new to astrophotography encounters is the concept of image stacking. Ever since the Charge Coupled Device (CCD) became the principal image capture device for amateur astrophotographers, it has become standard practice to take multiple images of the same object while in the field, in order to later combine them together in the digital darkroom to improve the image. This practice has been successfully applied to film images as well as digital captures. Stacking has become such a standard part of our current astrophotography lexicon that virtually all images are now created using this technique. So what is stacking and why is it beneficial?

Let's first discuss terminology. In this book stacking means mathematically combining two or more images to improve the signal-to-noise ratio (S/N) of the combined result. Typically, this involves either summing or adding image pixel values together, similar to the Track-and-Accumulate function in CCD cameras; or, alternatively, averaging the pixel values of the images. The term composite or compositing means selecting particular *areas* within different images to be combined into a new image. Creating a mosaic from several images is one way to make a composite.

A signal is the image that we are trying to capture while noise means any thing that degrades the signal. Noise can be airplane trails, dust, scratches, hot pixels, stray black or colored pixels, cosmic ray hits, sky glow, background color and luminance gradients, vignetting and uneven field illumination, thermal and bias artifacts, amplifier noise, artifacts from reading-out information on a CCD chip, quantization effects in analog/digital conversions, and so on.

Random noise elements are things that vary from frame-to-frame when taking multiple shots of the same subject. Film grain is an example — two different exposures of the same object do not exhibit the same background grain pattern. The quantum nature of light gives rise to photon noise, due to the uncertain arrival times of individual light quanta, and contributes to the mottled appearance in the background of digital imag-

es, similar to film grain (**Figure 5.1**). Shorter CCD exposures of faint objects will appear much grainier than longer ones. During a long exposure, enough photons arrive from a faint object to converge around a value of central tendency (in statistical parlance a Poisson distribution), to smooth out, but not completely eliminate, this random background graininess.

Our goal is to remove as much noise as possible from an image without degrading the image in the process. The war on noise is fought on several fronts, and we will explore techniques to reduce noise in this and subsequent chapters. With digital captures, the first step in this battle is to meticulously calibrate your images by applying dark frames, flat-field frames and bias subtraction to minimize thermal noise, uneven illumination and aberrations in the optical system, nonuniformities in the CCD chip and camera bias offsets. These procedures seldom are done in Photoshop and are beyond the scope of this book. Nevertheless, they are an essential first step in the battle against noise. There are many sources of information available to the reader covering this subject, and many excellent software packages are available (AIP for Windows, CCDSoft, Mira, MaximDL, and Ray Gralak's Sigma Combine are representative) that do the job better and easier than Photoshop can.

But now let's get back to our original question — what is stacking and why is it beneficial? Stacking consists of three steps.

- First, we must take multiple exposures of the same image subject.
- Second, we must align, or register, these images so that they "line up" — the same stars, galaxies and nebulae must appear in the same place in each frame down to the individual pixel level.
- Third, the aligned images are then arranged vertically, or stacked, and mathematically combined into a new single image.

The reason that this procedure is beneficial is that the stars, galaxies and nebulae (or any other image subject) remain essentially unchanged from frame to frame, but random noise does not. When we add two images to-

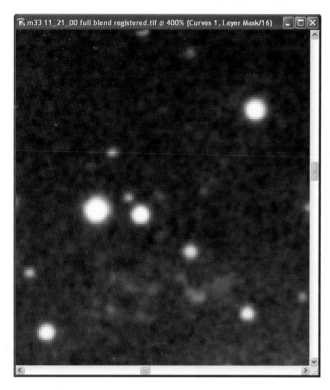 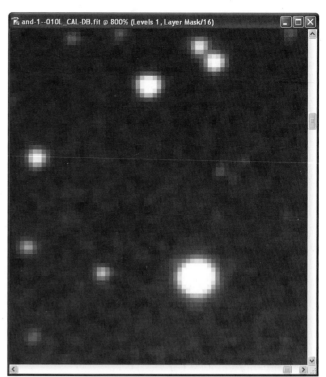

Fig. 5.1 Background noise in the form of film grain (left). On the right, a calibrated CCD image still shows background artifacts similar in appearance to film grain. Both are examples of random noise that can be significantly improved by stacking multiple images (film image courtesy of Herm Perez).

gether in a stack, the signal (galaxies, stars, nebulae, etc.) doubles (a 2x signal increase), but random noise only increases by the square root of 2 (a 1.4x noise increase) since it is governed by Poisson statistics. The signal-to-noise ratio has improved by 1.4 times (2x signal increase divided by 1.4x random noise increase). In other words, the brightness levels of the target have improved by a factor of 1.4 compared to the brightness levels of the background noise. If we stack 4 images, the signal increases 4x, but the noise only increases by the square root of 4, or 2x. So, the S/N ratio improves 2x (4x signal increase divided by 2x noise increase). We may therefore say that stacking improves the S/N ratio by the square root of the number of frames stacked:

- A 2 frame stack gives a 1.4x S/N improvement (the square root of 2)
- A 9 frame stack gives a 3x S/N improvement (the square root of 9)
- A 25 frame stack gives a 5x S/N improvement (the square root of 25)
- A 100 frame stack gives a 10x S/N improvement (the square root of 100).

This formula also holds true for increasing exposure time (doubling the exposure time improves the S/

N ratio by 1.4x). Stacking builds "exposure time" linearly by simply adding the luminance levels of multiple frames together. In essence, stacking *is* the same thing as increasing exposure. The real world, of course, is a little more complicated. Noise is also introduced each time that you read-out data from the CCD chip, so combining short exposures may not always be as good as taking longer ones. With film images there are issues arising from film's non-linear response to light. But when it comes to reducing noise, stacking equally-timed exposures improves the S/N regardless of capture source or total exposure time.

How many images should you stack? Should you go out every night for the next year and shoot 1,000 more images of the Orion Nebula in order to improve your S/N by 32x? Or 100 images to improve it 10x? Or maybe only 10 images to eke out a 3.2x improvement? As you can see from these numbers, stacking obeys another law — the law of diminishing returns. It takes 10 times the number of images to improve the S/N by 3.2 times. So you must find the best trade-off you can between improving image quality and the effort involved in obtaining additional images to stack.

Several factors come into play. Longer exposures

have higher S/N ratios than shorter ones, so fewer stacked images are necessary. Due to film's non-linear response curve, it takes a lot more exposure time to acquire film captures that are comparable to CCD captures. An entire night's work on one subject may only result in 3 or 4 film frames to stack. High quality astronomical CCD cameras produce higher S/N images than webcams or digital cameras. It is not uncommon to see planetary webcam stacks of 500 or 1,000 images, while CCD stacks typically run between 5 and 20 images per channel. The inexpensive webcam is a much noisier device than the expensive CCD camera, and webcam exposures are very short (since the planets are bright), generally around 1/10 second per video frame. You need to stack a lot of frames to reduce the high noise levels visible in the individual frames.

A common beginner's question is, "why can't I stack the same image together several times and achieve the same result as taking multiple exposures?" The answer is that the noise is no longer random. The same background noise appears in the same place in each of the frames and so will be summed together exactly like the signal. No S/N improvement will be obtained, no matter how many times you stack the same image. If you scan the same film image several times and stack the results nothing is gained. The film grain is in the same place in each frame, so stacking builds up noise and signal equally.

At what point in the image-processing workflow should you stack your images? Generally, this should be done very early, before engaging in processes such as setting the black and white points, color correcting and altering contrast. Your final results will be better if you stack before undertaking extensive pixel luminance manipulations. Some stretching may be necessary on high bit-depth images before stacking, but the idea is to minimize these steps, handle them with care, and stack as soon as possible. That way, the noise is not altered and "enhanced" along with the signal. With CCD images, stacking generally flows naturally from the calibration process. After applying darks and flats to the individual frames, most of the "CCD-specific" programs that are commonly used have built-in tools to align and stack the calibrated images. Be sure to stack at the highest bit-depth available. Perform stacking on 16-bit images before converting to 8-bits (assuming you have to convert to 8-bits at all — it's better if you don't!). For film images, if your scanner allows it, scan at 16-bits and do your stacking immediately after scanning.

There are several standalone software packages available that are specifically designed to stack astronomical images. One of the very best is *Registar* (**Figure 5.2**) from Auriga Imaging (see Appendix). This program works equally well with CCD or film images and literally counts and registers the position of the thousands of stars that may appear in an image. It makes superb alignments, even with images taken at different focal lengths. It also offers a crop/pad feature so that images may be easily aligned and cropped to the same pixel dimensions. This is very important with film scans, since each one will generally have different pixel dimensions. When combining images using Photoshop's Apply Image command, the individual images must have the same pixel dimensions in order for the command to work.

Methods for Combining Stacked Images

There are several techniques that may be used to mathematically combine images in a stack. The principal ones are as follows:

1. **Addition** directly adds the pixel values of each image in the stack. This is the same process used with the "track and accumulate" mode in CCD cameras. The problem with straight addition is that for images that already have a tonal range that extends over the full tonal scale, the highlight values quickly become clipped, since signal values are doubled with each additional image in the stack. Those values that lie near the maximum end of the tonal scale will "hit the wall" by reaching their maximum values (255 for 8-bit images; 65,535 for 16-bit images) resulting in loss of detail. As a practical matter, the final image stack will generally require application of a scaling factor (division by an integer value or application of a constant) in order to avoid highlight clipping, so the end result is the same as the Average method. Mathematically, there is no difference in S/N improvement between the Addition and Average methods — Average is merely the application of a constant to the Addition method. In Photoshop, Addition is performed using the Apply Image command (*Image|Apply Image*). This method will be covered with a tutorial example.

2. **Averaging** pixel values is the most straightforward and commonly used method to combine stacked images. Individual pixel values are added together and divided by the number of images in the stack to arrive at a final value. For images that

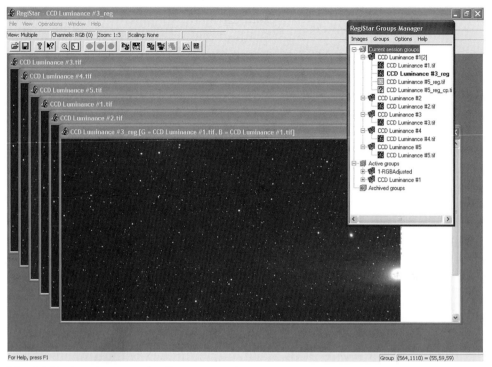

Fig. 5.2 Registar is a superb utility program for highly accurate alignment and stacking of astronomical images. It is also useful when images are to be stacked in Photoshop, since Registar easily allows aligned images to be cropped and padded to the same pixel dimensions.

were all taken with the same exposure, the combined and averaged signal values will be the same as the original signal values in each individual image, but the combined and averaged random noise will decrease according to the S/N formula we have already examined. Although average combines are typically performed more easily using third party software, I sometimes use Photoshop to combine and average two or more sets of images that were initially stacked using another program. Averaging a stack in Photoshop is done with layers and layer opacity settings, as will be demonstrated in a tutorial.

3. **Median** combine adjusts the pixel values so that they lie at the middle of the range of values exhibited in the individual images. In other words, for each median combined pixel value, half of the images in the stack have a higher pixel value and half have a lower value. The results of a median combine are similar to, but not exactly the same as, using average. The benefit of a median combine is that it will eliminate outlier events, such as cosmic ray hits, airplane trails or hot or black pixels. These extreme "one-off" pixel values tend to be

eliminated using median, but they are added into the result when the average or addition methods are used. The downside of the median method is that it produces less improvement in S/N than average (addition), leaving more evident background graininess. Performing median combines on groups of images, and then averaging the groups together improves this somewhat, but the S/N is still less than a straight average. Photoshop does not offer a way to stack using the median combine method.

4. **Sigma Combine,** Ray Gralak's Sigma freeware program (see Appendix), is popular among CCD imagers. By using two different noise reduction algorithms, Sigma purports to give results that are the best of both the average and median combine methods. The program also allows you to compare a sigma combine to an average or median combine with one mouse click. In my experience Sigma delivers on its promise — the CCD images I have stacked with Sigma exhibit a higher S/N than any other method. I highly recommend incorporating this program into your CCD image calibration workflow.

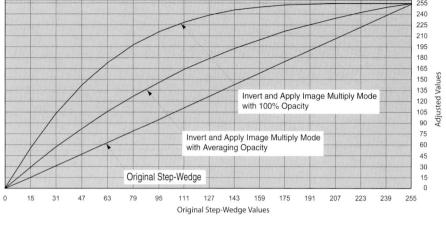

Fig. 5.3 The "Invert and Multiply" Hybrid stacking method. Photoshop's *Apply Image* command is used to combine inverted (negative) images with the Blending Mode set to Multiply. The effect is no different from applying a simple Curve to an Averaged set of images. Varying Opacity alters the steepness of the Curve.

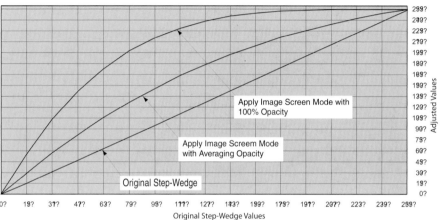

Fig. 5.4 Look familiar? This chart is the same as **Figure 5.3**. Using *Apply Image* with the Screen Blending Mode is identical to inverting the images and using Multiply mode, since Screen and Multiply are inverse processes — Screen lightens and Multiply darkens. It is better practice to improve the signal-to-noise ratio (S/N) of a stack by Averaging or Adding images. Apply your own Curve to the result. This will give you far more control over the process, and will avoid enhancing non-random noise, such as vignetting and background light gradients.

5. **Hybrid Methods (Multiply; Screen)** Some imagers achieve good results by using what I call hybrid stacking or combine methods. One popular process involves inverting the luminance portion of a set of images to obtain the equivalent of photographic negatives. These black and white negative images are then stacked using Photoshop's Apply Image command (*Image\Apply Image*), with the blending mode set to Multiply, instead of Add. Multiply mode gradually darkens the pixel values between black and white, leaving the black and white points themselves unchanged. Since the images are negatives, the fainter details of nebulae, galaxies and the like are rendered progressively darker with each image stacked. When the image stack is then inverted back into a positive, faint details are rendered more visible. A mask is often used in this process to apply the effect more subtly, and direct the enhancements to a particular area of the tonal range (**Figures 5.3 and 5.5**).

In fact, the same result may be achieved more easily by not inverting the images and just using the Screen Blending Mode instead (compare **Figures 5.3 and 5.4**). Screen mode gradually lightens all of the pixels between the black and white points, again leaving the endpoints unchanged. Screen is the exact inverse of Multiply. Therefore, nothing is gained by inverting, Multiplying and then re-inverting the combined images back into a positive. This just adds unnecessary processing steps.

I am not a big fan of the hybrid methods, although good results may be achieved. In truth, these methods combine two separate processing operations (hence the term "hybrid") that I prefer to handle individually. In addition to combining images mathematically to improve S/N, Multiply and Screen modes also apply a curve, selectively altering the brightness of a particular range of pixels (**Figures 5.3, 5.4 and 5.5**). I prefer to apply Curves myself as a separate step, to retain precise control over local contrast adjustments, rather than letting Photoshop apply a simple, generic curve that may or may not work best with a particular image. Allowing Photoshop to apply a curve at such an early processing stage may also result in accentuating non-random noise

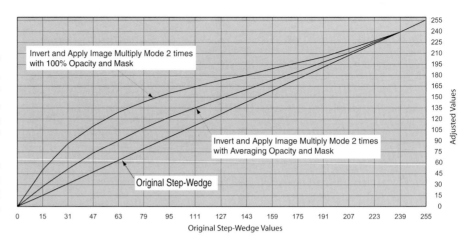

Fig. 5.5 Here the Apply Image "Mask" box is checked when combining inverted images using the Multiply Blending mode. By employing the original image as a mask, the Curve is skewed to enhance the brightness of the three-quarter tones and mid-tones. Here again, applying your own Curve directly and constructing your own mask provides more control and avoids potential pitfalls using "automated" processing steps.

like vignetting and sky gradients. Additional noise reduction techniques may need to be applied before adjustments are made with Curves.

In Photoshop, use Average or Addition to improve the S/N of a stack. Apply any additional noise reduction techniques needed and then enhance the fine details (the local contrast) by using separate curves layers. Trying to achieve a "one-punch knockout" using Multiply or Screen modes may sometimes work, but better results can often be achieved by taking control of the process directly using Curves.

Aligning and Stacking Images Using Photoshop

Let's now turn our attention to concrete examples. There are basically two different methods available to stack images in Photoshop. The first involves placing each image to be stacked into its own layer, aligning the layers so that the images are correctly registered and then adjusting each layer's opacity setting to average the individual images into a combined result. The second method requires first aligning the images, then cropping each one to the same pixel dimensions, then combining them directly, two at a time, using either the Apply Image or Calculations commands.

Averaging Images Using the Layer Method

On the tutorial disk, you will find a folder entitled Layer Stacking Example which contains five images taken by the author and Tim Khan. These are samples from a set of CCD luminance images that were used to construct an RGB mosaic of M31.[1]

1. From the Layer Stacking Example folder on the tutorial disc, open the files "Luminance #1" and "Luminance #2" (*File|Open*). If an Embedded Profile

Mismatch dialog box appears when opening any of these files, just accept the embedded profiles.

2. We will use Luminance #1 as our base image and construct a stack by adding the other four images as new layers. Make Luminance #1 the active image window (click on it) and add a new blank layer with *Layer|New|Layer* and click OK — or just click on the Create a New Layer icon at the bottom of the Layers Palette. A new, blank layer entitled Layer 1 appears above the Background Layer.

3. Now make Luminance #2 the active image. Select the entire image with *Select|All* (keyboard shortcut Ctrl+A). A "marching ants" selection border appears around the entire image. Copy the image to the Windows clipboard with Ctrl+C.

4. Make Luminance #1 active again. Be sure that the Layers Palette is visible (*Window|Layers*). Click on the blank Layer 1 to make it the active layer (the active layer is highlighted in blue). Now paste Luminance #2 into this blank layer with Ctrl+V. The image thumbnail window of Layer 1 now shows an image and not a blank pattern. Close the Luminance #2 file. We no longer need it since the image now resides in Layer 1, above the Luminance #1 image in the Background layer.[2]

5. Next open the file Luminance #3 (*File|Open*). This time, we will use a different method to copy

---

[1] The original 16-bit FITS files were converted to 8-bit grayscale TIFF files in order to be compatible with earlier versions of Photoshop. Only the newer versions — Photoshop CS and CS2 — allow for layering 16-bit files. Just remember that if you do use Photoshop CS or CS2, keep your own images in 16-bits when performing these processing steps.

[2] Note that it is not necessary to actually create the new blank layer first. After copying the image to the clipboard, pasting it into the new file will automatically place it into a new layer. I included it here to clearly illustrate the process.

the image into a layer in the Luminance #1 file. From the Toolbar, select the Move Tool (keyboard shortcut "V"). Arrange the Luminance #1 and Luminance #3 windows so that some portion of both images is visible on your screen. Make the Luminance #3 image window active. While holding down the Shift key, click in Luminance #3, hold and drag it over to the Luminance #1 image area, then release the left mouse key. The image is automatically copied into its own layer (Layer 2) in the Luminance #1 file using this drag-and-drop technique. By holding down the Shift key, the copied image is centered in the new layer. If you did not hold down the Shift key, the image would still be copied, but it would not be centered, which would create more work when aligning the images. Close Luminance #3.

6. Repeat step #5 for the Luminance #4 and Luminance #5 files. When completed, all five images to be stacked now appear in their own layers in the Luminance #1 file. The Layers Palette should look like **Figure 5.6**.

7. Now we will align the images, so that object positions are all registered directly on top of one another. We will also average the images together at the same time. Turn off the visibility of Layers 2 through 4 by clicking on the little "eyeball" icons at the left side of each of these layers in the Layers Palette. An "eyeball" icon should only appear next to the Background Layer and Layer 1.

8. Make Layer 1 active and lower its Opacity to 50% using the Opacity slider at the top right side of the Layers Palette. Select the Move Tool from the Toolbar (shortcut "V") and click once in the image window. Using the keyboard arrow keys, move the Layer 1 image around. Notice that you now have "ghost" images appearing on your screen. By lowering the opacity of Layer 1 it no longer obscures the Background layer completely. With the Opacity set at 100%, all you see is Layer 1, but by reducing the Opacity, Layer 1 becomes progressively more transparent, allowing the underlying layer to also show through. With the Move Tool, each stroke of the keyboard arrow keys moves the image one pixel at a time. This is most useful for precise registration of the images. Your Layers Palette and image should look something like **Figure 5.7**.

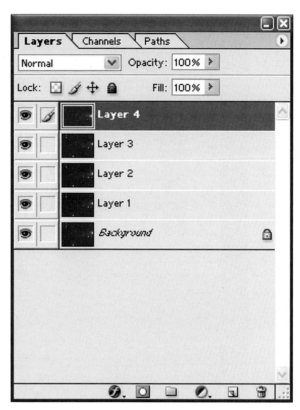

Fig. 5.6 The Layers Palette with all five images to be stacked arranged vertically, each in its own layer. Using "drag-and-drop" with the Move Tool will automatically copy an image into a new layer. Holding down the Shift key during the process will center it. Selecting an entire image (Ctrl+A) and then using "copy-and-paste" (Ctrl+C then Ctrl+V) may also be used.

9. Play around with the Move Tool by zooming into the image (Zoom Tool shortcut press Z) and aligning and mis-aligning the stars using the arrow keys. Notice that the stars from the Background layer and Layer 1 are both of equal brightness. By setting Layer 1 to 50% Opacity, the pixel values of both layers contribute equally to the image. When you are done playing, leave the images misaligned and Zoom the image back out to fit on the screen. In our next step, we will learn a much better way to align the images.

10. At the top left of the Layers Palette, there is a drop-down selection box that currently reads Normal. This is where you select the Layer Blending Mode. A layer's blending mode determines how its pixels will be blended with the underlying layers. Make Layer 1 active and re-set its Opacity to 100%. From the Layer Blending Mode drop-down selection box, choose Difference as the Blending

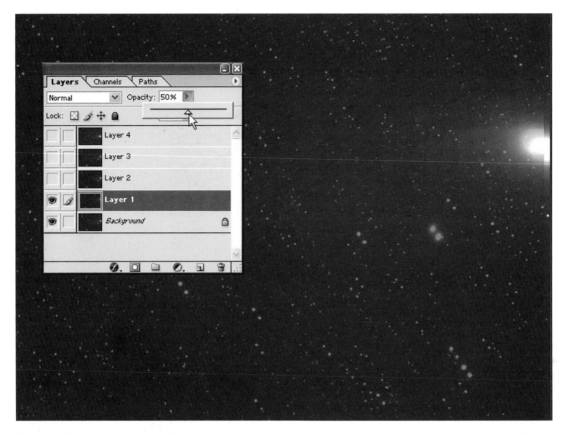

Fig. 5.7 Reducing a Layer's Opacity increases its transparency and allows underlying layers to "show through". Photoshop's layers work from the "top down". Here, only the Background and Layer 1 are visible (they are the only 2 layers with the "eyeball" icon turned on). If Layer 1 were set to 100% Opacity, then none of the Background image would be visible. Since Layer 1 is set to 50% Opacity, both Layer 1 and the Background contribute equally to the image.

Mode. Use the Move Tool with the keyboard arrow keys and move Layer 1 to line up with the Background layer. When the images are aligned, the image window will go completely (or almost completely) black (**Figure 5.8**). The Difference mode subtracts the pixel values of the two layers. When the images are aligned, the stars and galaxy are subtracted from themselves (e.g. there is no "difference"), resulting in a solid black image. It is easy to see when images are aligned this way, as the screen virtually snaps to black. The Background and Layer 1 are now aligned.

11. Save this file to your hard disk with a new file name. Select *File|Save As* and save the file in Photoshop format with the file name Stacking Example.psd. Be sure to leave the layers box checked in the Save As dialog box.

12. Now change the Layer 1 Blending Mode back to Normal and set the Opacity to 50%. Make sure that the Background and Layer 1 are still the only

two layers visible. The Background image and the Layer 1 image are now aligned and averaged. Using 50% Opacity for Layer 1 allows the pixel values of both layers to contribute equally, resulting in an average of the two layers.

13. Let's check to see how well our S/N is doing with only two images averaged thus far. Select the Zoom tool and Zoom well into the image, to around 600%, to get a good look at the background noise. Alternately click the visibility of Layer 1 on and off (click on the "eyeball" icon) and observe the background sky. Even with only two images stacked you should see that the background noise has been noticeably reduced and the sky background appears smoother.

14. Zoom the image back out to fit all of it on the screen. Select "Fit on Screen" from the Zoom Tool Options Bar near the top of the Photoshop window or just double-click on the Hand Tool icon (it looks like a gloved hand) in the Toolbox.

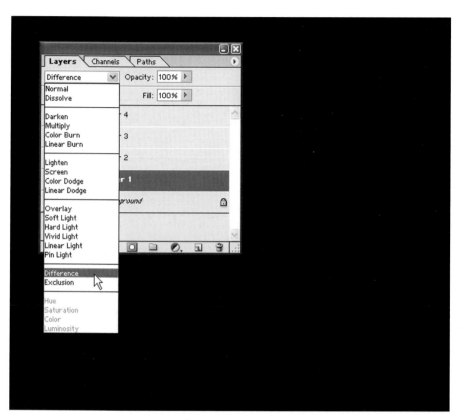

Fig. 5.8 Layer Blending Modes determine how a layer's pixels will be combined with pixels from the underlying layers. "Difference" mode subtracts pixel values. When a stacked image layer is aligned with the layers beneath, the screen goes black.

Now turn on the visibility of Layer 2. Make sure that the Background and Layer 1 are also still visible.

15. Change the Layer Blending Mode of Layer 2 to Difference. If you copied this image using centering, the screen will go black. This image is already aligned. Just to be sure, select the Move tool and use the keyboard arrow keys to move Layer 2 around a little. Objects immediately appear. Re-align the layer to black out the screen.

16. Change the Layer 2 Blending Mode back to Normal and set the Opacity to 33%. Notice that you may type in the Opacity setting directly, which is generally easier than using the tiny slider. Why do we use 33%? Why not 50% like we did with the first two layers? Because we want to average all of the images together. We want the pixel values of the third image in the stack (Layer 2) to contribute one-third toward the combined pixel values of the three images we have stacked thus far. Setting the Opacity of Layer 2 to 33% accomplishes this, and causes everything below Layer 2 to contribute two-thirds to the result. Both the Background and Layer 1 contributed 50% each to the two-stack. That **combined result** now contributes 66% to the

three-stack. Therefore, the contribution from the Background and Layer 1 is now 50% times 66%, or 33% each. Photoshop's layer stack works in a "top-down" manner. Top layers affect everything below them.

17. Repeat steps 14 through 16 for Layer 3 (the fourth image in the stack). But set the Layer 3 Opacity to 25%. The fourth image, Layer 3, now contributes 25% to the four-stack. Everything below it contributes 75%. Since we already know that each image in the three-stack contributed 33% to the total, each of them now contributes 75% times 33%, or 25% to the four-stack.

18. Now repeat steps 14 through 16 for Layer 4 (the fifth image in the stack). This one is quite a bit off (the telescope was re-positioned) and will not line up exactly. For our purposes in this exercise, just make do by "blacking out" the largest image area you can. Sometimes (although not in this case) using a rotational adjustment in conjunction with lateral movements can achieve alignment. To apply rotation, use the commands *Select|All* and then *Edit|Transform|Rotate*. Set the Opacity of this layer to 20%.

We may extrapolate a simple rule: To Average

R. Scott Ireland

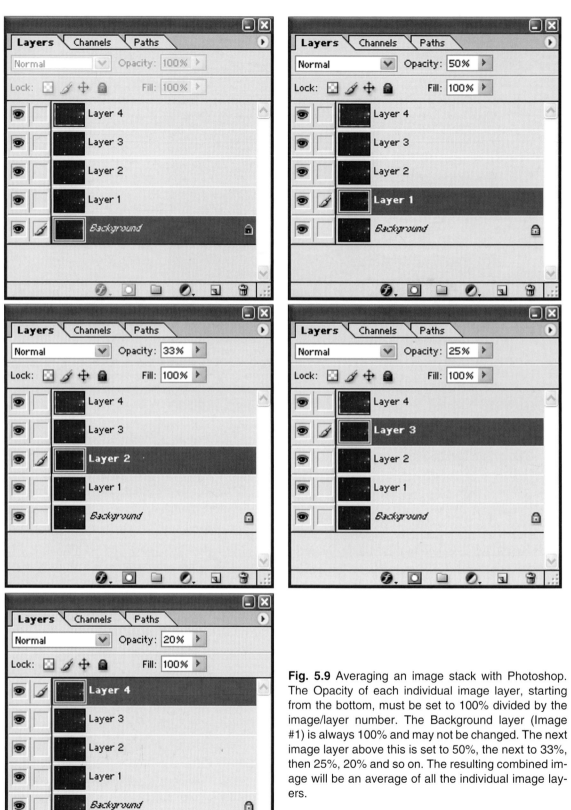

Fig. 5.9 Averaging an image stack with Photoshop. The Opacity of each individual image layer, starting from the bottom, must be set to 100% divided by the image/layer number. The Background layer (Image #1) is always 100% and may not be changed. The next image layer above this is set to 50%, the next to 33%, then 25%, 20% and so on. The resulting combined image will be an average of all the individual image layers.

Fig. 5.10 The left image shows a section of the first image in the stack (the Background layer). The right image shows the averaged result of the five-image stack. The noise in the sky background has been significantly reduced by stacking, making the background smoother and fainter stars more clearly visible. S/N has improved approximately 2 times.

images in a Photoshop layer stack, set the Opacity of each layer, starting from the bottom, to 100% divided by the layer (image) number.

The Background layer (the first layer/image) has no Opacity setting, it is automatically 100% (100% divided by 1) and cannot be changed (**Figure 5.9**).

- Layer 1 (the second layer/image) Opacity is set to 50% (100% divided by 2)
- Layer 2 (the third layer/image) Opacity is set to 33% (100% divided by 3)
- Layer 3 (the fourth layer/image) Opacity is set to 25% (100% divided by 4)
- Layer 4 (the fifth layer/image) Opacity is set to 20% (100% divided by 5)
- And so on.

19. Check each of the layers in your stack to be sure that the Blending Modes are all set to Normal and that each layer's Opacity is properly set according to the above rule. The image could now be flattened (don't flatten it right now though) using "Flatten Image" in the Layers Palette menu, and the result is a mathematical average of all the individual images.

20. Now let's take another look at our sky background. Zoom into the image to around 600% and

examine the background. Compare the noise in one image, the Background layer, to the noise level in the averaged five-stack (**Figure 5.10**). While holding down the Alt key, click repeatedly on the Background layer visibility icon (the little "eyeball"). Holding down the Alt key turns the visibility of all the other layers on and off with each click, allowing you to easily blink back and forth between only the first image and the entire five-stack. The S/N has improved significantly by averaging these images together. It theory, it has improved 2.24 times (the square root of 5). In reality, we have achieved a 2x improvement in S/N, which is well worth the effort.

Adding Images Using the Apply Image and Calculations Commands — Measuring Signal-to-Noise Values

The second method for stacking images in Photoshop utilizes the Apply Image command (*Image\Apply Image*) or its close relative, the Calculations command (*Image\Calculations*). These commands perform mathematical operations directly on the pixel values of two different channels. The channels to be combined may be selected from within a single image, or from two different images. Individual layers may also be se-

R. Scott Ireland

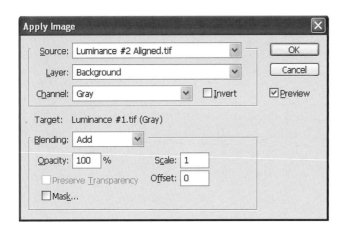

Fig. 5.11 The Apply Image command (*Image | Apply Image*) allows pixel values from two channels to be added or subtracted, combination methods not directly available using Layer Blending Modes. Scale is a "divide by" constant with a range from 1 to 2 setting it to the maximum value of 2 results in pixel values being averaged together (divided by 2). The number entered in the Offset box is added to (positive numbers up to +255) or subtracted from (negative numbers down to -255) the result after applying the Scale factor.

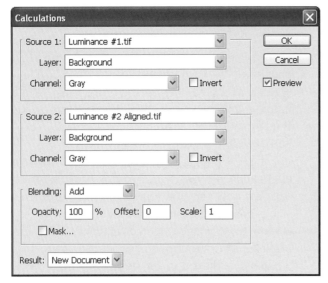

Fig. 5.12 The Calculations command (*Image | Calculations*) is very similar to Apply Image. The principal difference is that Calculations may only be used to combine single channels, while Apply Image can combine single or composite channels. It is necessary to use Apply Image when combining composite RGB color images.

lected, giving these commands quite a bit of flexibility over which pixels are to be combined (**Figures 5.11 and 5.12**).

Apply Image and Calculations offer most of the same Blending Modes (e.g. methods by which pixels will be mathematically combined) available in the Lay-

ers Palette, with two significant additions — "Add" and "Subtract." Using Apply Image or Calculations is the only way to add or subtract pixel values directly. There is no comparable Layer Blending Mode that allows us to accomplish this in a layer stack.

Let's now give the Apply Image and Calculations commands a try. We will use the aligned image layers that we created and saved as "Stacking Example.psd" in step 11 of our previous tutorial. Don't worry if you neglected to save this file; it is also on the tutorial disc.

1. Open "Stacking Example.psd" (*File | Open*). Use the file you created in the previous tutorial, or the one from the tutorial disk in the "Apply Image Example" folder.

2. Before using Apply Image or Calculations to stack images it is essential that you do two things: 1. Align all of the images so that the stars, galaxies, etc., are all in registration; and, 2. Be sure that all of the individual images have the same pixel dimensions. We have already aligned the five luminance images in our previous exercise. For this example, we need each of the aligned images to be saved as an individual file, and each of these files must have the same pixel dimensions. If the pixel dimensions differ, even by only one pixel, Apply Image and Calculations will not work.

3. As in the previous exercise, we will use Luminance #1 as our "base" image. Open Luminance #1.tif (*File | Open*) from the "Apply Image Example" folder.

4. Make Stacking Example.psd the active image window and be sure that the Layers Palette is visible (*Window | Layers* or keyboard shortcut F7). Delete Layers 2, 3 and 4 (click-hold and drag each one to the trash can icon at the bottom right of the Layers Palette, then release the mouse, or right click on each and select "Delete Layer"), so that only the Background and Layer 1 remain.

5. Change the Opacity of Layer 1 from 50% to 100% and make sure that the Layer Blending Mode is set to Normal.

6. Now Flatten the image (*Layer | Flatten Image* or choose "Flatten Image" from the Layers Palette Menu). Save the flattened image as "Luminance #2 Aligned.tif" (*File | Save As*).

Flattening an image causes all visible layers to become merged into the Background layer. In this case, you will recall that our original Luminance #1.tif image is the Background layer of Stacking Example.psd. Layer 1 is the Luminance #2.tif image. Layer 1 has already been aligned with the Background, and by setting the Opacity to 100% it becomes the only visible layer. Then by Flattening the file, Layer 1 (Luminance #2) is merged into the Background (Luminance #1), so we end up with a new version of Luminance #2 that is aligned with, and has the same pixel dimensions as, Luminance #1.

A word of caution. When using Photoshop to align images in a layer stack, attention must be given to images that vary significantly in orientation, scale, pixel dimensions or field of view. To preserve the most image detail, it is generally preferable to use the image that has the largest pixel dimensions as the base layer — the Background — and register all of the other images to it. However, if an image in the stack has a field that has shifted significantly from the Background image, then moving it to align with the other images will create areas of transparency in that layer. These areas contain no image information and appear as a "checkerboard" pattern in Photoshop. Remember, Photoshop layer stacks work from the top down, so any transparent areas in an image layer will allow information from the layers below it to show through into the final result. This can skew your averaging results and create edge areas that differ from the main image stack. In such cases, it may be necessary to judiciously crop the image stack using Photoshop's Crop Tool. In extreme cases, such as images that can't be lined up using small, lateral (*x-y*) movements, the only practical solution may be to employ third party software such as Registar to achieve initial alignment and registration.

7. You should now have two images on your screen, Luminance #1 and Luminance #2 Aligned. Make Luminance #1 the active image window (click on it) and select *Image\Apply Image*. Select Luminance #2 Aligned.tif in the Source drop-down selection box. The Layer will be set to Background; this is the only layer available. Channel is set to gray; since this is a grayscale image, that is the only channel available. When combining color images, the composite RGB channel would be used here. The active image window is automatically set as the Target image, so you need to be careful and make sure that you always set Source to the second image in the set. Otherwise, you will end up adding an image to itself, which will do nothing to improve the S/N! Select Add as the

Blending mode. For now, leave Opacity at 100%, Scale at 1 and Offset at 0, but **do not** close the Apply Image dialog box (**Figure 5.13**).

8. Click the Preview check box on and off to see the effect of the current settings. It is obvious that a straight Addition of these two images will result in clipped highlights around the galaxy core. The fainter galaxy arms are more visible, but we are losing highlight information (**Figure 5.13**). Let's try lowering all of the pixel values in the Added images. Enter a value of –100 (minus 100) in the Offset box. This doesn't work. Now we have lost subtle detail in the midtones and three-quarter tones and the highlights are still clipped more than the original images. Actually, we have clipped both the shadows and highlights, throwing out data at both ends of the tonal scale. If you are using Photoshop CS or later, you can see this graphically by keeping the Histogram Palette visible and refreshing the display (**Figure 5.14**). Try an Offset value of –50 (minus 50). This is better. We have eliminated the shadow clipping and have a better tonal range, but we are still losing some of the highlights.

9. Enter an Offset value of 0 and now set the Scale value to 2 (**Figure 5.15**). Click OK to accept these settings. This results in the two images being Averaged, just as they were in our Layer Stacking tutorial. Photoshop adds the image pixels together and then divides by the Scale factor, which may be set to a value from 1 to 2. Adding and then dividing by 2 gives us the same result as using a 50% Opacity setting for Layer 1 in our previous tutorial.

The Apply Image command has a setting for Opacity. Can't we just leave the Scale and Offset alone and set the Opacity to 50% to get the same Averaging result? Well, no, we can't. Apply Image does not work the same way a "top down" layer stack does. Apply Image and Calculations Opacity settings vary the amount of the overall effect; 0% renders no effect — the pixels in the Target image remain at their original values. 100% renders the full effect — the Source and Target image pixels are combined based upon the Blending Mode and other settings. Opacity settings between 0% and 100% vary the effect proportionately — ranging between the base Target values and the full effect. A setting of 50% (with Scale = 1 and Offset = 0) does not average the two images together, rather the result ends

R. Scott Ireland

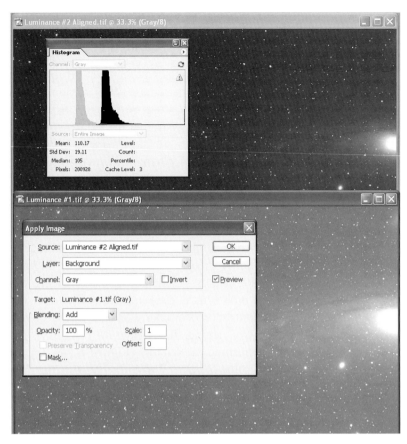

Fig. 5.13 Adding two images using the Apply Image command. Here we clearly see a problem associated with the Addition method — highlight clipping. More faint details are visible in the outer galaxy arms, but more of the central core area is clipped. Image details have been lost in this area. Note how the histogram has been shifted to the right.

up halfway between the original Target image values and a straight sum of the two images. The result differs, therefore, depending upon which image is set as the Target. This, of course, could not happen if the images were truly being averaged — selecting either one as the Target would render the same result. When using the Calculations command, "Source 1" is the Source image and "Source 2" is the Target image.

10. Now save this file under a new file name (*File|Save As*) — "Luminance 1 and 2 Averaged.tif". For this particular set of images, we are going to get our best result using the Average method, since these images only have a bit depth of 8-bits. With 16-bit images, the straight Addition method (Scale = 1) may often be used with good results. If you have Photoshop CS or later and would like to try your hand at combining 16-bit images with Addition, 16-bit versions of Luminance #1 and Luminance #2 are included on the tutorial disc. Apply Image and Calculations will not work with 16-bit images in Photoshop versions prior to CS.

11. Now repeat steps 4 and 5 to create individual files for Layers 2, 3 and 4. For example, to create the

individual file for Layer 2 (Luminance #3), re-open the Stacking Example.psd file (*File|Open*). Delete Layer 1, Layer 3 and Layer 4; then change the Opacity of Layer 2 to 100% and make sure that the Layer Blending Mode is set to Normal. Flatten the image and save it as (*File|Save As*) Luminance #3 Aligned.tif. Repeat the process with Layer 3 to create Luminance #4 Aligned.tif and with Layer 4 to create Luminance #5 Aligned.tif. If you would like to shortcut this process, all of these files are included on the tutorial disc.

12. Now let's try our hand at using Calculations in lieu of Apply Image. Open the files (*File|Open*) Luminance #3 Aligned.tif and Luminance #4 Aligned.tif. Open the Calculations command dialog box (*Image|Calculations*). Set Source 1 to Luminance #3 Aligned.tif and Source 2 to Luminance #4 Aligned.tif. Set the Blending Mode to "Add"; leave Opacity at 100% and Offset at 0. Set the Scale to 2. Set Result to "New Document". The Calculations dialog box is shown in **Figure 5.16**.

13. Click OK to accept these settings, and a new image window appears on the screen that contains

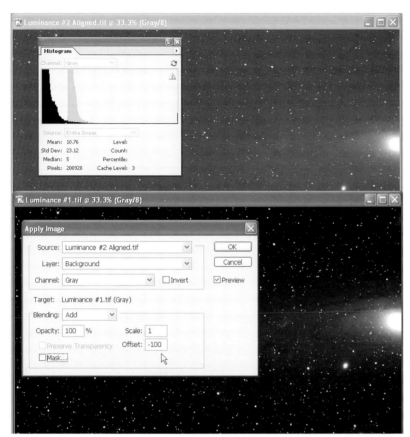

Fig. 5.14 Using an Offset value to lower all of the pixel values after an Addition does not solve the highlight clipping problem. Both shadows and highlights are now clipped in this example. Note the histogram "pushing" against the left side and the increased rise at the right.

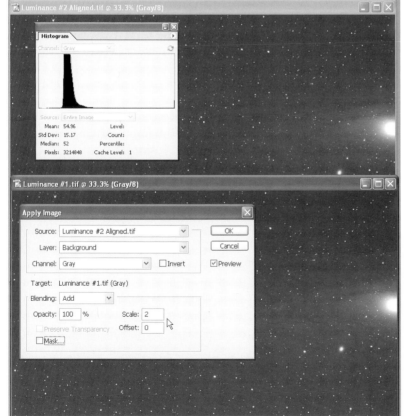

Fig. 5.15 Averaging two images using Apply Image. The images are first Added and then divided by the Scale factor. A Scale of 2 produces an Average of the two images. In this example, and with most 8-bit images, Averaging is the best solution. When working with the broader tonal scale of 16-bit images, straight Addition may often be employed with good results.

R. Scott Ireland

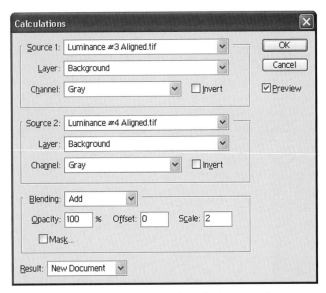

Fig. 5.16 With Apply Image and Calculations, stacks are created by adding two images at a time, and then adding these "two-stacks" together.

the Calculations result — an average of the two images. Make this new window active and save it (*File|Save As*) as Luminance 3 and 4 Averaged.tif. But wait a minute!! The "Save As" dialog is only offering us a few file format choices, and TIFF is not among them. What's going on here?? Well, when something like this happens, it is a clue that the file is not in the grayscale or color mode that you think it's in, or it's in 16-bit mode. Either way, *Image|Mode* is the way to find and fix the problem. Cancel out of the Save As dialog box and select *Image|Mode*. Note that the image is in Multichannel mode. Convert the image to Grayscale mode with *Image|Mode|Grayscale*. Now save the file as indicated above.

Remember that the Calculations command does not work on composite channels. If you were to combine two color images with Calculations, you would only have access to the individual color channels. Fortuitously, Calculations also offers access to grayscale luminance channels in addition to the individual color channels, making it useful for LRGB work. However, if you wish to combine color images directly (using the composite RGB "channels"), then you must use Apply Image instead.

14. So now we have "paired up" four of our five total luminance frames into two averaged images. The next step is to combine these "two-stacks" into a single "four-stack". Open the files Luminance 1

and 2 Averaged.tif and Luminance 3 and 4 Averaged.tif (*File|Open*). Next, open the Apply Image dialog (*Image|Apply Image*). The Calculations command would work equally well here. Make sure that the Source and Target images are different (it doesn't matter which is which since we are averaging the images). Set the Blending Mode to "Add", Opacity at 100%, Offset at 0 and Scale at 2. Click OK and save the file (*File|Save As*) under a new file name — Luminance 1 through 4 Averaged.tif. Close the other file.

Now we have 4 of our 5 images averaged together using the Apply Image/Calculations commands. So far, so good. But what do we do about the fifth image? Working with sets of two images is logical when using Apply Image and Calculations, since those commands are designed to combine two channels at a time. We are confident that the first four images have indeed been averaged together and our S/N improved proportionately. But what settings can we use to get a S/N benefit from the fifth image? We certainly cannot just average it together with the results of our first four combines. This would put too much emphasis on the fifth image, resulting in a lower combined S/N. Using the layer stacking method, as in our previous tutorial, is simpler — the fifth image layer is simply set to an Opacity of 20%. But as we have seen, Apply Image/Calculations settings do not work in the same manner. Let's perform an experiment with the last image — Photoshop actually provides a way for us to measure S/N improvements. We can try different Apply Image Opacity and Scale settings and then measure the results to determine the best settings for adding in the fifth image.

15. Open the Luminance #5 Aligned.tif file (*File|Open*). Luminance 1 through 4 Averaged.tif should already be open. If not, open that file now. With Luminance 1 through 4 Averaged.tif active, open the Histogram (*Image|Histogram*). If using Photoshop CS or later, make the Histogram Palette visible (*Window|Histogram*) (**Figure 5.17**).

Notice the information below the Histogram. Mean, Standard Deviation and Median pixel values are shown. Photoshop has already done the math for us! We may use Standard Deviation (abbreviated "Std Dev" or "SD") as a measure of noise. *A higher SD indicates more variability between pixel values, in other words, more noise.* Therefore, by comparing SD measurements or changes in the ratio of Mean/SD values, we can fairly well approximate whether or not we have improved the

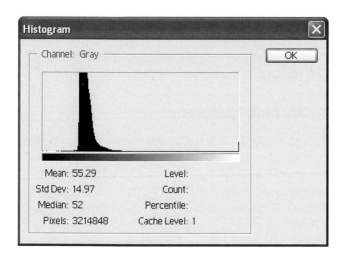

Fig. 5.17 The Histogram provides a measure of Standard Deviation (abbreviated "Std Dev" or "SD") indicating the degree of variability between pixel values. Lower SD is indicative of a higher S/N.

Signal-to-Noise ratio ("S/N") of our stack.

The overall SD of Luminance 1 through 4 Averaged.tif is 14.97. Now make Luminance #5 Aligned.tif active and open the Histogram again. The overall SD of this image is 17.59, higher than the four-stack, which is to be expected.

16. Make Luminance 1 through 4 Averaged.tif active and use the Zoom Tool (keyboard shortcut "Z") to Zoom well into the image (to around 600%). Find an area of the image that has a large section of blank sky background. Now select the Rectangular Marquee Tool (keyboard shortcut "M") from the Toolbox. Click-hold and drag to enclose an area that has only background sky, without stars, then release the mouse. A Selection Border ("marching ants") appears around the area. Any actions, tools, filters, commands or measurements will now apply only to the area within the Selection Border. Selections allow us to isolate and work on particular areas within an image.

17. Open the Histogram again and you will see that the selected sky background has a much lower SD. The area I selected has a SD of 1.36 (**Figure 5.18**). Focusing our attention on this background area, instead of the whole image, should give us a better indication of whether or not we are improving S/N by adding the fifth image.

The purpose of an Averaging stack is to improve S/N by reducing background noise ("N"). The value of the signal ("S") will remain relatively constant.

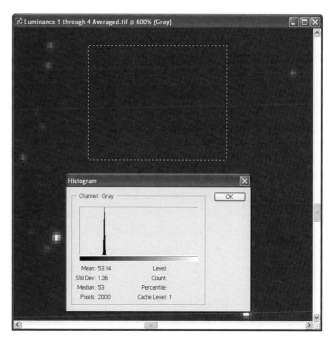

Fig. 5.18 The Rectangular Marquee Tool has been used to place a Selection Border around a blank area of background sky. Application of the Apply Image command and measurements of Standard Deviation and Mean values will now be limited to this area. The SD of the selected area is 1.36.

18. Select *Image | Apply Image*. Set Luminance #5 Aligned.tif as the Source; "Add" Blending Mode; Opacity 100%; Offset 0 and Scale 2. The Luminance #5 image is applied only to the area within the Selection Border. By clicking the Preview checkbox on and off, you may examine the before and after effect. Without even checking the SD, it is obvious that a straight average will significantly worsen the S/N of the four-stack. Let's prove it. Click OK to accept the above settings.

19. Open the Histogram again and check the SD. The area I selected went from 1.36 to 1.59. The SD has increased significantly, while the Mean value has not; therefore the S/N has been degraded. Make the History Palette visible (*Window | History*). Click-hold and drag the last History State (Apply Image) to the trash can icon at the bottom right of the Palette. This restores the image to its condition prior to using the Apply Image command.

20. Open Apply Image again (*Image | Apply Image*) and this time change the Opacity to 20%. Leave the other settings the same. Click OK and examine the Histogram. The SD of my selection has now improved; it dropped from 1.36 to 1.30. Great!

R. Scott Ireland

Mission accomplished! But wait, perhaps there is even more improvement to be had?

21. Repeat step 20 and try various Opacity and Scale settings. Before each iteration of Apply Image, use the History Palette or Undo command (*Edit|Undo*) to restore the image to its earlier state. Read the Histogram after each try and make notes of the settings used and the resulting SD and Mean values. Why do we need the Mean values too? Because a Scale setting of 1 results in a straightforward Addition of images. Relating changes in the Mean pixel values to changes in the SD is necessary to evaluate the results in this case, since the overall brightness levels are changing significantly with each new image added. At Scale settings of anything other than 2 (Averaging), pay attention to both the Mean and SD.

The Addition stacking method permits us to improve the S/N from the other direction — by increasing the signal ("S") more than the noise ("N").

This tabulating process is much easier with Photoshop CS and later. The results may be read directly from the active Histogram Palette as the Apply Image settings are changed, without having to close the dialog box and repeat the process.

I achieved my best result using a Scale of 2 (Averaging) with a 50% Opacity. This resulted in improving the SD from 1.36 for the four-stack to 1.29 for the five-stack.

If the Addition method were used (Scale set to 1), a 30% Opacity worked best, producing the highest Mean/SD ratio, and the highest delta Mean/delta SD ratio (change in Mean value related to change in SD).

In practice, achieving optimum settings is as much an art as it is a science, and this should always be kept in mind. In fact, Luminance #5 is not really a good candidate for stacking (using Photoshop). If you recall, this image was skewed quite a bit and had some uneven rotation of the field of view. It did not line up exactly with the other images. So while an area of background sky showed a S/N improvement (normally the best way to measure an Average stack), elongated stars in other areas of the image worked to reduce the overall image quality. In a broader way, the overall S/N was worsened by adding the fifth image. I would opt to leave it out of the stack.

Practical decisions like this one arise continually. Don't just mechanically follow a given procedure by rote because it worked before, or because someone rec-

ommends it. Understand what Photoshop is doing with each task performed and learn to critically evaluate the results for yourself. This is the surest path toward superior image-processing skill.

Some Final Thoughts

The increasingly popular procedure of using webcams to image the planets, with their characteristically high noise levels in each video frame, necessitates using specialized stacking programs such as Registax and K3CCD Tools, in order to conveniently stack hundreds of frames. The principles behind stacking are, of course, the same ones we have discussed here. It just takes a lot more images for effective noise reduction, and for that, Photoshop is not the best tool.

When selecting candidate images for stacking, attention must be paid to the quality of the individual frames. As a general rule, it is preferable to stack images of the same quality and exposure duration. There are circumstances, however, when it may be desirable to combine images with different exposures or S/N characteristics. In these cases, a "weighting factor" may be applied to accentuate the higher quality images in the stack. You have already seen how Photoshop may be employed for this purpose. When using the Layer Method, the Opacity of the individual layers may be adjusted to add weight to superior images. With Apply Image and Calculations, both the Opacity and Scale settings may be used to achieve weighting. Make measurements of standard deviation and mean to help you find the best settings, but do not rely exclusively on the numbers. Zoom into the sky background and visually inspect your results also. Use both your eyes and the numbers — a theme that you will hear me repeat often concerning most aspects of image processing.

When using Photoshop for stacking, it is preferable to utilize images that are as "clean" as possible. If they contain a lot of hot pixels, dark pixels, dust and scratches and so forth, it may be beneficial to do some touching up first before stacking, since Averaging the images together will provide some weight to these artifacts that will carry into the final stacked result. This is where a Median combine is beneficial. However, as we have seen, Photoshop does not offer a method for Median combines. When performing initial CCD image calibration, try to remove as many of these artifacts as possible. Most of the programs specifically designed for CCD image processing incorporate algorithms that will aid in this process. As an alternative, consider ap-

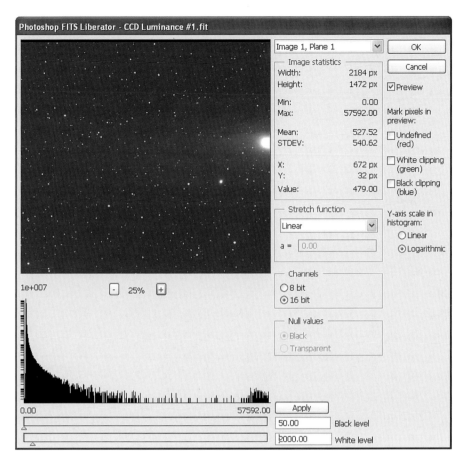

Fig. 5.19 Photoshop FITS Liberator is an excellent freeware Plug-In that provides consistent tonal scale stretches when opening 16-bit FITS files for stacking.

plying some judicious "dust and scratch" removal techniques with Photoshop prior to stacking. We will examine these methods in **Chapter 7.**

There is another popular image alignment technique that permits aligning images on a "sub-pixel" level. The procedure involves first "upsampling" the images by around 300–500%. In Photoshop, this is accomplished using the *Image |Image Size* command. The "Resample Image" checkbox is selected (use the Bicubic method) causing the pixel dimensions to be increased by resampling. Photoshop makes its best guess as to what the "in-between" pixels should look like and expands the image size accordingly. The images thus enlarged are then aligned in the manner described here, and then "downsampled" back to their original size using the same resampling procedure in reverse. The subject matter in the enlarged images covers more pixels than in the original, theoretically permitting a more precise "sub-pixel" alignment. In practice, and as a general rule, I am not fond of resampling images too often. Resampling operates to degrade the image as artificial "information" is added and subtracted, causing quantization errors and posterization. Resampling should be kept to a minimum and used only as necessary. However, in certain cases this procedure may help salvage images that are otherwise difficult to align. For more information on resampling, refer to **Chapter 11**.

When working with 16-bit FITS files (considerably easier with Photoshop CS and later), the images will appear very dark when initially opened. Photoshop does not provide an automatic "screen stretch" to compress the tonal values for easier visibility. In these cases, it may be desirable to modify the typical workflow procedure of stacking first, then adjusting the tonal scale. Use Levels or Curves to make some initial adjustments to the tonal scale of 16-bit images prior to stacking. Take care to achieve the same brightness levels for each of the images to be stacked. There is an excellent freeware Plug-In program available from the European Space Agency and NASA for working with FITS files in Photoshop. The program is called "Photoshop FITS Liberator" (see Appendix). When a FITS file is initially opened in Photoshop, the FITS Liberator screen appears and offers a wide array of settings (**Figure 5.19**). Using this utility, it is easy to achieve the initial tonal scale stretch and keep all of the images uniform in brightness.

R. Scott Ireland

Chapter 6
Anti-Vignetting — Balancing Uneven Illumination

In the previous Chapter, we discussed various sources of noise and explored some techniques to reduce random, background noise by stacking images. Now we will turn our attention to one of the principal sources of non-random noise — uneven field illumination.

Virtually all photographic images, regardless of the capture source or optical system used, exhibit differences in background illumination across the field of view. This holds true for "normal" daylight photographs as well as for astrophotographs. Since most daylight images are relatively bright, however, the effect is generally not noticeable. But small differences in luminosity become readily apparent when set against the near black background sky of an astrophotograph.

Uneven illumination is caused by many factors. Almost all lens/telescope systems exhibit light falloff to some degree. This manifests itself as a circular pattern in which the edges or corners of the field are darker than the central area (**Figure 6.1**). Obstructions in the optical path are another source of uneven illumination. The term vignetting is often used to describe both of these circumstances, although a more correct usage of the term describes only the effect of obstructions in the optical path, not light falloff. For simplicity, I will use the term vignetting to apply to all sources of uneven illumination, and the term anti-vignetting (abbreviated "A/V") to refer to all techniques used to combat uneven illumination, regardless of the cause.

Other common sources of uneven field illumination include out-of-focus dust motes on a CCD sensor, differences in pixel-to-pixel sensitivity of a CCD chip and background sky gradients. Gradients result from light sources that vary in brightness across the sky, such as light pollution from cities, moonlight or clouds.

When working with CCD images, the first bastion

Fig. 6.1 Vignetting from light falloff is clearly evident in this film image of the Double Cluster made by the author. The image was highly stretched to clearly illustrate the problem.

against vignetting, as always, is to carefully calibrate the images using dark frames and flat field frames. But even after careful flat-fielding, uneven illumination may still appear, particularly in the form of linear gradients caused by sky glow.

In order to combat vignetting, we need to employ a new set of techniques. Stacking will not work, since vignetting is not random noise. Uneven illumination will generally appear in the same place from frame to frame, so stacking will increase this non-random noise in the same manner as the signal. In fact, some would say that non-random noise is signal. It is just a part of the signal that we do not wish to keep in our final image!

In essence, A/V techniques are just another form of flat-fielding. Our goal is to create a customized flat-field frame that takes into account the conditions present on a given night, at a given moment, using a particular array of equipment to image a particular area of sky. One of the simplest ways to accomplish this is to use the information that is already contained within the image itself. Let me restate and generalize this very important concept;

Whenever possible, let the image do the work for you.

What does this mean, exactly? In the case of A/V, it means using the vignetting pattern in the image itself to create a "map", or mask, of the uneven illumination. This mask is then subtracted from the image to balance the luminosity. We cannot divide the A/V mask into the image, as we would with a CCD flat-field frame, since Photoshop does not offer us a way to perform pixel division. However, we can make do with subtraction, since it is essentially the same process. The Apply Image or Calculations commands can be used to perform pixel subtraction directly (the "Subtraction Method"). Or, we may balance illumination by adding an A/V mask into the image layer stack (the "A/V Layer Mask method").

Sometimes an image contains large or complex subject matter that makes it difficult or impossible to extract an adequate A/V mask directly from the image. In such cases, we may create a "synthetic" A/V mask using Photoshop's Gradient Tool (the "Synthetic Mask method").

We will explore each of these techniques in the following examples. As with any mask in Photoshop, an A/V mask may be edited and fine-tuned until it achieves the desired result. This is one reason why

masking is such a powerful and useful technique to master. In this chapter, you will have the opportunity to further expand upon your masking knowledge, the application of which extends to countless other areas of image processing as well.

Where does A/V fit into the image-processing workflow? Ideally, A/V should be applied early in the process, right after stacking. When images are stacked using the Average or Addition methods, vignetting is not altered significantly in the final stack. It is averaged in the same manner as the other signals. Therefore, it is generally unnecessary to perform A/V on the individual frames prior to stacking. An exception to this is when the individual images exhibit different vignetting characteristics, such as a sky gradient that changes between exposures, or when combining images taken on different nights. In these cases, it may be desirable to balance the illumination of the individual frames prior to stacking.

While we are on the subject, this is another reason why stacking images using hybrid methods, such as multiplication, may be undesirable. An unintended consequence is enhancement of the brightness differences across the frame, exaggerating vignetting and requiring stronger A/V processing.

The Subtraction Method — Introduction to Cloning

OK, let's get down to work! We will start with the Subtraction A/V method, which directly subtracts the A/V mask pixels from the base image using the Apply Image command.

1. From the tutorial disc, open the file "AV Base Image.tif" (*File|Open*). This is a widefield shot of the Double Cluster in Perseus. I used a 300mm camera lens to take this film image, and the vignetting pattern (light falloff at the edges of the field) is readily apparent since I used the lens at its widest aperture.

2. Duplicate the image with *Image|Duplicate* and click OK. A new image, "AV Base Image copy" appears on the screen. We will use this image to create our A/V mask.

3. Make AV Base Image copy the active image window and open *Filter|Blur|Gaussian Blur*. Set the Radius to 90 pixels and make sure the Preview box is checked. ***Do not*** click OK yet. The image now looks like **Figure 6.2**. Notice what has hap-

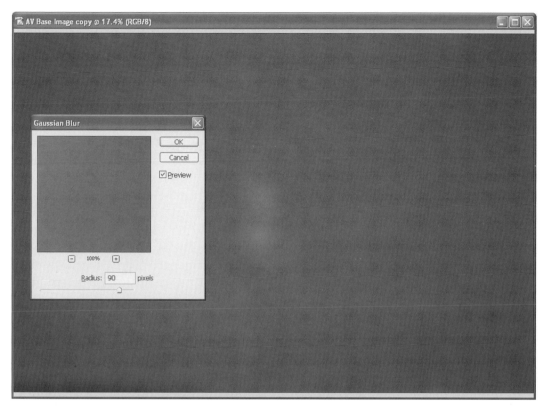

Fig. 6.2 A Gaussian Blur is applied to the image to create an A/V mask. In this case, the mask is not satisfactory because of the two "hot spots" in the center. The Double Cluster was not removed from the image prior to blurring.

pened. By selecting a wide blur radius, all of the individual stars have disappeared and "blended" into the background. What remains is a broad, soft rendition of the overall field illumination. The vignetting pattern is clearly evident, but we have handily eliminated the details, except for one area. The center of the image has two "hot spots", the Double Cluster itself. If we eliminate these hot spots, we should have an excellent A/V mask.

4. Click Cancel to close the Gaussian Blur dialog box without applying the filter. Select the Clone Stamp Tool from the Toolbox (keyboard shortcut "S"). This tool used to be called the Rubber Stamp Tool, but since everyone else on the planet called it the Clone Tool, the Photoshop guys finally acquiesced and changed its name (they couldn't resist leaving the "Stamp" in though). Using the Clone Stamp Tool starts with the user placing a "sampling point" in the image. As the mouse is then moved around in the image, the sampling point moves with it synchronously. When the left mouse button is clicked and held, the area under the sampling point is copied to the new mouse location. Why is this good? Because it lets us sam-

ple areas very close to the objects we want to eliminate. The cloned areas thereby remain smooth, without obvious artifacts, since the colors and luminosities of the sampled areas are very nearly the same as the areas being replaced. The secret to good cloning technique is to continuously set new sampling points and keep those points very close to the areas being cloned. This is much harder to describe than it is to do. Once learned, cloning can be done very quickly.

5. With the Clone Stamp Tool selected, choose a 100 pixel soft-edged round brush from the Tool Options Bar at the top of the Photoshop window (**Figure 6.3**). If the Tool Options Bar is not displayed, select *Window|Options*. Also make sure that the Mode is set to Normal, that both the Opacity and Flow are set to 100% and the "Aligned" box is checked. Now press "Z" to select the Zoom Tool and zoom well into the image so that the Double Cluster is prominent in the center of the image window. This will be a display setting of around 67%. Press "S" to re-select the Clone Stamp Tool.

R. Scott Ireland

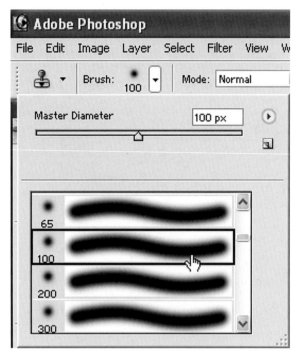

Fig. 6.3 The Tool Options Bar is used to select a brush size and style for the Clone Stamp Tool. Brush sizes may also be changed "on the fly" from the keyboard using the left and right bracket keys, a very handy shortcut that you will use often.

6. Start by selecting a background area outside of, but near, one of the star clusters. Hold down the Alt key, and a little "target" icon appears on the screen. Set a sampling point by holding down the Alt key and left-clicking once. Then release the Alt key, move the mouse over an area of the cluster, left-click-hold and move the mouse to "paint" starting from the sampling point. Notice that the sampling point, indicated by a small "+", moves as you paint. The image area under the "+" is being copied to the mouse location.

7. Proceed to "paint out" the clusters, and be sure to make a lot of sampling point selections. In time, you will develop a facility and a rhythm for "Alt-click sampling then release Alt and click painting" and things will go much faster. Don't worry if your cloning technique is a little sloppy at this point. Precision is not needed for this example. You merely need to reduce the centralized brightness of the cluster stars somewhat.

8. When you are satisfied that the clusters have been satisfactorily eliminated (see **Figure 6.4** — the cluster on top has been eliminated), once again open the Gaussian Blur filter (*Filter\Blur\Gauss-*

ian Blur). Set the Radius to 90 pixels and click OK. This is now your A/V mask.

9. Make the AV Base Image.tif window active (click once on it). Select *Image\Apply Image*, set the Source to AV Base Image copy, Layer to Background, Channel to RGB and Blending to Subtract. Leave Opacity at 100%, Scale at 1 and change the Offset to 50. Leave the Invert and Mask boxes unchecked. ***Do not*** click OK just yet. Click the Preview check box on and off to see the effect on the image. The vignetting disappears almost magically! Notice that the star colors remain true to the original. There is only one small problem. One area of the image is still too bright. It runs along the bottom edge from the left corner to about the center of the image. The A/V mask needs to be tweaked a little more.

10. Click Cancel to close the Apply Image dialog box without subtracting the mask. Now switch to the mask window. The area along the bottom left is too dark, so you will once again use your new-found cloning skills to lighten it up a bit.

11. Fit the A/V mask window to the screen (double-click on the Hand Tool icon — the little white glove — in the Toolbox), select the Clone Stamp Tool and use a soft brush of around 250 pixels. Notice that the area above the dark line is a consistent neutral gray color. Use this area to clone out the dark line and replace it with gray.

12. Make AV Base Image.tif active and once again open the Apply Image dialog (*Image\Apply Image*). Use the settings indicated in step 9. Click the Preview box on and off to see how well you did with your additional cloning efforts. If you are satisfied with the result, click OK to subtract the A/V mask from the original image. I have included a file on the tutorial disc called "AV Subtraction Mask.tif". This is my version of the A/V mask, prepared exactly as described above, that you may try for comparison purposes.

Feel free to try the alternate Blending Modes and mask settings available in the Apply Image and Calculations dialog boxes. While it is my preference to use Subtract and fine-tune the A/V mask directly, you may find that other settings work better for a particular image. Try the "Difference" or "Exclusion" Blending Modes, and experiment with additional masking using the "Mask" check box. Try "Invert" to invert the mask too.

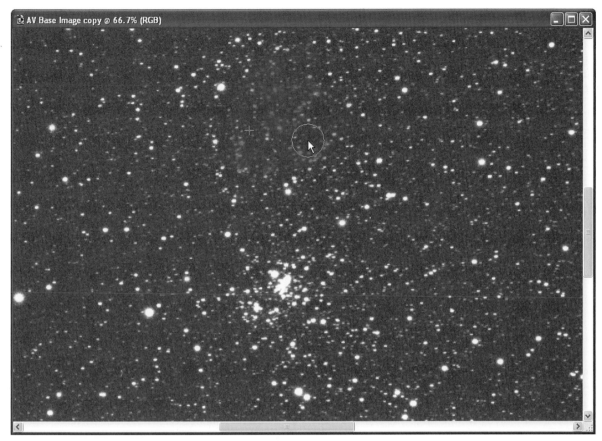

Fig. 6.4 The upper star cluster has been "painted out" using the Clone Stamp Tool. The circle under the cursor arrow is the area being cloned. The small "+" sign to the left indicates the sampling point. Removing prominent, bright objects eliminates A/V mask "hot spots" when blurring is applied.

Notice that even when using a destructive edit, such as the Apply Image command, it is possible to preview the effect of the A/V mask that you create and then fine-tune it to achieve the desired result. Learn to use image and layer duplicates whenever possible to "un-destructify" (apologies to Noah Webster) destructive editing procedures.

A/V Layer Mask Methods

In case you have not figured it out by now, I'll let you in on a little secret. I love layers. I use them wherever and however I can to perform tasks in Photoshop. To me, layering is what makes Photoshop such a powerful tool. Building layer structures adds a third, vertical "dimension" to the art of image processing, permitting a level of digital darkroom control unattainable by other means. Mastering the use of layers is time well spent. It is the single most important factor in unleashing the power of Photoshop.

There are many different ways in which A/V lay-

ers and masks may be constructed. We will explore some of these techniques in the following examples. Use these as guidelines when creating your own masks, not as dogmatic "do this and then do that" procedures. The goal is for you to develop a facility for working with layers and masks.

Here are two relatively quick and easy methods:

Multiply Layers

1. Open the file "AV Base Image.tif" from the tutorial disc (*File|Open*).

2. Duplicate the image by copying the Background layer into a new layer. Make the Layers Palette visible (*Window|Layers*). Click-hold and drag the Background Layer to the "Create a New Layer" icon at the bottom of the Layers Palette (this looks like two overlapping pages), then release the mouse. A Background copy layer appears above the Background layer.

3. Set the Background copy layer Blending Mode (the drop-down selection box at the top left of the

R. Scott Ireland

Layers Palette) to "Multiply" and adjust the layer Opacity (at the top right of the Layers Palette) to the point where vignetting disappears. For this example, set the Opacity to around 66%.

The Difference Layer A/V Mask

1. Again open the file "AV Base Image.tif" from the tutorial disc (*File|Open*).

2. Duplicate the Background layer as described in step 2 of the Multiply Layers example.

3. With the Background copy layer active (click once on it to make it active; active layers are highlighted in blue), select the Clone Stamp Tool from the Toolbox and use it in the manner described in steps 4–7 of the Subtraction Method example to remove the two star clusters from the Background copy layer. This will avoid hot spots appearing in the A/V mask.

4. Blur the Background copy layer with *Filter|Blur|Gaussian Blur*. Set the Radius to 90 pixels and click OK. Double-click on the layer name ("Background copy"), rename the layer to A/V Layer and press enter.

Note that the pixel radius used with the Gaussian Blur filter will vary depending upon the size (pixel dimensions) and content of the image. Larger images will generally require a larger radius. Use whatever radius is necessary to blur the image to a point just beyond where the individual details are lost. Remember, the ideal A/V mask is a background luminosity map of the image, but without the individual stars, nebulae, galaxies and so forth.

5. Set the new A/V Layer Blending Mode (the drop-down selection box at the top left of the Layers Palette) to "Difference" and adjust the layer Opacity to about 35% (**Figure 6.5**).

6. Click the A/V Layer visibility on and off (by clicking on the little "eyeball" icon at the left of the Layers Palette) to judge the result and further adjust the Opacity of the A/V layer if necessary.

Each of these examples employs a different layer blending mode. Layer blending modes govern how a layer's pixels will be combined with the underlying image layers. The "Multiply" mode is used in the first example — the color value of each pixel in the layer is multiplied by the underlying image pixel value and then divided by the tonal scale (255 for 8-bit images). Multiply darkens all image values except black (it is al-

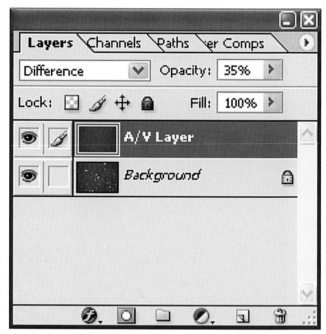

Fig. 6.5 A simple A/V Layer Mask. The original image is copied into a new layer (the A/V Layer) and a Gaussian Blur is applied. The A/V Layer Blending Mode is set to "Difference" and the layer Opacity is adjusted to achieve the desired effect.

ready as dark as it can get) and white. The effect is more noticeable in the shadows and midtones than it is in the highlights.

In the second example, the "Difference" layer blending mode was used. This mode subtracts the blend color (the top layer) and the base color (the combination of all lower layers) and returns the absolute value of the difference. Basically, large differences are rendered lighter and smaller differences darker. While this method does not always work for A/V, it can prove satisfactory in many cases and is certainly easy to apply. It is also possible to apply additional manual adjustments to the A/V Layer, if desired, to fine-tune the effect. One problem to watch out for is unintended color shifts or loss of the fainter stars. The task is to remove vignetting without creating processing artifacts or losing image details. Check your stars and colors carefully.

In truth, a Curves adjustment layer could have been used to achieve a level of A/V correction comparable to either of the previous two examples. Simply lowering the midpoint of the Curve would have produced similar results (try it for yourself). So why did we examine these two methods?

Because they illustrate several important points

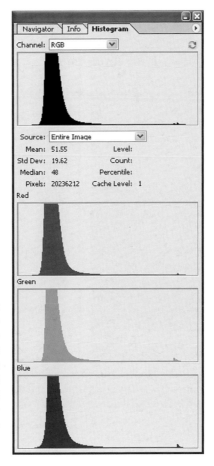 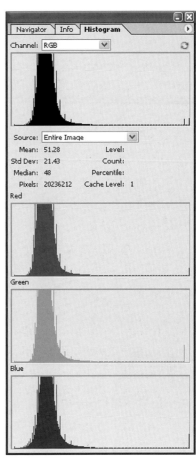

Fig. 6.6 The histograms on the left result from using the Difference Layer A/V Mask in the tutorial exercise. The histograms on the right reflect application of a simple Curves brightness reduction. The resulting images appear the same to the eye. Even the center/edge RGB values look similar. But in this case, using Curves has caused more damage to the image, as evidenced by the shadow tone spikes, midtone/highlight gaps and highlight clipping.

for us to consider:

a. First, remember that our A/V goal is to balance the background field illumination, not just to reduce the overall image brightness until the vignetting is not as noticeable. Pay attention to the edge vs. center brightness values. Set Color Sampler Points with the Eyedropper Tool and watch the Info Palette RGB numbers. Try to even out the background, don't just darken it.

b. In each of the above examples, the image was darkened in order to make A/V corrections. It is much easier to see small brightness differences when the background is lightened, rather than darkened. We will soon see how exaggerating the overall image brightness (temporarily, of course!) helps us to quickly see and correct subtle vignetting patterns.

c. I have said this before, but it bears repeating. It is important to have as many image-processing techniques and tools at your disposal as possible. Each image presents a unique processing challenge, and the more techniques you know, the more prob-

lems you will be able to solve. Generally, Photoshop provides many different ways to accomplish any given task. Sometimes the end result is the same, sometimes not. Which brings us to our next and most important point.

d. I just indicated that applying a simple Curve can produce the same result as using the Difference Layer A/V Mask that we created in our tutorial example. To the eye, this is true. It also appears true if you cursorily examine the RGB values of the center vs. the edge of the image. But refer now to **Figure 6.6**. The histograms tell us a different story. Using Curves has damaged the image more than using the Difference Layer A/V Mask. There is some spiking in the shadow tones and three-quarter tones. If you look carefully, you will see that gapping appears from the midtones through the highlights. Highlight clipping is also evident. The damage is slight, not catastrophic. The image still looks fine. But image processing is a cumulative affair. Slight damage at this point will be exacerbated as you continue to apply subsequent

R. Scott Ireland

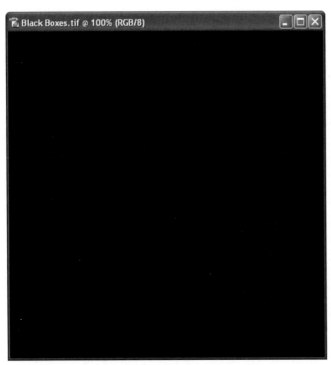

Fig. 6.7 It is much easier to detect and adjust brightness differences when working with lighter tones than it is with darker ones. The two boxes in each image vary in luminance by 2 RGB steps and are set 13 and 15 steps from the tonal scale endpoints. Can you even see the two black boxes, let alone the 2-step difference between them? Even with a well-calibrated monitor it is not easy.

image-processing steps. Among competing techniques, choose the one that accomplishes the goal but creates the least damage to the image. By the way, in case you're wondering, the Multiply Layers method produces a histogram similar to using Curves, since it is merely applying a "standard" Curve itself, and does not involve a luminance mask. It is not really a masking technique at all, but merely a type of Curves adjustment layer.

e. And so one final point is illustrated. Use everything at your disposal to keep track of the "health" of your image. Your eyes, the RGB numbers and especially the histogram. The histogram is your image's heart-rate monitor and EKG. Always check on the patient after dispensing any treatment.

The best A/V results are generally obtained when time is taken to work directly in the mask itself to make fine tonal adjustments. This is certainly the case when using the Gradient Tool to make a "synthetic" mask, but it can also improve a mask derived from the image itself. There are many ways to refine a mask. Any of the standard image adjustment tools may be applied directly to the mask, such as Levels and Curves. These are often used to increase the contrast between light and dark areas of the mask. Painting the mask directly using black, white and various shades of gray (or even colors) is another common technique. Let us now examine some of these methods in our next tutorial.

The Screen Layer A/V Mask

I mentioned in point "b" above that it is easier to see small brightness differences when an image is bright than when it is dark. This is illustrated in **Figure 6.7**. It is easy to detect the brightness difference between the two white boxes and the white background. It is not easy to even see the black boxes against the black background, let alone detect their individual brightness differences. The top-left white box has an RGB value of (240, 240, 240). The bottom-right one is (242, 242, 242), and the background is pure white — (255, 255, 255). The top-left black box has an RGB value of (13, 13, 13). The bottom-right one is (15, 15, 15) and the background is pure black — (0, 0, 0). The brightness differences and range from the tonal scale endpoints are the same. But I'll wager that most of you cannot detect the difference between the black boxes on your monitor, even if it is well calibrated. It will be nearly impossible to see them on the printed page (**Figure 6.7**). I've included both files on the tutorial disc for

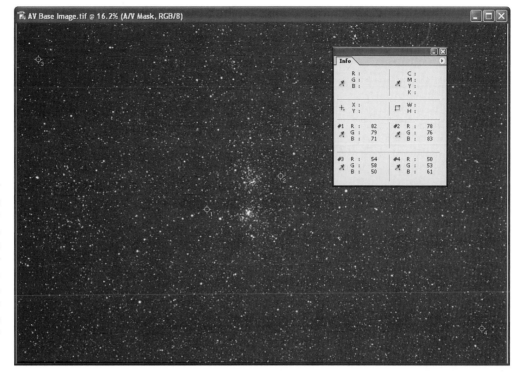

Fig. 6.8 Color Sampler points #1 and #2 are placed in areas of sky background close to the center of the field. Points #3 and #4 are placed near the edges of the field. Luminance values at the edge are approximately 50–60, while those in the center are approximately 70–80.

your edification ("White Boxes.tif" and "Black Boxes.tif"). Give it a try.

So how can we use this to our advantage? By brightening the entire image in order to more carefully adjust our A/V mask to balance the uneven illumination.

1. Once again, open the file "AV Base Image.tif" from the tutorial disc (*File|Open*).

2. Duplicate the Background Layer as described in the previous examples.

3. Next, we will remove the color information from the Background copy layer. In this example, we are going to construct a grayscale mask in order to avoid any potential color shifts in our base image. Make sure the Background copy layer is the active layer and select *Image|Adjustments|Desaturate*. The color information disappears and we are left with a grayscale version of our original image.

4. Now Invert the Background copy layer with *Image|Adjustments|Invert* (keyboard shortcut Ctrl+I). We are going to lighten the image to correct the vignetting, rather than darken it as in our previous examples. We need to reverse the tonalities to create a "negative" mask that applies more adjustment to the edges of the field than the center. Remember, with a mask, "black conceals and white reveals".

5. Use the Clone Stamp Tool, also as described previously, to remove the two star clusters (they are dark clusters now!) from the Background copy layer. Double-click on the layer name ("Background copy") and rename the layer to A/V Mask.

6. Blur the A/V Mask layer with *Filter|Blur|Gaussian Blur*. Set the Radius to 90 pixels and click OK.

7. Now let's set some Color Sampler points, so that we may compare the brightness values of the background sky at the center and edge of the frame. Turn off the visibility of the A/V Mask Layer (click once on the "eyeball" icon at the left side of the A/V Mask Layer in the Layers Palette — when the "eyeball" is not visible, the layer is not visible), so once again we have our original image in view. Select the Eyedropper Tool from the Toolbox (keyboard shortcut "I"). Make sure the Sample Size is set to "3 by 3 Average" in the Tool Options bar at the top of the Photoshop Window (select *Window|Options* if it is not visible). Remember that we have a total of four Color Samplers that we may place, so place two of them near the center of the field and the other two at each outer edge. Zoom into the image and select areas of sky background without stars. Hold down the Shift key and click once to place each Color Sampler point. **Figure 6.8** shows the four points that I

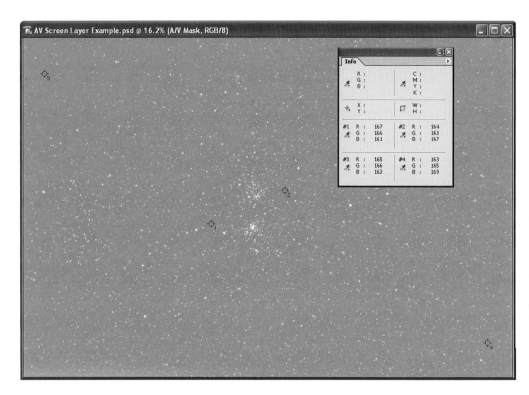

Fig. 6.9 The A/V Mask Layer has been set to the Screen Blending Mode and the Opacity adjusted to 72%. The edge areas have been lightened more than the central areas due to the mask. The RGB values of the four Color Sampler points are now very close, although further adjustments may be necessary as we darken the image. It is now easy to see small brightness differences. Painting directly into the mask will balance these areas.

chose, as well as the Info Palette RGB values for those points. Notice that the luminance values at the edge of the field are around 20 steps darker than at the center.

8. Turn the visibility of the A/V Mask Layer back on (click once to bring back the "eyeball"). Change the Layer Blending Mode from "Normal" to "Screen". The image immediately becomes very bright. You will recall that Screen is the inverse process to Multiply; Multiply darkens values while Screen lightens them. We will of course reduce this brightness later. For now, we merely want to easily see where we need to make adjustments.

9. Vary the A/V Mask Layer Opacity slider from 0% through 100%. Notice that while the entire image brightens as the Opacity is increased, the center of the image does not change as much as the edges, due to the mask. Make the Info Palette visible (*Window|Info*) and now adjust the Opacity more carefully, using the up and down arrow keys, until the four Color Sampler points are closest to each other in luminosity value. For the points I placed, this Opacity setting is 72% (**Figure 6.9**).

10. Now we can easily see where the A/V Mask is deficient and requires adjustment. Notice the bright line along the bottom-left of the image. Let's fix

this area. We will do so by directly altering our A/V Mask. Make sure the A/V Mask Layer is active and select the Brush Tool from the Toolbox (keyboard shortcut "B"). From the Tool Options Bar (*Window|Options*) select a wide, soft-edged brush of around 400 pixels or so. Leave the Mode at Normal, Opacity at 100% and change the Flow to 1%. Click once on the Airbrush icon at the right side of the Options Bar to enable airbrushing. When engaged, the Airbrush icon will appear surrounded in white, rather than gray.

11. We are almost ready to "paint" our mask. From the Toolbox, make sure that the Foreground and Background colors are set to black and white by clicking on little black/white icon at the bottom-left of the Foreground and Background color boxes. Use the keyboard shortcut "X" to quickly reverse the Foreground and Background colors. This is a very handy shortcut to remember when working with masks, as you will frequently go back and forth between black and white (or other selected shades of gray) to add to or delete from your mask. For now, make black the Foreground Color (the top-left box). We want to darken our mask to eliminate the white line.

12. Leave the image Zoomed out to full view and left-click and hold to paint the A/V Mask along the

white line at the bottom. Paint in several small steps to monitor the effect as you go. Use the left and right keyboard bracket keys to decrease and increase your brush size. In this case, after making a few strokes with the larger 400 pixel brush, you will likely need to fine-tune the mask with a smaller brush of around 200 pixels. Balance the luminosity by eye, but also remember to check the Info Palette after painting. Don't worry about being too precise at this point, but try to bring the RGB values roughly into the 160–170 range.

13. Don't worry if you overdo it and make the area too dark. You have a couple of ways of correcting mistakes when working with masks (this is one of the really nice things about them!). First, you may use the History Palette (*Window\History*) to step back through individual Brush Tool strokes. Go back to the History State prior to the problem, and then click-hold and drag the steps below that to the trash can icon at the bottom-right of the History Palette. Or, you may simply reverse the Foreground Color to white (use the "X" key shortcut) and paint the mask with white to lighten it. Painting a mask "in and out" by reversing colors is a technique that you will soon master, and it allows you to create a mask of considerable refinement.

14. When you are satisfied that you have altered your mask to eliminate the bright line, this would be a good time to save your work. Select *File\Save As*, rename the file to another name, and then save it as a Photoshop Format (*.psd) file. Be sure that the Layers box is checked so that the individual layers are saved.

15. So now we have evened-out the vignetting. Great! But, the image is way too bright. How do we deal with that? If we just use a Levels or Curves adjustment layer at the top of the layer stack to darken the entire image, our Histogram will have an unacceptable amount of gapping (try it for yourself and see). So what do we do? We start by darkening the A/V Mask itself instead of the overall image.

16. With the A/V Mask Layer active, add a Curves Adjustment Layer with *Layer\New Adjustment Layer\Curves*. Click OK to accept the default settings in the New Layer dialog box, and click OK again in the Curves dialog box to close it without making any changes. You may also add an adjustment layer by clicking on the "Create new fill or

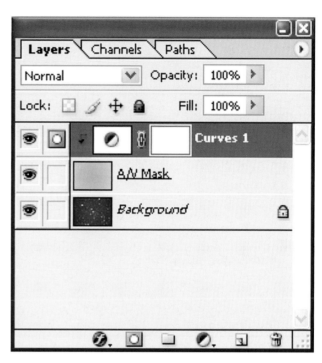

Fig. 6.10 A Clipping Mask has been created with the A/V Mask Layer as the base. Changes made in the Curves 1 Adjustment Layer will now be directed to the A/V Mask and not the overall image. Notice the Clipping Mask icon — a down arrow at the left of the Curves 1 layer. Any number of layers may be added to the Clipping Mask. The Clipping Mask base layer ("A/V Mask") is underlined.

adjustment layer" icon (small half-black/half-white circle) at the bottom-center of the Layers Palette.

17. Now we will set up the Curves Adjustment Layer so that it only affects the A/V Mask and not the entire image. One easy way for us to do this is to create a Clipping Mask. With the A/V Mask Layer active, hold down the Alt key and move the mouse cursor over the area between the A/V Mask Layer and the Curves Adjustment Layer. When the cursor changes from a small, white hand to two overlapping circles (one dark, one clear), left-click once. Immediately, the Curves layer icon indents and a downward-facing arrow (the Clipping Mask icon) appears at the left (**Figure 6.10**). Notice too that the A/V Mask Layer name is now underlined. This indicates that it is the base layer of the Clipping Mask. Now, any changes we make in the Curves Adjustment Layer will only affect the A/V Mask Layer and not the whole image.

18. Re-open the Curves 1 Adjustment Layer dialog box by double-clicking on the layer icon (it has a

R. Scott Ireland

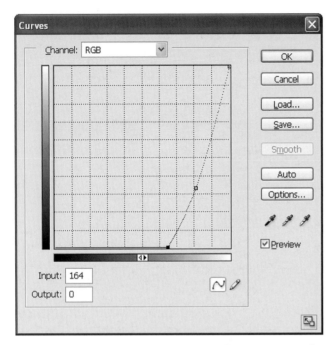

Fig. 6.11 The A/V Mask Layer is darkened and its contrast increased by applying a very steep Curve. It is often a useful technique to apply image adjustment tools directly to a mask in order to increase its effectiveness at separating the underlying image tonal values.

half black/half white circle in it). Notice too that there is another box at the right of the Curves 1 layer. This is a mask that affects the adjustment layer. When you set up an adjustment layer, an adjustment layer mask is automatically added and filled with white ("reveal all"). This mask may be used to regulate how the adjustment is applied to the underlying layer or layers. For now, we want our Curves adjustment to apply to the entire A/V Mask Layer, so we will leave the adjustment layer mask filled with white. We could just as easily delete this mask by dragging it to the trash can icon, but let's leave it for now. We may need to fine-tune this adjustment layer later.

19. Now darken the A/V Mask by sliding the Curves black point far to the right (Input 164; Output 0), and then apply an additional slight downward adjustment by placing another point on the Curve (Input 206; Output 84). The Curve is shown in **Figure 6.11**. When you have entered these points, click OK to accept this Curve. You will recall from the discussion on Curves on **page 58**, that steepening a Curve increases image contrast. Here we have both darkened the A/V Mask and increased its contrast, so that the separation between

darker and lighter tones has been exaggerated. This is worth remembering. You will often have occasion to apply image adjustment tools directly to masks in order to increase their power to separate different tonal areas of an image.

20. Let's pause and examine what has happened. The overall image has darkened considerably. Check your Color Sampler values in the Info Palette. If you've made adjustments to your A/V Mask similar to mine, all four points now lie in the RGB range around 80–90. This compares to a range of 160–170 prior to making the Curves adjustment. We are halfway home. Ultimately, we want the background sky to be in the range of 40–50 or so. Click the Curves 1 Layer "eyeball" icon on and off (to toggle its visibility), and examine the brighter and darker versions of the image. Now you have two ways to visually check the effectiveness of your A/V Mask artistry! If you need to, go ahead and apply further adjustments to the A/V Mask by painting in the A/V Mask Layer with white or black, as described in steps 10 through 13. Use your eye (with both the dark and bright versions of the image) and the Color Sampler values to guide you. The image and color values should look similar to **Figure 6.12**.

21. Before moving on, check the status of the image Histogram in the Histogram Palette (*Window|Histogram*) if you have Photoshop CS or later, or with *Image|Histogram* in earlier versions of Photoshop (make the Background layer active). By applying the Curve to the A/V Mask and not to the image itself, we have maintained a healthy histogram. There is no evidence of gapping. The image is still too light, however. We need to bring the tonal value of the background sky down to a level of around 40–50.

22. So how can we bring our sky background level down to 40–50? We could add either a Levels or Curves adjustment layer to the top of the layer stack and alter the black point from an Input of 51 to an Output of 0. The problem is that this will result in significant gapping in the Histogram. Try this for yourself and see. But what if we applied the same black point setting to just the original image (the Background layer only), rather than the entire layer stack (Background Layer + A/V Mask Layer + Curves 1 Adjustment Layer)? Remember, Photoshop layers work in a "top-down" fashion.

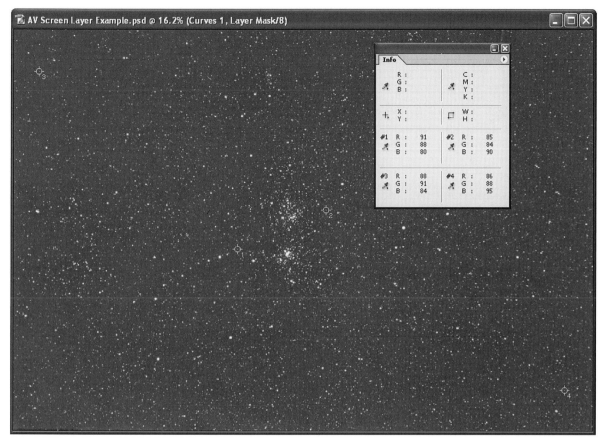

Fig. 6.12 The image after applying the Curve in **Figure 6.11** to the A/V Mask Layer. Vignetting has been removed. The background sky values have dropped from approximately 160–170 to 80–90, and the Histogram remains intact. Had the Curve been applied directly to the overall image, Histogram gapping (posterization) would have occurred.

A layer at the top of the stack affects everything below it. That is why we created a Clipping Mask with the Curves 1 Adjustment Layer. We wanted to apply the Curve only to the mask and not to the rest of the image below it. In this case, we don't even have to create a Clipping Mask, we can just add a Levels or Curves adjustment layer directly above the Background Layer. There is nothing below the Background Layer to worry about, but by placing the Adjustment Layer here it will not affect the layers above it.

23. Make the Background Layer active (click once on it). Add a Levels (or Curves — your choice, indulge yourself) Adjustment Layer directly above the Background Layer. Set the RGB channel black point to an Input of 51 and an Output of 0 and click OK to accept these settings. Just type these numbers into the left-most Input and Output boxes in the Levels dialog box. In the Curves dialog box, use Ctrl+Tab to cycle between points on the Curve (there are only two, the black and white points). Select the black point and then type in the Input and Output numbers.

24. Now check the Histogram. It looks good! There is a little spiking starting to occur in the shadow tones, but it is not serious. There is no gapping evident, and the slight highlight clipping was already there in the original image. The Info Palette shows us that our background sky values are all pretty much in the range we wanted, 40–50. If you experimented with a Curves or Levels adjustment layer at the top of the layer stack, as suggested in step 22, you may have noticed that the final RGB background sky values were exactly the same as the ones we now have (with some single-digit quantization errors as evidence of the gapped Histogram). But now we have the same background sky values without gapping (**Figure 6.13**). You may even check this now by dragging the Adjustment Layer you just created to the top of the layer stack in the Layers Palette (click-hold and drag it to the top and then release the mouse), and then

R. Scott Ireland

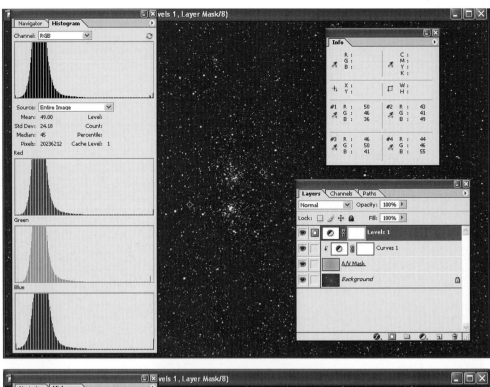

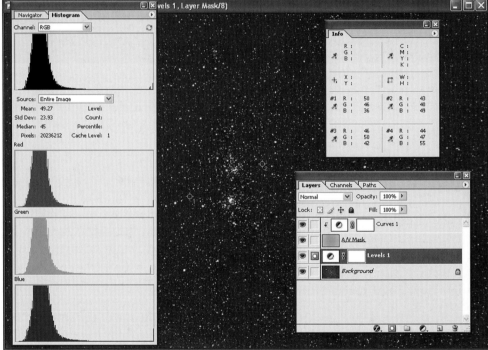

Fig. 6.13 The same Levels Adjustment Layer applied at two different places in the layer stack. The background sky levels are the same in either case, but by applying the adjustment to the Background Layer only (bottom), the quality of the Histogram is preserved. It is important to keep in mind that the position of an adjustment layer or image layer in the layer stack can yield strikingly different results.

dragging it back again to just above the Background Layer.

This is an important lesson to remember. *We have achieved the same result, but maintained a healthy Histogram, merely by applying the adjustment at a different place in the layer stack.*

25. Well, we are finally done. Check on the results of your work by holding down the Alt key and repeatedly clicking on the "eyeball" icon (the layer visibility icon) of the Background Layer. Holding down the Alt key causes all of the other layers to turn off and on at once. Be sure to save your file if you want to go back later and work with it some more. At this point, it would save file space to go ahead and delete the unused adjustment layer masks (in the Curves and/or Levels Adjustment Layers). We did not need them. Just click-hold and drag them to the trash can icon at the bottom of the Layers Palette.

The Synthetic A/V Layer Mask

In some cases it may be easier and more effective to create an A/V mask "from scratch", rather than extracting a mask from the image itself. With a synthetic mask, we may choose the grayscale or color values used to create the mask, giving us an additional degree of control over the process. Synthetic masks frequently prove useful when the original image contains large, complex subject matter, such as nebulae that vary in brightness across the entire frame or dense star clusters that comprise a significant portion of the frame. In these cases it may be difficult or impossible to "clone out" the subject and obtain a good blurred luminance mask using the original image. The Synthetic A/V Mask is completely "custom made" and is, therefore, the ultimate A/V masking method.

For this technique we will employ Photoshop's Gradient Tool to create our initial A/V mask. We will then adjust and fine-tune the mask using skills already learned from our previous examples.

1. Once again, open the file "AV Base Image.tif" from the tutorial disc (*File|Open*).

2. Create a new, blank layer by clicking once on the "Create a New Layer" Icon at the bottom of the Layers Palette.

3. Select the Gradient Tool from the Toolbox (keyboard shortcut "G"). The Gradient Tool shares the same Toolbox location as the Paint Bucket Tool,

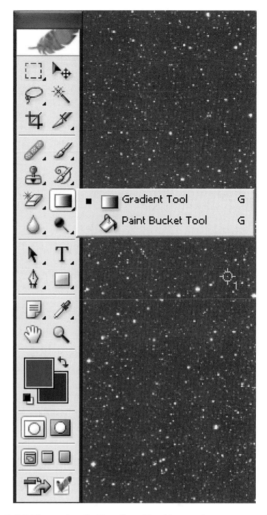

Fig. 6.14 Photoshop's Gradient Tool is used to create a Synthetic A/V Layer Mask. Using a Radial Gradient creates a circular mask with smooth, even transitions between grayscale or color values, typical of vignetting patterns. A Linear Gradient is used to create an A/V mask for non-circular brightness or color gradients.

so if the Paint Bucket is displayed, click-hold on the Toolbox icon and a flyout selection box will appear allowing you to select the Gradient Tool (**Figure 6.14**). Alternatively, use the keyboard shortcut "Shift+G" to cycle between the two tools. Once the Gradient Tool is selected, be sure that the Tool Options are displayed (*Window|Options*; or double-click on the Gradient Tool icon in the Toolbox).

4. In the Gradient Tool Options at the top of the Photoshop window, click on the drop-down selection box next to the rectangular gradient display (the "Gradient Picker") to select a preset gradient pattern. Choose the "Foreground to Background"

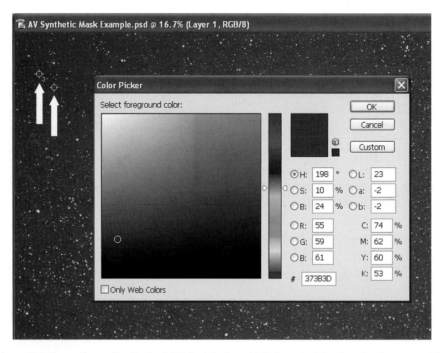

Fig. 6.15 One of the benefits of creating a Synthetic A/V Mask is the ability to select the tonal values used for the mask. Here the Foreground Color Picker is used in conjunction with the Eyedropper Tool to select the gradient Foreground Color by clicking on one of the Color Sampler points. The Eyedropper icon (cursor) and Color Sampler point #3 are indicated with white arrows above. Note the precise cursor mode chosen for the Eyedropper Tool (press the Caps Lock key). When aligned over the Color Sampler, the Eyedropper icon will disappear. Typing specific RGB values into the dialog box may also be used to choose the Foreground and Background gradient colors.

preset. This will apply a gradient starting with the foreground color and creating a smooth tonal transition to the background color.

5. Next, choose a Radial Gradient from the Tool Options. This is the second of five icons located to the right of the Gradient Picker. The Radial Gradient shades in a circular pattern between the starting and ending points of the gradient. The first icon is a Linear Gradient, which shades in a linear pattern. This should be used when an A/V mask is needed to correct for sky brightness gradients or other non-circular patterns. For now, leave the Tool Blending Mode set to "Normal", the Opacity set to 100% and check the "Dither" box.

6. Place Color Sampler points at both the brighter central areas of the image and also at the darker outside edges. Select the Eyedropper Tool from the Toolbox (keyboard shortcut "I"), set the Sample Size to "3 by 3 Average", hold down the Shift key and click to place the Color Samplers. Place two representative points in each area. You are limited to a total of four Color Sampler points.

Figure 6.8 and **6.9** show the locations of the Color Sampler points that I placed. These are the same points used in our previous tutorial example.

7. Make sure that the Eyedropper Tool is still selected, and click once on the "Set Foreground Color" icon in the Toolbox. This is the topmost of two large color square icons located near the bottom of the Toolbox. A Color Picker dialog box appears with the words "Select Foreground Color" (**Figure 6.15**). We will apply our Radial Gradient starting from the center of the image and moving out to the edge. Therefore, we need to select a darker tone for the Foreground Color, since we want to mask the brighter central areas of the image more than the darker edge areas. If necessary, change your Eyedropper Tool icon from the "little eyedropper" to a precise cursor (a small target-like circle with a dot in the center) by pressing the Caps Lock key once. Move the Eyedropper icon over one of your edge Color Sampler points (the precise cursor will "blank out" when it is exactly over the point) and click once. Click OK to close the Color Picker dialog box and accept the new Foreground Color.

Fig. 6.16 The A/V Mask created using a Radial Gradient and Foreground/Background colors selected from the image. (Note: Brightness has been exaggerated to make the image mask more visible.)

8. In the same manner, set the background color by clicking on one of the central Color Sampler points.

9. Make the blank Layer 1 active and re-select the Gradient Tool. Starting from the center of the image, click-hold and drag to the upper left edge of the image, then release the mouse. Notice that as you drag the cursor, a solid line indicates the starting and ending points of the Radial Gradient. You should now have an A/V mask in Layer 1 that looks something like **Figure 6.16**. The mask is pretty dark in all areas, since the difference between the foreground and background RGB values is only about 20 steps.

10. Rename Layer 1 to "A/V Mask". Select the entire layer (*Select|All* or Ctrl+A). Convert the mask to grayscale by removing the color information with *Image|Adjustments|Desaturate*. As in our previous example, we want our mask to be grayscale (a luminance mask), in order to avoid any unintended color shifts.

It is worth noting here that an A/V mask may be used to correct color gradients as well as brightness differences. Often, an image's vignetting pattern skews color as well as luminance information. By subtly painting (or otherwise creating) a mask with colors complementary to the offending colors, the same mask may be used as a color correction tool in addition to performing its function as a luminance mask. Or, a separate color-correcting mask may be created. However, in general my preference is to use Curves, rather than color masks, to perform color-balancing tasks. I find it much easier than trying to "paint" with just the right offsetting complementary color. Later in this example, we will explore how to use the A/V grayscale mask that we create as a Curves adjustment layer mask, so that color corrections are targeted directly to the vignetted areas of the image.

In steps 7 and 8 above, it is also possible to type RGB values directly into the Color Picker to establish the Foreground and Background colors for the Radial Gradient. This would actually save a step, since grayscale values could be entered, making desaturation of the image unnecessary. In this example, the edge values range between 50 and 60, approximately, while the center values range between 70 and 80. In the Color Picker dialog box, we could try using Foreground RGB values of (55, 55, 55) and Background values of (75, 75, 75). Give this a try for yourself and see which method you prefer.

11. Next, change the A/V Mask Layer Blending Mode (the top-left drop-down selection box in the Layers Palette) from "Normal" to "Overlay". By using the Overlay Layer Blending Mode, middle gray (50% gray) tones in the mask (128, 128, 128) will have no effect upon the underlying image. Any mask tones darker than middle gray will darken the underlying image proportionately. Mask tones lighter than middle gray will lighten it. The mask we created darkens the entire image, but selectively darkens the center more than the outside edges. Click the visibility (the little "eyeball" icon in the Layers Palette) of the A/V Mask Layer on and off and examine the RGB values in the Info Palette (*Window|Info*). The values of all Color Samplers should now lie in the range of 30–40. These values are a little darker than we ultimately want (40–50), but we will fix that shortly.

12. Now let's exaggerate the brightness of the image (temporarily, of course!) to examine the A/V mask more closely, and make any final touch-ups that are needed. Add a Curves Adjustment Layer to the top of the Layer Stack (above the A/V Mask Layer) by clicking on the "Create new fill or adjustment layer" icon at the bottom-center of the Layers Palette (it looks like a half black/half white circle) and choosing "Curves". Place a point on the Curve, in the RGB Channel, with an Input Value of 90 and an Output value of 180 (click to place a point anywhere on the Curve and then type these values into the Input/Output boxes) and click OK to accept these values and close the Curves dialog box. Make the Info Palette visible (*Window|Info*). The image has brightened up quite a bit — the Color Sampler values have increased from 30–40 to 70–80. Select the Eyedropper Tool from the Toolbox (shortcut "I") and examine the RGB values in different parts of the image to evaluate the effectiveness of your mask. Use your eyes too! My mask looks pretty good. It is just a little too dark in the central areas of the image.

13. Since my mask requires a very subtle adjustment, I am going to touch it up by painting with a very low brush "flow" and also use a dark-gray color, rather than white, to lighten it very slightly. Your mask may differ somewhat from mine, but it is in-

structive nevertheless to follow along with this technique. With the A/V Mask layer active, select the Brush Tool (shortcut "B") from the Toolbox. Choose a very wide (around 700 pixels) soft-edged Brush (use the keyboard bracket keys as a shortcut to alter the Brush size). Set the Foreground Color (click on the Foreground Color swatch in the Toolbox to bring up the Color Picker) to a dark-gray by typing the RGB values 70, 70, 70 into the Color Picker dialog, and click OK. In the Tool Options, set the Brush Flow to 1%, and click on the Airbrush icon to turn on this feature. Now paint the A/V Mask with smooth, circular motions in the darker central areas to lighten them slightly. Note that the Brush paints cumulatively — the longer you hold on an area, the more paint is applied. That is why it is beneficial to use the old darkroom dodging/burning technique of constantly moving the Brush around in small, circular motions. It will produce a smoother, more blended result and avoid "hotspots" or "darkspots". This effect is very subtle due to the low Brush Flow. To see the changes clearly, bring up the History Palette (*Window|History*) and go back and forth between the History States before and after using the Brush Tool. Use different grayscale values for the foreground color, and different Brush flows and sizes, as necessary, for your A/V Mask. If you make a mistake, simply back up in the History Palette and delete the undesired Brush strokes. Or, just paint with a different grayscale value. It is helpful to set the Background Color to a different value, so that you can "paint" with a darker and lighter color by simply using the "X" key to switch the Foreground and Background Colors.

14. When you are satisfied with your A/V Mask, delete the Curves Adjustment Layer by dragging it to the trash can Icon at the bottom of the Layers Palette. We don't need it anymore.

15. Now we are done altering our A/V Mask, but the overall image is still too dark. Set up another Curves Adjustment Layer at the top of the Layer Stack, and enter a point (in the RGB Channel) with Input/Output Values of 108/135. This brings up the Color Sampler background values from around 30–40 to 40–50. Now the image looks right. Check the "before and after" effect of your A/V Mask by holding down the Alt key and repeatedly clicking the visibility (the little "eyeball"

icon) of the Background Layer. This turns all of the other layers on and off.

16. Everything looks good, so we are done, right? Wrong. We forgot to check our Histogram! Make the Histogram visible with *Window|Histogram* (Photoshop CS and later) or *Image|Histogram* (Photoshop 7 and earlier). The Histogram shows some noticeable gapping. Where did we go wrong? Actually, it was the last step — adding the Curves Adjustment Layer to raise the overall image brightness. Confirm this for yourself by turning the visibility of the Curves layer on and off and checking the respective Histograms. So how do we get the brightness correct without creating problems? The answer is to associate the brightness increase with one layer, rather than both the Background and A/V mask layers. Remember, a layer affects every layer below it in the Layer Stack. Perhaps by raising the brightness of only the A/V Mask or the Background Layer, we may be able to solve our problem.

17. We can do this in either of two ways. First, create a Clipping Mask by associating the Curves Adjustment Layer with the A/V Mask Layer only. Hold down the Alt key and move the mouse cursor to the area between the A/V Mask Layer and the Curves Layer in the Layers Palette. When the cursor changes into an icon with a dark and light circle, click once. The Curves Layer now shows a down arrow icon, and it is applied only to the A/V Mask Layer, not the overall Layer Stack. Voila! Our Histogram is now fine.

18. But there is another way. Undo the Clipping Mask you created in step 17 (the same way you created it). Now, click-hold and drag the Curves layer to place it between the Background Layer and the A/V Mask Layer. Now, the Curves Layer brightens only the Background Layer, and not the A/V Mask Layer, since it appears in the Layer Stack "before" the A/V Mask Layer is applied. The Histogram looks good.

19. So which way is better? Compare the two solutions by using the History Palette (*Window|History*) and alternately clicking on the "Create Clipping Mask" and "Layer Order" History States. Examine the respective Histograms. While both methods produce acceptable results, placing the Curves layer between the other two layers is the better method. With the Clipping Mask in step

17, the Histogram is slightly jagged (although no longer gapped) and the image is just a little too dark. Repositioning the Curves Layer reduces the jagged Histogram and produces a better overall brightness (**Figure 6.17**). By the way, in case you're wondering, creating a Clipping Mask between the Curves Layer and the Background Layer does not change anything here. The RGB values stay the same. There are no other layers below the Background Layer, so placing the Curves Layer as the second layer in the Stack produces the same result as a Clipping Mask — the Curve affects only the Background Layer.

Do not just accept the first solution that works. Try different layer arrangements. Frequently, you will find that you can improve upon your results.

20. Our Synthetic A/V Layer Mask is now complete. Save this file (*File|Save As*) in Photoshop *.psd format, to retain the layers intact, and give it a different file name. We will use it again in our last tutorial example.

Selective Color Correction using a Synthetic A/V Layer Mask

Up to now, we have employed mostly grayscale (luminance) masks to correct vignetting. But there are a couple of additional techniques that you should know about. Recall from our earlier discussion that I made reference to a procedure whereby an A/V Mask Layer may be used to correct color as well as luminance values. Frequently, vignetted areas of an image will exhibit skewed colors ("color gradients") in addition to differing brightness values. These areas may be corrected by using colors, instead of grayscale values, to create a "color correcting" A/V Mask. The procedure is essentially the same as creating a Synthetic A/V Mask Layer. An additional A/V Layer is created using the Gradient Tool but the Foreground and Background are set to colors, rather than just grayscale values. Complementary colors are used to correct errant color biases in the underlying image. For example, if the central vignetted area of the image has a cyan cast, and the edges are too blue, then a gradient should be created using a red tone in the center grading to a yellow tone at the edges. If the central area has a magenta cast, and the edges are correct, the gradient should employ a green tone in the center, grading to a neutral gray at the edges. For a red cast, use cyan; for a green cast use

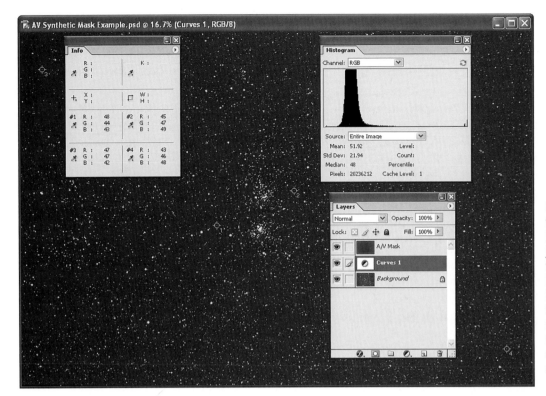

Fig. 6.17 The final Synthetic A/V Layer Mask. Placing the Curves Adjustment Layer between the Background Layer and the A/V Mask Layer creates fewer processing artifacts than placing it on top of the Layer Stack, as evidenced by the smoother Histogram.

magenta, and so forth. Try the "Soft Light" or "Overlay" Layer Blending Modes for the color-correcting A/V Mask Layer, and vary the Layer Opacity setting to achieve the best level of correction. Then fine-tune the mask by painting it with a low-flow airbrush using the appropriate colors, just as we did in our previous tutorial using gray tones.

Here again, you may try to use the existing image information to make your job easier. Create a copy of the Background Layer, clone out the bright objects and then apply a fairly strong Gaussian Blur, just as in our tutorial examples. But this time, do not remove the color information by desaturating the image. Instead, merely invert it, and the complementary colors will automatically appear. Try this as the starting point for your color-correcting A/V Mask Layer.

In practice, I find it a little difficult to get my colors perfectly balanced using this method. However, many experienced imagers use it and achieve excellent results. I encourage you to experiment and develop your own preferred working methods and techniques.

There is one final technique for us to look at that employs the A/V Mask to selectively apply color corrections. In this method, one or more Curves Adjustment Layers are used with the A/V Mask utilized as a Layer Mask. Color adjustments are therefore applied selectively and differentially following the underlying vignetting pattern. We will examine this method in our final example.

1. Open the *. psd file that you saved as the last step in our previous tutorial example (*File|Open*). Now we will create our very own color problem! We will add a magenta cast to the central vignetted area of the original image.

2. Add a blank layer to the top of the Layer Stack by clicking on the "Create a new layer" icon at the bottom of the Layers Palette.

3. Next, select a medium magenta tone for the Foreground Color using the Color Picker. The RGB values I used were (161, 86, 178). Set the Background Color to a middle-toned neutral gray (128, 128, 128).

4. Select the Gradient Tool (shortcut "G") and use the following settings: Foreground to Background pattern; Radial Gradient; Normal Mode; 100% Opacity and check the Dither box.

5. With the blank layer active, apply a radial gradient starting at the center of the image and ending at the top-left corner. Change the Layer Blending Mode to "Overlay" and set the Layer Opacity to 55%. The image now has a vignette with a distinct magenta cast.

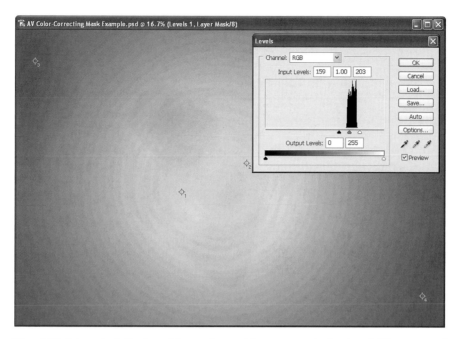

Fig. 6.18 A Levels Adjustment Layer is used to exaggerate the tonal differences of the A/V Mask. This version of the A/V Mask will be used to selectively apply color corrections with a Curves Adjustment Layer.

6. Now we will use the A/V Mask that we created in our last example to construct a new Curves Layer Mask. Click-hold on the A/V Mask Layer and drag it to the "Create a new layer" icon at the bottom of the Layers Palette. Release the mouse to create a new layer called "A/V Mask copy". Move the A/V Mask copy Layer to the top of the Layer Stack (click-hold and drag it to the top).

7. Make the A/V Mask copy Layer active, and turn off the visibility of all of the other Layers (Alt-click on the visibility icon of the A/V Mask copy Layer). Select the entire Layer (Ctrl+A) and invert the tonalities with *Image\Adjustments\Invert* (shortcut Ctrl+I). Deselect with Ctrl+D. We are going to apply a Curve to counteract the magenta cast that is now in the center of our image, so we want our mask to apply more of the correction to the center than to the edges. This is why we inverted the mask.

8. Next, we will increase the tonal contrast of the mask (e.g. "stretch" it) to make it more effective at separating the center and edge areas of the image. Exaggerating the tonal differences in a mask is a good technique to remember. It is possible to create very useful luminance masks that can serve a wide variety of purposes in this way. Create a Levels Adjustment Layer at the top of the Layer

Stack (*Layer\New Adjustment Layer\Levels*), above the A/V Mask copy Layer. Create a Clipping Mask linking the Levels and A/V Mask copy layers by holding down the Alt key and moving the mouse between the two layers in the Layers Palette until a dark circle/light circle icon appears, and then left-click once.

9. Make sure that the A/V Mask copy Layer and the Levels Adjustment Layer are the only layers visible. Open the Levels Adjustment Layer dialog box and Increase the mask contrast by dragging the shadow slider to an Input value around 159 and the highlight slider to an Input value of around 203 (or enter these Input values directly; see **Figure 6.18**).

10. With the A/V Mask copy layer active, open the Layers Palette Menu (click on the little right-facing arrow at the top-right of the Layers Palette) and choose "Merge Clipping Mask". This closes your Levels Adjustment Layer and applies the adjustment to the underlying A/V Mask copy Layer. Note that you could also have combined these two layers by making sure that they are the only two visible layers and choosing "Merge Visible".

11. Create a new Curves Adjustment Layer at the top of the Layer Stack ("Curves 2"). Make the A/V

R. Scott Ireland

Mask copy layer active and select all of it with Ctrl+A. Then copy it to the clipboard with Ctrl+C. Then deselect with Ctrl+D.

12. Open the Curves 2 Layer Mask into the main window by holding down the Alt key and clicking on it (In the Layers Palette, it is the right window in the Curves 2 Layer). Paste the A/V mask into the main window with Ctrl+V. Again deselect with Ctrl+D. The mask now appears in the Curves 2 mask icon. Curves adjustments will be selectively applied according to the tonalities of the A/V Mask copy that we created.

13. Discard the A/V Mask copy layer (click-hold and drag it to the trash can icon at the bottom of the Layers Palette). We no longer need it.

14. Now make all of the Layers visible by Alt-clicking on the visibility icon of the Curves 2 Layer (or Alt-clicking twice on any layer).

15. The Info Palette shows us that the green values in the center of the image (Color Sampler points #1 and #2) are too low (the magenta cast), while the edge areas are fairly neutral (Color Sampler points #3 and #4). Open the Curves 2 dialog box and create Curve points in the color Channels using the following Input/Output values: RGB Channel — no points; Red Channel — (55,49); Green Channel — (36,48); Blue Channel — (59,52). Be sure to set new points so that you do not inadvertently alter the black or white points. We are reducing the magenta cast by using a Curve that adds a fair amount of green, and slightly reduces both red and blue (remember, red + blue = magenta). Click OK to accept these settings and close the dialog. Most of the magenta cast is now gone. But our mask adjustments were not perfect. The edge areas are now a little too green and some of the central areas are still a bit too magenta. No problem! We will simply make some adjustments to our Layer Mask to "dial in" the correct colors.

16. Select the Brush Tool and use a very wide soft-edged brush of around 900 pixels. Reduce the Brush Flow to 1% and enable the Airbrush. Click once on the Curves 2 mask window to be sure that you are painting into the mask, and not the image. Paint the edge areas with black while keeping an eye on Color Sampler points #3 and #4 in the Info Palette. Paint the central mask areas with white while referring to Color Sampler points #1 and #2.

Use the Eyedropper Tool (shortcut "I") to check color values in the other background sky areas of the image. You may observe the effect of your adjustments by alternating the visibility of Layer 1 (the magenta layer) and the Curves 2 Layer.

17. When you are satisfied with your mask, check the Histogram (*Window|Histogram* or *Image|Histogram*). My Histogram looks fine after these adjustments, so no further steps should be necessary. The final color-correcting mask and Layers Palette are shown in **Figure 6.19**.

To obtain even more precise color-correction, it is possible to add additional Curves Adjustment Layers and Layer Masks. I encourage you to experiment for yourself by trying different Curves settings in the Curves 2 Adjustment Layer, and also by adding an additional Curves Adjustment Layer. Try masking out the entire second Curves Layer (fill the Layer Mask with black) and just "painting in" some final corrections, particularly to the blue and red channels, which could use some more tweaking.

You may find that painting a mask directly with complementary colors is easier than making Curves adjustments, and then altering the effect with grayscale masks. Again, I encourage you to try your hand at making a direct, color-correcting mask layer using complementary colors and see for yourself which you prefer. You should now have enough masking skills to handle the task easily.

Some Final Thoughts

There are other methods that may be used to select and mask the vignetted areas of an image. For example, it is possible to use a selection tool, such as Color Range (*Select|Color Range*) to create a selection border around the vignetted area and then convert this selection into a mask (*Select|Save Selection*, or "Save selection as channel" in the Channels Palette are two ways to do this). In cases of extreme vignetting, this may be an easier way to create a starting point for your A/V mask. In subsequent chapters, we will examine selection methods in greater detail.

Masks and selections are related. A selection may be saved as a grayscale image (an Alpha Channel). So it is possible to create a mask by first making a selection and then converting the selection into an Alpha Channel. It is also possible to convert an Alpha Channel into a selection. Selections are "activated" Alpha

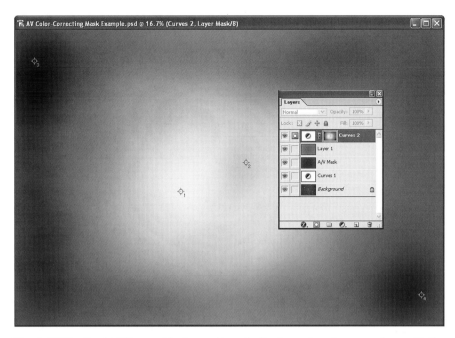

Fig. 6.19 The final A/V Layer Mask used to selectively apply color corrections with the Curves 2 Adjustment Layer. Final color adjustments were made using a very low-flow airbrush and painting the mask with white, black and gray. Multiple Curves Adjustment Layers may be used to obtain an even more precise color balance.

Channels. Alpha Channels are "frozen" selections. They are, in essence, the same thing. The "static" nature of Alpha Channels and masks makes them generally easier to work with than selections. Masks are the ultimate tools with which to identify and separate image areas and characteristics in order to precisely target your adjustments.

In certain cases, it may be desirable to actually create a vignette around the edges of an image. Ansel Adams advocated slightly darkening the edges of a print, to provide the viewer with a psychological "border" that directs the eye to the central subject area. A subtle vignette can provide a framework to keep the eye from "wandering" off the edge of the image. While this technique is generally not applicable to astropho-

tographs, it may nevertheless be used to enhance some images. It can certainly improve many daylight photographs.

Finally, you must always consider the time tradeoff between obtaining the "perfect" image, versus one that is "good enough". None of us has an unlimited amount of time to devote to processing each image. Often one of the quicker techniques discussed above can produce completely adequate, albeit not perfect, results. However, it is important to understand and master the more complicated techniques as well. Having facility with both simple and complicated methods will enable you to consistently and efficiently produce photographs of high quality, no matter what types of image-processing problems you may encounter.

Chapter 7
Additional Noise Reduction Techniques

In the last two Chapters, we explored Stacking and Anti-Vignetting, two fundamental methods to reduce image noise. We have seen the importance of maximizing the image signal-to-noise ratio (S/N) by reducing random background noise through Stacking. We have also examined methods used to create Anti-Vignetting masks in order to balance background field illumination and thereby minimize a principal source of non-random noise.

However, even after employing these methods, we find that most of our images will still contain elements of residual noise. *Remember, an original image capture contains the most information that we will ever have about that image. The procedure of image processing is one in which we selectively alter the original image information in order to optimize its appearance. It is essentially a reductive process. The final image will contain less information than the original, but if we have done our job well it will highlight those image elements that we consider most important and produce a more aesthetically pleasing result.*

So, image processing itself can introduce noise. The more processing steps that are involved, and the greater the degree of processing applied in these steps, the more chance there is that image artifacts will be introduced. Film grain and digital image background noise may be more accentuated after applying contrast stretching and Curves adjustments. Calibrating and processing digital captures often results in "wrong-colored" pixels, hot (white) pixels, dark (black) pixels, and other artifacts. Film scanning can introduce green pixels and other background noise. Dust motes, minute film scratches, hairs, airplanes and all kinds of other environmental bogeymen conspire to degrade our images. *Image processing is a constant battle to increase signal while keeping noise at bay.*

In this Chapter we will "buff up" our arsenal of noise fighting techniques. We will explore specific methods to remove dust and scratches, black speckles and colored pixels. We will learn some additional methods, beyond Stacking, to smooth out our sky backgrounds and reduce graininess and digital noise.

At what point in the image-processing workflow should we administer these techniques? Well, there are no hard and fast rules. Any particular image may dictate a different procedure. However, in general, it is advisable to employ dust and scratch removal early, right after Stacking, and sometimes even earlier on the individual frames. The other techniques are best administered after all Stacking, Anti-Vignetting and contrast and color adjustments have been performed, but before final sizing and sharpening of the image.

Dust and Scratch Removal

Dust and scratch removal has been with us since the first caveman processed the first digital image sometime in the dim, dark past (probably around 1980). It is a necessary evil that is universally despised by those who do a lot of image processing. It can take a considerable amount of time to "retouch" an image and remove all of the little nasty spots, lines, blots and stray colored pixels that inevitably appear, no matter how carefully we clean our digital sensors and film. With the rapid rise in digital camera use, the problem has become even more acute, since these devices are notorious for attracting dust onto the image sensor.

What is the best way for us to retouch our images and remove the wide array of artifacts that we label "dust and scratches"? The traditional, time-honored method is *"Cloning"*. We outlined the basic steps in **Chapter 6**, and I refer you there now to brush up on this methodology. Cloning replaces small areas of the image where artifacts appear with adjacent "clean" image areas using Photoshop's Clone Stamp (a/k/a Rubber Stamp) Tool or Healing Brush Tool. Using a small, soft-edged brush, we hold down the Alt key and left-click to make selections and then release the Alt key and left click to "paint" from the selected area to the problem area. The trick is to make many small "selection/paint" steps very close by the problem area in order to retain smoothness in texture, tone and color, and avoid obvious cloning artifacts. Cloning is an impor-

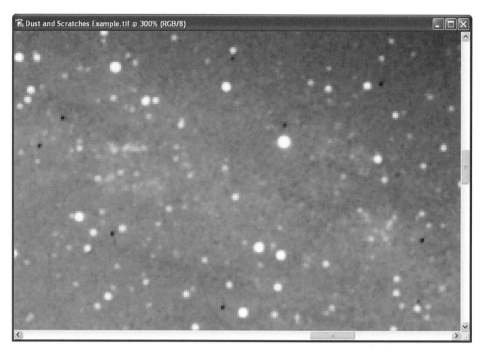

Fig. 7.1 The term "dust and scratches" is used to describe a multitude of small artifacts that appear in virtually all images, regardless of the capture method. Here we see black "speckles" scattered throughout a CCD image.

tant technique to master, since it may be the only viable way to fix certain problems. A deft "hand" with the Clone Stamp Tool can successfully remove large, offending image elements, such as star blooms, telephone wires, airplane trails and the like, in addition to dust and scratches. Unfortunately, there is no tutorial that will improve your cloning technique. This only comes with practice.

But there is another technique that may be used to remove the majority of dust and scratch problems, and it is a lot faster than cloning. Used in conjunction with cloning (to remove the larger scale problems), this technique will speed up your image retouching work considerably. Let's work through an example.

The Dust and Scratches Layer

Rather than copying over dust spots with adjacent image areas, as in cloning, the Dust and Scratches Layer instead utilizes a slightly blurred version of the original image to fix these problems. A blurred copy of the Background layer is applied on top of the original image. By using a layer mask, the blurred version is applied only to the problem areas. Since the same image pixels are used to hide the dust spots (rather than adjacent pixels), they are in perfect alignment and the color matching problems and other visible artifacts inherent

in the cloning method are eliminated. Remember, whenever possible let the image do the work for you.

1. From the tutorial disc, open the file "Dust and Scratches Example.tif" (*File|Open*). This is a portion of the CCD image composite we have worked with before — an Andromeda Galaxy mosaic created by the author and Tim Khan. In this version of the image, the dust and scratch retouching work has not yet been performed.

2. From the Toolbox, select the Zoom Tool and increase the screen display to 100% ("Actual Pixels"). Now examine the galaxy carefully. There are quite a few small, dark spots scattered throughout the image. You don't notice them in the dark sky background, but they stand out clearly against the bright galaxy (**Figure 7.1**).

3. Next, make a copy of the Background layer and place it at the top of the layer stack. From the Layers Palette, click-hold on the Background Layer and drag it to the "Create a new layer" icon (this is the little "double square" icon at the bottom-right of the Layers Palette, next to the trash can icon) and then release the mouse. A Background copy layer appears at the top of the layer stack. This is an exact copy of the original image, with each pixel in the same position as in the original.

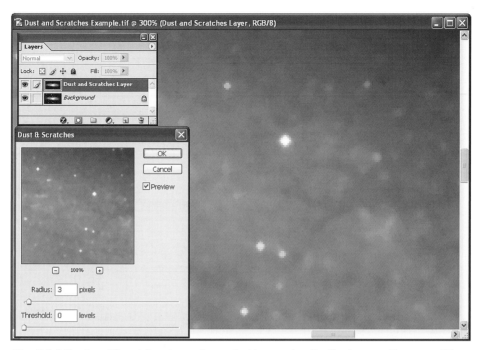

Fig. 7.2 A Dust and Scratches Layer is created by copying the Background Layer and then blurring it slightly by applying the Dust and Scratches Filter (*Filter | Noise | Dust and Scratches*). The pixel Radius chosen should be just enough to eliminate the dust spots and speckles.

Turning the visibility of either of these layers on and off produces no change. This is a very good thing, as we'll soon see!

4. Rename the Background copy layer to "Dust and Scratches Layer" by double-clicking on the Layer name and typing in the new one.

5. With the Dust and Scratches Layer active (highlighted in blue), select *Filter | Noise | Dust & Scratches*. Adjust the Radius setting until the black spots just disappear. For this image the setting should be 3 pixels (**Figure 7.2**). Leave the Threshold setting at 0 levels and click OK.

Photoshop's Dust & Scratches filter reduces noise by modifying dissimilar pixels. As with other filters, the Threshold command identifies how much difference there must be between pixel values before the effect is applied. In most cases, I find that leaving the Threshold set to 0 levels is best. The pixel radius should be set to the minimum value that just eliminates the dust spots/speckles. A setting of between 3 and 5 pixels will usually suffice.

Why not use the Gaussian Blur filter instead of the Dust & Scratches filter? Well, we could. This noise reduction technique, as with most others, utilizes a blurred version of the original image to smooth out and eliminate unwanted artifacts. You will find as you gain experience with Photoshop that much about image processing is a "yin and yang" dialectic tug-of-war between blurring and sharpening. We blur to smooth out imperfections and transitions and sharpen to enhance detail, direct emphasis and give the appearance of photographic quality. The final result is a balance between these two opposing methods.

Here we use the Dust & Scratches filter because it is more "targeted" to our immediate needs. The Dust & Scratches filter will eliminate the dust spots with a smaller radius setting. To blur this image sufficiently with the Gaussian Blur filter would require a Radius setting of around 6.5 pixels, compared to the 3 pixel Dust & Scratches filter setting (try this for yourself and see). We should always employ tools and methods that create the least amount of disruption to the image. In this case, the Dust & Scratches filter accomplishes our task with less blurring of the background than the Gaussian Blur filter would render.

6. Now we will create a layer mask that hides all of the Dust and Scratches Layer. With the Dust and Scratches Layer active, select *Layer | Add Layer Mask | Hide All*. A layer mask window appears to the right of the image icon, and it is filled with

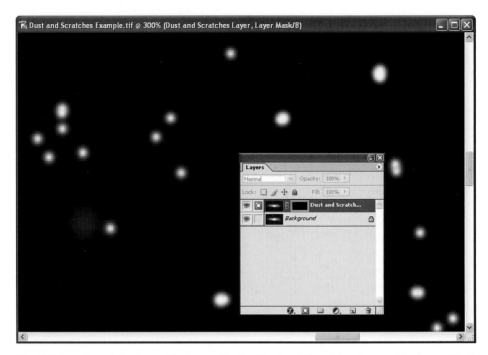

Fig. 7.3 A portion of the Layer Mask used for the Dust and Scratches Layer. The Layer Mask is painted with white only where speckles, dust spots or other artifacts appear. This allows the blurred/filtered image to show through into the Layer Stack only where it is needed.

black ("hide all"). Our image immediately returns from blurred to normal, because the layer mask hides the entire Dust and Scratches Layer. Now, only the Background Layer (the original image) shows through the Layer Stack.

7. Here's the good part! From the Toolbox, select the Brush Tool (keyboard shortcut "B"). In the Tool Options Bar, choose a soft-edged brush of around 10 pixels diameter. Leave the Mode set to "Normal", the Opacity and Flow each set to 100%, and make sure that the Airbrush is disabled. Zoom into the image to around 300% and center on a bright area of the galaxy that has a lot of black speckles (to the right of the galaxy is a good area). Click once on the Dust and Scratches Layer Mask window to make it active. We are going to paint in the Layer Mask, not in the image. In the Toolbox, make the Foreground Color White (click on the little black/white icon at the lower left of the Foreground/Background Color boxes to set the Foreground and Background to White and Black, respectively). Now, wherever a dark speckle appears in the image, paint with White in the Dust and Scratches Layer Mask. Voila! The black speckles just disappear! This is much faster than

trying to clone out each individual speck! And the image appears perfect, since we are using a blurred version of the same pixels. The colors are the same (**Figure 7.3** and **7.4**).

By the way, Photoshop also contains a "Despeckle" noise filter (*Filter|Noise|Despeckle*). So, one might think that this would be the ideal filter to use when removing dark "speckles". Wrong. There are several problems with it. First, it seldom works well. You will end up softening your background sky and all of the black spots will remain anyway. Give it a try on the previous tutorial image and see for yourself. Second, there is no pixel radius or threshold adjustment setting for the Despeckle filter. Also, a reminder — set up your adjustments as non-destructive edits. Use duplicate layers, adjustment layers and masks whenever possible, rather than applying filters or other destructive edits directly to the underlying image pixels.

What about the other Photoshop filters listed under the *Filter|Noise* menu? Well, we certainly do not want to use the "Add Noise" filter, for obvious reasons. We've already examined Despeckle and Dust & Scratches. That leaves one more — Median —and this filter can be very useful, as we'll see in our next example.

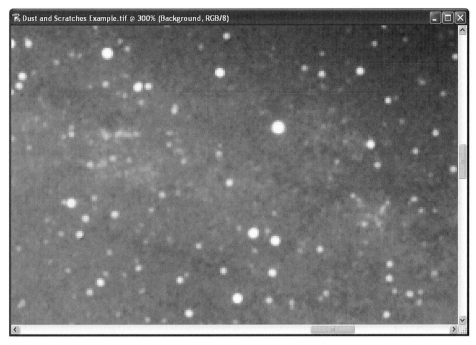

Fig. 7.4 The final result using the Dust and Scratches Layer Mask. Compare this with the "before" image of **Figure 7.1**. This method produces a perfect, seamless result when dealing with small-scale dust, black speckles, scratches and the like. The process is much faster than Cloning and produces superior results.

Using Photoshop's Median Filter for Noise Reduction

1. Once again, open the file "Dust and Scratches Example.tif" (*File\Open*) from the tutorial disc.

2. Duplicate the Background layer. From the Layers Palette (*Window\Layers*), click-hold and drag the Background layer to the "Create a new layer" icon at the bottom-right of the Layers Palette and then release the mouse. A Background copy layer appears at the top of the Layer Stack. Double-click on the Background copy layer name and change it to "Median Filter".

3. Zoom well into the image (to around 300%) and select an area of the galaxy that displays a lot of black speckles.

4. With the Median Filter Layer active (highlighted in blue in the Layers Palette), select *Filter\Noise\Median*. The Median filter dialog box appears. Make certain that the Preview box is checked (to view the filter's effect in the main image window). Now adjust the Radius by moving the slider, or by clicking once on the Radius value and using the up and down arrow keys on the keyboard (this method is easier to control). The first thing that you notice is that this is one powerful filter! At a Radius setting of only 2 pixels, the black speckles are pretty much gone. However, for our purposes, let's make sure that we have blurred the image a good bit. Choose a Radius of 5 pixels and click OK to apply the filter.

5. Next, change the Median Filter Layer Blending Mode from "Normal" to "Lighten". The Layer Blending Mode is found in the drop-down selection box (click on the little down-facing arrow) at the top-left of the Layers Palette. As we have already seen in previous Chapters, the Layer Blending Mode governs how a layer's pixels are blended with the underlying pixels in the Layer Stack.

6. Now we will fine-tune the effect of the Median Filter. Adjust the Opacity of the Median Filter Layer until the black speckles just disappear. The Opacity adjustment is located to the right of the Layer Blending Mode. Clicking on the right-facing arrow produces an adjustment slider. Use this slider to get close to your desired Opacity, and then use the up and down arrow keys for more precise control. In this case, an Opacity setting of 90% to 92% is correct.

Look at what has happened! We have not only

Fig. 7.5 Photoshop's Median Filter (*Filter | Noise | Median*) is here used to both remove black speckles and smooth out background graininess. The key is to change the Median Filter Layer Blending Mode to "Lighten" and use the layer's Opacity setting to fine-tune the effect.

eliminated the black speckles, we have also smoothed out the grainy sky background! Two for one! (**Figure 7.5**). Try turning the visibility of the Median Filter layer on and off (click the little "eyeball" icon at the left in the Layers Palette) and check the small details. Adjust the layer Opacity further if needed. Unsharp masking could now be applied to this image as a final step to give it a touch more definition, without exaggerating the background graininess. We will cover unsharp masking in great detail in **Chapter 12**.

The Median Filter searches within the defined Radius for pixels of similar brightness, eliminates those pixels that vary significantly, and replaces each pixel with the median value found within the search Radius. This results in significant blurring, as the averaging takes place throughout the image (unless a selection or mask is used to limit the effect to a particular area). However, the real magic comes when we use "Lighten" as the Layer Blending Mode. Lighten examines the pixels in each layer and allows the lighter pixels to show through (the "blend color"). Pixels darker than this blend color are replaced (dark speckles), while pixels lighter than the blend color do not change (stars). Similar colors (grainy sky background) are rendered as a smoother, slightly blurred result.

While the Median Filter is not a panacea for all images, it is a very handy technique to have in your arsenal and can sometimes solve multiple noise problems very quickly and easily.

It is instructive at this point to show you another way to apply filters. Even though this next example is a destructive edit, which I generally do not recommend, it is nevertheless useful in many circumstances where non-destructive edits are difficult or impossible to set up.

In this example, we will once again use the Median Filter to accomplish the same result as in our previous tutorial. This time, however, we will not set up a separate layer, but rather employ Photoshop's *Edit|Fade* command after applying the Median filter directly to the Background layer. By using the *Edit|Fade* command, we retain the ability to alter and regulate a destructive edit by choosing different Blending Modes and Opacity settings.

Using the Edit/Fade Command

1. Once again, open the file "Dust and Scratches Example.tif" (*File|Open*) from the tutorial disc.

2. Zoom well into the image (to around 300%) and select an area of the galaxy that displays a lot of

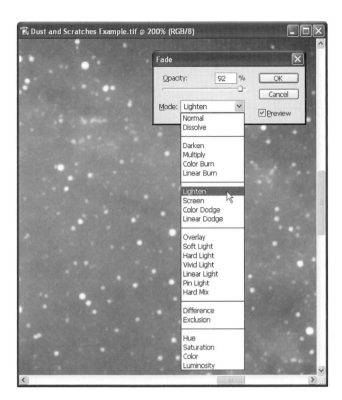

Fig. 7.6 The *Edit| Fade* Command may be used to modify the effect of a filter, painting tool or other adjustment. It is applied immediately after making the adjustment and allows the user to modify the edit by using various Blending Modes (as with Layers). It also allows an Opacity adjustment to regulate the magnitude of the edit.

black speckles.

3. Select *Filter|Noise|Median*. Set the Radius to 5 pixels and click OK.

4. Immediately select *Edit|Fade Median*. A Fade dialog box appears (**Figure 7.6**). Even though we have performed a destructive edit and applied the Median filter to the underlying image pixels (the Background layer), immediately selecting the Fade command allows us to alter the previous edit. We may change the Blending Mode and Opacity, just as with Layers, but in this case "after the deed is done".

5. As in our previous example, set the Blending Mode to "Lighten" and the Opacity to around 91%, then click OK.

The *Edit|Fade* command may be used after applying any filter, painting tool, erasing tool or color adjustment. It allows us to regulate the Opacity from 0% (no effect from the edit) to 100% (full effect), as well as alter the Blending Mode to govern how the edit will interact with the "before" image pixels. It is a very useful

and powerful command to know, and it can solve certain problems that are difficult to fix in other ways, as we shall see in later Chapters.

Removing Stray Colored Pixels Using the Color Range Command

It is not uncommon to encounter stray, colored pixels in many astrophotographs. A typical occurrence is to find seemingly random, green pixels scattered throughout the background of deep-sky film or CCD images. These may sometimes be cleaned up using a Dust and Scratches layer, or by Cloning, but finding them all can quickly become very tedious work. The Median Filter works fine for black speckles, but it does not do well on colored pixels, as they exhibit brightness levels similar to normal, faint stars.

So, in our next tutorial example, we will examine a new noise reduction technique using Photoshop's Color Range Command, which allows us to make a selection based upon a particular color or set of colors. We will use this to target unwanted stray green pixels and then use a Curve to blend these pixels seamlessly into the star field. To my knowledge, this technique was first described online by Tony Hallas and thus has come to be known as "Tony Hallas' Green Pixel Gun".

1. From the tutorial disc open the file "Green Pixel Noise.tif" (*File|Open*). This is a small star field section extracted from a larger deep-sky image. I have put in some additional stray green pixels of differing colors to make our job more interesting!

2. Duplicate the Background layer. From the Layers Palette (*Window|Layers*), click-hold and drag the Background layer to the "Create a new layer" icon at the bottom-right of the Layers Palette and then release the mouse. A Background copy layer appears at the top of the Layer Stack. Double-click on the Background copy layer name and change it to "Green Pixel Gun". This way we always retain the original image pixels intact in the Background Layer. If we do not like our results, we can always delete the Green Pixel Gun layer and start over.

3. Next, Zoom deeply into the image, to around 600%, so that the green pixels will be easier to spot and select.

4. Select the Eyedropper Tool from the Toolbox (keyboard shortcut "I"). In the Tool Options Bar (at the top of the Photoshop Window) set the Sample Size to "Point Sample". Remember to reset

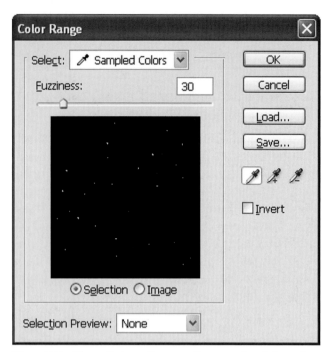

Fig. 7.7 The Color Range Command dialog box (*Select | Color Range*). This highly useful tool creates a selection based upon specific colors sampled from within the image using the Eyedroppers. A low "Fuzziness" setting narrows the range of colors selected. A higher setting broadens the color range selected. The Preview Window indicates the selected pixels. The Selection Preview may also be set to display the selection in the image window as a mask.

Fig. 7.8 The Color Range Command has created a selection border around only the offending green pixels located throughout the image.

this option back to "3 x 3 Average" when you are finished with this technique. For 95% of the Eyedropper sampling tasks you will perform, you will want to use the 3 x 3 Average setting. In this case, we want to target very specific colors, so a Point Sample is preferable.

5. Choose *Select|Color Range*. The Color Range dialog box appears (**Figure 7.7**). Notice the 3 Eyedroppers at the right side of the dialog box. The Eyedropper on the left is used to make an initial color selection by clicking once in the image window. The + Eyedropper adds colors to the selection, while the – Eyedropper deletes colors from the selection. The + Eyedropper may be temporarily selected by holding down the Shift key while using the "initial selection" Eyedropper (I find this the most convenient way to use this tool). Make sure that the dialog box Preview Window is set to "Selection". Click on the left Eyedropper (initial selection), move the cursor into the image window and click once on some green pixels. If the Color Range dialog already contains a selec-

tion (the settings are "sticky"), you may first have to clear the previous selection by clicking on a different color entirely, and then begin again. Now move around the entire image and make several selections (about 15 or 20 should do) by holding down the Shift key (the Eyedropper changes to a "+" Eyedropper) and clicking once on more green pixels of different shades. You will notice that white dots start to appear in the Color Range dialog Preview Window and grow in number as you move through the image adding additional shades of green to the selection.

6. When you are done making Eyedropper selections, adjust the "Fuzziness" slider to around 35 or 40 and click OK to close the dialog (**Figure 7.8**). Fuzziness adjusts the sensitivity of the selection. Lower numbers narrow the selection, while higher numbers expand the range of colors selected.

7. Now move around the image to see how well your selection turned out. If too many "non-offending" pixels were selected, merely cancel the selection (*Select|Deselect* or keyboard shortcut Ctrl+D) and repeat steps 5 and 6, perhaps using a lower Fuzziness setting.

8. If your selection is mostly on-target, then you may easily deselect any "correct" pixels that were accidentally selected, by using the Lasso Tool. From the Toolbox, select the Lasso Tool (keyboard shortcut "L"). Hold down the Alt key (a little "minus" sign appears next to the Lasso icon) and draw a circle with the Lasso Tool around any image pixels that were incorrectly selected. When you complete the circle and release the mouse, those pixels will be deselected. Don't worry about being careful drawing circles with the Lasso. Anything that surrounds the pixels will do. If you accidentally deselect a set of "bad" green pixels, then just use the History Palette to delete the last Lasso action. For images where the main subject contains green areas, such as the Dumbell or Veil Nebulae, simply hold down the Alt key and Lasso around the entire subject area to remove it from the selection.

9. When you are satisfied that only the "bad" green pixels have been selected, create a Curves Adjustment Layer by clicking on the "Create new fill or adjustment layer" icon (a little half black/half white circle) at the bottom of the Layers Palette, and selecting "Curves". A Curves dialog box opens and a new Curves Adjustment Layer (Curves 1) appears at the top of the Layer Stack. A layer mask is automatically applied to this adjustment layer, incorporating your selection. Curves adjustments will only apply to the selected green pixels.

10. Now, make Curves adjustments until the green pixels blend into the background. You will reduce the Green Channel, and also the RGB Channel. In the Green Channel try setting a Curves point with Input/Output values of (118, 63). In the RGB Channel try a point with Input/Output values of (138, 110). Your particular settings may vary, of course, depending upon how you handled the Color Range selection, but these settings should give you a starting point. When you are satisfied that you have reduced the green pixel values sufficiently, click OK to accept the Curves settings. But don't expect perfection just yet. Despite your best efforts, there may still be some green pixels or artifacts in the image. As you reduce the Curves Channels, you may see some "black halo" artifacts appear around the unmasked green pixels. Try to make adjustments to the point just before

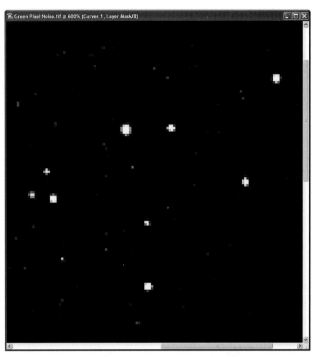

Fig. 7.9 When an Adjustment Layer is created, a Layer Mask is automatically applied, based upon an active selection. In this case, a Curves Adjustment Layer mask was created that will apply adjustments only to the green pixels selected with the Color Range Command. Compare this mask to the selection borders in **Figure 7.8**.

these artifacts become distinct. Again, it will be helpful to Zoom well into the image (600% or so) to see the effects more clearly. You may even find it necessary to make some tweaks to the Red and Blue Channels to balance the colors.

11. In order to smooth out the effect of the Curves Adjustment Layer Mask, it may be helpful to apply a slight blur to the mask. With the Curves 1 Layer active, hold down the Alt key and click once inside the Layer Mask Window (it is the Window to the right that looks mostly black). The Curves Adjustment Layer Mask now appears in the main image window (**Figure 7.9**).

12. Select *Filter\Blur\Gaussian Blur*, set the Radius to 1 pixel, and click OK. Now restore the image in the main window by clicking once on the Background Layer Eyeball icon (layer visibility). Then immediately select *Edit\Fade Gaussian Blur*. Remember the *Edit\Fade Command*? This allows us to tweak and fine-tune the blur we just applied to the layer mask (a destructive edit). Now try different Blending Modes and Opacity settings until

R. Scott Ireland

you achieve the best result that minimizes the artifacts and visibility of the green pixels. For this example, I found that a "Normal" Blending Mode and an Opacity setting of 30% worked best.

13. Finally, re-open the Curves dialog box and make your final adjustments. After blurring the Layer Mask, I found that making another Curves adjustment allowed me to completely eliminate the visibility of the green pixels. My final Curves points were as follows: In the RGB Channel, points at Input/Output values of (41, 17) and (138, 86); no adjustment to the Red Channel; in the Green Channel, a single point at (118, 51); and no adjustment to the Blue Channel.

Once you've practiced this technique, it will become second nature and easy to implement. You will quickly develop a sense of what settings will work best in a given situation. The method will generally prove faster than trying to use the Clone Tool to remove stray, colored pixels

The Color Range Command is a tool well worth mastering. By providing a method to create selections based on specific, targeted colors, it may be used to solve a myriad of image-processing problems that are difficult to deal with in any other way. Remember that selections and alpha channels are different sides of the same coin. Once Color Range has been used to make a selection, the selection may be saved, creating a grayscale alpha channel. The selection or alpha channel may then be re-loaded, inverted, used as a mask, or otherwise modified to help you define and differentiate image areas for precise, targeted correction.

Reducing Background Noise

Film grain and its analog, CCD background "mottling", are sources of noise that appear in virtually every astrophotograph. The dark background of most images serves to exaggerate its appearance. We saw in **Chapter 5** how this random source of noise may be mitigated by Stacking images. Even after Stacking, however, residual background noise will remain. And sometimes it is difficult or impossible to obtain multiple images to stack. Limited time windows, dynamic subjects such as comets or meteors and other factors may limit the number of images available. It is useful, therefore, to have some additional techniques at our disposal for reducing background noise. I shall use the term "grain" hereafter to refer to both film grain and

CCD background noise.

What we want to do is smooth the background sky without altering the appearance of the stars, nebulae, galaxies and other image subjects. We will explore Photoshop techniques to accomplish this, but it is also worth mentioning at this point some of the many grain reduction software packages available that are specialized for this task.

Very popular among astrophotographers is SGB-NR ("Selective Gaussian Blur Noise Reduction"), by Pleiades Astrophoto (see Appendix). Previously available as a stand-alone program, an updated version of the SGBNR algorithm is now included in the freeware program PixInsight LE.

Many other grain reduction programs and Photoshop plug-ins are commercially available. Some of the more popular include Visual Infinity's Grain Surgery (a Photoshop plug-in, see Appendix); Neat Image (http://www.neatimage.com/), available as both a stand-alone program and a Photoshop plug-in; and Picture Code's Noise Ninja (see Appendix), also available as both a stand-alone program and Photoshop plug-in. I encourage you to experiment with any of these to the extent that your time and budget allow. They can be amazingly effective, and are excellent at reducing background noise/digital camera noise in regular "daylight" images too.

Photoshop Grain Reduction Technique

Once again, we will put your Layer Masking skills to the test! In this procedure, we will use the original image (here again, let the image do the work for you whenever possible) to create separate masks for both the image subjects (stars and meteors, in this case) and the background sky (where the grain/noise is!). Utilizing these masks, we will apply blurring to the background sky only, in order to smooth out the grain, and then restore subject brightness by masking out the background sky and applying a Curve only to the image subjects.

1. From the tutorial disc, open the file "Grain Reduction Example.tif" (*File|Open*). This is a Leonid Meteor Radiant composite image by the author.

2. Zoom into the image with the Zoom Tool (keyboard shortcut "Z") to around 100% ("Actual Pixels"). Notice all of the grain, speckles and other artifacts that reside in the background, even though this is a "blue sky", rather than a "black sky", image.

3. Make the Layers Palette visible (*Window\Layers*), and create a copy of the Background Layer by click-holding and dragging it to the "Create a new layer" icon at the bottom-right of the Layers Palette and then releasing the mouse.

4. With the Background copy Layer active, select *Image\Adjustments\Desaturate*. This command removes the color information from the image, leaving us with a grayscale version of our original image.

5. Now, select the entire Background copy Layer with *Select\All* (keyboard shortcut "Ctrl+A"). Copy this selection to the Clipboard with *Edit\Copy* (shortcut "Ctrl+C").

6. Discard the Background copy Layer by click-holding and dragging it over the trash can icon at the bottom right of the Layers Palette, then release the mouse. We no longer need it, as we have copied our black and white version of the image to the Clipboard. Remove the remaining selection border ("marching ants") with *Select\Deselect* (shortcut "Ctrl+D").

7. Make two new copies of the Background Layer. Double-click on the layer names and name the first layer above the Background Layer "Stars" and the topmost layer "Sky."

8. Add a Layer Mask to both the Stars and Sky Layers by making each one active, in turn, and clicking on the "Add layer mask" icon (a small circle inside a shaded square at the bottom left of the Layers Palette). The Layer Masks are filled with white initially, so they "reveal all" image pixels at this point. Your Layers Palette should now look like **Figure 7.10**.

9. Alt-click on the Stars Layer Mask Icon (the small window to the right of the layer icon) to load the Layer Mask into the main image window. Select *Edit\Paste* (shortcut "Ctrl+V") to paste the grayscale version of the image from the Clipboard into the Layer Mask. Clear the selection border with Ctrl+D. We have used the black and white version of the original image to create a layer mask that "reveals" only the image subject elements and "hides" the background sky. Remember, when working with masks, "white reveals and black conceals".

10. Next, click once on the Sky Layer to make it active. Alt-click on the Sky Layer Mask Icon to load

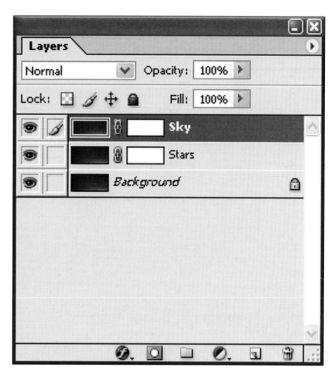

Fig. 7.10 Layer Masks have been added to the Stars and Sky Layers. The Masks are initially filled with white, which "reveals all" pixels into the Layer Stack.

it into the main image window. Once again paste the grayscale image into the mask with Ctrl+V. Invert the Layer Mask tonalities with *Image\Adjustments\Invert* (shortcut "Ctrl+I"). Clear the selection border with Ctrl+D. We have now reversed the black and white version of the image and created a mask that "hides" the image subjects and "reveals" the background sky.

11. While still in the Sky Layer Mask, select *Image\Adjustments\Levels*. Move the shadow and highlight sliders into the histogram to increase the contrast of the mask (see **Figure 7.11**). The Input Levels should be adjusted to approximately (68, 1.00, 221). Click OK to apply the Levels Adjustment. By increasing the contrast of the Layer Mask, we will get a cleaner separation between the sky background and the stars when we smooth the background grain.

It is often advisable to enhance the contrast of a mask derived from the underlying image. This strengthens the mask's ability to differentiate and separate image areas.

12. With the Sky Layer still active, make the Channels Palette visible. Notice that there is a new Alpha Channel called "Sky Mask". When the Stars

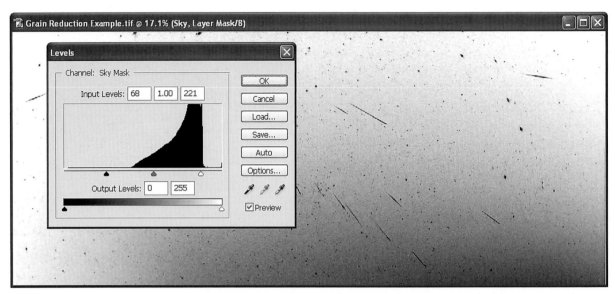

Fig. 7.11 A Levels Adjustment is applied to the Sky Layer Mask to compress the tonalities and increase contrast. This enhances the ability of the mask to separate sky and subject areas.

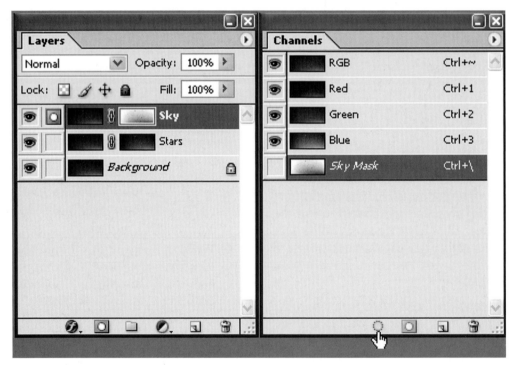

Fig. 7.12 Saved Selections and Layer Masks appear as "Alpha Channels" in the Channels Palette. Alpha Channels are grayscale bitmaps that contain "non-image" information; the RGB Channels contain the image information. Alpha Channels may be edited with Photoshop filters, commands and painting tools and may also be loaded as selections. The cursor is located over the "Load channel as selection" icon in the Channels Palette. Selections are merely "activated" Alpha Channels/Masks; Alpha Channels are "passive" or "frozen" selections.

Layer is activated, the Channels palette shows another Alpha Channel called "Stars Mask". An Alpha Channel is created whenever a selection is saved or a Layer Mask is created. Alpha Channels may be loaded as selections by clicking on the "Load channel as selection" icon (small dotted circle) at the bottom-left of the Channels Palette (**Figure 7.12**).

13. In the Layers Palette, Unlink the Sky Layer Mask from the image information in the Sky layer by

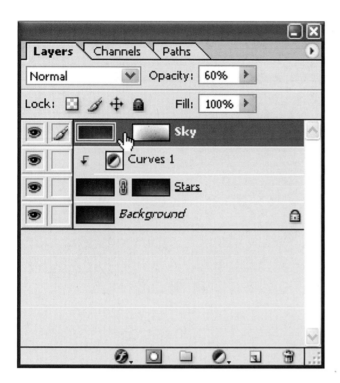

Fig. 7.13 A Layer Mask is unlinked from the image information in that Layer by clicking on the "chain-link" icon located between the Layer image icon and the Layer Mask icon. Here the Sky Layer Mask is unlinked, but the Stars Layer Mask remains linked. When unlinked, changes applied to that layer's image pixels will not affect the Layer Mask.

clicking on the little "chain-link" icon (it will disappear) located between the image icon and the Layer Mask icon. Do the same thing for the Stars Layer (**Figure 7.13**). This will allow us to alter the image information in each of these layers without affecting the layer masks.

14. Click once in the Stars Layer to make it active. Create a Curves Adjustment Layer with *Layer|New Adjustment Layer|Curves*. In the New Layer dialog box that appears, check the "Use Previous Layer to Create Clipping Mask" box ("Group with Previous Layer" in earlier versions of Photoshop), leave the other settings at their defaults and click OK. A Curves dialog box opens and a "Curves 1" Adjustment Layer appears above the Stars Layer. Note the little down arrow symbol in the Curves 1 Layer. We have created a Clipping Mask, and the Curves 1 Layer is now "attached" to the Stars layer below it. Curves adjustments will be directed only to the Stars layer. We will adjust this Curve later, but for now, click OK in the Curves dialog box to close it without

making any adjustments. Discard the Curves 1 Layer Mask (click-hold, drag it to the trash can then release the mouse) since it will not be needed.

15. Make the Sky Layer active, and make certain that you are working on the image and not the Layer Mask. Select *Filter|Blur|Gaussian Blur*, set the Radius to 150 pixels (yes, that's one hundred fifty, not fifteen) and click OK. The idea is to apply a very strong blur to the sky background. We will adjust the amount of blurring in the next step. Notice that the sky background gets very soft, but the meteors and stars remain relatively untouched, thanks to the Layer Mask.

16. Now, Zoom well into the image (to around 100%) and reduce the Opacity of the Sky Layer until you are satisfied with the result. I find that a setting of between 65% and 75% works best. Try not to smooth the background too much and make the image look unnatural. A little bit of unevenness and grain is a good thing!

Note that if we had not unlinked the Sky Layer Mask in Step #13, the Gaussian Blur would have affected both the image information on that layer and the Layer Mask. We would have defeated the purpose of our high contrast Layer Mask and both the Stars and the Background would have been softened.

17. Make the Curves 1 Layer active and open the Curves dialog box (double-click on the layer icon). In the RGB Channel, create an adjustment point with an Input/Output value of (211, 240). Even though our Sky Layer Mask was very effective, there is still a bit of softening in the fainter background stars, reducing their brightness. We have now restored most of that lost brightness.

18. Finally, fine-tune the Stars Layer Mask by painting directly in the Mask. Step #17 not only brightened the stars, it also made the sky background a bit too bright in the center/bottom-right of the image. Zoom out to fit the entire image on the screen, start with a large (600 pixel), soft-edged Brush, set the Brush Flow to 5% and enable the Airbrush capability. Paint with black in the Stars Layer Mask to reduce the background sky brightness in the lower-right part of the image. Vary your brush size, if necessary, by using the left and right keyboard bracket keys. Try to restore this area to its original brightness level. It will help to have an on-screen duplicate of the image (*Image|Duplicate*). In the

Fig. 7.14 Background smoothing has been applied to the top image. The bottom image is the original (the visibility of all layers except the Background Layer has been turned off). It is a good practice to use on-screen duplicates of an image (*Image | Duplicate*) to compare your adjustments to the original while you work.

duplicate image, turn off the visibility of all layers except the Background Layer, and arrange the two image windows so that you may compare your adjustments to the original image while you work (**Figure 7.14**).

Why didn't we use Levels to increase the contrast of the Stars layer mask, like we did with the Sky Layer Mask? When applying Curves to the image subject, it is generally best to leave the masked areas a little "looser". This avoids harshness and unnatural-looking artifacts. Some grain may be introduced back into the image, but what you are trying to achieve is a natural-looking balance. As with most image-processing techniques, this one involves making tradeoffs.

Try experimenting with different settings. Change Opacity; try different Curves settings; use other image adjustment tools on both masks, and observe the effects. Develop your own working procedure to achieve the results that suit you best.

A Quick Grain Reduction Method

The following is a "quick and dirty" method for selecting the highlights in an image, and therefore, by extension, selecting the sky background in an astrophotograph.

Many times, a selection (or mask) may be considered as "two selections in one". Selecting all of the stars, nebulae and galaxies in an image means that the sky background is also selected. All you have to do is invert the subject selection (*Select|Inverse*) or the subject mask (*Image|Adjustments|Invert*). In order to isolate an area or tonal range within an image, it is often easier to select the areas that lie outside of the desired area or tones, and then simply invert the selection. You may save file space by saving only one such selection or mask. If, for example, you have obtained a good, clean sky background selection, just save this one selection or mask to use for both sky and stars/subject selections.

Let's work through a brief example.

1. From the tutorial disc, once again open the file "Grain Reduction Example.tif" (*File|Open*).

2. Duplicate the Background Layer.

3. With the Background copy Layer active, Press "Ctrl + Alt + ~ (the "tilde" key). Selection borders appear around the image highlights (stars and meteors, in this case). Wow! Pretty quick, huh?

4. Zoom well into the image to get a good look at a starfield containing some of the fainter stars. The initial selection missed many of these. Expand the selection with *Select|Similar*. The final result is far from perfect, but remember, it is quick and easy! There are always tradeoffs in image processing.

5. At this point, you may wish to feather the selection a little. Feathering expands the selection borders by a specified number of pixels, and often improves the result by smoothing out a selection. Not all selections are improved by feathering however, so do not just apply feathering as a matter of course. Check your results carefully. Choose *Select|Feather*, enter a Feather Radius of 1 pixel and click OK.

6. Now invert the selection with *Select|Inverse* (keyboard shortcut Shift+Ctrl+I). We now have a selection that, for the most part, encompasses only the sky background areas.

7. Select *Filter|Noise|Median*, set a Radius of 50 pixels and click OK. Now go get yourself a cup of coffee or something as this filter processing will take awhile.

8. Immediately select *Edit|Fade Median*. Set the Blending Mode to "Lighten", leave the Opacity at 100% and click OK. By changing the Blending Mode, we have restored the fainter stars that were smoothed out by the application of the Median Filter.

9. Clear the selection borders with *Select|Deselect* or Ctrl+D.

10. Now you may wish to fine-tune the amount of the background smoothing by adjusting the Opacity of the Background copy Layer. In this case, I prefer to leave it at 100%. We have achieved a modest level of background smoothing without creating any artifacts or losing the fainter stars.

You may want to experiment by using different Radius settings and different *Edit|Fade* Blending Modes with the Median filter to see if you can improve the result. I also encourage you to try using the Dust & Scratches Filter (*Filter|Noise|Dust & Scratches*) or the Minimum Filter (*Filter|Other|Minimum*) in lieu of the Median Filter.

Why didn't we use the Gaussian Blur filter here, as we did in our previous example? In this case, Gaussian Blur tends to create "halo" artifacts around the brighter objects. We could use Gaussian Blur and then employ the *Edit|Fade* command with a Blending Mode of "Dissolve" or "Lighten" to minimize these artifacts, but Median produces better results in this case. Gaussian Blur worked when we extracted a mask from the image, since the mask contained various grayscale tones that operated to smooth out the application of the filter. A selection border is more "black and white", literally. If you were to convert the selection made in Step #6 above into a mask, you would see a high-contrast mask with a narrow range of transitional tones. Selections generally have sharper boundaries than masks (**Figure 7.15**).

One problem in using this quick and dirty method is that fainter nebulae and the outer areas of galaxies may not be adequately selected. In these cases, you may wish to convert your selection into a temporary mask using Quick Mask Mode, and paint to adjust the selection; or use the full layer masking method to separate image elements as described in our previous example.

Reducing Green Background Noise

Now we will examine a more comprehensive method to reduce green in sky backgrounds. This technique utilizes "Channel Mixing" to combine the information

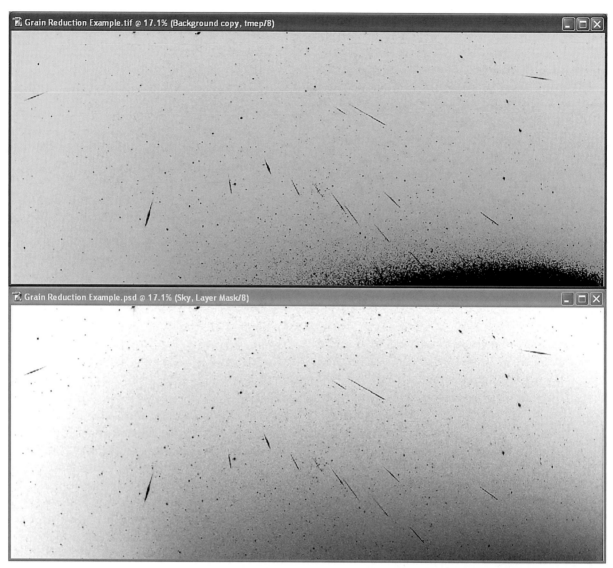

Fig. 7.15 Using selection tools generally produces sharper selection boundaries than image-derived masks. The top mask represents the Ctrl + Alt+ ~ selection made in the Quick Grain Reduction example. The bottom mask is the Sky mask derived from the image itself in the Photoshop Grain Reduction Technique example. Note the higher contrast in the selection, compared to the range of gray tones in the image-derived mask.

contained within the Red and Blue Channels of an image. The result is then used as a mask to reduce or eliminate green from the sky background. This is a variation on the green channel substitution technique used in planetary image processing, as described in **Chapter 9**.

The principle behind this method assumes that the majority of astrophoto subjects do not contain the color green in the sky background or shadow tones. Only noise-related phenomena, such as skyglow and light pollution, contribute significantly to green background color. Therefore, the desired image elements (signal) should be improved by reducing or replacing the green

channel (noise) in the sky background. The mask created by combining the Red and Blue Channels is used to apply adjustments only to the background sky (shadow tones) and "hold" the midtones and highlight areas in the image. This technique was first described, to my knowledge, by Juan Conejero and Vicent Peris of Pleiades Astrophoto (makers of SGBNR). They dub the technique SCNR ("Subtractive Chromatic Noise Reduction").

1. From the tutorial disc, open the file "Green Background Example.tif" (*File|Open*). This is an unprocessed film image of the North America Nebula taken by the author. It contains an extreme

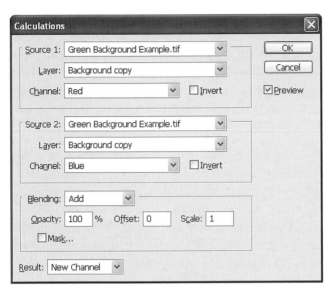

Fig. 7.16 The Calculations Command (*Image|Calculations*) is used to "Channel Mix" the Red and Blue Channels. The result will be used as a mask to reduce the overall green image background while retaining the original color of the image subjects.

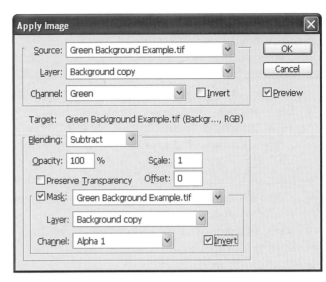

Fig. 7.17 The Apply Image Command (*Image|Apply Image*) is used to subtract the Green Channel from the image using an inverted mask to target the background and not the image subjects. The original mask is comprised of the combined luminance values of the Red and Blue Channels. The result — green is reduced in the background without creating an overall magenta cast in the image.

amount of green background noise due to the film's reciprocity characteristics.

2. With the Layers Palette visible (*Window|Layers*), Duplicate the Background Layer by click-holding and dragging the Background Layer to the "Create a new layer" icon at the bottom of the Layers Palette, then releasing the mouse. This isolates the Background Layer (the original image pixels) so that if we do not like our results, we can delete or modify the Background copy Layer and begin again.

3. Select *Image|Calculations*. A dialog box appears as shown in **Figure 7.16**. Since we only have one image file open, "Source 1" and "Source 2" are both the same. Set the Source 1 Channel to "Red" and the Source 2 Channel to "Blue" (this could be reversed, it does not matter, as long as one is red and the other blue). Set both the Source 1 Layer and the Source 2 Layer to "Background copy". Set the Blending mode to "Add" with an Offset of 0 and Scale of 1. The Result selection box should be set to "New Channel". Click OK.

4. Now take a look at the Channels Palette (*Window|Channels*). A new Alpha Channel has been created called "Alpha 1". It represents the addition of the Red and Blue pixel values in the image. In the next steps, we will invert this and use it as a

mask to adjust only the background luminance values.

5. Return to the Layers Palette and click once on the Background copy Layer. This should restore the color image to the main image window.

6. Select *Image|Apply Image*. Once again, there is only one "Source", since there is only one image file open. Set the Source Layer to "Background copy" and the Source Channel to "Green". Set the Blending Mode to "Subtract", leave the Opacity at 100%, the Scale at 1 and the Offset at 0. Check the "Mask" selection box. This expands the selection possibilities. In the Mask area, set the Layer to "Background copy" and choose "Alpha 1" as the Channel. Finally, check the box entitled "Invert". Make sure that you invert the mask (the "Invert" box near the bottom of the dialog box) and not the image Channel (near the top). The settings are shown in **Figure 7.17**.

7. Click OK to accept these settings and implement the Apply Image Command.

The severe green background is immediately reduced. We have subtracted the luminance values in the Green Channel from the image, using an inverted version of our Red + Blue mask ("Alpha 1"). This mask applies the effect primarily to the background areas (where the

R. Scott Ireland

green is), while retaining and restoring correct colors in the image subjects (stars and nebula).

8. Immediately select *Edit\Fade Apply Image*. Now you may vary the Blending Mode and Opacity to suit the particular requirements of your image. In this case, leave the Opacity at 100%, choose "Soft Light" as the Mode and click OK. I prefer the Soft Light Blending Mode for this image, but "Normal" also works well. Note too that you may further adjust the effect of the Apply Image Command by varying the Layer Opacity of the Background copy Layer. This is another reason to work with a copy of the Background Layer. It allows you to adjust your destructive edits.

9. Now make final adjustments to the image with Levels, Curves and Hue/Saturation. You may wish to place some Color Sampler points in the sky background and one within a star and use these to set your black and white points first, then follow-up with Curves and Hue/Saturation. I was able to achieve a good color balance, after setting the black and white points, by applying a slight additional correction to the Green Channel (Curve Input/Output point (57, 53)). I then increased the nebula brightness and contrast in the Curves RGB Channel and added a +20 increase in overall Saturation.

Do you see the similarity in procedure between this technique and the Photoshop Grain Reduction technique? In both cases, we used information from the image itself to create masks that allowed us to work primarily on the sky background. In this case, our purpose was to reduce green, so we constructed a mask from the red and blue color channels, but the concept is the same. As you work more and more with various Photoshop techniques, you will find many such recurrent "themes" and relationships, and will develop the skill and facility necessary to expand upon them in ways of your own.

Chapter 8
Star Techniques

Each of us enjoys capturing many different types and forms of celestial objects as subject matter for our astrophotographs. However, except for planetary images, all of our images have a very important co-subject, or co-star (if you'll allow me the pun!) that demands our attention — Stars. Stars are the ubiquitous co-subjects of our photographs whether we like it or not. They are ever-present. And, they are equal in importance to the main subject. No matter how wonderfully you have rendered a galaxy or nebula, if the stars do not look "right" the image will fail. You've heard the oft-quoted aphorism "There are only three things certain in life — birth, death and taxes". Well, for astrophotographers, it is "birth, death, taxes and stars . . . and taxes may be optional". You might not have recorded the nebula or galaxy you were after, but one thing's for sure, your image will contain stars.

In this Chapter, we will examine some Photoshop methods for altering and improving the appearance of stars. But, "improving" is a subjective term. What looks great to one person may not to another. Some of the following techniques will help correct obvious problems. But others will allow you to invoke your artistic side. You may create and soften colored star "halos", or you may choose to eliminate them. You may enlarge stars, to draw more attention to them, or you may reduce their apparent size, to direct emphasis to the main image subject. The choice is yours, and the final result will depend only on your personal artistic conception.

Fixing Elongated Stars ("Star Shaping")

Many astrophotos contain slightly elongated stars (usually at the edges of the field), due to small tracking errors or optical aberrations. As a general rule, we find round stars to be more aesthetically pleasing than oval ones. There are, of course, exceptions. With meteors and comets, our main subjects move independently among the background stars and we have come to "accept" star trails in these types of images. Night landscapes with long, colored star trails in the background

can also be quite beautiful. But in the majority of cases, elongated stars detract from an otherwise pleasing image.

In the following tutorials, we will employ Photoshop techniques to "reshape" slightly elongated stars. I say "slightly", since an image containing severe tracking errors may simply not be repairable. There is no panacea in these cases, other than to re-shoot the subject. But many images are only mildly flawed, with slightly elongated stars throughout or elongated stars in the corners only. In these cases, we may employ the following techniques to good effect.

Fixing Elongated Stars — The Basics

1. From the tutorial disc, open the file "Elongated Stars1.tif" (*File|Open*). This is a portion of a CCD image of Omega Centauri taken by Tim Khan. Here we see the image before all processing steps have been completed (including re-shaping the elongated stars).

2. Select the Zoom Tool from the Toolbox and Zoom into the image (to around 300%). We see that the stars are oval in shape, and they are all elongated in the same general direction (**Figure 8.1**).

3. Open the Image Size dialog box with *Image|Image Size*. Make sure that the "Resample Image", "Constrain Proportions" and "Scale Styles" (if available) checkboxes at the bottom of the dialog box are checked. In the drop-down box next to "Resample Image", select "Bicubic" as the interpolation method. In the "Document Size" area of the dialog, be sure that the Resolution is 300 pixels/inch and that both the Width and Height dimensions are displayed in "inches". Change the Width of the image from 1.517 inches to 6 inches. The dialog box should now look like **Figure 8.2**.

Notice what happens when you change the dimension. The other dimension and the pixel count automatically change. Since "Constrain Proportions" was checked, Photoshop maintains exactly the same ratio of

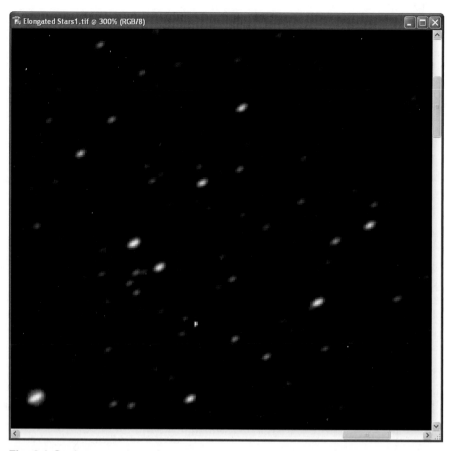

Fig. 8.1 Oval stars are a common problem in many astrophotographs. The problem may be corrected, to some extent, by using Photoshop's Layers and Move Tool to re-register the stars in a copy of the image laid over the original.

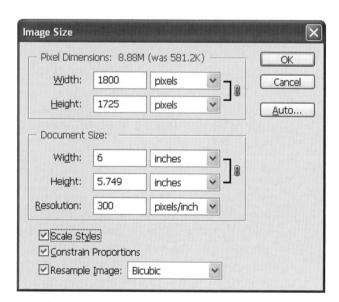

Fig. 8.2 *Image\Image Size* is used to "resample" the image upward by a factor of 3x or 4x, significantly increasing the pixel dimensions. Since Photoshop's Move Tool only permits one-pixel movements, resampling allows us to effectively achieve more precise, sub-pixel movement of the image.

Width to Height as in the original image. By entering one dimension at 4x, the other dimension will automatically be entered at 4 times the original amount. Multiplying one of the Pixel Dimensions by 4 does the same thing. It does not matter whether you change the Pixel Dimensions or the Document Size, you will get the same result.

So why did we do this? In order achieve a more precise, *sub-pixel* image movement. By physically enlarging the image dimensions 400%, each 1-pixel movement in the enlarged image will represent a ¼ pixel ("sub-pixel") movement of the original image when we later reduce it back to its original size.

Upward resampling, or "upsampling" physically enlarges the image by adding pixels in each dimension. Photoshop fills in the missing pixels using its interpolation algorithm (here we used "Bicubic"). Basically, Photoshop makes its "best guess" as to what these in-between pixels should look like. Yes, this is cheating. We are not really creating any new image information. But this shortcut will allow us to make smaller image movements and thereby give us finer adjustment capabilities.

As always, this procedure is a tradeoff. Resampling upward and then downward again increases the potential for artifacts in the image. The tradeoff is round vs. oval stars. Pick your poison.

4. Click OK to accept the settings and close the *Image/Image Size* dialog box.

> The image gets much bigger. Now you may notice color fringing around the stars; the color channels are not precisely aligned. But that is a subject we will cover in **Chapter 9** on LRGB and Channel Mixing. For now, we just want to try our hand at changing the oval stars into circular ones.

5. Make a duplicate of the Background Layer (from the Layers Palette, click-hold and drag the Background Layer to the "Create a new layer" icon at the bottom-right of the Layers Palette (it looks like two, overlapping squares), then release the mouse). A "Background copy" layer appears at the top of the Layer Stack.

6. Make sure that the Background copy Layer is the active layer (active layers are highlighted in blue in the Layers Palette) by clicking on it once. In the drop-down selection box at the top-left of the Layers Palette, change the Layer Blending Mode from "Normal" to "Darken" (**Figure 8.3**).

As we have seen in earlier Chapters, Layer Blending Modes determine how a layer's pixels will blend with the underlying pixels in the Layer Stack. "Darken" compares the pixels in the top layer to the pixels below and chooses the darkest value for the final image.

7. From the Toolbox (*Window/Tools*), select the Move Tool (keyboard shortcut "V"). With the Background copy Layer still active, click once in the main image window to activate the Move Tool. Now use the keyboard arrow keys to re-position the layer until the stars appear more circular. Try moving 6 pixels to the left and 3 pixels down as a starting point.

By using the arrow keys with the Move Tool, Photoshop moves a selection or a layer one pixel at a time. This is far more precise than click-holding in the image window and moving the image "by hand" with the mouse.

We end up re-shaping the stars by moving the

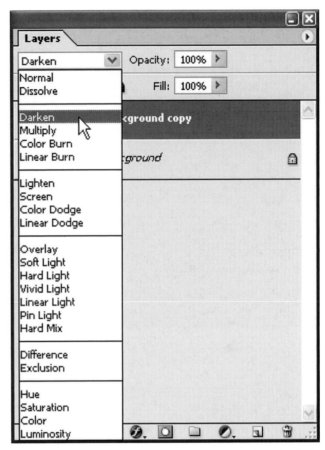

Fig. 8.3 Layer Blending Modes determine how a layer's pixels will be blended into the underlying Layer Stack. "Darken" is used here so that the dark sky background will be selected as the top layer is moved out of registration. The stars are re-shaped by gradually covering them with sky background, one pixel at a time.

dark sky background "over" a portion of each star. This occurs because the Darken Layer Blending Mode compares each layer and chooses the darkest pixel.

8. Move around the image window and Zoom in and out to examine how the stars appear. You will not get all of them perfectly round. The idea is to find the best compromise that improves the overall appearance without eliminating the fainter stars. Click the visibility of the Background copy Layer on and off (click on the little "eyeball" icon at the left side of the layer in the Layers Palette) to see the before and after effect.

9. Now we will restore some of the brightness that we lost by shifting the star positions. With the Background copy Layer still active, create a Curves Adjustment Layer at the top of the Layer Stack by clicking on the "Create new fill or adjust-

Fig. 8.4 The image before (left) and after (right) applying Star-Shaping. This technique permits only subtle changes, but they can significantly improve the overall appearance of the image.

ment layer" icon (a little half black/half white circle) at the bottom of the Layers Palette and choosing "Curves". In the RGB Channel, click once anywhere on the Curve to place a control point, then enter the Input/Output values (160, 208). Click OK to accept this setting and close the Curves dialog box. The brightness of the stars has been restored. Hold down the Alt key and click repeatedly on the Background Layer visibility icon (the little "eyeball") to see the before and after effect of all your adjustments. By holding down the Alt key, you turn on and off the visibility of all of the other layers.

10. The image now looks pretty good (**Figure 8.4**). We have managed to minimize the unpleasant oval appearance of the stars and still retain their original brightness. If you are satisfied with your results, you may want to Flatten the image (to reduce file size) with *Layer|Flatten Image*. Flatten Image is also accessible from the Layers Palette menu (click on the small, right-facing arrow at the top-right of the Layers Palette). Flattening an image "collapses" the Layer Stack and applies all of the changes therein. This saves a lot of file space, since layers, masks and alpha channels all take up space. However, you may also save the file and retain the individual layers, masks and alpha channels by saving the file in Photoshop *.psd format,

in case you want to go back and do more editing later. The tradeoff is larger file size.

11. Now let's resize the image back to its original pixel dimensions. Select *Image|Image Size*, again make sure that "Resample Image" and "Constrain Proportions" are checked and "Bicubic" is used, change the Width from 6 inches back to 1.517 inches and click OK.

As a practical matter, you do not want to over-do these star-shaping movements, since the important elements in your image may begin to soften and degrade. A few pixels of movement are all you will get, but this is frequently sufficient to greatly improve the look of the image.

Fixing Elongated Stars with Selective Shaping

In our previous example, the image contained only stars, and they were all elongated in the same direction. But what do we do when we have another subject in the image, such as a nebula or galaxy? How do we re-shape the stars without blurring the main subject? And what do we do when different areas of the image have stars elongated in different directions? Or when some stars are perfectly round and others are elongated?

Well, we do the same thing that we did in our first example! But, we do it *selectively*. Masks or selections

Fig. 8.5 A freehand selection border is drawn around the central image area using the Lasso Tool. By inverting this selection, only the left and right edges will be affected by star shaping (or any other edit). Selection borders can be used in this manner to restrict edits to specific areas.

are used to isolate portions of the image, and star-shaping is selectively applied, as needed, to these individual areas. Let's work through a few examples.

Isolating an Image Area for Editing

1. From the tutorial disc, open the file "Elongated Stars2.tif" (*File|Open*). This is another CCD image by Tim Khan, a luminance frame of M101.

2. Using the same procedure in Steps #2 and #3 of the first tutorial, resample the image upward by 400% using *Image|Image Size*. The image Width should be increased from 7.28 inches to 28 inches.

3. Duplicate the Background Layer and set the Layer Blending Mode to "Darken", following Steps #5 and #6 in the first tutorial.

4. From the Toolbox, select the Lasso Tool (keyboard shortcut "L"). The Lasso Tool allows you to draw freehand selection borders. Draw a wide border around the galaxy, similar to that shown in **Figure 8.5**, so that only the left and right outside edges of the image lie outside the border. Don't worry about being precise. Close enough will do in this case. The stars in and around the galaxy look good — we merely want to isolate this area and apply star shaping to the outside edges only.

5. Now choose *Select|Inverse*. The selection border is inverted — now the left and right edges are selected. Feather the selection (*Select|Feather*) by 6 pixels.

6. Make sure that the Background copy Layer is active (highlighted in blue) and select the Move Tool from the Toolbox (shortcut "V"). Click once in the image window and use the keyboard arrow keys to star-shape the edge areas.

You will not be able to correct all of the stars. They are elongated in slightly different directions as you move throughout the selected areas. Just do the best you can. The point is that *only* the stars in the selected areas are shaped. The galaxy and stars in the central region are not affected.

Remember this technique and use it to temporarily isolate and protect image areas when making edits of all sorts.

7. When you are satisfied with your star-shaping efforts, add a Curves Adjustment Layer to the top of the Layer Stack (see Step #9 in the previous tutorial). Click OK to close the Curves dialog box without making any adjustments. Since a selection is active, a mask is automatically created for the adjustment layer that applies the Curve only to

the star-shaped areas.

8. Now create a Clipping Mask by holding down the Alt key and moving the cursor in between the Background copy Layer and the Curves 1 Layer in the Layers Palette until a half black/half clear circle appears, then click once. The Curves 1 Layer is indented and a down-arrow appears. Curves adjustments will now apply only to the Background copy layer.

9. Re-open the Curves dialog box and apply an appropriate adjustment to the RGB Channel to restore the brightness of the shaped stars.

10. Finally, restore the original pixel dimensions using *Image|Image Size*.

This technique may be used to isolate various sections of an image. In this example, we made a simple selection and applied star-shaping equally to both the left and right sides. But we could have done a better job by creating separate selections and star-shaping each side individually. In our next example, we will use layer masks to isolate and adjust several different areas within an image.

Selective Star Shaping Using Layer Masks

1. From the tutorial disc, open the file "Baby Nebula.tif" (*File|Open*). This is a film image by Herm Perez.

2. From the Toolbox, select the Zoom Tool and enlarge the image to around 200%. Move throughout the image and examine the different areas carefully. The star elongations exhibit a radial pattern, with the greatest elongations at the outside edges. The stars all "point" toward the center of the image, but this makes our task more difficult, since the stars are elongated in different directions. Global corrections or simple selections will not work. What we need to do is isolate at least four different regions (the four corner areas) and apply star-shaping corrections to each of these areas independently. How do we accomplish this? There are a few ways, but the easiest is to use layer masks.

3. Resample the image upward (using Bicubic interpolation) to around 4x with *Image|Image Size*. Change the Width from 6 inches to 24 inches and click OK. The image pixel dimensions should now be 7200 x 4952 pixels. An easy shortcut to check the pixel dimensions is to hold down the Alt key and click in the "Doc" area at the bottom-left of the main Photoshop window. A small box pops up indicating the pixel dimensions, number of channels, color model and resolution.

4. Let's begin work on the upper-right corner of the image. Duplicate the Background Layer and rename the new Layer to "Upper Right" (double-click on the Layer name to change it). Change the Upper Right Layer Blending Mode from Normal to "Darken". Make sure the Upper Right Layer is active, select the Move Tool (shortcut "V") and click once in the image window. Now use the arrow keys to move the layer and re-shape the stars in the upper right corner. 7 pixels to the left and 4 pixels down should do the job. Next, create a Layer Mask that hides the entire layer with *Layer|Add Layer Mask|Hide All*. Since we only want to apply our correction to the upper-right, it will be easier to "paint in" the correction than it will be to "paint out" the remainder of the image. Choose the Brush Tool (shortcut "B"), and select a soft-edged Brush of around 300 pixels diameter. Leave the Brush Opacity and Flow at 100%. In the Toolbox, set the Foreground Color to White. Now, make sure that the Upper Right Layer Mask is active (click once in the layer mask window), and paint the mask with white to "reveal" your star-shaping corrections. When finished, your mask should look something like **Figure 8.6**

5. Once again, make a duplicate of the Background Layer. Move this new Layer to the top of the Layer Stack, by click-holding and dragging it to the top in the Layers Palette, then release the mouse. Change the Layer name to "Bottom Right" and set the Layer Blending Mode to "Darken". Make sure that the Bottom Right Layer is active, select the Move Tool and re-shape the stars in the bottom-right image area. This will require a move of about 4 pixels to the left and 1 pixel up. Create a Layer Mask with *Layer|Add Layer Mask|Hide All*, and paint the Mask with white to apply shaping only to the bottom-right corner.

But wait a minute! Aren't we undoing the corrections we made in the Upper Right Layer by duplicating the Background Layer and putting it at the top of the Layer Stack (remember, layers work from the top down)? No, because we are using a Layer Mask to hide the entire layer, *except for*, the bottom-right area. Only that area will show through into the final image, just as only the upper-right area will show through from the

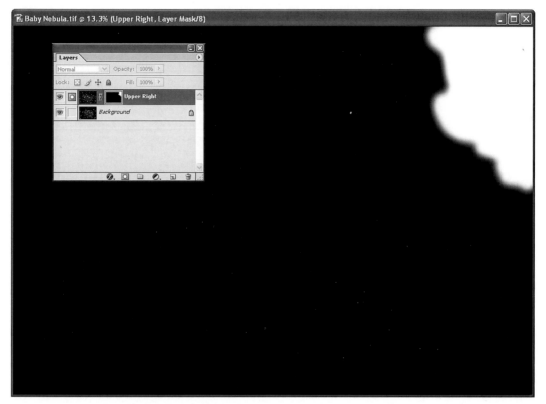

Fig. 8.6 The Layer Mask used to apply star-shaping only to the upper-right region of the image. The Layer Mask icon in the Layers Palette shows a miniature version of the actual mask. Mask areas painted in white will cause any corrections made in that Layer to "reveal" or "show through" into the overall image. Areas painted with black will be hidden.

Upper Right Layer. By using Layer Masks, we are creating little "windows" for each layer, allowing only the parts that we want to show through.

If you make a mistake with your mask, simply paint it out with black and try again. Don't worry about the fact that the corrected areas are getting darker. We will fix this when we are finished re-shaping the stars.

6. Repeat Steps #4 and #5 to create an "Upper Left" Layer at the top of the Layer Stack, set the Blending Mode to "Darken" and use the Move Tool to shift the stars about 4 pixels to the right and 3 pixels down. But, in this area we see that the stars "change directions" quickly as you move down from the corner. It would be ideal if we could apply our star-shaping a little more to the corner stars and a little less to the stars farther down the left side. Well, we can!

7. Create a Layer Mask for the Upper Left Layer with *Layer|Add Layer Mask|Hide All*. Using the Brush Tool, paint the extreme upper-left area of the Mask with white to correct those stars. But now, in the Toolbox, click on the "Set background color" box to bring up the Color Picker, type in the RGB values 128, 128, 128 and click OK. The Background Color changes to a middle-toned neutral gray. Use the keyboard "X" key as a shortcut to quickly toggle the Foreground and Background colors. Toggle the Foreground Color to gray and paint the Layer Mask a little farther down the left side. Try to create a Mask approximately like the one shown in **Figure 8.7**.

In a layer mask, gray tones "partially reveal and partially conceal" the layer, governing how much of it shows through into the Layer Stack. *We capitalize on this by using gray tones in a mask to target opacity changes to specific locations within a layer.* We are no longer limited to one opacity setting per layer.

In this example, using a middle-gray in our mask results in 50% opacity for that area. Half of the overall star-shaping adjustment is applied there. If we used darker gray tones ("hide more"), less star-shaping would be applied, since we are "hiding" more of the adjustment we made. This is the same as lowering the layer opacity *in that specific* area to allow more of the

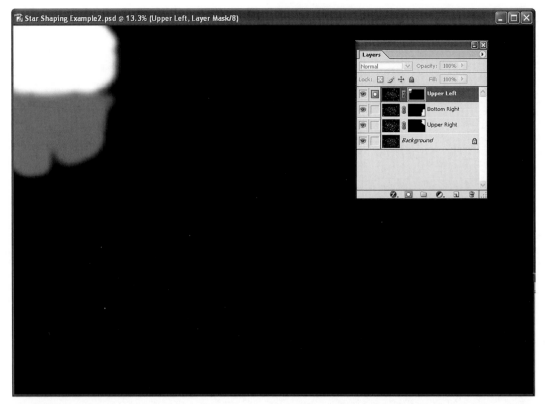

Fig. 8.7 A full star-shaping correction is applied to the uppermost part of the left corner. Less correction is applied to the stars below by painting the Layer Mask with gray instead of white. In a layer mask, gray tones "partially reveal and partially conceal" the layer, allowing for targeted opacity adjustments. Middle gray is equivalent to a using 50% layer opacity. Darker gray tones progressively hide more of the layer (equivalent to moving the layer opacity setting toward 0%). Lighter gray tones progressively reveal more (equivalent to moving the layer opacity setting toward 100%).

uncorrected stars to show through into the final image. Had we used lighter gray tones ("reveal more"), more re-shaping correction would be applied. This is the same as increasing the layer opacity in that area to show more of that layer and less of the other layers. White ("reveal all") is, of course, 100% opacity; all corrections made on that layer are applied. Black ("hide all") is 0% opacity; none of the layer is applied.

It is also possible to vary the opacity and flow of the Brush Tool while painting with black to achieve the same result. One of the reasons Photoshop is such a powerful image-editing tool is that it provides many different ways to accomplish things.

8. Repeat Step #4 to create a "Bottom Left" Layer, set the Blending Mode to "Darken" and use the Move Tool to shift the stars about 5 pixels to the right and 2 pixels up. Create a Layer Mask (*Layer\Add Layer Mask\Hide All*) and paint the mask with white in the bottom-left corner to shape only those stars. If you wish, paint with gray tones to apply a little less shaping to the stars as you move towards the right along the bottom.

Now we have accomplished our "selective star-shaping", but in the process, we have considerably darkened the shaped areas. We could use a Curves Adjustment Layer to fix this, as we have already seen. But instead, we will learn a new technique that is extremely useful and has many applications beyond this particular example. We will set up a "Dodge and Burn" Layer.

9. Create a new layer at the top of the Layer Stack with *Layer\New\Layer*. Be sure to use the menu commands and not the shortcut in the Layers Palette. In the New Layer dialog box, change the Layer Blending Mode to "Overlay". You will notice that a checkbox at the bottom of the dialog now becomes available, entitled "Fill with Overlay-neutral color (50% gray)". Activate this option by clicking on the checkbox, and then click OK to close the dialog box (**Figure 8.8**). Double-click on the Layer name and change it to "Dodge and Burn".

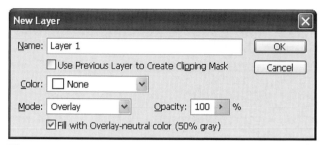

Fig. 8.8 A "Dodge and Burn" Layer is created using *Layer|New|Layer* to open this dialog box. "Overlay" is selected as the Layer Blending Mode and the checkbox "Fill with Overlay-neutral color (50% gray)" is selected. The Layer is filled with a middle-toned gray (RGB values 128, 128, 128). Initially, this layer has no effect on the underlying pixels. But by painting the layer with gray tones darker than middle-gray, overall image brightness is reduced. Painting with gray tones lighter than middle-gray increases image brightness.

As you will recall from earlier Chapters, using the "Multiply" layer blending mode darkens underlying pixels, while using the "Screen" mode lightens them. The "Overlay" mode combines both of these blending modes into one. Middle-gray tones have no effect on the underlying pixels, but gray tones darker than middle-gray will reduce the underlying image brightness, without affecting the colors. Conversely, gray tones lighter than middle-gray will brighten the image without affecting the color.

We may use these properties of the "Overlay" mode to our advantage by creating a Dodge and Burn layer, which allows us to apply subtle, targeted brightness changes to an image non-destructively. This is much better than using Photoshop's Dodge and Burn Tools. These Tools apply destructive edits, directly altering the pixels to which they are applied. But a Dodge and Burn layer can be modified and corrected indefinitely, providing a tool with far greater subtlety and control.

10. Make sure that the Dodge and Burn Layer is active and at the top of the Layer Stack. Zoom the image out so that the entire image is visible on the screen. From the Toolbox, select the Brush Tool (keyboard shortcut "B"). In the Tool Options bar at the top of the main Photoshop window, choose a soft-edged Brush and set the diameter to around 800 pixels. Leave the Brush Mode set to "Normal" and the Opacity at 100%. Set the Brush Flow to 5% and engage the Airbrush feature (click on the little airbrush icon). In the Toolbox, set the Foreground Color to white and the Background

color to black (click on the little white/black icon or use the keyboard shortcut "D"; toggle between black and white using the keyboard shortcut "X").

11. Now, paint the Dodge and Burn layer with white in the areas that were star-shaped to restore brightness. Hold down the left mouse key and make small, circular motions as you paint (just like dodging and burning in the good old chemical darkroom days!). You may find it helpful to create a duplicate image window on-screen (*Image|Duplicate*) and turn off all layers except the Background Layer. This way, you can compare your adjustments to the original image brightness.

12. If you over-adjust brightness, change the Foreground color to black or gray and "paint out" some of the increased brightness. You may find that using a slightly lower Brush Flow (2%) provides more control when painting with black. My final Dodge and Burn layer is shown in **Figure 8.9**. I also used it to apply some brightening to parts of the nebula.

13. By now, our image file is getting very large! Let's resample the file back down to its original size. Open *Image|Image Size*, make sure that "Resample Image" and "Constrain Proportions" are both checked and that Bicubic is the interpolation method. Change the Width from 24 inches back to 6 inches and click OK. You may want to flatten the image first. If you wish to retain the ability to go back and re-edit, then it is best to save the upsampled (4x) version of the image (in Photoshop *.psd format) with all of the layers intact. The tradeoff is that you will have to store a ***really*** large file.

If you now check the status of the image Histogram, you will be relieved to see that it is entirely intact, even though we were working with an 8-bit image. The shadows are clipped somewhat, but they were already clipped in the original.

It is worth remembering the Dodge and Burn Layer technique as a method to apply selective and precise brightening changes. It is often an effective substitute for Curves adjustments, and may result in less damage to the Histogram.

Star "Shrinking"

In many circumstances, it is advantageous to reduce, or "shrink", the sizes of stars in an astrophotograph. "Bloated" stars appear for various reasons. With CCD

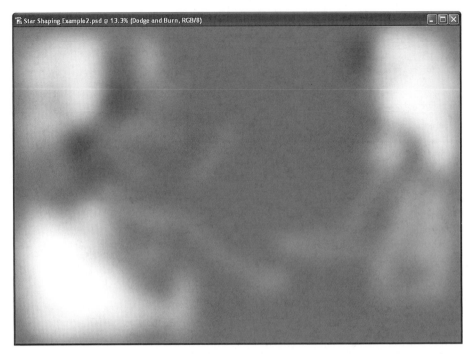

Fig. 8.9 My final Dodge and Burn Layer for "Baby Nebula.tif". This is a powerful technique that offers very subtle and precisely targeted brightness adjustments.

images, star sizes may differ between color channels. High-resolution luminance images, particularly those taken in hydrogen-alpha light, may exhibit smaller stars than the comparable RGB data, making LRGB combinations problematic. Some star fields are so populated and bright that they overwhelm a nebula or galaxy that also appears in them. Reducing star sizes can draw more attention to the main subject in these cases. Film response curves, CCD sensor response, filters, various types of optical systems, chromatic aberration and atmospheric conditions may all, at one time or another, conspire to create bloated stars or colored star halos (bloated stars in one color channel).

In the following examples, we will examine some Photoshop methods to reduce the size of stars. I use the term "Star Shrinking" to collectively describe these techniques.

Selective Star Shrinking Using Photoshop's Minimum Filter

In this exercise, we will employ Photoshop's Minimum Filter to "star-shrink" a crowded star field. In this way, we may subtly re-direct the viewer's attention to the fainter nebulae in the image. Photoshop's Minimum Filter operates by "spreading out" black areas and shrinking white ones. The Filter replaces each target pixel with the darkest pixel found within a user-speci-

fied Radius setting.

1. From the tutorial disc, open the file "Star Shrinking Example1.tif" (*File|Open*). This is an image of IC443 taken by Herm Perez.

2. Duplicate the Background Layer by click-holding and dragging it to the "Create a new layer" icon in the Layers Palette, then release the mouse.

3. Zoom into the image (to around 50%) and select a field with 4 or 5 of the brightest stars in the image. With the Background copy Layer active (highlighted in blue), choose *Select|Color Range*. In the Color Range dialog box, use the initial selection Eyedropper (the one on the left) to select one of the brightest stars, then use the "+" Eyedropper to add 5 or 6 more of the brightest stars to the selected colors. Look at the Preview window and adjust the Fuzziness slider until the brighter stars are selected. When you are satisfied with the Preview, click OK.

For this example, I recommend a Fuzziness setting of 40. You want your selection to include all of the brighter stars, but not the very faint ones. These are already "shrunk", and application of the Minimum Filter could cause them to disappear! With some images, you will find that you have to remove areas or objects inadvertently selected by Color Range, such as a bright central galaxy core that has a similar color and brightness to the selected stars. In these cases, use the Lasso Tool while holding down the Alt key (a little "minus" sign appears) and draw a rough circle around the areas you wish to exclude. You may also use other selection tools for this purpose, such as the Magic Wand Tool or Elliptical Marquee Tool. With all of selection tools, holding down the Alt key causes the defined areas to be de-selected.

4. Now expand the Color Range selection with *Select|Modify|Expand*. In the "Expand by" dialog box, enter 6 pixels, and click OK. The selection borders now expand to include the colored star halos. This will minimize artifacts when we apply the Minimum Filter. This setting will vary depending upon the image and your initial selection. Generally start with a low setting — 1 or 2 pixels — and work up from there.

5. At the bottom of the Layers Palette click on the "Add layer mask" icon (a circle inside a shaded square) to convert the selection into a Layer Mask for the Background copy Layer. You may also create the same mask with *Layer|Add Layer Mask|Reveal Selection*. The mask will now cause any changes made to the Background copy Layer to be applied only to the brighter stars and not to the background.

6. Load your newly created Layer Mask into the main window by holding down the Alt key and clicking on the Background copy Layer Mask icon (the small window on the right side of the Layer in the Layers Palette). Choose *Filter|Blur|Gaussian Blur*, set the Radius to 3 pixels and click OK. This will smooth the mask and help minimize the appearance of artifacts around the stars.

7. In the Background copy Layer, click on the image icon (the one on the left) to restore the image to the main window (you want to work on the image, not the layer mask). Choose *Filter|Other|Minimum*. Enter a Radius of 2 pixels and click OK. Don't worry about how the image looks, we will adjust that in the next step.

8. Adjust the Opacity of the Background copy Layer to fine-tune the star-shrinking effect. What you want to avoid is exaggerated "dark halos" or other artifacts around the stars. You also do not want to overdo the shrinking effect. It should be a subtle adjustment. For this example, I reduced the Background copy Layer Opacity to 60%.

9. Now make the final touches using a Curves Adjustment Layer (or a Dodge and Burn Layer, as in our previous example) and a Hue/Saturation Adjustment Layer. We want to brighten the faint nebula slightly to bring it out from the background a little (don't overdo it!). Using a Curves Adjustment Layer (*Layer|New Adjustment Layer|Curves*), I placed one control point in the RGB Channel at Input/Output (48,52), and used a Layer Mask (*Layer|Add Layer Mask|Reveal All*) to "paint out" the background sky areas (paint the mask with black using a low-flow brush) that were overly affected by the Curves adjustment. I then added a Hue/Saturation Adjustment Layer and used the same Layer Mask that I created for the Curves Layer (I loaded it as a selection just before creating the Hue/Saturation Adjustment Layer). I applied +15 Saturation to the "Master" Channel and +10 Saturation to the "Reds" Channel.

This is a lot of adjustment! But it works because the Layer Mask mitigates the effect. You would generally not want to apply this much Saturation increase to an entire image. You may also try your hand at using a Dodge and Burn Layer, instead of the Curves Adjustment Layer. For this image, I prefer the results I obtained by using Curves.

The Minimum Filter is a strong filter, so you will want to use a small pixel radius. Try to use a setting where artifacts just begin to appear. Then you may reduce the effect by lowering the layer opacity. I will repeat myself — this technique is best applied sparingly. It is most beneficial when used with a light hand, to gently re-direct the viewer's attention from a crowded star field to the fainter objects that lie within.

We could just as easily have applied the Minimum Filter to our Color Range selection, without creating a layer mask. However, a mask offers us far more control and flexibility. You can always re-paint the mask, blur it, or adjust it in some other manner to fine tune the application of the filter. This level of control is more difficult to achieve using only selections.

Star Shrinking to Reduce Blue/Violet Fringing

In our next exercise, we will apply star shrinking to one color channel, rather than all three channels, in order to reduce color fringing around the stars.

1. From the tutorial disc, open the file "Star Shrinking Example2.tif" (*File|Open*).

R. Scott Ireland

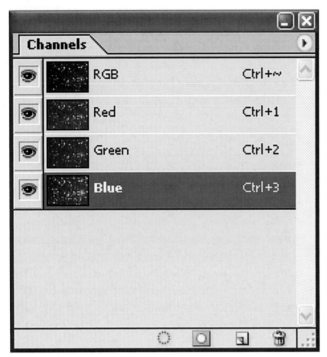

Fig. 8.10 In this example, only the Blue Channel is "active", so edits will only be applied to the Blue Channel. However, all of the color Channels are visible. The little "eyeball" icons at the left side of each Channel indicate visibility, just as in the Layers Palette.

Here we see an excerpt from a larger image that displays a severe case of "blue bloat". Most of the stars have significant blue/violet fringes around their outer edges.

2. Make the Channels Palette visible (*Window|Channels*). Click back and forth on each of the Color Channels (Red, Green and Blue) and examine the stars. Be sure that only one Channel is visible at a time (the little "eyeball" icon at the left of each Channel toggles visibility — just as in the Layers Palette). You will notice that when compared to the other Channels, the Blue Channel stars appear more bloated and have outer halos.

3. Make the Blue Channel active by clicking on it (it should be the only Channel highlighted in blue). But now, turn on the visibility of the other Channels by clicking "on" the visibility of the RGB Channel to make all of the little "eyeball" icons visible. Your Channels Palette should look like **Figure 8.10**. Since only the Blue Channel is active, edits will only be applied here. However, since the visibility of the other Channels is on, we can view the effect of our adjustments in full color.

4. Select *Filter|Other|Minimum*, set the Radius to 3 pixels and click OK. The blue/violet fringing has disappeared, but now the image has a yellow cast.

5. Immediately select *Edit|Fade Minimum*, leave the Mode set to "Normal" and adjust the Opacity slider to eliminate the color fringing without adding a yellow cast. A setting of 65% should suffice. Experiment by trying other Blending Modes, such as "Overlay" and see if you can improve your result. The before and after Blue Channels are shown in **Figure 8.11**.

To fine-tune the application of the Minimum Filter, you may use the Color Range Command to select the brighter stars in the Blue Channel before applying the filter. Follow the same procedures that we outlined in the Selective Star Shrinking example to create, modify and expand the selection. This allows for a more precise adjustment, which may be necessary with some images. It will also help to minimize background color casts.

6. We have effectively removed the blue/violet fringing by applying star shrinking to the Blue Channel only. However, our sky background black point is wrong. The image is not color balanced. If we set some sky background Color Sampler Points with the Eyedropper Tool and refer to the RGB values, we see that there is still a slight yellow cast in the image. Create a Curves Adjustment Layer with *Layer|New Adjustment Layer|Curves* and click OK. In the Curves dialog box, set the Channel to "Red" and place a point on the Curve (click anywhere on the Curve once to place a point) and then type in the Input/Output values of (33, 29). Then set the Curves Channel to "Blue", place a point on the Curve and type in the Input/Output values of (23, 29).

Now the image is pretty well color balanced. Just in case you did not notice the yellow cast remaining before applying Curves, click the visibility of the Curves Adjustment Layer on and off and take a look. *It is amazing the degree to which our minds will adjust the colors we perceive, to make them appear the way we "think" they are supposed to appear. It is always a good idea to double-check RGB numbers to look for color casts, since often we will not notice them otherwise.*

Star "Softening" — Restoring and Enhancing Colored Star Halos

We have examined techniques to re-shape stars, to re-

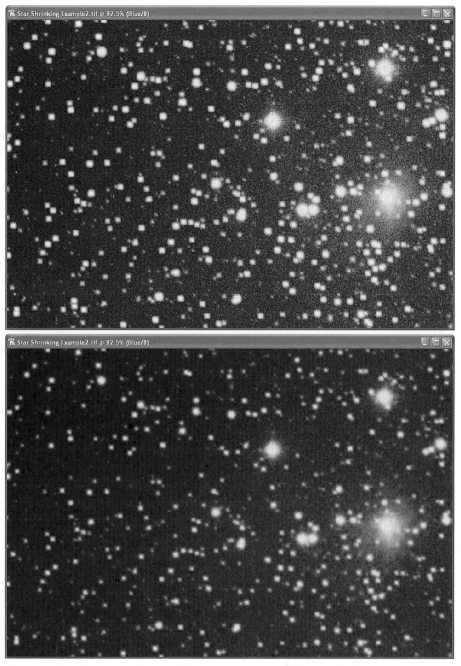

Fig. 8.11 Star Shrinking using the Minimum Filter and the *Edit | Fade* Command has been applied to the Blue Channel only (bottom image) to reduce blue/violet star halos. The top image shows the Blue Channel before application of the filter.

duce star sizes and to minimize unwanted color halos. But now it's time to unleash your artistic instincts! In the following examples, we will explore ways to create and enhance the colored halos that appear around stars. Why would we want to do this? In some images, the stars *are* the subject, such as constellation photographs or nightscapes containing star fields. Often, such imag-

es seem flat and lack that special "something". If we increase the exposure to capture more faint stars, then the brighter stars burn out, clipping the highlights and producing too much contrast. With Milky Way photographs, an image often contains so many stars that the overall impression is harsh. It lacks a central "focus" to anchor the viewer's attention and provide a sense of balance and repose. In these cases, you may find that softening and enhancing the colored halos around stars will produce a more aesthetically pleasing and beautiful result, consistent with your artistic vision of the night sky.

Selective Star Softening using Curves

In our first exercise, we will create selections and masks to separate the stars and sky background in an image, and then use Curves Adjustment Layers to apply selective, local contrast adjustments. Our goal is to build overall image contrast (in technical parlance — to give it some snap, crackle and pop!), yet at the same time reduce the amount of contrast applied to the bright, clipped stars. This softens the appearance of the clipped stars and helps retain as much color as possible in their halos.

This technique was first described by Matt Ben-Daniel, and he dubs it "Star Shaping". With apologies to Matt, I have appropriated the term "star shaping" to refer to techniques that actually re-shape stars. I prefer to think of Matt's technique as one that employs star *softening* since, to me, this is the essence of the procedure.

1. From the tutorial disc, open the file "Star Softening Example1.tif" (*File|Open*).

This is a widefield image of the Double Cluster taken by the author. We worked on this image in **Chapter 6**. In this version, Anti-Vignetting has been applied, but it still requires more contrast enhancement. However, we see that the brighter stars are already clipped. This is a normal occurrence. As we process an astrophotograph, we attempt to extract faint image detail or improve the overall look by enhancing contrast. In the process, bright stars can become clipped, taking on a harsh appearance. They "burn out", resulting in a loss of subtle edge coloration.

2. From the Toolbox, select the Zoom Tool (shortcut "Z") and Zoom into the central cluster region of the image (to around 100%, or "Actual Pixels"). Notice that the bright stars and their color halos appear harsh and somewhat garish.

3. From the Toolbox, select the Magic Wand Tool (shortcut "W"). In the Tool Options at the top of the main window, make sure that the "Contiguous" box is unchecked and that the "Use All Layers" and "Anti-aliased" boxes are checked. Anti-aliasing helps smooth the edges of a selection and reduce "jaggedness". Set the "Tolerance" to 60.

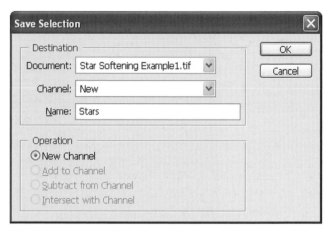

Fig. 8.12 The Save Selection dialog box (*Select|Save Selection*). It is often convenient to save a complex selection for later use. Saved selections appear as Alpha Channels in the Channels Palette.

A low Tolerance setting narrows the selection based on the selected color. A higher Tolerance setting encompasses a broader range of colors. Notice the four boxes near the left of the Tool Options. The first box on the left is the "New Selection" box. The next box to the right adds to the initial selection, the following one subtracts from the selection and the final box on the right selects an area that intersects an already active selection. Make sure that the "New Selection" box is highlighted and click once on a bright, white star at the center of one of the clusters. Now move around the image and check your selection. The brighter stars that contain colored halos have been selected. The faint stars have not been selected, which is appropriate; they do not require softening. If you need to modify your selection, de-select with Ctrl+D and start over, or use the "add to" or "subtract from" Tool Options. With some images, it may be necessary to remove objects from the selection (such as nebulae and galaxies). Use the Lasso tool while holding down the Alt key to subtract these areas from the selection.

4. Choose *Select|Modify|Expand*, enter a Radius of 4 pixels and click OK. This opens up our selection to encompass both the stars and their colored halos.

5. Save your selection with *Select|Save Selection*. The Save Selection dialog box appears (**Figure 8.12**). Make sure that the "Document" is Star Softening Example1.tif, the "Channel" is New, type in the word "Stars" to name the selection and click OK. It is often a good idea to save a selection for use in later processing steps, particularly if it is

a complex selection requiring multiple steps.

6. Make the Layers Palette visible (*Window\Layers*). Create a Curves Adjustment Layer at the top of the Layer Stack with *Layer\New Adjustment Layer\Curves* and click OK in the New Layer dialog box. A Curves dialog box opens and a "Curves 1" Adjustment Layer appears in the Layers Palette. This layer automatically has a Layer Mask applied, since we had a selection active when we created the layer. Click OK to close the Curves dialog box. We will make our adjustments later. Double-click on the Curves 1 Layer name and rename the Layer to "Stars".

7. Re-load your saved selection with *Select\Load Selection*, set the "Channel" to "Stars" check the "Invert" box and click OK. This selection is inverted. Now everything except the stars is selected (sky background and fainter stars).

Take note of this fact — once you have created a selection or mask, you have actually created *two* selections — the selection and its inverse. It is not necessary to increase file space by creating and saving a sky background selection. We already have it. It is the inverse of the stars selection.

8. Create a second Curves Adjustment Layer at the top of the Layer Stack with *Layer\New Adjustment Layer\Curves* and click OK. Re-name this Layer to "Sky". The inverted selection is automatically added as a layer mask. You can see the difference between the two Curves masks in their thumbnail icons — one is black with white stars (reveals stars and hides background) and the other is white with black stars (reveals background and hides stars).

9. Open the Star Layer Curves dialog box (double-click on the left thumbnail with the half black/half white circle). In the Curves RGB Channel, create five control points with the following Input/Output values: (96, 100), (155, 155), (211, 165), (242, 203) and (250, 230). Make sure that you do not inadvertently modify either the white or black points — there should be five points on the RGB Curve in addition to the white and black points. Click OK to accept these settings and close the Curves dialog box.

The easiest way to place Curves control points is to click once on the Curve in the "general vicinity" of the input value, and then just type in the input/output numbers. Use Ctrl+Tab to move between control points. Once placed, do not try to access or adjust control points by clicking on them; they WILL move no matter how careful you are. That is a real exercise in frustration! Only move the Curve directly for quick, broad adjustments. For precise control, use the keyboard — type in the numbers or use the arrow keys.

10. Open the Sky Layer Curves dialog box. In the Curves RGB Channel, create two control points (in addition to the black and white points) with the following Input/Output values: (72, 53) and (197, 216). Click OK to close the dialog. This simple "S" Curve boosts image contrast and darkens the background sky without affecting the brighter stars and their halos (because of the layer mask).

If we had just applied this "S" Curve to the original image, without segregating the stars and sky and without softening the stars/halos, the bright stars would have become even larger, reducing smoothness and color (**Figure 8.13**).

There is no special magic to the input/output Curves values listed above. I just wanted to be sure that "you see what I see". You may come up with better settings. Indulge yourself!

This type of star softening is quite subtle. If you Zoom in and examine the results by turning the adjustment layers on and off, you may wonder if it was worth all the trouble. The more skilled you become with image processing, the more you will come to realize that the difference between a superb image and just a "good" one lies in the small details. You don't build a Patek Philippe watch by just throwing some small parts together and you don't build a fine image by just slapping on a Curve. You must love the process of seeing a beautiful image unfold before your eyes, step by painstaking step. This is the true satisfaction that comes from mastering digital darkroom techniques.

Enhancing Star Halos

OK, now we're really going to have some fun! If you have ever seen Akira Fuji's constellation photographs, then you are familiar with those lovely, diffuse colored glows that surround his stars. And, the brighter stars appear even *larger* than normal! One way to achieve this "look" is to use a diffusing filter when capturing the image. But in the following examples, we will explore some Photoshop techniques that let us create diffuse halos without having to employ special methods in the field.

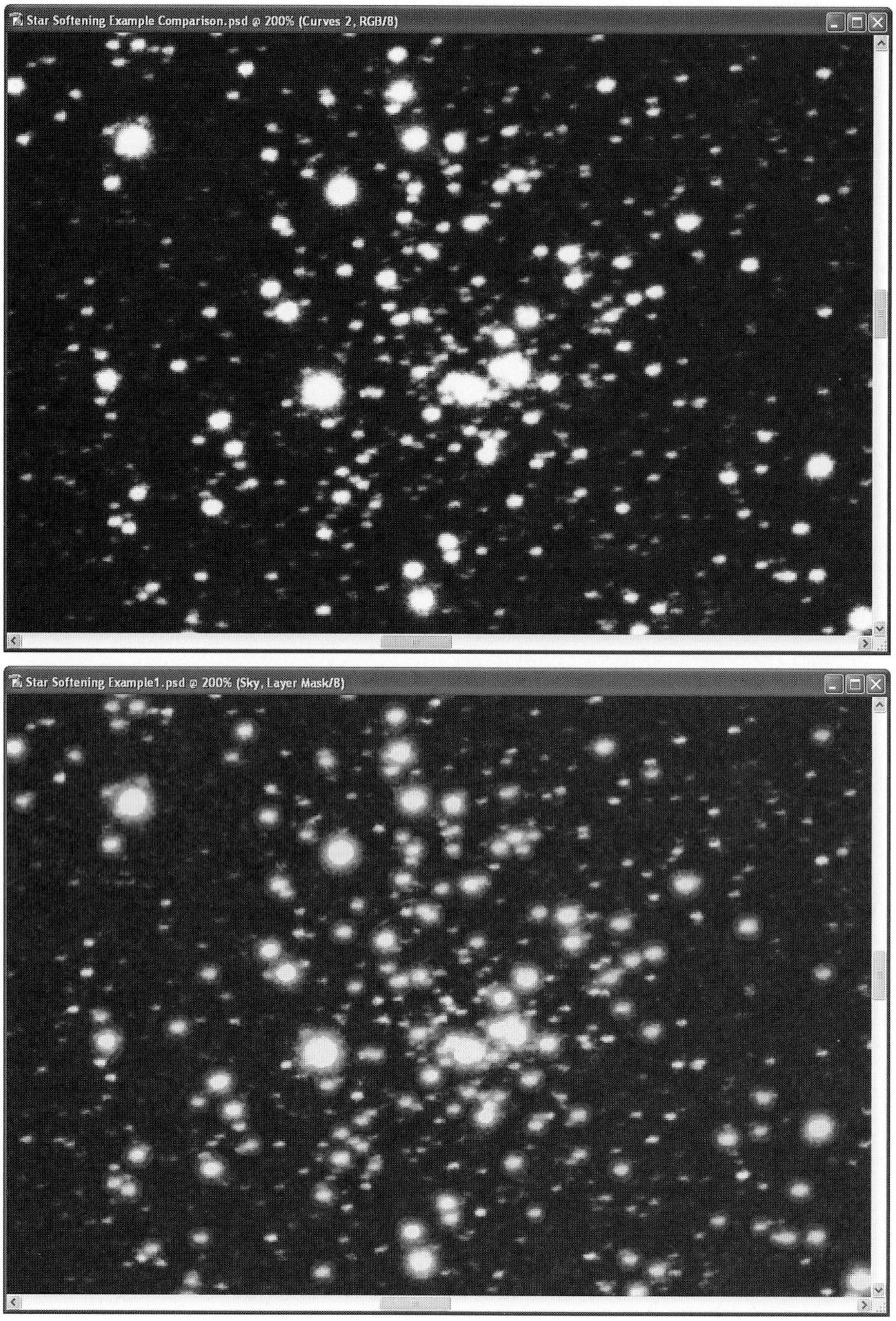

Fig. 8.13 *The final image with (bottom) and without (top) selective star softening.*

Using Photoshop's Artistic Filters to Enhance Star Halos

1. From the tutorial disc, open the file "Star Softening Example1.tif" (*File|Open*). Since this image is already in our "mind's eye" from the last exercise, it will be helpful to compare the results of this procedure to selective star softening.

2. From the Layers Palette, create a copy of the Background Layer by click-holding and dragging it to the "Create a new layer" icon, then release the mouse.

3. From the Toolbox, select the Rectangular Marquee Tool (shortcut "M") and draw a small selection border around one of the central star clusters (see **Figure 8.14**). When applying processor-intensive edits, it is helpful to select a small portion of the image to work on. This way, the preview

Fig. 8.14 When applying processor-intensive filters, use a selection border to isolate a small part of the image first. This way, previews will update quickly as you change settings. Once the desired settings are determined, cancel the selection and apply them to the whole image.

display will update quickly as you change settings. After you have decided on the filter parameters to use, cancel the selection, un-do any edits and apply the filter to the entire image. Then go ice skating or have a cup of coffee while Photoshop applies the filter!

4. Make sure that the Background copy layer is active and choose *Filter\Artistic\Underpainting*. Move the "Scaling" and "Relief" sliders to their lowest settings, set the "Texture" to Sandstone, the "Brush Size" to 6, "Texture Coverage" to 3 and click OK. The filter is applied to the selection.

5. Change the Background copy Layer Blending Mode to "Lighten". Zoom in to 100% ("Actual Pixels") and compare the filtered area to the surrounding stars. We've definitely given the stars a glow! But the effect is far too "paint-like". Reduce the Layer Opacity to between 30% and 50%, depending upon your preference (**Figure 8.15**). Another reason to apply the filter to a selection is to have a side-by-side comparison to the original, unfiltered image. This helps when fine-tuning the opacity to obtain a realistic, photographic look.

6. When you are satisfied with your settings, record

them and then open the History Palette (*Window\History*) and delete all of the History States after duplicating the Background Layer (click-hold on the "Rectangular Marquee" History State and drag to the trash can icon at the bottom of the History Palette, then release the mouse). See **Figure 8.16**.

7. Repeat Step #4, but now apply the Underpainting Filter to the entire image. The settings you used previously should appear (they are "sticky" settings) when you re-open the filter. Once again, change the Background copy Layer Blending Mode to "Lighten" and adjust the Opacity to suit.

8. Zoom into the image to 300% and center one of the star clusters in the window. Create a Hue/Saturation Adjustment Layer at the top of the Layer Stack (*Layer\New Adjustment Layer\Hue/Saturation*). Open the Hue/Saturation dialog box and choose "Reds" as the Channel to edit. Click on the initial selection Eyedropper (the one on the left) and click once on an orange star halo. Expand the selection by choosing the "+" Eyedropper and click on three or four more orange halos. Increase the "Reds" saturation to +15. Next, choose the "Magentas" Channel and use the initial and "+"

R. Scott Ireland

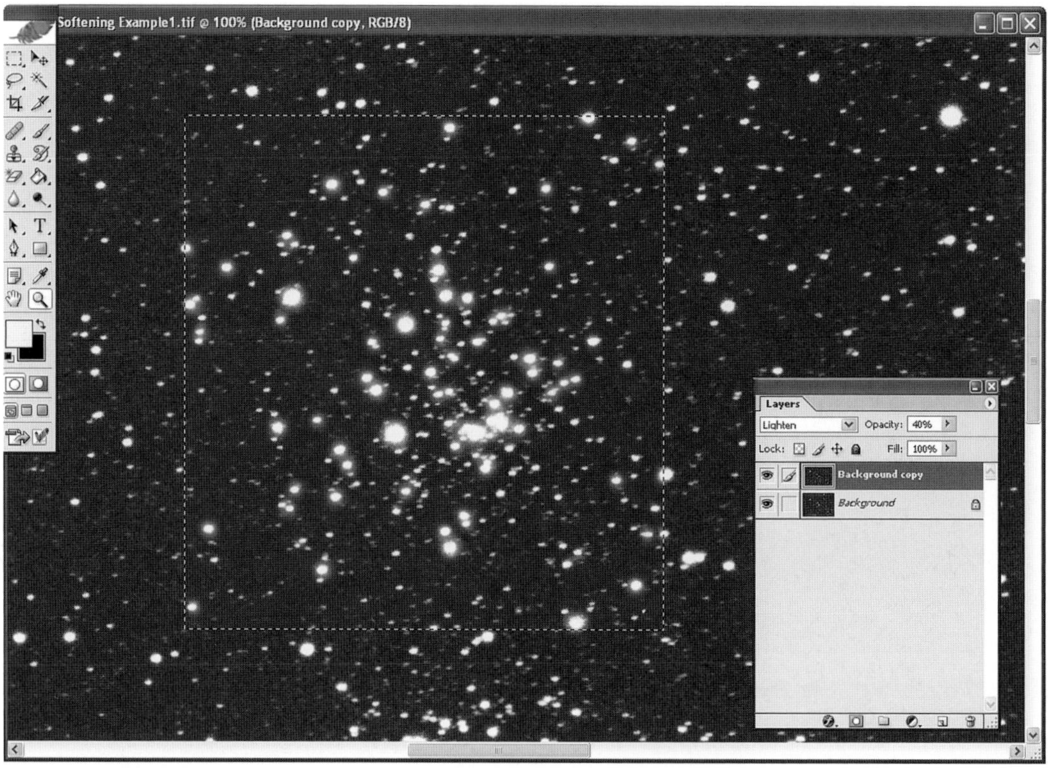

Fig. 8.15 The Underpainting Filter has been applied to the selected area using "Lighten" as the Layer Blending Mode and reducing the Layer Opacity to 40%. Applying a processor-intensive filter such as this to a selected area speeds up previews and allows for comparing the result side-by-side with the original image.

Eyedroppers to select several blue/violet halos. Increase the "Magentas" saturation to +20 and click OK to close the dialog box.

This adds a touch more color intensity to our halos. Notice the linear color "wheel" across the bottom of the Hue/Saturation dialog box. The two vertical inner bars control the range of tif hues that will be affected by any adjustments. The two outer triangles control the "falloff".

Falloff is basically feathering applied to hues. Color adjustments are tapered off gradually across the falloff range. You may select colors and range with the Eyedroppers or by manually adjusting the bars in the color wheel.

9. Now we will apply an "S" Curve as the final step, to boost the contrast a bit. Create a Curves Adjustment Layer (*Layer |New Adjustment Layer |Curves*) and place two additional control points (leave the black and white points alone) in the RGB Channel with Input/Output values of (72, 53) and (197, 216). Click OK to close the dialog.

We have created a soft, outer "glow" around the brighter stars. The settings used in this example are for illustrative purposes only. I encourage you to experiment using different textures and settings. It may also be worthwhile to create a selection encompassing the brighter stars and their initial halos, as we did with the Color Range Command in earlier examples, and then apply an Artistic Filter (try other filters too!).

Using Gaussian Blur to Enhance Star Halos — Floating Selections

1. From the tutorial disc, open the file "Star Softening Example2.tif" (*File|Open*). This is a lovely southern-sky Milky Way image by Monte Wilson.

Our strategy for applying star softening to this image will be as follows: 1. We will make a "hard" selection (no expansion) of the bright stars, and then run a narrow Gaussian Blur. This will soften the stars and reduce their intensity. 2. Next we will make another selection to include most of the stars, along with their halos. We will float this selection to a new layer and then run a wider Gaussian Blur. This will expand and soften the colored halos and further smooth out the stars. 3. Finally, we will adjust Layer Blending Modes

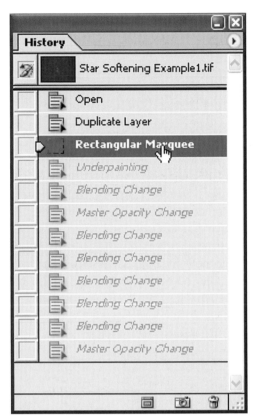

Fig. 8.16 Photoshop's History Palette allows you to "step back" through each processing step and undo image History "States". Find the desired State, then click-hold on the State below it and drag to the trash can. All of the subsequent States will be deleted.

and Opacities to suit our artistic sensibilities (!) and apply final touch-ups with Curves and Hue/Saturation. So let's get started!

2. From the Toolbox, select the Zoom Tool and Zoom in to 200%. Bring the bright stars around the upper nebula into view.

3. Make a copy of the Background layer with *Layer|Duplicate Layer*.

4. Open *Select|Color Range* and click on one of the bright stars with the initial selection Eyedropper. Set "Fuzziness" to 40 and click OK to close the dialog.

5. Save this selection with *Select|Save Selection*, name the selection "Stars" and click OK.

6. With the Background copy Layer active, open *Filter|Blur|Gaussian Blur*, enter a 2 pixel Radius and click OK. De-select with Ctrl+D.

7. Reduce the Background copy Layer Opacity to 30%. Double-click on the Layer name and change

it to "Stars 2 pxl GB".

8. Make the Background Layer active and turn off the visibility of the Stars 2 pxl GB Layer (click off the "eyeball" icon).

9. Again open the Color Range dialog (*Select|Color Range*). Clear the previous selection by clicking on the background and then click on a bright star with the initial selection Eyedropper. Select the "+" Eyedropper and click on about six more stars, including some stars fainter than the brightest ones. Set "Fuzziness" to 90 and click OK. Check your selection. This time, you should have selected all but the faintest of stars.

10. Choose *Select|Modify|Expand*, enter a 2 pixel expansion and click OK. Save the selection with *Select|Save Selection*, and name it "Stars and Halos".

11. Float this selection to a new layer with Ctrl+J. A new layer, "Layer 1" appears. If you turn off the visibility of the other layers and examine it, you see that the star selection you made has been copied into this layer without the other image elements. The stars have been "removed" from the sky background. These other areas are now "transparent". Move Layer 1 to the top of the Layer Stack (in the Layers Palette, click-hold and drag it to the top).

12. Make sure that Layer 1 is active, and that the visibility of Layer 1 and the Background Layer are turned on. The visibility of the Stars 2 pxl GB layer should still be turned off.

13. Open *Filter|Blur|Gaussian Blur*, enter a 5 pixel Radius and click OK. Change the Layer Blending Mode to "Lighten" and re-name this layer to "Stars/Halos 5 pxl GB".

14. Create a Curves Adjustment Layer at the top of the Layer Stack (*Layer|New Adjustment Layer|Curves*) and enter RGB control points (in addition to the black and white points — do not adjust these) with Input/Output values of (38, 28), (72, 68) and (198, 211).

15. Finally, let's add some additional color saturation. Create a Hue/Saturation Adjustment Layer at the top of the Layer Stack (*Layer|New Adjustment Layer|Hue/Saturation*) and increase the saturation to +15 in the "Master" Channel. The final Layers Palette is shown in **Figure 8.17**.

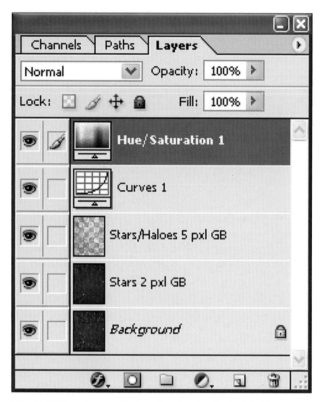

Fig. 8.17 The Layers Palette for the final tutorial. More control was achieved over the star softening effect by using two different star selections and applying the Gaussian Blur Filter with different Radii.

Now you must decide if you like what we've done! And, how much star softening you wish to use, if any. The Opacities of the Gaussian Blur layers may be modified to suit your taste. Or, you may decide that you prefer sharper, pinpoint stars instead — turn off the visibility of the Gaussian Blur layers and see.

I think that I prefer this image with star softening applied. It takes on a "painterly", ethereal quality, and the star clouds actually become cloud-like.

As I said previously, there is no "magic" in the settings or the procedures that we used in these exercises. There are countless creative possibilities. My goal is not to have you slavishly follow rote image-processing steps. Instead, I hope that these examples will expose you to new ideas about how to use the various tools available to you in Photoshop. And, I hope that some of them have gotten your creative juices flowing, so that you may find new ways of your own to make beautiful images.

Chapter 9
LRGB and Channel Mixing

As a man is, so he sees. As the eye is formed, such are its powers.

William Blake

Human vision is a collaborative effort between the eye and brain, as we have discussed before in this book. This eye/brain system behaves in remarkably *adaptive and interpretive* ways to construct our visual models of the outside world. Images formed in the mind are abstractions of reality. Photographs are further abstractions of the world and how we see it.

This is not just philosophical pontificating. The point is that we can understand and capitalize on certain aspects of how we "see" to create more effective and pleasing photographs. Since the Renaissance, artists have utilized perspective, color relationships, contrast effects and many other "tricks" to exploit the peculiarities of human vision and thereby enhance their two-dimensional representations of the world. Although our canvas is now the computer screen, we still deal with color, value, line, shape, space, form, and texture. Instead of brushes, we use things like Levels, Curves, Gaussian Blur and Unsharp Masking to adjust contrast, emphasis, balance and proportion. The tools of construction have changed, but the fundamental principles of art and vision remain the same.

So what does this have to do with LRGB and Channel Mixing? Simple. We capitalize on one of the peculiarities of human vision by recognizing that the eye/brain system is much more responsive to brightness, or *luminance*, than it is to color, or *chrominance*. Luminance information is the Big Kahuna of vision. It is how we perceive spatial relationships. It is where all of the fine detail resides. By comparison, our color perceptions are crude and coarse. Monochrome is the rapier. Color is the broadsword.

LRGB is an acronym for "Luminance, Red, Green and Blue". It is a procedure that combines high-resolution, high signal-to-noise ratio grayscale information ("L") with lower resolution; lower S/N color information ("RGB"). By combining the two, we "trick" the

mind into seeing a high-resolution, high S/N color image. This ruse works well enough to warm the heart of any Renaissance master. And, we save boodles of time in the process. Instead of having to capture three, long-exposure red, green and blue CCD images, we may instead capture one deep unfiltered luminance image and make do with shorter (e.g. "noisier") red, green and blue filtered exposures. Or, we may combine a CCD luminance image with a color film image. Or enhance a color image by synthesizing a luminance layer. There are many possibilities based upon this concept.

Channel Mixing is a term that I use to broadly describe techniques that involve working within individual color channels. These methods segregate and recombine channel data in an image, or among different images, in order to achieve greater detail, clarity, perceived resolution or some other improvement in the final image. Combining color channels to make a grayscale image, creating false color channels, substituting one or more color channels for another, sharpening or otherwise enhancing one channel and mixing color channels to create a luminance layer are all examples of Channel Mixing.

LRGB and Channel Mixing are related in that they both deal with grayscale (luminance) images and how they interrelate to enhance color and detail. The individual RGB (or CMYK) color channels are grayscale. So, on a fundamental level, all image processing deals only with luminance constructs. The world really is black and white, with shades of gray, after all!

LRGB ("Luminance Layering")

LRGB — Photoshop Procedure

I. From the tutorial disc, open the files M51Red.tif, M51Green.tif, M51Blue.tif and M51Luminance.tif (*File|Open*). These are CCD frames of the Whirlpool Galaxy taken by Tim Khan. The exposures are each five minutes, with the red, green and blue images having been taken through each respective color

Fig. 9.1 A color image is created by placing the individual, color-filtered monochrome CCD images into the appropriate R, G and B color Channels. Colors are then rendered based upon a composite of the varying gray-scale levels contained within each filtered image. Here, the green image is copied and pasted into the Green Channel of the "base" RGB image.

filter and the luminance frame being unfiltered. The images have already been dark subtracted, aligned and stacked. They are 8-bit TIFF conversions of the original 16-bit FITS files. They have each been contrast stretched using the same settings with Photoshop FITS Liberator. Use Ctrl+Tab to cycle through the images in the main window and note the greater brightness and detail contained in the unfiltered luminance image.

2. Now we have to select one image to use as our "base". Let's use the red image, although the green or blue one would work equally well. Make M51Red.tif the active image (*Window|M51Red.tif*). Convert the image from Grayscale to RGB with *Image|Mode|RGB Color*. We have now created a color image that appears monochrome, since each of the color channels contains the same information (check this for yourself in the Channels Palette). We will fix that in our next step!

3. Make M51Green the active image (*Window|M51Green.tif*). Select the entire image with *Select|All* (shortcut Ctrl+A) and copy it to the Clipboard with *Edit|Copy* (shortcut Ctrl+C).

4. Once again, make M51Red.tif the active image. Open the Channels Palette (*Window|Channels*) and select the Green Channel (click on it once; it will then be the only Channel highlighted in blue).

Paste M51Green.tif into the Green Channel with *Edit|Paste* (shortcut Ctrl+V). Then Deselect (Ctrl+D). See **Figure 9.1**.

5. Repeat the procedure in steps #3 and #4 to copy M51Blue.tif into the Blue Channel of M51Red.tif. Now we have our color composite (albeit a little dark!). Save this file (using the Photoshop *.psd format) with a new name — "M51LRGB.psd" (*File|Save As*). Close the files M51Green.tif and M51Blue.tif. Their job is done.

6. Now we will begin a sequence of adjustments to the image tonal range and color balance by initially establishing the black and white points. Make the Layers Palette visible (*Window|Layers*) and create a Levels Adjustment Layer with *Layer|New Adjustment Layer|Levels*. Click OK in the New Layer dialog to open the Levels dialog box. Double-click on the "Set Black Point" Eyedropper, enter RGB values of 25, 25, 25 in the Color Picker and click OK. Double-click on the "Set White Point" Eyedropper, enter RGB values of 245, 245, 245 and click OK. Select the Black Point Eyedropper in the Levels dialog and click once on a blank area of background sky. Select the White Point Eyedropper and click once at the center of a bright, white star. It will be helpful to first temporarily close the Levels dialog box and Zoom into the image to make the White Point selection. When the Black and White points have been set,

click OK to close the Levels dialog box. The image has now brightened up considerably, and the colors are more apparent.

Do not be overly concerned about the Histogram here. I have used 8-bit files for this example in order to allow for the use of Adjustment Layers with versions of Photoshop earlier than CS. Since we are performing a considerable amount of processing, the Histogram will get a little "ragged". When processing your own images, it is highly advisable to perform these steps with 16-bit data, if possible. In Photoshop CS or later, there will be no problem using Adjustment Layers with 16-bit files. With earlier versions, as you become more confident of your adjustments, leave the images in 16-bit mode and apply direct edits in lieu of using Adjustment Layers.

7. Now we will add our Luminance layer (the "L" in "LRGB"). Position the image Windows (M51LRGB.psd and M51Luminance.tif) so that both are visible. Make M51Luminance.tif the active image, hold down the Shift key and click-hold and drag the Background layer (from the Layers Palette) to the M51LRGB.psd image Window, then release the mouse. The luminance image is copied to the RGB file and automatically centered and placed into a new layer at the top of the Layer Stack ("Layer 1"). Change the Layer Blending Mode of Layer 1 from "Normal" to "Luminosity" (**Figure 9.2**). Layer Blending Modes are accessed through a drop-down selection box at the top-left of the Layers Palette. Close the M51Luminance.tif image (*File|Close*). From the M51LRGB.psd Layers Palette, double-click on the "Layer 1" name and change it to "Luminance". As we build multiple layer files, it is helpful to name the key individual layers to keep track of them.

Our LRGB is now constructed. The "Luminosity" Layer Blending Mode allows us to use the higher-resolution luminance image and combine it with color information from the lower-resolution RGB composite (located below it in the Layer Stack). Note that we could have achieved the same result by placing the RGB composite above the luminance image in the Layer Stack. In this case, "Color" should be used as the Layer Blending Mode. This instructs Photoshop to use the color information from the top layer and the luminance information from everything below it in the Layer Stack.

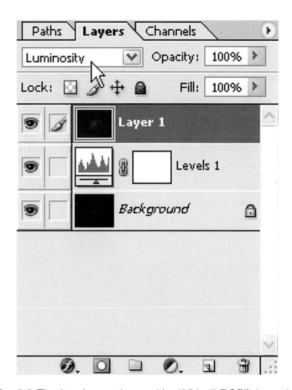

Fig. 9.2 The Luminance image (the "L" in "LRGB") is copied to the top of the Layer Stack ("Layer 1") and the Layer Blending Mode is set to "Luminosity". The luminance information in this Layer will be blended with the color information from the Layers below. Conversely, the same result may be achieved by placing the RGB image above the Luminance image and setting the RGB Layer Blending Mode to "Color".

8. Now we need to build up the brightness and color in this image. Let's start by working with the color information. Turn off the visibility of the Luminance Layer (click the "eyeball" icon at the left side of the layer in the Layers Palette to turn it off). Add a Curves Adjustment Layer above the Levels 1 Layer (*Layer|New Adjustment Layer|Curves*). In the RGB Channel, enter the Input/Output point (127, 210) and click OK to close the Curves dialog box. The overall image has been brightened, but the sky background level is now too bright. Re-open the Levels 1 dialog and adjust the black point slider in the RGB Channel until the sky background levels are around 30 to 40 in each Channel. This point will be about where the left slider intersects the first shadow pixels shown in the histogram.

9. Next, add a Hue/Saturation Adjustment Layer above Curves 1 in the Layer Stack, raise the Master Channel Saturation to +40, and close the dialog box.

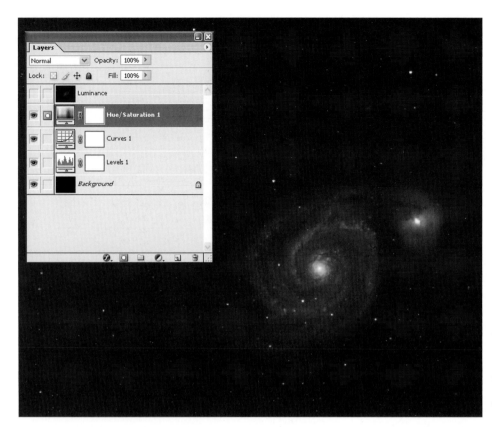

Fig. 9.3 Levels, Curves and Hue/Saturation Adjustment Layers have been created above the RGB composite image (the Background layer). These Adjustment Layers will be used to fine-tune the LRGB color information.

An issue with LRGB combinations is a loss of color richness due to the lower spatial resolution of the color composite. It is necessary to provide a hefty boost to color saturation to overcome the effect.

We now have all of our color Adjustment Layers — Levels, Curves and Hue/Saturation — located above our RGB color composite (the Background layer in this case). As we work through completion of the LRGB image, we will likely need to come back to the color information and perform further adjustments or try different settings, so it is important to retain all of these Adjustment Layers. Your Layers Palette should now look like **Figure 9.3**.

10. Next, we will shift gears and work on the overall image. Turn on the visibility of the Luminance Layer (click to turn on the "eyeball" icon). Add a Curves Adjustment Layer at the top of the Layer Stack. In the RGB Channel create the Input/Output points (14, 0), (41, 98) and (87, 185) and then close the dialog. Note that with the point (14, 0) we are adjusting the existing black point (at the bottom left of the Curve).

The galaxy brightness and color is starting to look good, but wow! The color noise is really bad. How on earth can we get the color and brightness correct without so much noise?

11. Turn off the visibility of the Luminance Layer and the Curves 2 Layer. We will now composite all of our color adjustments into one image layer. Make Hue/Saturation 1 the active layer. Hold down Shift+Ctrl+Alt, then press N, then E. A new layer, Layer 1, appears directly above Hue/Saturation 1. It is a pixel layer that combines all visible layers into one. The settings contained in the three Adjustment Layers above the Background layer have been applied to it and the adjusted pixels are conveniently copied into a new layer, leaving the Background layer untouched and intact.

This is a very important shortcut to remember, so I will repeat it. To combine all visible layers (both pixel layers and Adjustment Layer settings) into one, new pixel layer, hold down "Shift+Ctrl+Alt" then press "N", then press "E". It may help to remember this shortcut using the mnemonic "N"ew / "E"verything.

12. Turn on the visibility of the Luminance Layer and the Curves 2 Adjustment Layer so that all Layers are now visible, and Zoom well into the image (300% to 400%). We want to get a good look at what happens to the color noise as we apply this

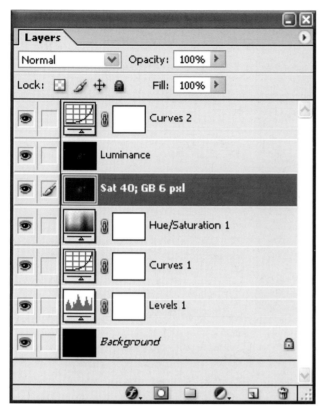

Fig. 9.4 Shift+Ctrl+Alt+N+E has been used to combine all of the color layer adjustments into one new pixel layer. The Gaussian Blur filter was then applied to reduce color noise. This layer (Sat 40; GB 6 pxl — meaning "Saturation +40 and a Gaussian Blur of 6 pixels") is now **the** color layer, since it contains everything below it in the Layer Stack. No adjustments made below this Layer will be visible now, unless new combination layers are created.

step. Make sure Layer 1 is the active layer (highlighted in blue), and open *Filter\Blur\Gaussian Blur*. Adjust the blur Radius to obtain the best tradeoff between reduction of color noise and loss of color information. In this case, a 6 pixel Gaussian Blur looks to be about right, so enter 6 pixels and click OK. Change the name of Layer 1 to "Sat 40; GB 6 pxls". We may want to alter our color settings and try again, so this will keep track of the settings we used this time. Your Layers Palette should now look like **Figure 9.4**.

Notice how "layer thinking" builds flexibility into making destructive edits. The Gaussian Blur filter is a "one-shot" procedure. But by creating layers that combine all previous processing steps (Shift + Ctrl + Alt + N + E), we can easily try different color settings (Saturation, Curves, etc.), and then create new combination layers to compare and fine-tune our results. As an

independent exercise, I encourage you to experiment with different Saturation or Curves settings and try this for yourself.

Note, however, that the Sat 40; GB 6 pxl Layer (shorthand for "Saturation of +40 and a Gaussian Blur of 6 pixels") is now effectively our bottom layer. We no longer "see through" it to any layers below. If we make a change in any of the color layers, we will have to create another composite layer and make it the new "base" (turn on its visibility and turn off the visibility of the Sat 40; GB 6 pxl Layer). See why it's a good idea to give descriptive names to layers?

The image now looks like the Whirlpool we know and love, but there is still a lot of pixelization noise, and our Histogram looks like Swiss cheese. Not to worry, we will fix this in our last step. But first, we need to do a little more color correcting. All of the color adjustments and blurring we performed have shifted the color balance somewhat.

13. Select the Eyedropper Tool (shortcut "I") and place two Color Sampler points in different areas of the background sky and one in the center of a bright, white star. We will observe the black and white points while we adjust Curves to re-establish a neutral color balance.

14. Open the Curves 2 dialog box and place the following additional adjustment points:
Red Channel — one point with an Input/Output value of (20, 19)
Green Channel — one point with an Input/Output value of (20, 21)
Blue Channel — two points with Input/Output values of (16, 17) and (251, 250)

The magenta cast, which you may not have noticed, should now be gone. Remember to always check and adjust color balance "by the numbers".

15. If you wish, you may now add another Hue/Saturation Adjustment Layer at the top of the Layer Stack to give the galaxy some additional color saturation. I created this layer and added +25 saturation to "Reds" and +20 saturation to "Blues". In both cases, I expanded the color bars at the bottom of the dialog box to encompass a broader range of colors. Finally, I applied a "hide all" layer mask to this layer (filled with black) and applied these saturation adjustments only to the galaxy by "painting it in" with white in the layer mask. For good order's sake, I also deleted all of the unused layer

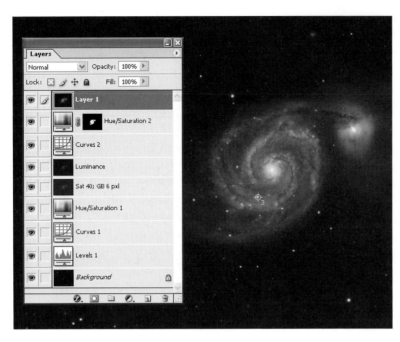

Fig. 9.5 The final LRGB Layers Palette. Layer 1 is a composite of all layers below (all previous processing steps). A very light Gaussian Blur was applied to this layer (0.3 pixel) to eliminate posterization ("gapped" Histogram) in the final image.

masks from the other adjustment layers.

16. Make a composite image containing all of your adjustments at the top of the Layer Stack with Shift+Ctrl+Alt+N+E. All layers from Sat 40; GB 6 pxl and above should be visible. The layers below may also be visible — it will not make any difference. Open *Filter|Blur|Gaussian Blur* and apply a 0.3 pixel blur to this composite layer ("Layer 1").

17. Save your work on this file (M51LRGB.psd) with *File|Save*. We will use it for our next tutorial example.

Now if you check the Histogram, you should find that all is well. By applying a very light final blur, we have "smoothed out" the overall image and eliminated the horrendous posterization (gapped Histogram) we created by applying all of these processing steps to 8-bit files. My final Layers Palette is shown in **Figure 9.5**.

LLRGB ("Multiple Luminance Layering")

There are many variations based upon the theme of luminance layering (LRGB). Sometimes high-quality luminance information so greatly exceeds the brightness and resolution of the color data that the colors become "washed out" or too noisy when combined. This occurs when imaging very faint objects, since it is difficult to obtain exposures long enough for good S/N ratio color information.

In such cases, results may be improved by reducing the Opacity of the luminance layer, but this discards valuable detail. Attempting to "boost" the color information sufficiently results in too many processing artifacts, background noise and loss of color resolution. A better procedure is to add an additional luminance layer and match the luminance to color in two steps, rather than one. This technique was developed by Robert Gendler, and he dubs it LLRGB, or "Multiple Luminance Layering".

Let's explore how to build an LLRGB image with Photoshop's layers, using the LRGB image you created in the previous tutorial.

LLRGB — Photoshop Procedure

1. Open the final LRGB file (M51LRGB.psd) that you created in the previous tutorial example (*File|Open*).

2. Discard "Layer 1" (the composite layer at the top of the Layer Stack) and the "Sat 40; GB 6 pxl" Layer by click-holding and dragging them to the trash can icon at the bottom-right of the Layers Palette, then releasing the mouse.

3. Turn off the visibility of the Curves 2 and Hue/Saturation 2 Adjustment Layers (click the little "eyeball" icons off).

4. Duplicate the Luminance Layer by click-holding and dragging it to the "Create a new layer" icon in the Layers Palette, then release the mouse. Double-click on this new Layer name and change it to

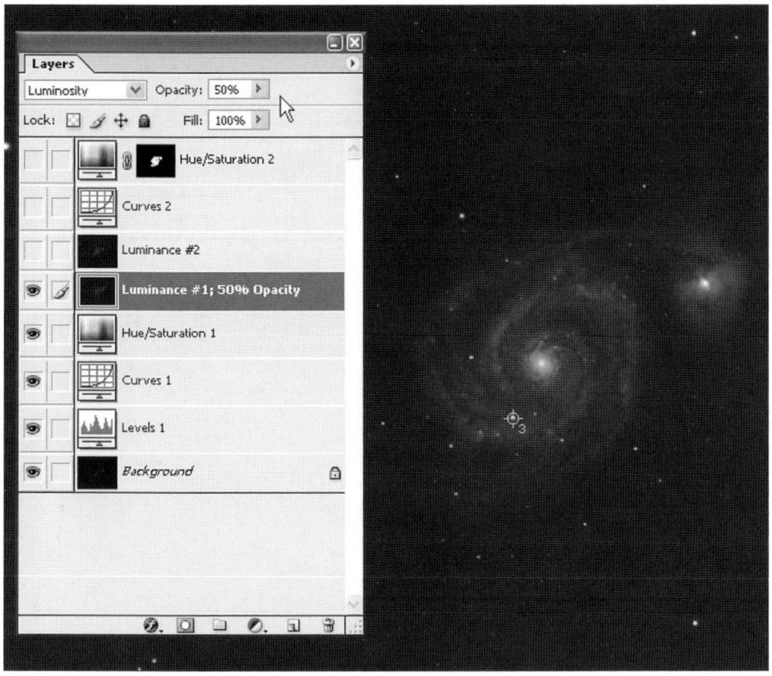

Fig. 9.6 Rob Gendler's LLRGB Technique ("Multiple Luminance Layering") adds luminance to color in two discrete steps. The first luminance layer is created by applying the luminance image at a 50% Opacity, as shown here. The result will be used as the new color image "base" for application of the second luminance layer (Luminance #2) at 100% Opacity.

"Luminance #2". Now turn off the visibility of this layer.

5. Reduce the Opacity of the original "Luminance" layer from 100% to 50%. Double-click on the Layer name and change it to "Luminance #1; 50% Opacity". Check the Layer Blending Mode to be sure that it is still set to "Luminosity". This layer and the ones below it will comprise our "new and improved" color image (**Figure 9.6**).

6. Since we are using a portion of our luminance frame to strengthen the color data, we may now apply more adjustments to the original color data. The luminance component will help to maintain detail/spatial resolution in the color component. Make sure that the visibility of the Luminance #1; 50% Opacity Layer and all layers below it are turned on and that all layers above it are turned off. Open the Levels 1 Adjustment Layer dialog and re-establish the image black and white points (refer to step #6 in the LRGB procedure above if you've forgotten how to do this). Open the Hue/Saturation 1 Adjustment Layer dialog and apply some additional color saturation to the Master Channel. I increased it from +40 to +60.

7. Add a new Curves Adjustment Layer (*Layer|New Adjustment Layer|Curves*) and place it above the Hue/Saturation 1 Layer in the Layer Stack. This new layer should be named "Curves 3" automatically. We will use this layer to apply final color

balance and brightness changes to our color base image (our new and improved color image using the 50% luminance layer!).

It is easier to add a new Curves layer for these adjustments than to try to alter the Curves 1 layer. We need some additional brightness in the color image to compensate for the 50% luminance layer, but the Curves 1 RGB Channel is already set about as high as we can reasonably make it.

The following are the Input/Output points (in addition to the black and white points, which were not altered since we already set them in Levels) that I entered into the Curves 3 Adjustment Layer. Your points, however, may need to vary from these:

- RGB Channel (115, 176)
- Red Channel (48, 44) and (251, 253)
- Green Channel (None)
- Blue Channel (82, 82) a lockdown point, and (251, 248).

8. Now we will combine all of our color work into a new image layer so that we may apply a blur to reduce color noise. Again, make sure that the visibility of the Luminance #1; 50% Opacity Layer and all layers below it is turned on and that all layers above it are turned off. Press Shift + Ctrl + Alt + N + E. A new layer ("Layer 1") should now appear above the "Luminance #1; 50% Opacity" Layer. This layer combines all of the processing steps in the visible layers into one, new image lay-

R. Scott Ireland

er. Your Layers Palette should now look like **Figure 9.7**.

9. Now turn on the visibility of the Luminance #2 Layer and the Curves 2 Layer. Make sure that the Luminance #2 Layer has the Layer Blending Mode set to "Luminosity" and that the Opacity is set at 100%. Yes, the image looks awful, but don't fret! By turning on the final luminance layer and the brightness/contrast adjustments, we can now see just how much we need to blur the color information ("Layer 1").

10. Zoom into the image to get a good look at the galaxy detail and background noise. Make Layer 1 the active layer and open *Filter|Blur|Gaussian Blur*. Enter a 30 pixel Radius and click OK. We may now vary the Opacity of this layer to "dial in" the exact amount of blurring that we need. For now, leave the Opacity at 100%. Re-name this Layer to "CAB; GB 30 pxls" (shorthand for combine all layers below; Gaussian Blur 30 pixels). While you're at it, change the name of Luminance #2 to "Luminance #2; 100% Opacity". This may seem tedious, but it is a good workflow habit, when working with complex, multiple layer operations, to clearly label the function of each layer.

11. Open the Curves 2 dialog box and make final brightness and color balance adjustments. Here again, your points may need to be different, but my final Input/Output points are as follows:

    • RGB Channel (15, 0) a black point change; (37, 101); (117, 231) and (255, 255)

    • Red Channel (0, 0); (20, 21); (154, 105); (251, 247) and (255, 255)

    • Green Channel (0, 0); (20, 21); (233; 230); (248; 246) and (255; 255)

    • Blue Channel (0, 0); (9, 15); (24, 18); (28, 22); (251; 247) and (255, 255).

    Note that here I have listed all of the black and white points too, since I modified the black point in the RGB Channel.

12. Turn on the visibility of the Hue/Saturation 2 Layer, open the dialog box and make your final Saturation adjustments to the galaxy. Since our color image is now so "strong" with the addition of the partial luminance frame, I actually reduced Saturation here. I set the Master Channel Saturation to –20 and set all of the other Channels to 0.

13. Now adjust the Opacity of the CAB; GB 30 pxls

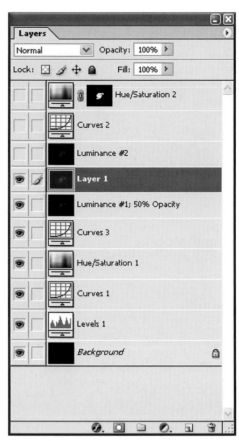

Fig. 9.7 The first step in creating an LLRGB is complete. The 50% Opacity luminance frame has been applied to the color data, additional brightness and saturation adjustments have been made, and the result has been combined into a new image layer ("Layer 1") using Shift+Ctrl+Alt+N+E.

Layer for optimum results. I used an Opacity setting of 75%.

14. With all Layers visible, create a final combination layer at the top of the Layer Stack with Shift+Ctrl+Alt+N+E. Open *Filter|Blur|Gaussian Blur*, enter a pixel Radius of 0.3 and click OK. Re-name this layer to "CAB; GB 0.3 pxl". Your final Layers Palette should look like **Figure 9.8**.

Whew!! Our LLRGB is done. Take a well-deserved break!

This has been quite an exercise. Was it worth it? My final LLRGB has stronger color definition than the LRGB version, but admittedly, the improvements are marginal. The technique is best used with fainter objects. But this exercise clearly demonstrates the power of "3 dimensional thinking" in Photoshop. We have performed a very complex array of combinations and image adjustments, all without having to flatten the image or combine it with other images in separate steps.

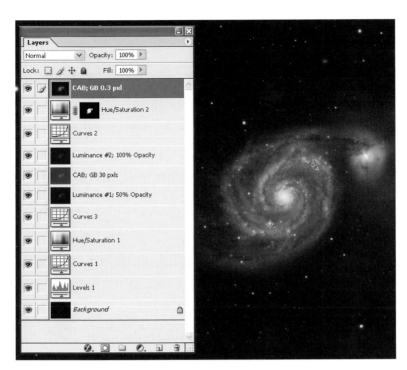

Fig. 9.8 The final LLRGB composite. Strengthening the color image with a partial application of the luminance frame provides more color definition, and is particularly useful when working with very faint objects. By using "3 dimensional layer thinking", all of the complex processing steps have been contained within one Photoshop *.psd file. It would be easy to make additional editing changes in the future.

All processing is contained within one Photoshop *.psd file. It would be relatively easy to come back later and try different settings to fine-tune the result.

This exercise also demonstrates another important concept that is worth remembering. It is often beneficial to apply image-processing edits in multiple small steps, rather than one large step. If a one-step procedure does not produce good results, try "breaking it up" and applying it in stages. This theme recurs in many different areas of image processing, such as the application of Unsharp Masking, and resampling an image to increase its pixel dimensions.

Synthetic LRGB ("Synthetic Luminance Layering")

We may derive the "L" in our LRGB or LLRGB images from a variety of sources. As long as the luminance information exceeds the definition and S/N characteristics of the color information, such combinations should prove fruitful. Luminance sources include narrow-band images, such as hydrogen-alpha ("HaRGB"). A hydrogen-alpha frame may also be substituted for the red channel of a color image. We open up a lot of possibilities when we delve into the individual color channels in search of improvement.

One such technique involves creating a "synthetic" luminance layer. Even when we lack a separate, high-quality luminance frame, it is often possible to improve the color image. As often as not, one color channel exhibits higher subject definition and a better S/N ratio than the other channels, and may be used as the luminance component of an LRGB. Or, channel mixing can be used to re-combine two or more color channels, using different proportions of each, into a new grayscale luminance layer.

Synthetic LRGB — Photoshop Procedure

1. From the tutorial disc, open the file "Rosette1.psd" (*File|Open*). This is Herm Perez's image of the Rosette nebula that we have worked with before in **Chapter 4**. The image was created in the sRGB color space, so if you have correctly set your default working color space to Adobe RGB (1998), you should now be confronted with an embedded profile mismatch dialog box. Choose "convert document's colors to the working space" and click OK. The file is now correctly displayed in our working color space.

2. Open the Channels Palette (*Window|Channels*) and look at the individual color channels. Which one do you think might make a good choice for our synthetic luminance layer? Well, of course the Red Channel! Virtually all of the nebula detail is contained here. The Green Channel shows very little and the Blue Channel almost none. So, the Red Channel meets our first synthetic LRGB criterion — higher subject definition. But what about

the signal-to-noise ratio ("S/N")?

3. Zoom into the image to around 500%. From the Toolbox, select the Rectangular Marquee Tool. Move around the image and create multiple, rectangular or square selections of background sky only (after the first selection, hold down the shift key to add new selection rectangles). The selections will of necessity be small, since there are a lot of stars to avoid in this image! Four or five selection rectangles should suffice. What you want to do is create a sampling of some background sky areas, devoid of any significant detail, in order to provide an overall measure of S/N.

4. Save your background sky selections as a new Channel with *Select|Save Selection*. Name the selection "Background Sky S/N" and click OK. An alpha channel representing this selection appears at the bottom of the Channels Palette. Now you may reload this background sky selection anytime you need it to check S/N.

5. Make the Histogram Palette visible (in Photoshop CS and later) with *Window|Histogram*. If you are using an earlier version of Photoshop you will have to use *Image|Histogram* repeatedly to perform the following analysis. Select "Expanded View" in the Histogram Palette drop-down menu. This menu is accessed by clicking on the little right-facing arrow at the top-right of the Histogram Palette.

6. With your selection active and both the Histogram and Channels Palettes visible, examine the Std. Dev. for each individual color channel in the Channels Palette. Standard Deviation is a statistical measure of variation from central tendency. Lower Standard Deviation numbers indicate a higher S/N ratio for the selected background sky areas. Higher Standard Deviations indicate more variability in pixel values, in other words, more noise. My background sky selections show that the Red Channel also meets our second synthetic LRGB criterion — a higher S/N ratio than the other color channels. See **Figure 9.9**.

7. Clear your background sky selections with Ctrl+D. From the Channels Palette, make only the Red Channel visible. Select the entire Red Channel with Ctrl+A, and copy it to the clipboard with Ctrl+C. Now Click on the RGB "Channel" to make all color Channels visible.

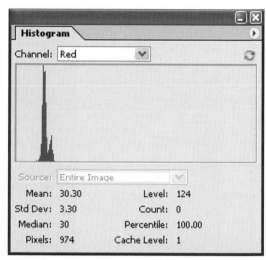

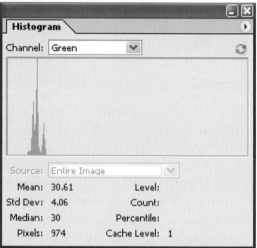

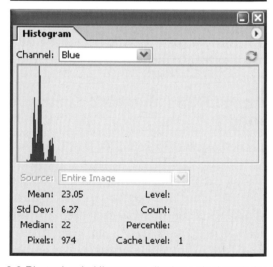

Fig. 9.9 Photoshop's Histogram displays pixel statistics useful for measuring signal-to-noise ratios ("S/N"). Here, the Red Channel Standard Deviation ("Std. Dev.") is lower than the other Channels, indicating a higher S/N for the selected background sky areas.

8. Open the Layers Palette and press Ctrl+V. The Red Channel is now copied from the clipboard into a new layer ("Layer 1") above the Background Layer. Rename Layer 1 to "Luminance — Red Channel", and change the Layer Blending Mode from "Normal" to "Luminosity". We have constructed our synthetic LRGB. Now we will make final color and contrast adjustments.

9. The nebula has brightened up considerably, but the color has become too muted and pink. Create a Hue/Saturation Adjustment Layer above the Background Layer (*Layer|New Adjustment Layer|Hue/Saturation*). Choose "Edit: Reds" and use the initial selection Eyedropper (on the left) to select a bright central region of the nebula. Use the "+" Eyedropper and/or expand the selection color bars (in the color wheel at the bottom of the dialog box) to be sure that adjustments will be applied to the entire nebula. Adjust the "Reds" saturation to +35 and click OK. You might wish to experiment with further color adjustments. For example, Color Range could be used to select the nebula and create a layer mask for further Curves or Hue/Saturation adjustments.

10. Turn off the visibility of the Luminance — Red Channel Layer (click off the little "eyeball" icon) and press Shift+Ctrl+Alt+N+E. We now have an image layer that includes our color adjustments. Make sure Layer 1 is the active layer and choose *Filter|Blur|Gaussian Blur*. Enter a pixel Radius of 12 pixels and click OK. Change the name of Layer 1 to "CAB; GB 12 pxls" (shorthand for "combine all layers below; Gaussian Blur with a 12 pixel Radius"). As you will recall from earlier examples, it is usually beneficial to blur the color information in an LRGB. Turn the visibility of the Luminance — Red Channel Layer back on.

11. If you wish, apply a final contrast adjustment using a Curves Adjustment Layer at the top of the Layer Stack. A slight "S" Curve in the RGB Channel may be used.

12. Now let's check the background sky sample again to see how our adjustments have affected the S/N. Choose *Select|Load Selection* with Background Sky S/N as the Channel and click OK (**Figure 9.10**). In the Histogram Palette, examine the Standard Deviation of the original image (only the Background Layer visible) and your Synthetic

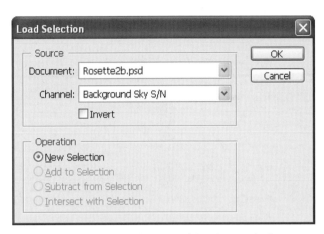

Fig. 9.10 A representative set of background sky areas throughout an image may be saved as a selection and reloaded at any time to check the signal-to-noise ratio as processing steps are applied.

LRGB (all Layers visible). The background sky Standard Deviation of my finished image is 4.04, compared to 5.87 in the original image, a significant improvement. Any reasonable contrast or brightness adjustment in my final Curves Layer produces an improvement in S/N over the original. This is even more impressive given the large increase in nebula brightness.

As an independent exercise, try applying a Curve to the original image (Background Layer) and increase the nebula brightness close to that of your Synthetic LRGB. Then check the S/N. The Standard Deviation was 7.01 when I tried this, higher than both the original (5.87) and the Synthetic LRGB (4.04). Clearly, using the Red Channel as a synthetic luminance layer is a better way to improve the appearance and signal-to-noise characteristics of this image (**Figure 9.11**).

You may remember from **Chapter 5** on Stacking that combining an image with itself does not improve the S/N, since the random noise elements are no longer random, they are located in the same place. Synthetic LRGB, however, is not the same thing. By delving into the individual color channels to create a luminance layer, we are not overlaying the same data — *we are selectively recombining different elements of information contained within the image*. S/N may indeed be improved this way, as we have just demonstrated.

It is also possible to "mix" the information from more than one color channel to create a luminance layer, which leads us to our next topic.

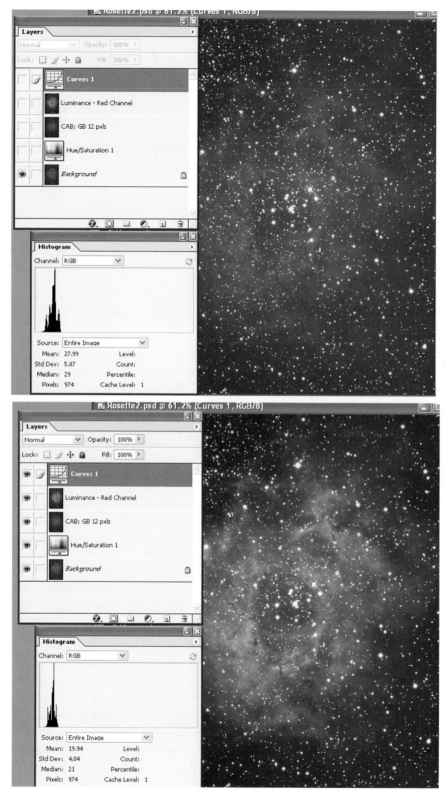

Fig. 9.11 The original image (top) and the final Synthetic LRGB (bottom). Both nebula detail and background S/N have improved by using the Red Channel as a synthetic luminance layer.

Channel Mixing

Color to Monochrome Conversions Using Photoshop's Channel Mixer

The previous tutorial demonstrates how using monochrome information contained within individual color channels can sometimes improve an image. In this section, we will explore the "best" method for converting a color image to monochrome (black and white).

In the non-astrophotographic world of image processing, it is a well-known secret among cognoscenti that Photoshop's Channel Mixer is the ideal method for producing beautifully-toned black and white images from full-color originals. There are other ways to go from color to monochrome, of course. We have seen some of these in earlier chapters, including *Image|Adjustments|Desaturate*, converting an image from RGB to Grayscale, or converting to the LAB color model, which separates luminance and chrominance information. But Channel Mixer offers us a far greater degree of control over how we use the grayscale information from individual color channels. This command allows us to *specify the percentage contribution of each original color channel* in the final result (**Figure 9.12**). In this way, our grayscale palette is extended across all channels, and we may judiciously combine them to produce the greatest amount of detail and tonal range possible.

Channel Mixer — Photoshop Procedure

1. From the tutorial disc, open the file Channel Mixer Example.tif (*File|Open*). This is a lovely, wide-field image of the Small Magellanic Cloud taken by Monte Wilson. Depending upon how you have set up your default color settings (*Edit|Color Settings*), you may be presented with an embedded profile mismatch dialog box. If so, choose "Use the embedded profile" in order to display the image in the color space in which it was created. This is a CMYK image in the "U.S. Web Coated (SWOP) v2" color space.

2. Open the Channels Palette (*Window|Channels*). Whoaa . . . what's this? Where's red, green and blue? Well, they're not here. The CMYK color model uses the subtractive primary colors — cyan, magenta and yellow. Black is added to the mix to improve tonal rendition on the printed page. As we discussed in an earlier chapter, CMYK is the

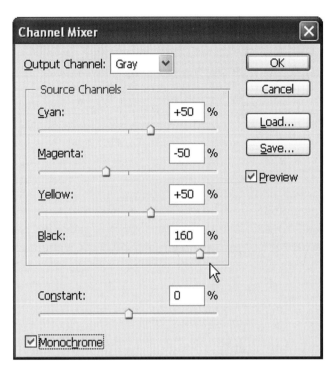

Fig. 9.12 Photoshop's Channel Mixer (*Image|Adjustments|Channel Mixer*) is the ultimate way to create a black and white image from a color original. The grayscale information contained within each color channel is re-combined by specifying the percentage of each channel used for the final output. Maximum detail and tonal range can be achieved.

principal color model used in the printing industry. As such, its logic is based upon color separations and ink application percentages. Photoshop's tools, commands and information may look different and a little strange when you are used to working in RGB. A detailed examination of CMYK is beyond the scope of this book, but it is worth having at least some exposure to this universal color model. It can solve many problems not easily handled in RGB.

3. Look through the individual CMYK color channels. Clearly, the yellow channel provides the most vivid rendition of the SMC stars. Look carefully and you will see that the cyan channel provides almost all of the detail for the H-II regions. The magenta doesn't seem to contribute much detail to any area in particular.

Now here's the neat part. The bright areas in the yellow channel represent areas of the image that contain more blue. Bright cyan areas correspond to more red. And bright magenta areas correspond to more green. *If we were to examine the color channels of this image in RGB, we would see the same tonal relationships.* In CMYK, brighter tones in a color channel represent *less* of that color, in other words, less ink is applied. In RGB, bright areas represent *more* of a color, since RGB is modeled on light transmission rather than light reflection from ink on a page. *So, the yellow channel in CMYK will look quite a bit like the blue channel in RGB. Blue areas appear brighter in both. It is the same with the Cyan-Red and Magenta-Green channels.* This makes it much easier to envision how CMYK edits will look. If you are accustomed to thinking in RGB, just think "blue" for yellow, "red" for cyan and "green" for magenta, and CMYK suddenly becomes much easier to understand and work with.

4. Make a copy of the Background Layer (to preserve the original image pixels in the bottom layer). Create a Levels Adjustment Layer above the Background copy Layer (*Layer\New Adjustment Layer\Levels*). We will set the black and white points, which should provide most of the color correction we need for this image. In the Levels dialog box, double-click on the "set black point" Eyedropper. In the Color Picker set the CMYK values to (80%, 70%, 70%, 70%) and click OK. Similarly, set the white point Eyedropper values to (4%, 2%, 2%, 0%). Color sampler points have already been placed in this image for the black and white points. Be sure that your Eyedropper Sample Size is set to 3 by 3 Average. Click on Color Sampler point #1 or #3 (two alternative background sky points) with the black point Eyedropper and click on Color Sampler point #2 with the white point Eyedropper. Notice that the slight red cast in the image is gone (did you notice it before making the adjustment?). To achieve neutral values in CMYK, a higher percentage of Cyan ink (the "weak" ink) must be used. Before the Levels adjustment, Cyan values were similar to the other color channels, which gave the image a red cast.

5. Next, create a new "combine all" layer at the top of the Layer Stack with Shift+Ctrl+Alt+N+E and re-name this layer to "CAB" (combine all below). You must remember when using combine layers, that nothing below this layer will now show through into the image. If you want to make another Levels change, for instance, you will have to discard the CAB layer and make a new one after re-adjusting Levels.

6. Create a Hue/Saturation Adjustment Layer (*Lay-*er\New Adjustment Layer\Hue/Saturation*) above the CAB Layer. Increase Master Saturation to +20 and click OK. We will be using Channel Mixer to create a synthetic luminance layer, so we want to bolster the saturation of the color information.

7. Now create a Channel Mixer Adjustment Layer (*Layer\New Adjustment Layer\Channel Mixer*) at the top of the Layer Stack. In the Channel Mixer dialog box, check the "Monochrome" box at the bottom-left. Change the "Source Channel" percentages to increase Cyan and Yellow to +50% each. Reduce Magenta to –50% and increase Black to +160%. These settings are shown in **Figure 9.12**. Click OK to accept these settings and close the Channel Mixer dialog box.

Since the important image details reside in the Cyan and Yellow Channels, we have increased these and reduced Magenta in our luminance "mix". If we were working with an RGB image, we would typically set the percentages so that the three channels add up to around 0. If the total were less than 0, overall luminance levels would be reduced and the image would get darker. Conversely, if the three channels totaled over 100%, the image would get brighter.

I encourage you to play with the Channel Mixer settings and see if you can improve on those given above. When working on your own images, it is helpful to create on-screen duplicates (*Image\Duplicate*) and compare them as you change settings. The goal is to mix the channels until you get the most detail and tonal range in the subjects of interest.

8. Now change the Layer Blending Mode of the Channel Mixer 1 Layer from "Normal" to "Overlay". This brings the color information into our synthetic LCMYK. Lower the Opacity of the Channel Mixer 1 Layer to 75%. This is the final setting that I preferred. You may prefer a different setting. I also applied a 0.5 pixel Gaussian Blur to the CAB Layer in order to smooth the image a bit. You could also try creating a duplicate of the CAB Layer set to Luminosity mode and then just blurring the color information below it. Experiment and see what works best for you.

9. Finally, hold down the Alt key and click repeatedly on the visibility icon (the little "eyeball" icon) of the Background Layer to toggle the other layers on and off and compare your final LCMYK to the original image. This is another good reason to leave the original image in the Background Layer.

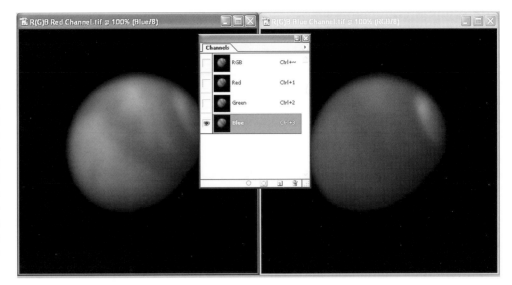

Fig. 9.13 The first step in constructing a Synthetic Green Channel is to join the red and blue data in one image file. Here, the blue-filtered image is selected (Ctrl+A), copied (Ctrl+C) and then pasted (Ctrl+V) into the Blue Channel of the red-filtered image. Note that the red image may first need to be converted from Grayscale to RGB.

Would it be possible to get a similar result using only Curves? Perhaps, but I did better using the above method. Try it for yourself and see.

Here we used the Channel Mixer to create a synthetic luminance overlay for a color image.

We could just as easily have left it as a grayscale if the goal was to create a high quality black and white image. Keep this tool in mind when making black and white conversions from color originals.

Synthetic Color Channels — R(G)B Photoshop Example

It may be useful in certain circumstances to create an "artificial" color channel. Don Parker described the following method to me in connection with tri-color imaging of Mars. Due to planetary rotation, limited moments of good "seeing" and other factors, there may be insufficient time to collect enough color-filtered sub-frames for a full RGB composite. Since the important details on Mars are visible primarily in red and blue light, it may be a reasonable trade-off to use the limited time available to collect only high-quality red and blue exposures. A "synthetic" green channel can then be constructed using the red and blue data.

1. From the tutorial disc, open the files R(G)B Red Channel.tif and R(G)B Blue Channel.tif (*File*|*Open*). These are red and blue filtered monochrome images of Mars taken by Tim Khan and me using a Philips ToUCam webcam. They are unprocessed composites of 400 video frames each, stacked using the K3CCD Tools program.

2. Make R(G)B Blue Channel.tif the active image window, select the entire image with Ctrl+A, then copy it to the clipboard with Ctrl+C.

3. Make R(G)B Red Channel.tif the active image window and display the Channels Palette (*Window*|*Channels*). Click on the Blue Channel to make it the active channel (it should be the only one highlighted in blue) and paste the blue image here with Ctrl+V (**Figure 9.13**). Close the R(G)B Blue Channel file, we no longer need it. Clear the Selection Border ("marching ants") with Ctrl+D. Note that these files are already RGB images, they are just monochrome RGB images (they contain the same information in each color channel). When working with your own files, it may first be necessary to convert the base image (the red one in this example) from Grayscale mode to RGB using *Image*|*Mode*|*RGB Color*.

4. Turn on all of the color channels by clicking on the RGB Channel in the Channels Palette. We now have an RRB image. Both the Red and Green Channels contain the same red-filtered information, and the Blue Channel contains the blue-filtered image. The image is an awful shade of green at this point, but don't worry. We'll fix that soon!

5. Open the Layers Palette (*Window*|*Layers*) and duplicate the Background Layer (click-hold and drag it to the "create a new layer" icon at the bottom-right of the Layers Palette, then release the mouse). Create a Channel Mixer Adjustment Layer above the Background copy Layer (click on the half black/ half white icon at the bottom of the Layers Palette and select "Channel Mixer").

R. Scott Ireland

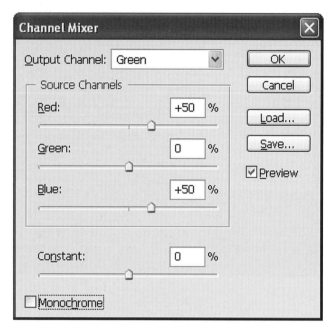

Fig. 9.14 A Synthetic Green Channel is created with Channel Mixer using 50% of the Red Channel and 50% of the Blue Channel.

6. In the Channel Mixer dialog box, select Green as the "Output Channel". Under "Source Channels", set Red to +50%, Green to 0% and Blue to +50% (**Figure 9.14**). We have now created our synthetic Green Channel by combining equal amounts of the red and blue images. Click OK to close the Channel Mixer dialog box.

7. The color now looks much better, but the image is still too dark and a bit too red. Create a Curves Adjustment Layer at the top of the Layer Stack and enter the Input/Output point (76, 148) in the RGB Channel. Enter the point (127, 124) in the Red Channel. Click OK to close the Curves dialog. This brings up the brightness and lowers the red levels slightly.

8. Add a Hue/Saturation Adjustment Layer at the top of the Layer Stack, lower the Master Saturation to –15, and click OK.

This image is now ready for re-orientation using *Image|Rotate Canvas* and sharpening using various methods that we will explore in **Chapter 12**.

Correcting for Prismatic Dispersion and Misaligned Color Channels

It is quite common to have red and blue "fringes" on opposite sides of a planetary image. This is the result of *prismatic dispersion* — a differential refraction of the red and blue wavelengths as light passes through the Earth's atmosphere. The effect is most acute with objects near the horizon, since the light is traveling through more atmosphere before reaching our eye, telescope or imaging device. This is the same effect that causes a bright star at low elevation to shimmer in red and blue.

There are optical devices available to counteract the effect of prismatic dispersion. But it is also possible, and considerably easier, to solve the problem in the digital darkroom by re-aligning the individual color channels. There are other cases too that require color channel re-alignment, and the following procedure should prove satisfactory in most circumstances.

Re-aligning Color Channels — Photoshop Procedure

1. From the tutorial disc, open the file Realignment Example.tif (*File|Open*). This is an image of Mars taken by Tippy D'Auria and myself using a Philips ToUCam webcam on a 3.5-inch Maksutov-Cassegrain. It is a composite of 150 video frames stacked using the K3CCDTools program. No adjustments have been made other than a preliminary unsharp masking. It is a good idea in these cases to re-align the color channels near the beginning of your processing workflow, prior to engaging in extensive sharpening or color adjustments.

2. From the Toolbox, select the Zoom tool and Zoom into the image to around 200%. It is obvious that there is red fringing along the top half (in its initial orientation) of the planet's disc. There is also a problem with green/blue fringing along the bottom.

3. Open the Channels Palette (*Window|Channels*). Click on the Red Channel to make it active (highlighted in blue), and make sure that the visibility of the other Channels is turned off (click the little "eyeball" icons at the left side of each Channel to turn them on and off). Now toggle the visibility of the Green Channel on and off (click the little "eyeball" for the Green Channel on and off). By "blinking" these two Channels, we see that the Green Channel is positioned lower than the Red Channel (**Figure 9.15**).

4. Make the Green Channel active (click on the Channel name; the Green Channel should then be highlighted in blue) and make sure that the visibil-

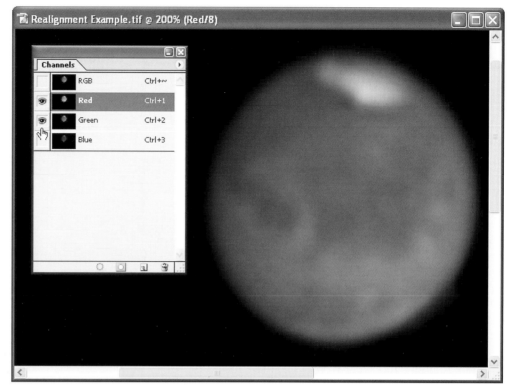

Fig. 9.15 It is helpful to "blink" the visibility of color Channels on and off when performing re-alignments. Only the highlighted Channel (Red in this example) is active and may be altered, but any of the other Channels may be made visible by clicking to turn on their "eyeball" icons. By blinking two Channels at a time it is easier to see and correct misalignments.

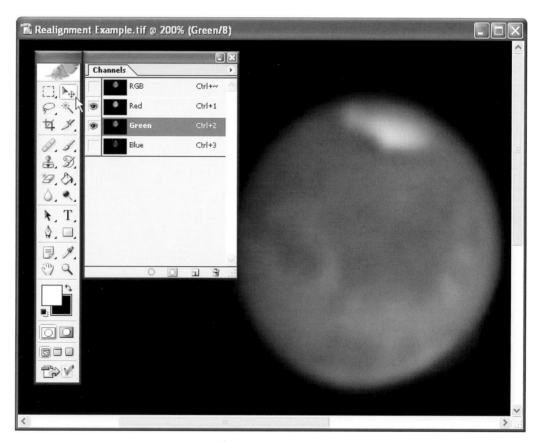

Fig. 9.16 The Move Tool (top right in the Toolbox) is used to re-align the individual color Channels. Click once in the main image window and use the keyboard arrow keys to reposition a Channel one pixel at a time.

ity of only the Red and Green Channels is turned on. From the Toolbox, select the Move Tool (keyboard shortcut "V"). Click once in the main image window and use the keyboard arrow keys to move the Green Channel one pixel at a time. It will require movement of about 3 pixels up and 1 pixel to the right. See **Figure 9.16**.

5. Now make the Blue Channel active and only the Red and Blue Channels visible. Blink the visibility of the Red one on and off. It is obvious that the Blue Channel is also positioned lower than the Red. Use the Move tool and arrow keys to reposition the Blue Channel upward by 6 pixels.

This is about as good as we can do with this image. There is still some slight red fringing on the left and bottom-right, but any movement we make in the Red Channel exacerbates the problem to one side or the other (try this for yourself and see). There are also some data missing along the top and right side, but there is nothing we can do about that. Nevertheless, our Channel realignments were worthwhile. The image is now ready for further processing with Curves, Hue/Saturation and the Unsharp Mask filter.

6. Open the History Palette and click on the original History State ("Open"). This shows the original image file before the Channel realignments. Click back and forth between the first and last History States to "blink" the image before and after realignment (**Figure 9.17**). The final result is indeed an improvement.

It is a good workflow habit to always examine the individual color channels when working on any image. As this Chapter has demonstrated, there are many po-

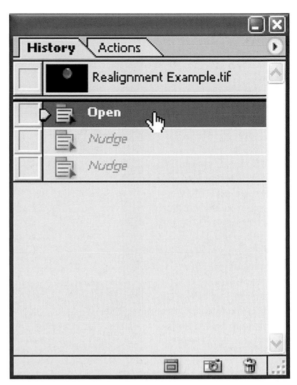

Fig. 9.17 The History Palette may be used to see the before and after effect of edits and other image adjustments. Just click on a different History State to display the status of the image at that point. Each change has its own History Palette "layer".

tential image-processing tools that reside within the individual grayscale channels of our color images. Luminance layers, monochrome conversions, synthetic channels, selections, luminance masks and contrast masks are just some of the possibilities. Use your skill and imagination to find others and expand your processing repertoire.

Chapter 10
Composites and Mosaics

A basic problem all photographers face is the limited dynamic range of their recording devices. The human eye can perceive a 15-stop range of brightness, from black to white. This is a 30,000:1 brightness ratio. Positive (slide) films are only capable of recording a brightness range of 4 to 5 stops (32:1 ratio). Color negative films extend the range to around 6 or 7 stops (128:1). The current crop of digital cameras lays claim to 8 or even 9 stops (512:1). High quality low-noise astronomical CCD cameras can achieve a range of around 13 stops (8,000:1). The best instruments available cannot achieve the range of brightness that we are able to see. And even with the broad dynamic range of a CCD camera, faint image details become lost in the surrounding brightness levels, and are only visible if we differentially stretch the image tonal scale to reveal them. There are many subjects with brightness ranges that cannot be recorded with a single exposure, or cannot be rendered visually complete without separating several tonal ranges from within a single exposure, which is tantamount to the same problem.

Do not confuse bit-depth and tonal scale with the ability to record subject dynamic range. Even though we use 16-bit devices that can record 65,535 grayscale levels, this does not mean that these devices are capable of rendering discrete subject brightness levels to the same extent.

The way to circumvent this problem is to create multiple exposures of the same subject and make a *composite image*. Shorter exposures used to capture faint image elements are combined with longer exposures that capture the brighter elements. The composite image blends these elements together to effectively extend the camera's dynamic range. This technique is as useful for landscapes as it is for astrophotographs.

Composites may also be used to combine images of transient phenomena, such as meteor showers, eclipses, transits and occultations. Changing image elements within a fixed field of view can be rendered together to better illustrate the dynamic nature of the event.

Another limitation of our recording devices is imposed by the size of the imaging sensor (film is a "sensor" also). We are limited to a specific field-of-view using a particular optical configuration. Other things being equal, the smaller the sensor, the narrower the field-of-view. We may overcome this limitation by combining several images taken "side-by-side" into a *mosaic image*. A wider-field, high-resolution image may be constructed even when using a relatively low-resolution instrument, such as a webcam.

In this Chapter, we will explore some basic Photoshop techniques that allow us to transcend both dynamic range and field-of-view limitations by constructing Composites and Mosaics.

Creating a Composite using Layer Masks

In this example, we will construct a Composite image of the Orion Nebula. M42 is the classic example of a subject that encompasses a brightness range that cannot be completely rendered with a single exposure. We will place the various exposures into one image file, with each exposure in its own layer, and then blend together the details from each image using Layer Masks. In this way, we will create a composite image that encompasses the full subject dynamic range, from the bright Trapezium region to the faint outer nebulosity.

1. On the tutorial disc are five images of the Orion Nebula, taken by Rick Krejci. Rick used a Canon EOS 10D digital camera to take this series of 5-minute exposures. He bracketed using different camera ISO speed settings (100, 200, 400 and 800) in order to capture the full brightness range of the Nebula. The digital camera RAW files were converted to 16-bit TIFF files using the Adobe Camera RAW converter in Photoshop CS (**Figure 10.1**). These files were then converted to 8-bits and saved as the TIFF files you now have on the tutorial disc. No other processing changes were applied to these RAW captures. In practice, you should keep digital camera files in 16-bits when-

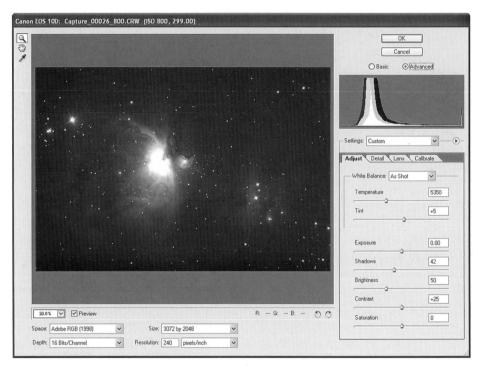

Fig. 10.1 Adobe's Camera RAW converter is a powerful tool for processing digital camera RAW files. It is included as a Plug-In in Photoshop CS and CS2.

ever possible. I have only converted them to 8-bits here in order to allow for Layer processing with versions of Photoshop earlier than CS (**Figure 10.2**).

2. From the tutorial disc, open the files "Orion 1.tif" and "Orion 2.tif" (*File|Open*). These are the two "shortest" exposures in the sequence. We will use Orion 1.tif as our base image, and add the progressively brighter exposures vertically into the Layer Stack. Place the image windows so that both are visible. Make Orion 2.tif the active image and open the Layers Palette (*Window|Layers*). Hold down the Shift key, click-hold on the Orion 2 Background Layer, drag it into the Orion 1 main image window and release the mouse. Orion 2 is copied into a new layer, Layer 1, in the Orion 1 image. Holding down the Shift key centers it. Close Orion 2.tif.

3. Following the procedure in step 2, copy "Orion 3.tif", "Orion 4.tif" and "Orion 5.tif", in that order, into the Orion 1.tif Layer Stack. Rename the Layers (double-click on their names in the Layers Palette to change them) to the image file names. Your Orion 1.tif Layers Palette should now look like **Figure 10.3**.

4. Now is a good time to save Orion 1.tif under a dif-

ferent name as a Photoshop *.psd file. This exercise will involve quite a few layers and steps, so you should save your work periodically. Save Orion 1.tif as "Orion Mask Composite.psd" (*File|Save As*) and be sure to check the "Layers" box to save all Layers intact.

5. We now need to check the alignment of the images and re-align them if necessary. Turn off the visibility of all Layers except Orion 1 and Orion 2 (click off the little "eyeball" icons at the left side of each Layer in the Layers Palette to turn off visibility). Use the Zoom Tool to Zoom into an area of bright stars — zoom to around 300%. Change the Layer Blending Mode of the Orion 2 Layer from "Normal" to "Difference". Select the Move Tool from the Toolbox (keyboard shortcut "V"), click once in the image window and use the keyboard arrow keys to reposition the Orion 2 Layer until it is in register with the underlying Orion 1 Layer. If you find it easier, you may also align the images by leaving the layer blending mode of Orion 2 as "Normal" and temporarily lowering its Opacity (to around 50%) to get a "ghost" view of both layers. When Orion 2 is aligned with Orion 1 change its Layer Blending Mode back to "Normal" and its Opacity back to 100%.

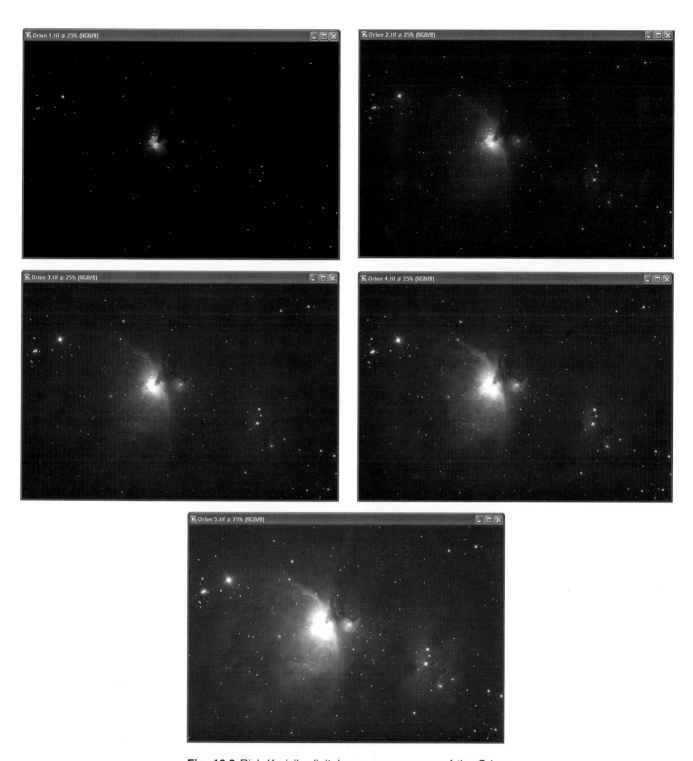

Fig. 10.2 Rick Krejci's digital camera sequence of the Orion Nebula region. These five RAW images display a wide subject brightness range that cannot be captured in a single exposure. By creating a Composite image, highlights that are burned out in the deeper exposures will be retained by progressively blending in the shorter exposures.

R. Scott Ireland

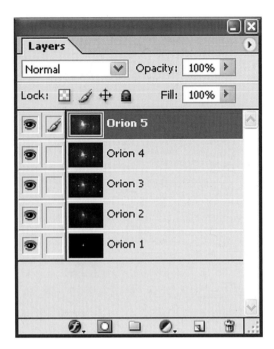

Fig. 10.3 The other four images for the Composite have been copied into the Orion 1 image by Shift-click-holding and dragging their Background Layers into the Orion 1 main image window. Holding down the Shift key centers each one. It is important to arrange the images by increasing brightness level, with the brightest one at the top of the Layer Stack and the faintest at the bottom.

6. Leave the visibility of the Orion 1 and Orion 2 Layers on, and now Make Orion 3 the active Layer (its visibility will turn on automatically). Follow the procedure of step 5 to align this Layer to the underlying Layers. Then proceed to align the

Orion 4 and Orion 5 Layers in the same fashion. After aligning all of the Layers, remember to re-set their Layer Blending Modes to "Normal" and their Opacities to 100%. Don't worry about achieving an exact alignment, just do the best you can. We could perform a sub-pixel alignment for more precision, as outlined in **Chapter 5**, but it is not necessary for this exercise.

7. Now we need to establish the same color balance among the various images in the stack, to be sure that any color-casts are eliminated. We can most easily accomplish this by creating a Levels Adjustment Layer for each image and setting the Black and White points. Turn off the visibility of all Layers except Orion 1. From the Toolbox, select the Eyedropper Tool (keyboard shortcut "I"), hold down the Shift key and click in the main image window to place three Color Sampler Points in representative background sky areas. I chose a point at the left edge, a point at the right edge and a point near the center. Zoom into the bright stars in the Trapezium region and place the fourth Color Sampler here. The bright stars in this Layer have RGB values of around (217, 217, 217). Be sure that the Eyedropper Tool Sample Size is set to "3 by 3 Average". **Figure 10.4** shows the Color Sampler points that I placed.

8. Create a Levels Adjustment Layer (*Layer|New Adjustment Layer|Levels*) directly above the Orion 1 Layer and click OK to close the Levels dialog box. In the Layers Palette, hold down the Alt key

Fig. 10.4 Three Color Sampler Points are placed in different areas of background sky using the Eyedropper Tool. The fourth Color Sampler is placed in the center of a bright Trapezium star. Levels Adjustment Layers are used to independently set the Black and White points of each image Layer, establishing uniform tonal range and color balance.

and move the mouse cursor between the Levels 1 Layer and the Orion 1 Layer until the cursor changes to two overlapping circles, then left-click once. A Clipping Mask is created that links the Levels 1 Layer to the Orion 1 Layer. You may delete the Levels 1 Layer Mask (click-hold and drag it to the trash can icon in the Layers Palette) as we will not need it. Re-open the Levels 1 dialog box (double-click on the Layer Thumbnail). Double-click on the "Set Black Point" Eyedropper and the Color Picker appears. Enter RGB values of (20, 20, 20) and click OK. Double-click on the "Set White Point" Eyedropper, enter RGB values of (245, 245, 245) and click OK. Click on the Black Point Eyedropper in the Levels dialog box, Zoom into the image to one of the background sky Color Samplers (I recommend using the one near the middle of the image) and click once on the Sampler Point. This sets the Black Point. Select the White Point Eyedropper and click once on the Sampler in the Trapezium area to establish the White Point.

9. Repeat step 8 to create Levels Adjustment Layer Clipping Masks for each image Layer and set the Black and White points of each one. Your Layers Palette should now look like **Figure 10.5**.

Yes, this is a lot of work. But if we had used only one Levels Adjustment Layer (or a Curves Layer) at the top of the Layer Stack, and made one overall adjustment, the lower Layers would have been darkened too much and details would have been obscured. Try it and see for yourself. Here, one size does not fit all. We have also removed a Cyan cast in the brighter images that did not appear in the fainter ones.

10. Now we will create our first Layer Mask to blend the details in Orion 1 into Orion 2. Turn off the visibility of all Layers (click off the little "eyeballs" in the Layers Palette) except Orion 1 and Orion 2 and their associated Levels Clipping Masks. Make Orion 2 the active Layer and add a Layer Mask with *Layer|Add Layer Mask|Reveal All*. Zoom the image to 100% and center the Trapezium region in the image window. Activate the Orion 2 Layer Mask by clicking on its Thumbnail in the Layers Palette. From the Toolbox, select the Brush Tool (keyboard shortcut "B"). In the Tool Options (at the top of the Photoshop window), choose a 90 pixel soft-edged Brush and set the Brush Opacity to 20%. Set the Foreground color

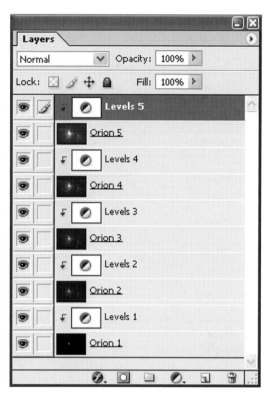

Fig. 10.5 Levels Adjustment Layers have been created and linked to each underlying image by creating Clipping Masks. This permits the color balance of each image to be controlled individually by setting the Black and White points. A single Levels or Curves Layer at the top of the Layer Stack would darken the lower layers too much and obscure detail.

in the Toolbox to black, and paint the Mask in the Trapezium region to reveal details from the Orion 1 Layer. You may want to increase the Opacity of the Brush when painting in the very center of the Trapezium to completely reveal the underlying Layer. Paint with black at 20% Opacity to gradually reveal underlying details. Paint with white to restore details from the Orion 2 Layer. It is helpful to turn the Layer Mask on and off by holding down the Shift key and clicking on its Thumbnail in the Layers Palette (a red "X" appears when it's off). This makes it easier gauge the effect of the Mask. Mask painting is an art that improves the more you do it, and there's no worry about making mistakes. Just keep painting with black or white until it's the way you want it. Lower Brush Opacity to paint with gray and feather the effect. My mask is shown in **Figure 10.6**.

11. Repeat the procedures in step 10 to create Layer Masks for the Orion 3, Orion 4 and Orion 5 Layers. Work to retain the important details from each

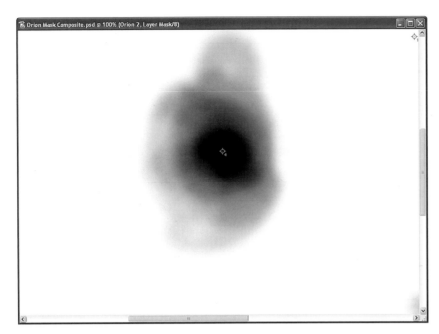

Fig. 10.6 My Layer Mask for the Orion 2 Layer. Painting with black in the center (at 100% Brush Opacity) completely reveals the underlying Trapezium area in the Orion 1 Layer (by hiding this area in the Orion 2 Layer). Using a 20% Opacity Brush produces gray tones that blend both Layers together to create a smooth, seamless transition between images.

underlying Layer that are overexposed and featureless in the Layers above, while still making a smooth and seamless transition between Layers. Make an on-screen duplicate image (*Image|Duplicate*) if it helps your visualization, and turn Layer visibilities and Mask visibilities on and off for the same purpose. Your "eye" becomes accustomed to the on-screen contrast, so A–B comparisons are essential.

12. When you are satisfied with your Layer Masks, re-save the Orion Mask Composite.psd file (*File|Save*). You will need this file for the next tutorial example.

13. Take a look at the Color Sampler points. My white point looks fine. My background sky near the center of the image is a good neutral color also. But the left edge of the image has a red cast and the right edge has an even worse reddish-yellow (orange) cast. Create a Curves Adjustment Layer (*Layer|New Adjustment Layer|Curves*) at the top of the Layer Stack. Let's fix the area on the right, the worse of the two edges. From the Curves dialog box go to the Red Channel and enter a new point with Input/Output values of (19, 8). Go to the Blue Channel and change the Black point to an Input/Output value of (0, 7) and click OK to close the Curves dialog. Yes, the image is an awful shade of Cyan, but the right edge is now neutral. Activate the Curves Layer Mask by clicking on its Thumbnail. From the Toolbox, select the Gradient

Tool (it may be hidden under the Paint Bucket Tool — click-hold to access the Tool flyout selection box). In the *Tool |Options*, choose a "Foreground to Background" pattern and a Linear Gradient. Set the Foreground color to white and the Background color to black. Click-hold at the right edge of the image, drag out a line to around the beginning of the Running Man Nebula (NGC 1977) and release the mouse. Voila. The red-yellow cast at the right is gone and the image is restored to normal. The Curves Layer Mask that I created with the Gradient Tool is shown in **Figure 10.7**. The red cast on the left is not nearly as noticeable. You may similarly correct it, if you wish. There is also a streak on the image (Orion 5) that can be removed with the Clone Stamp Tool or Healing Brush Tool. I will leave it to you to repair it if you wish, although it is not necessary for this example.

14. Now we can make our final contrast and saturation adjustments. Create another Curves Adjustment Layer (*Layer|New Adjustment Layer|Curves*) at the top of the Layer Stack. In the RGB Channel, enter a new point with an Input/Output value of (20, 36) and click OK. If you would like to increase the color saturation, set up a Hue/Saturation Adjustment Layer at the top of the Stack. I preferred the saturation unchanged.

15. If you check the Histogram, you will see that all of our edits have created significant gapping. The

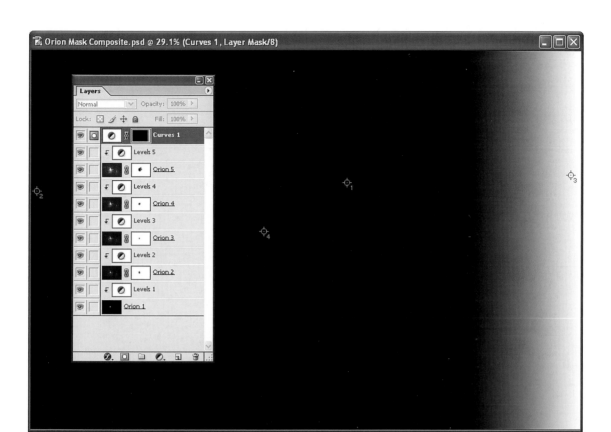

Fig. 10.7 A Curves Adjustment Layer has been set up to correct a strong red-yellow cast at the right side of the image. The Gradient Tool was used to make a linear gradient Layer Mask that applies the correction to the right side only. The gradient tapers off from white to black, allowing the correction to "feather" seamlessly into the rest of the image.

background is also quite noisy. The gapping could have been minimized if we had been able to retain the RAW files in their original 16-bit form. Create a new "combine all" pixel Layer at the top of the Layer Stack by making sure that all Layers are visible and then pressing Shift+Ctrl+Alt+N+E. Apply a light blur to this Layer with *Filter|Blur|Gaussian Blur*, enter a Radius of 0.5 pixels and click OK.

16. Re-save this file (Orion Mask Composite.psd; *File|Save*). We will use it for our next tutorial. The final image compared with the brightest exposure (Orion 5) is shown in **Figure 10.8**.

Creating a Composite using the Layer Style "Blend-If" Sliders

In this example, we will be working with the same Orion Nebula images that we combined with Layer Masks in our first example. Now we will employ a different method to blend together selected tonal ranges from the individual images.

Photoshop provides a wide variety of effects and styles that may be applied to the contents of individual Layers. These Layer Styles are powerful tools that work as informational edits (as compared to pixel edits), much like Adjustment Layers. A particularly useful feature available in the Layer Styles dialog box is the "Blend If" sliders. By varying these sliders, we specify the particular luminance ranges from each Layer that will be blended together in the final image. The Blend If sliders provide a different "look and feel" to the image, compared to using Layer Masks applied to pixel Layers. It is a valuable technique to add to your image-processing repertoire.

1. Once again, we will use Rick Krejci's Orion Nebula digital camera image sequence for our composite. Open the layered file that you created in the first tutorial example (*File|Open*; "Orion Mask Composite.psd"). If you did not save this file, then you will need to combine, align and color balance the individual exposures following steps 1 through 9 of the first tutorial ("Creating a Composite using Lay-

Fig. 10.8 Shown at the top is the brightest single exposure (Orion 5). Below is the Composite of five exposures blended together using Layer Masks. The Composite has a more natural appearance than any of the individual exposures.

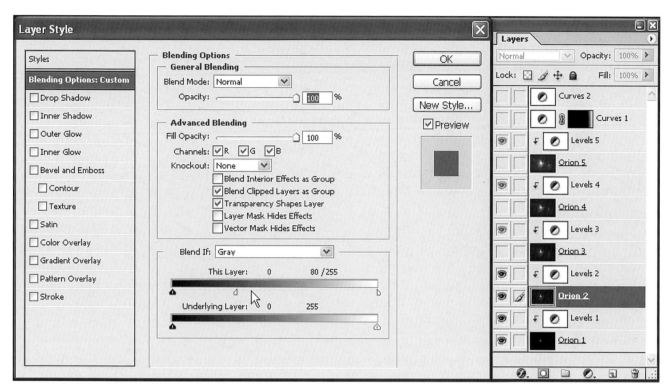

Fig. 10.9 The Layer Style Blending Options "Blend If" sliders regulate how tonal regions between two Layers are combined. Here, luminance values between 80 and 255 in the Orion 2 Layer will be gradually blended into the entire Orion 1 Layer. Holding down the Alt key and clicking on a slider splits it into two sliders. The second "falloff" slider feathers the effect to create smooth, gradual tonal transitions.

er Masks"). Delete the "combine all" Layer at the top of the Layer Stack (click-hold and drag it to the trash can icon at the bottom of the Layers Palette, then release the mouse). Similarly delete the individual Layer Masks from the Orion 2 through Orion 5 Layers. If you delete the masks by dragging them to the trash can, be sure to select "discard" when a dialog box appears asking if you wish to apply the mask before removing it. You may also activate the mask, right-click and select "discard layer mask".

2. In the Layers Palette, turn off the visibility of all Layers (click the "eyeball" icons off) except Orion 1 and Orion 2 and their associated Levels Layers. Zoom into the Trapezium area to a 100% view and make Orion 2 the active layer (click on it — it will be highlighted in blue). Click on the "Add a layer style" icon at the bottom-left of the Layers Palette (it looks like a small "f" surrounded by a black circle). Choose "Blending Options" to open the Layer Style dialog box (**Figure 10.9**). You may also open the Blending Options dialog from the Layers flyout menu (click on the small right-

facing arrow at the top-right of the Layers Palette) or by double-clicking on the Layer image icon.

3. Make sure that the "Blend If" Channel is set to Gray, then click-hold and drag the white slider (the highlight slider) in "This Layer" to the left until the highlight luminance value reads 80 (shadow and highlight values are located directly above the slider scale). The Trapezium area and bright stars darken, since the Blend If sliders drop out everything in the Orion 2 Layer that has a luminance value above 80 (**Figure 10.10**). This makes it fairly easy to preview which tonal areas are being used from each Layer.

4. Hold down the Alt key and click once on the highlight (white) slider for "This Layer". The slider splits into two sliders. Drag the outer white slider all the way to the right. The highlight value now reads 80/255. Tonal values above 80 are gradually tapered off ("falloff") between 80 and 255 (the maximum white value). These pixel values are partially blended with the underlying Layer to create smooth tonal transitions over this range. Click OK to close the Layer Style dialog box.

R. Scott Ireland

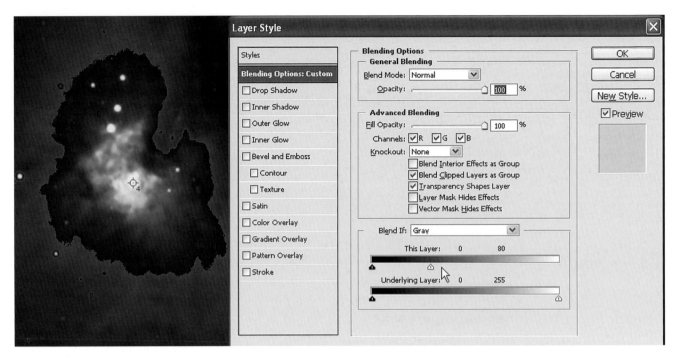

Fig. 10.10 It is easy to preview how Layers will combine using the Blend If sliders without a falloff adjustment. Here, only tonal values between 0 and 80 from the Orion 2 Layer are used, with a hard cutoff at 80. Compare this to the setting in **Figure 10.9**, where the falloff slider was used to feather the effect.

5. Now click on Orion 3 to make it the active Layer (the visibility of the whole Clipping Group turns on automatically). Open the Layer Style Blending Options dialog box for this Layer. Hold down the Alt key and click on the highlight (white) slider for "This Layer" to split it, then drag the left white slider all the way to the left so that the highlight value reads 0/255. Split the highlight (white) slider for the "Underlying Layer" and drag the left white slider to the left until the highlight value reads 19/255. This blends the entire Orion 3 Layer into the shadow regions of Orion 2 with a falloff that extends across the full tonal scale of both Layers. Note that we have not moved the black (shadow) sliders. The shadow values should remain at 0 for both "This Layer" and the "Underlying Layer". Click OK to close the Orion 3 Layer Style dialog.

6. Repeat the process in step 5 for the Orion 4 Layer. Split the white slider for "This Layer" and drag the left white slider to the left until the highlight value reads 20/255. Split the white slider for the "Underlying Layer" and drag the left white slider all the way to the left, so that the highlight value reads 0/255. We continue to gradually blend highlights from the brighter layers into the darker images below. Click OK to close the Layer Style dialog.

7. Repeat the process in step 5 for the Orion 5 Layer. In the General Blending options at the top of the Layer Style dialog, select "Screen" as the Layer Blending Mode and set the Opacity to 80%. Split the white Blend If sliders and move them to establish highlight/falloff values of 23/255 for "This Layer" and 20/116 for the "Underlying Layer" (See **Figure 10.11**). Click OK to close the Orion 5 Layer Style dialog.

We have employed the Blend If sliders to progressively add the brighter areas of each image into the shadow areas of the underlying images. Wide falloff settings maintained smooth tonal transitions from each image to the next. In the brightest image (the Orion 5 Layer), a Screen Layer Blending Mode was used, at a slightly lowered Opacity, to help bring out details in the faint outer areas of the Nebula.

8. Turn on the visibility of the Curves 1 Adjustment Layer. This is the Layer we created with a Gradient Mask to correct the reddish-yellow (orange) cast at the right side of the image. If you did not keep this Layer from the first tutorial, don't worry

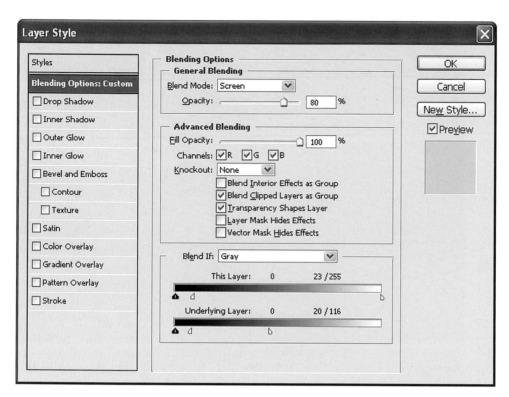

Fig. 10.11 The Layer Blending Options for the brightest image (the Orion 5 Layer). The Blend If sliders have been used to progressively add the brighter areas from each image into the shadow areas of the underlying images. Here we have set the Layer Blending Mode to Screen in order to bring out detail in the faint outer regions of the Nebula.

about re-creating it for this example.

9. Create a Levels Adjustment Layer at the top of the Layer Stack ("Levels 6"). Make sure that the Black Point target RGB values are (20, 20, 20) and the White Point target values are (245, 245, 245), then click on Color Sampler 1 with the Black Point Eyedropper and Color Sampler 4 with the White Point Eyedropper. Click OK to close the Levels dialog. This establishes the overall color balance for the composite image.

10. Create a Curves Adjustment Layer at the top of the Layer Stack. In the RGB Channel, enter two new points (leave the Black and White points alone) with Input/Output values of (13, 19) and (129, 178). Click OK to close the Curves dialog. This increases the brightness and contrast of the three-quarter tones and midtones to bring out the Nebula.

11. Finally, create a new "combine all" pixel Layer at the top of the Layer Stack by making sure that all Layers are visible and then pressing Shift+Ctrl+Alt+N+E. Apply a light blur to this Layer with *Filter\Blur\Gaussian Blur*, enter a Radius of 0.6 pixels and click OK. This smoothes out the posterization (gapped Histogram) caused from processing 8-bit images. The finished Layers Pal-

ette is shown in **Figure 10.12**. The final composite image is compared to the composite created using Layer Masks in **Figure 10.13**.

Compared to the Layer Mask composite, this image is much softer and has a "painterly" feeling. It conveys a diaphanous and ethereal quality. Some days I prefer one version over the other, but I like both renditions. Use whichever method best suits a particular image and your artistic sensibilities.

As this book goes to press, Adobe has released its newest version of Photoshop, Photoshop CS 2. A new function, "Merge to HDR" (*File\Automate\Merge to HDR*) has been added that may greatly simplify the process of creating image composites. HDR stands for "high dynamic range". The tool is designed to combine multiple images with different exposures into a single composite image that spans the full brightness range (dynamic range) of the individual images. In other words, it performs the same function as the methods we examined above. Of particular interest is the fact that the Merge to HDR function uses 32-bit depth floating point arithmetic. This provides an initial tonal scale (you will ultimately want to convert the image to a 16-bit or 8-bit file for printing and other purposes) that should provide smoother tonal transitions, with less posterization and higher image quality. If you plan to do a lot of composites, it may be worth your while to

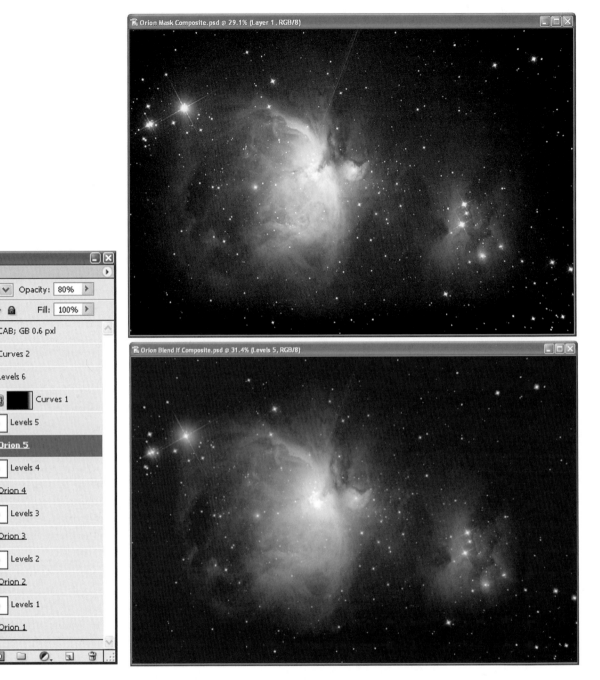

Fig. 10.12 My final Layers Palette for the Orion Composite, created using the Layer Style Blend If sliders.

Fig. 10.13 The top image is the Orion Composite created in the first tutorial using Layer Masks. The bottom image is the Composite from the second tutorial using the Layer Style Blend If sliders. The top image, having greater edge definition, appears sharper and more detailed, while the bottom image conveys a softer, "painterly", more ethereal effect.

invest in this latest incarnation of Photoshop.

Color Channel Composites

In earlier Chapters, we have seen the benefits of working within individual color channels to improve an im-

age. LRGB, channel mixing and similar techniques are in reality composites, whether the information is gleaned from one image or from combinations of separate exposures. Our next tutorial will build on this concept by combining enhanced details obtained in a longer, color-specific exposure with an underlying

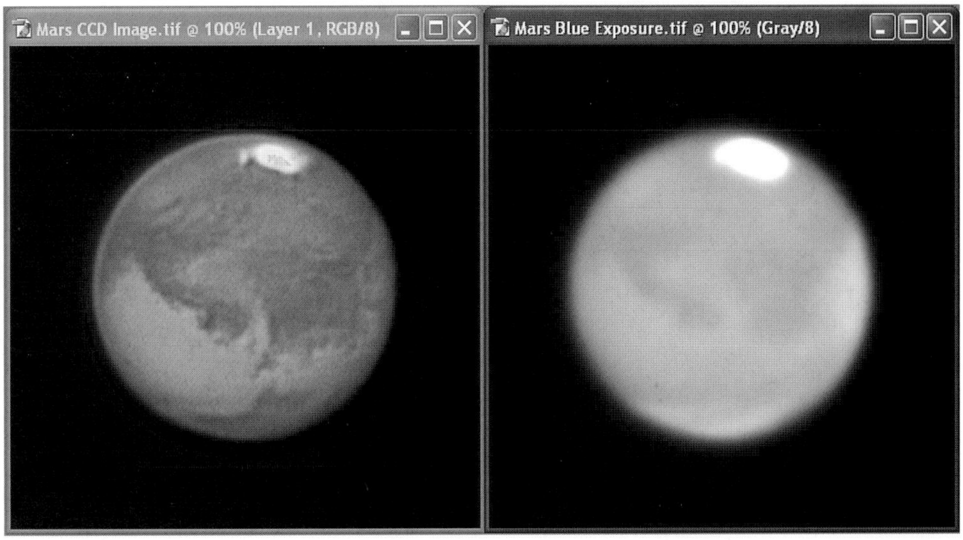

Fig. 10.14 The problem here is to combine the brighter atmospheric features displayed in the deeper blue light exposure (on the right) with a tricolor image of Mars that is properly exposed to show surface features (on the left). Don Parker's solution employs the use of contrast-enhancing Layer Blending Modes to create a Composite of the two images.

RGB image. Don Parker originated this technique to improve the visibility of Martian clouds and limb haze in his images.

1. From the tutorial disc, open the file "Mars CCD Image.tif" (*File|Open*). This is a tri-color image of Mars by Don, taken with an SBIG ST9XE CCD camera through individual RGB filters (**Figure 10.14 Left**). Look closely and you can detect blue limb haze/clouds and a front coming off of the north polar cap. These features are quite faint, and the image could be improved by enhancing their visibility. Open the Channels Palette (*Window|Channels*) and examine the individual color channels. The Blue Channel contains the majority of tonal information for these features. But the clouds are still too faint. No amount of Blue Channel manipulation will give us a usable rendition to blend into the base image. There is simply not enough tonal separation between the Martian surface features and the cloud formations. What we need is a longer blue light exposure.

2. Open the file "Mars Blue Exposure.tif" (*File|Open*) on the tutorial disc (also by Don). This is the exposure we need for the cloud features (**Figure 10.14 Right**). It is, of course, too bright to use as the Blue Channel in the RGB composite. If we merely copied and pasted it into the Blue Channel, the entire image would take on a strong magenta cast (try it). It might be possible to create masks to isolate the clouds and restore proper color balance to the planet's surface, but there is an easier way. We will create a Composite.

3. Make sure that both image windows are visible on your screen. Click on Mars Blue Exposure.tif to make it the active image. Select the Move Tool from the Toolbox (keyboard shortcut "V"). Hold down the Shift key, click-hold in the Mars Blue Exposure.tif image window, drag into the Mars CCD Image.tif window and release the mouse. The blue exposure is copied into a new Layer ("Layer 1") and centered above the Background Layer in the RGB image. These images are already pretty well aligned. If they were not, you could lower the Opacity of Layer 1 and/or set its Layer Blending Mode to "Difference", then use the Move Tool to move Layer 1 into alignment with the Background. Close the Mars Blue Exposure.tif file.

4. Open the Layers Palette of Mars CCD Image.tif (*Window|Layers*). Change the Layer Blending Mode of Layer 1 from "Normal" to "Hard Light" (click on the drop-down selection box at the top-left of the Layers Palette to access Layer Blending Modes). Lower the Opacity of Layer 1 to 75%.

"Hard Light" is one of the contrast-enhancing Layer Blending Modes. It is a member of the same family as "Overlay", "Soft Light" and others grouped together in one section of the Layer Blending Mode list. Hard Light will either darken (Multiply) or lighten (Screen) the base image Layer, depending upon the tonality of the overlying Layer. In this case, the entire blue exposure (Layer 1) is lighter than 50% gray, so the whole image is lightened. More contrast is retained, however, than would be the case if Screen mode were used.

R. Scott Ireland

5. Application of the blue exposure in Layer 1 has caused us to lose too much edge detail in the polar cap. Make sure Layer 1 is the active Layer and choose *Layer\Add Layer Mask\Reveal All*. In the Toolbox, set the Foreground color to black and choose the Brush Tool (keyboard shortcut "B"). In the Brush Tool Options at the top of the Photoshop window, choose a soft-edged 20 pixel Brush and set the Brush Opacity to 10%. Click on the mask icon to make it active and "paint" the polar cap with black to restore details. In actuality, because of the low Brush Opacity, you will be painting with gray to gradually blend in detail from the underlying Layer. If you "overshoot" and darken the cap too much, just change the Foreground color to white and paint the mask to make corrections.

6. When you are satisfied with your mask, Duplicate Layer 1 by click-holding and dragging it to the "Create a new layer" icon (two overlapping squares) at the bottom of the Layers Palette, then release the mouse. "Layer 1 copy" appears at the top of the Layers Palette. Note that the Layer Mask, Blending Mode and Layer Opacity were copied also. Lower the Opacity of the Layer 1 copy Layer to 20%.

7. Add a Curves Adjustment Layer at the top of the Layer Stack (*Layer\New Adjustment Layer\Curves*). In the RGB Channel, enter a new adjustment point with Input/Output values of (146, 102) and click OK to close the Curves dialog. The image was getting too bright to continue work. Now back to our cloud layers.

8. Make Layer 1 copy the active layer (click on it) and open the Unsharp Mask filter (*Filter\Sharpen\Unsharp Mask*). Enter an Amount of 500%, a Radius of 5 pixels, set Threshold to 0 and click OK. This sharpens up the clouds a bit and gives them more definition. You may wish to rename this Layer to "USM 500, 5, 0" in order to keep track of the pixel edit applied. This is a good habit to get into. At this point, make any final adjustments to your Layer Masks.

9. The last thing needed is to add just a touch of blue/cyan to the cloud features. Normally, I would handle this with Curves and Layer Masks, but here we can manage it using a coarser adjustment tool. Add a Color Balance Adjustment Layer at the top of the Layer Stack (*Layer\New Adjustment Lay-*

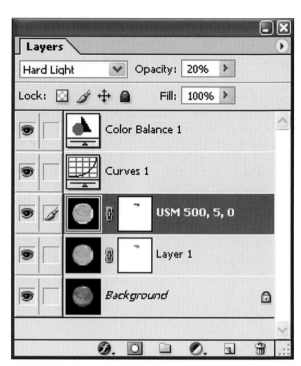

Fig. 10.15 The Layers Palette for the Color Channel Composite of Mars.

er\Color Balance). In the Color Balance dialog box, click the "Highlights" button, enter a Magenta/Green value of +11 and a Yellow/Blue value of +26. Leave Cyan/Red at 0. Now click the "Midtones" button and enter a Cyan/Red value of +16 and a Magenta/Green value of +9. Leave the Yellow/Blue Midtones at 0. Make sure that the "Preserve Luminosity" box is checked and click OK to close the dialog. **Figure 10.15** shows my completed Layers Palette. The final Composite image is shown in **Figure 10.16**.

Creating a Mosaic

While composites allow us to transcend the dynamic range and temporal limitations of our imaging devices, mosaics deal with plain, old-fashioned geography (or celestial cartography). We take multiple "side-by-side" and/or "up-and-down" frames, with each frame slightly overlapping the ones next to it, then we "stitch" them together. It is Quilting for photographers.

Mosaics allow us to widen our photographic field-of-view without resorting to the use of a shorter focal length optical system. We simply move the lens or telescope and photograph the adjacent fields. The end result is a wide-field image with much higher resolution.

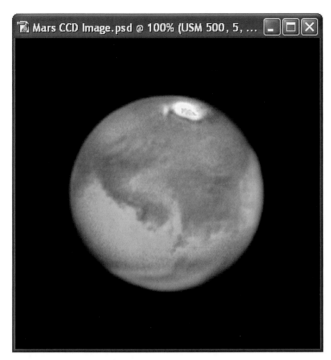

Fig. 10.16 The final Color Channel Composite of the two images shown in **Figure 10.14**. Clouds, atmospheric haze and surface features are all clearly visible.

Consider the humble webcam image containing 640 pixels by 480 pixels. To capture a wider field, we could of course employ a shorter focal length lens. But the total field-of-view would still be rendered within those 640 by 480 pixels. If, however, we moved the optical/ camera system and took 6 images — 3 side-by-side and then moved "down" and took another 3 side-by-side — we will have elevated our modest webcam resolution to a more respectable 1,920 pixels (3 side by side columns of 640 pixels) by 960 pixels (2 up and down rows of 480 pixels). Well, actually the pixel dimensions would be a little lower than this, since we have to overlap the images to line them up in Photoshop, but you get the idea.

As you can see, mosaics allow us to overcome some of the limitations of a small imaging sensor. The tradeoff is the time and trouble required to take multiple images and then stitch them together.

In our next example, we will build a partial lunar mosaic using a selection of frames taken by Robert Reeves with a ToUCam webcam.

1. On the tutorial disc you will find a folder entitled "Mosaic". It contains nine individual stacked webcam images. These were selected from a larger group of images taken by Robert Reeves in order

to construct a mosaic of the entire lunar surface. There is also a file on disc entitled "Moon Mosaic.psd". This is one of those rare instances when I am providing you with the finished product. Moon Mosaic.psd is the mosaic I created using the same nine frames, with all layers, adjustment layers and masks intact. There are quite a few steps and complications in this exercise, so I felt that having a finished file for comparison might prove instructive.

2. Before we go any further, we must do a little math (sorry). Capturing images for a mosaic, and then constructing one, takes a little forward planning. During capture, you will want to overlap the adjacent images by 20% to 30% or so to make stacking and blending them together in Photoshop (or any other program) more expeditious. It is also helpful to lay out your exposures in advance with a simple graphic on paper. Here we already have the images, so next we need to make a canvas in Photoshop that will accommodate them. If you examine the individual frames in the Mosaic folder, you will find that they have the following pixel dimensions:

row 1-1.tif	637 x 477 pixels
row 1-2.tif	636 x 476 pixels
row 1-3.tif	635 x 476 pixels
row 1-4.tif	636 x 476 pixels
row 2-1.tif	636 x 476 pixels
row 2-2.tif	636 x 474 pixels
row 2-3.tif	636 x 476 pixels
row 2-4.tif	616 x 476 pixels
row 2-5.tif	636 x 476 pixels

The images were taken with a "landscape" orientation in mind, so if we combine the long dimensions of the first row, we see that row 1 requires a canvas 2,544 pixels wide and 477 pixels high. Since we don't really know how may pixels overlap between images, we must be conservative in our estimates. We can easily crop out any excess canvas when we are finished. Similarly, row 2 requires a canvas 3,160 pixels wide and 476 pixels high. The combination of rows 1 and 2 will require a canvas of at least 3,160 by 953 pixels. In order to leave ourselves plenty of "breathing room", we will use a canvas 3,800 pixels wide by 1,600 pixels high.

3. Open a new file in Photoshop with *File|New*. A di-

R. Scott Ireland

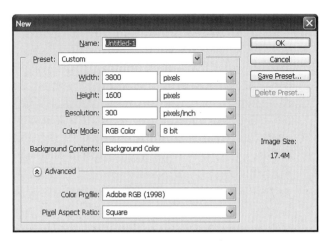

Fig. 10.17 The *File|New* dialog box is used to create a Photoshop canvas with sufficient size to contain the finished mosaic.

alog box appears similar to **Figure 10.17**. Enter the following values: a width of 3800 pixels; a height of 1600 pixels; 300 pixels/inch; set "Color Mode" or "Mode" to RGB Color and set the "Background Contents" or "Contents" to Background Color. If you have additional choices (Photoshop CS or later) use 8-bit mode, the Adobe RGB (1998) color space and a square pixel aspect ratio. Note that you must also have the Toolbox Background Color set to Black, since we want our canvas to have a black background. When all settings are entered, click OK to close the dialog box. A long, rectangular image window should appear, filled with black. Save this file (*File|Save As*) in the Photoshop "*.psd" format with the name "Mosaic.psd".

4. From the tutorial disc, open the four images in row 1 (*File|Open*), "row 1-1.tif" through "row 1-4.tif". If missing profile dialog boxes appear, just select "Leave as is (don't color manage)" — it will not matter in this case.

5. Make row 1-1.tif the active image and access the Layers Palette (*Window|Layers*). Click-hold and drag the Background Layer from row 1-1.tif into the Mosaic.psd image window, then release the mouse. The image is automatically copied into a new Layer ("Layer 1"). Close the row 1-1.tif file.

6. Repeat step 5 and copy the row 1-2.tif image into the mosaic. Our canvas now contains the two top-left images of our mosaic, each in its own Layer. Now we will roughly place and align them. Acti-

vate Layer 1 (click on it) and select the Move Tool from the Toolbox (keyboard shortcut "V"). In the image window, click-hold and drag the image to move it into the desired position. Do the same for Layer 2. You can see the overlap between these images easily, which facilitates rough alignment. Don't worry about being precise. We will carefully align the images once we have copied all of them into the Layer Stack. Your mosaic should now look like **Figure 10.18**.

7. Repeat steps 4 through 6 to copy, in order, the remaining row 1 images and all five of the row 2 images into the Layer Stack of Mosaic.psd. In order to move multiple Layers together as one unit, you may link them by clicking on the small box to the right of the visibility ("Eyeball") box in the Layers Palette. A small "chain link" icon is displayed for all linked layers. Click again to unlink them (the chain link icon disappears). Leave the Background Layer unlinked. In Photoshop CS2 this procedure has been changed. You must first select layers to be linked, and then click on the "Link Layers" icon at the bottom of the Layers Palette. Linked Layers make it easy to reposition the entire mosaic. Just remember to unlink them when you are done. See **Figure 10.19**.

8. In the Layers Palette, be sure that all Layers are unlinked (no "chain link" icons are visible) and turn off the visibility of all Layers (click off the "Eyeball" icons) except for the Background Layer, Layer 1 and Layer 2. Set the Layer 2 Blending Mode to "Difference" (click on the drop-down selection box at the top-left of the Layers Palette to access Layer Blending Modes). Zoom into the image to around 100%. Use the Move Tool and the keyboard arrow keys to reposition Layer 2 until it is carefully aligned with Layer 1. This is the same technique we learned in **Chapter 5** on Stacking. Move Layer 2 until the area that overlaps Layer 1 "blanks out" and becomes predominantly black. Use the keyboard arrow keys to move one pixel at a time. When the Layers are aligned, change the Layer 2 Blending Mode back to "Normal".

9. Turn on the visibility of Layer 3, change the Blending Mode to "Difference", and align it with the underlying Layers using the Move Tool and keyboard arrow keys. Do the same thing for Layers 4 through 9, working progressively up the Layer Stack. Don't forget to reset all of the Layer

Blending Modes back to "Normal" after they are aligned.

10. Create a Threshold Adjustment Layer (*Layer|New Adjustment Layer|Threshold*) and place it at the top of the Layer Stack, above Layer 9. In the Threshold dialog box, move the slider to estimate the darkest and lightest points in the combined set of images. Move the cursor into the image window (it automatically changes to an Eyedropper), hold down the Shift key and click to place Color Samplers for the Black and White points. My Black point resides in the Layer 5 image, and my White point is in Layer 3.

Determining the Black and White points requires some thought, since there are several possible candidates in these images. The idea is to identify the darkest and lightest areas that may be able to hold image detail. These points often prove to be useful anchors when determining how to array the tonalities of the mosaic. With color images, they also aid in achieving color balance.

After setting the Black and White points, you may discard the Threshold Adjustment Layer. If you want to leave it for later reference, turn off its visibility for the remainder of this exercise.

11. In the Layers Palette, place a Levels Adjustment Layer (*Layer|New Adjustment Layer|Levels*) di-rectly above Layer 1. Create a Clipping Mask with Layer 1 by holding down the Alt key and moving the cursor between Layer 1 and the Levels Adjustment Layer until the cursor changes into two, overlapping circles, then click once. A down arrow appears next to the Adjustment Layer icon and the Layer 1 name is underlined, indicating a Clipping Mask. Levels adjustments made here will apply only to Layer 1. In the same way, create Levels Adjustment Layers/Clipping Masks for each of Layers 2 through 9. When finished, your Layers Palette should look like **Figure 10.20**.

It is of course possible to adjust the tonal range of each image prior to combining them in the mosaic file, or even before bringing them into Photoshop. However, my preference is to minimize destructive edits and retain as much control as possible over each image for fine-tuning the overall mosaic tonal range. This is best accomplished using individual Adjustment Layers. If the Layer Stack becomes too unwieldy, Layer Sets (Layer Groups in Photoshop CS2) may be created to streamline its appearance.

12. Turn off the visibility of all Layers except the Background, Layer 1, Levels 1 and Layer 5. Open the Levels 1 dialog box and in the RGB Channel, move the Input Levels midtone slider (the middle slider under the Histogram) until Layer 1 blends smoothly into Layer 5. You should end up with a

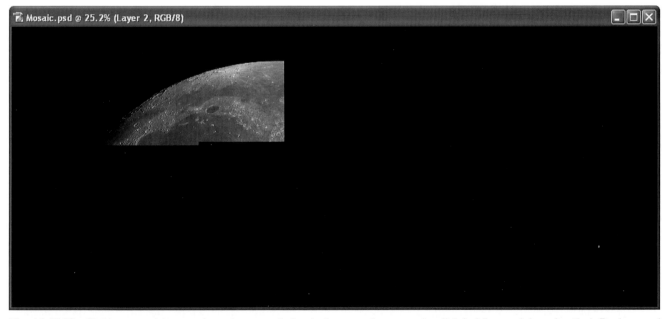

Fig. 10.18 The first two row 1 images have been copied onto the mosaic canvas by click-holding and dragging their Background layers into the mosaic image window. Each is automatically placed into its own Layer. Using the Move Tool, the images have been roughly aligned and placed on the canvas.

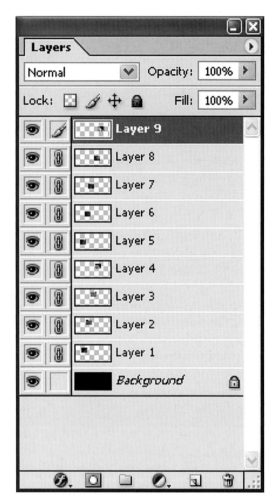

Fig. 10.19 The Layers Palette after all images have been copied into the mosaic canvas. Note that Layers 1 through 9 have been linked (the small "chain link" icons are displayed) and the Background is **not** linked. In this configuration, the Move Tool will move all of the linked Layers together as one unit, allowing the entire mosaic to be repositioned easily. Be sure to unlink the Layers after repositioning. In Photoshop CS2, layers are first selected (Control+Click) and then linked by clicking on the "Link layers" icon at the bottom-left of the Layers Palette.

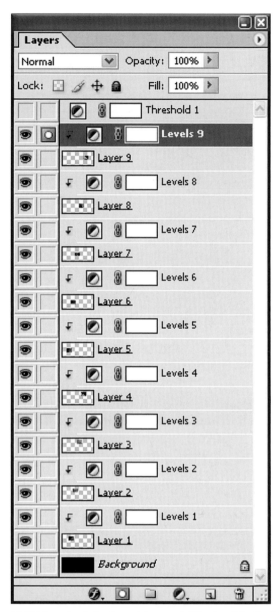

Fig. 10.20 Levels Adjustment Layers/ Clipping Masks have been created that allow the tonal range of each image to be adjusted and re-adjusted independently of the other images. Layer Sets (Layer groups in Photoshop CS2) could also be used to streamline the appearance of the Layers Palette.

midtone Input Level of around 1.17. You may find it helpful to Zoom into the image to around 100% when making these tonal adjustments.

13. Make Layer 2 and Levels 2 visible (leave the underlying Layers and Layer 5 visible) and blend the brightness of Layer 2 into Layer 1 using the Levels 2 midtone slider. In this case, a midtone Input Level of around 1.21 blends the darker areas well (at the bottom of the frame) but leaves the upper part of the frame too dark. A value of 1.28 works better for the upper areas. Move the midtone slider

to set a value of 1.28 and click OK to close the Levels 2 dialog box. In the Toolbox, set the Foreground Color to Black and the Background Color to White. Select the Gradient Tool (keyboard shortcut "G"). In the Tool Options at the top of the Photoshop window, select "Foreground to Background" from the drop-down selection box; choose a Linear Gradient, check the "Dither" box and set the Tool Opacity to 25%. Click on the

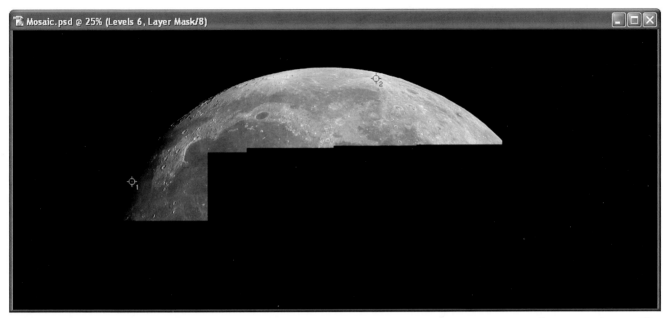

Fig. 10.21 The tonal ranges of all the first row images have been matched using the individual Levels Adjustment Layers. The frame containing the darkest areas with detail (adjacent to the Black point) was used as the starting point.

Levels 2 Layer Mask thumbnail to activate the mask (if you do not have a Layer Mask, create one with *Layer\Add Layer Mask\Reveal All*). In the image window, click-hold near the bottom of the Layer 2 image and drag about 2/3 of the way up the frame, then release the mouse. The bottom of Layer 2 should now darken slightly and blend into the adjacent frame. The Gradient Tool smoothly matches the differing brightness levels across the frame by "holding back" some of the Levels adjustment near the bottom, but allowing the full adjustment at the top. Creating a good Gradient blend is an art that improves with practice. It is helpful to turn the mask on and off (Shift-click on the Layer Mask thumbnail) to evaluate the result. If you need some guidance, open "Moon Mosaic.psd" and examine my Levels 2 Layer Mask.

Do you see the pattern in this procedure? In this case, we start from the Black point, the area around which contains the darkest areas of the image where we want to hold detail. My Black point is in Layer 5. If your Black point is in a different layer, you could change the matching sequence and start from there. For the purposes of this exercise, we are using Layer 5 as the starting point. We then work outward one section at a time and blend each image into the previous one using the individual Levels Adjustment Layers and Masks. We are only adjusting grayscale brightness lev-

els and not color, since the original frames are all grayscale. We did not really need to set this image up in RGB Mode, it could just as well have been a Grayscale image. But, when working on color mosaics, you will need to balance color as well as brightness. In these cases, Curves Adjustment Layers may be created above the Levels layers and added to the Clipping Masks. A Levels/Curves combination for each layer provides a great deal of control over color balance, contrast and brightness.

14. Make Layer 3 and Levels 3 visible and adjust Levels 3 to blend Layer 3 into Layer 2. Here a midtone setting of 1.31 works well without the necessity of a Layer Mask.

15. Now make Layer 4 and Levels 4 visible and blend Layer 4 (using Levels 4) into Layer 3. A midtone setting of 1.37 for Levels 4 will do the job without a Layer Mask.

OK, take a break. The easy part is finished! Your mosaic should now resemble **Figure 10.21**.

16. Turn on the visibility of Layer 6 and Levels 6 (and leave the visibility of all underlying Layers on). This image is going to require more than just a midtone adjustment. Open the Levels 6 dialog box and move the Output Levels Black point (shadow) slider from 0 to 72. Move the Input Levels midtone slider to 0.76 and click OK to close the dia-

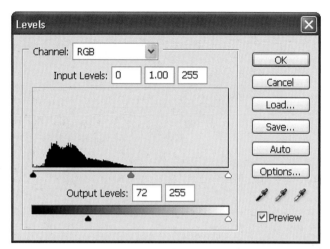

Fig. 10.22 Moving the Output Levels Black and White sliders redefines the tonal range between Black and White. Moving the Input Levels Black and White sliders remaps image pixels over that tonal range. The above setting is equivalent to the Curves adjustment of **Figure 10.23**.

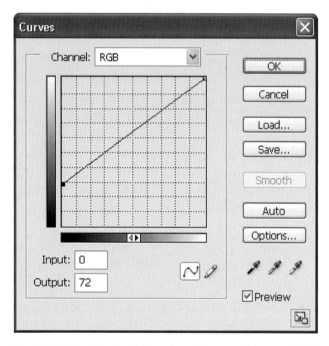

Fig. 10.23 The Black point has been increased from a brightness level of 0 to 72. This is equivalent to the Levels setting of **Figure 10.22**. Because the Curve has been flattened in all areas, overall contrast is decreased.

log. We have used Output Levels to redefine the Black point to begin at a brightness Level of 72. This raises overall brightness while flattening the Curve between black and white, reducing overall contrast (**Figures 10.22** and **10.23**).

17. Make Layer 6 active and add a Layer Mask with

Layer\Add Layer Mask\Reveal All. We will use this Layer Mask to blend the seams between images together. But before continuing, step back and examine Layer 6 in context. The image quality is not as high as the adjacent frames. We should try to use less of this image in the overlapping areas, and blend in more of the adjacent images.

18. Activate the Layer 6 Mask (click on its thumbnail). In the Toolbox, set the Foreground color to black and choose an 80 pixel soft-edged Brush (keyboard shortcut "B"). Set the Brush Opacity to 50%. Paint the Layer Mask with black in the overlapping areas to reveal more of the adjacent layers. Fine-tune the Mask by painting with black or white until the images blend together seamlessly. Lower the Brush Opacity for an even finer level of control.

19. Turn on the visibility of Layer 7 and Levels 7. Open the Levels 7 dialog box, move the Output Levels Black point slider from 0 to 77 and click OK to close the dialog. Add a Layer Mask to Layer 7 and follow the procedures outlined in step 18 to paint the Mask and blend the seams. You may wish to go back and fine-tune the Layer 6 Layer Mask at this point also, in the areas where Layers 6 and 7 intersect.

20. Follow the same procedure with Layer 8 and Levels 8. Open Levels 8 and reset the Output Levels Black point from 0 to 79. Create a Layer 8 Layer Mask and paint the Mask to blend the seams.

21. With Layer 9, you may once again match the images using only the midtone slider. Turn on the visibility of Layer 9 and Levels 9. Open the Levels 9 dialog, move the midtone slider to a value of 1.30 and click OK to close the dialog. Use a 100 pixel soft-edged Brush at a 10% to 20% Opacity and paint the Levels 9 Layer Mask with Black to blend it into the adjacent image.

Our mosaic is almost complete! All that remains is to make final global and local contrast adjustments, and apply some sharpening.

22. Add a Curves Adjustment Layer (*Layer\New Adjustment Layer\Curves*) at the top of the Layer Stack. If you kept the Threshold Layer, put the Curves Layer just below it. In the RGB Channel of the Curves dialog box, adjust the Input/Output value of the Black point to (0,9); adjust the Input/Output value of the White point to (255, 250) and

Fig. 10.24 The final mosaic created from Robert Reeves' nine individually stacked webcam images. Mosaics provide a means to transcend resolution and field limitations inherent in an image capture system.

add two new points with Input/Output values of (20, 16) and (229, 243). The Black/White point adjustments bring our tonal range endpoints together a bit, while the other two points build an "S" Curve to enhance overall contrast. Paint the Curves 1 Layer Mask with black, using a 10–20% Opacity soft-edged Brush, wherever you want to reduce the effect of this Curve. I applied some masking to the brightest highlight/quarter tone areas, in order to hold these tonal values as we make another Curves adjustment.

23. The image looks fine at this point, but I would like to darken the maria regions more and increase contrast in these areas without blowing out the highlights. Create another Curves Adjustment Layer above the Curves 1 Layer. In the RGB Channel, enter three new points with Input/Output values as follows: (30, 9), (151, 135) and (235, 247). Leave the Black and White points unchanged. This is another "S" Curve that gives the image too much contrast, but we can easily adjust it to suit our taste. Reduce the Layer Opacity of the Curves 2 Layer to 65%. Now paint the Curves 2 Layer Mask with black (using a 10–20% Opacity soft-edged Brush) wherever you want to reduce the effect of this Curve. The maria regions

are located in the three-quarter tone/midtone region, so I masked the darker shadow areas (near the Black point/Eyedropper #1) which had become too dark after making this adjustment.

24. Create a "combine all" Layer at the top of the Layer Stack with Shift+Ctrl+Alt+N+E. Open *Filter|Blur|Gaussian Blur*, enter a Radius of 0.4 pixels and click OK. Rename this Layer to "CAB; GB 0.4 pxls" ("combine all below; Gaussian Blur 0.4 pixels"). This slight blur will help to smooth out the Histogram and improve the cosmetic sharpening we are going to perform in the next step.

25. Duplicate the CAB; GB 0.4 pxls Layer (click-hold and drag it to the "Create a new layer" icon at the bottom of the Layers Palette, then release the mouse). Open *Filter|Sharpen|Unsharp Mask*, enter an Amount of 300%, a Radius of 1.0 pixels and a Threshold of 5 levels and click OK to close the dialog and apply sharpening.

26. Finally, select the Crop Tool from the Toolbox (keyboard shortcut "C"), then click-hold and drag to create a Crop marquee (border) around the part of the image that you wish to keep. Placement does not have to be precise, since you can apply adjustments to it prior to actually performing the

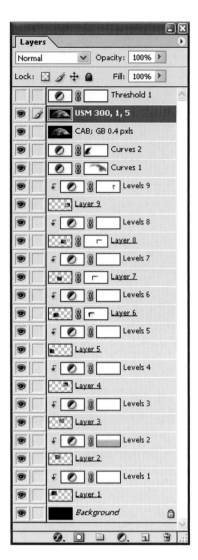

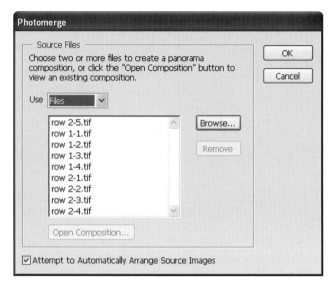

Fig. 10.25 (Left) The final Layers Palette for the mosaic. Yes, it's a whopper. But by working in Layers, we retain the maximum amount of flexibility and creative control over the end result.

Fig. 10.26 Photomerge (*File | Automate | Photomerge*) is an automated tool that greatly simplifies arranging images for a mosaic/panorama. It is available in Photoshop CS and has been upgraded to handle 16-bit images in Photoshop CS2.

crop. Reposition the Crop marquee by click-dragging inside it, or change its dimensions by click-holding and dragging any of the corner or side "handles" (small boxes). When you are satisfied with the composition, press the Enter key to execute the crop.

The final mosaic is shown in **Figure 10.24**. **Figure 10.25** shows the final Layers Palette. The Photoshop file — Moon Mosaic.psd — is on the tutorial disc for your reference.

Adobe has incorporated an automatic mosaic/panorama maker into Photoshop CS, known as "Photomerge" (*File\Automate\Photomerge*). In Photoshop CS2, Photomerge has been further enhanced to handle 16-bit images. This tool can be a real time-saver and it is well worth your time to explore its capabilities. The initial dialog box allows you to select the images or folder of images to be combined (**Figure 10.26**). When you click "OK", Photoshop automatically opens the images, places them into individual layers and aligns them. You are then presented with the dialog box shown in **Figure 10.27**. If you check the "Advanced Blending" box, Photoshop will try to match the tonalities of the various images. One nice feature is that you may preview this adjustment before accepting it. Although it does a remarkably good job of balancing disparate tones, as with all such automated tonal and color adjustments you can probably do a better job yourself. Instead, check "Keep as Layers" and let Photoshop set up all of your mosaic images in layers and align them. You may then fine-tune the alignment, if necessary, and proceed to make tonal, color and contrast adjustments. This is a very worthwhile and time-saving tool.

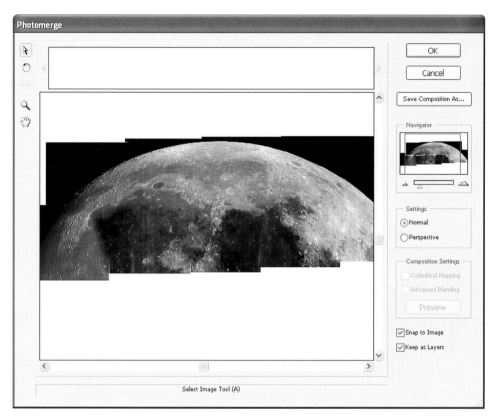

Fig. 10.27 Photomerge does a very nice job of lining up the mosaic images, although its automated tonal adjustments are not sufficient to handle the darkest images in this set. Check the "Keep as Layers" box and use this tool to set up individual image Layers and perform an initial alignment. Rely on your own judgment for final alignment, tonal and color adjustments.

Chapter 11
Sizing Images for Printing and Web Display

If you have been working through this book from the beginning you know how to make a "finished" image. You have applied all of your newfound image-processing skills and your virtuosity has produced an image that looks great on your computer monitor. You now want to share it with others and to bask in the "oooo-hhs" and "aaaahhhs" you so richly deserve. After all, capturing an astronomical image and processing it is no cakewalk.

But you are not quite done — there's a little bit more that we need to know about pixels, paper and computer monitors before your image is completely "finished". This chapter will explore how to finalize your image in order to make a print, or to display it on the Web. Web display is really the same thing as computer monitor display, so an image prepared for the Web should also be suitable for email and other convenient methods of sharing digital images.

It is always advisable to perform as many image-processing steps as you can on the largest practical *original* file. Put simply, having a larger bundle of information (pixels) to work on is better than working on a smaller bundle. A larger file can "handle" more processing manipulations than a smaller one, with less potential for introducing processing artifacts. Having more pixels to work with also facilitates making larger prints and other high-quality output. Especially when working with astrophotos it is better to work on 16-bit images and only convert them to 8-bits when necessary. The 16-bit information will maintain smoother tonal gradations and will hold up to more post-processing steps than an 8-bit file. Since the introduction of Photoshop CS, it is easier to work directly on 16-bit files.

So, what do I mean by the largest "original" file size? I mean starting off with a file containing all the pixels available from your CCD camera, film scanner, digital camera, webcam or other image capture device (input sources). If your input source is a 4000 dpi (dots per inch — pixels per inch, or ppi is a more correct description) film scanner, and you are scanning a 35mm image (1.5 inches wide by 1 inch high), then by using the full resolution of your scanner the resulting pixel dimensions of your image will be approximately 6000 x 4000 pixels. It is the physical, optical/mechanical resolution of the scanner that is important. You want the maximum number of pixels that the hardware (not the interpolation software) can deliver.

If you are using an SBIG ST10 CCD camera, using the chip to its full capacity will deliver an image of 2184 x 1472 pixels. A Philips ToUCam webcam set to its full capability will produce video files with individual frame sizes of 640 x 480 pixels. With both of these cameras it is possible to set the device to deliver fewer pixels. The ST10 may be set to deliver a partial frame image, rather than the full frame. The ToUCam may be set to deliver half-frame video (320 x 240 pixels). Similarly, my film scanner can be set to 2000 dpi, 2800 dpi, or some other resolution lower than 4000 dpi. However, as a general rule, you should always capture as much information (pixels) as your input source can deliver.

As with every rule, there are exceptions. You may decide that capturing a 2¼-inch medium format film image in 16 bits at 4000 dpi, is simply not worth the huge file sizes (500 to 600 megabytes). Perhaps you are satisfied with the print sizes that can be obtained from a 2000 dpi file instead. Be sure to consider the fact that this technology will continue to change rapidly. Making a smaller film scan today, with the idea that you can always go back and make a larger one in the future may not be a wise policy. Scanners may become a thing of the past. Your current scanner may not be supported by future computers or software. The original film may become lost or damaged or faded. Similar arguments can be made for digital cameras and other input devices.

The point you should take away from this discussion is to be informed on this subject and to make intelligent choices in your workflow, based upon your particular needs and goals. It is my general practice to capture the highest resolution optical/mechanical output (not by using the device's interpolation software) that is available from the imaging devices that I use (film scanner, CCD camera, digital camera, webcam). I always scan slides and transparencies at my film scanner's full 4000 dpi output. I always capture video from my webcam at 640 x 480 pixels with settings for as little video compression as possible. I always capture full resolution RAW files with my digital camera. This results in much larger file sizes, but you never know how big you may wish to ultimately print the image, or how much more image processing you may wish to perform on it later. More pixels are good insurance.

PPI, DPI, Size and Resolution

The concepts of ppi, dpi and a resolution are common sources of confusion. It is worth reviewing these concepts again to see how they impact the sizing and printing of images.

Put simply, pixels (picture elements) are the defining characteristic of a digital image. Period. A digital image consists of one thing and one thing only — a two dimensional matrix of pixels defined as a certain number of pixels in width and height (the "pixel dimensions"). Once you know the pixel dimensions of an image, that's it, you're done! Everything else is just jockeying those pixels around to create the type of video display or output that you need for a particular purpose.

For example, a 4000 *dpi* scanner is really a 4000 *ppi* scanner, in other words, it scans a piece of film and produces an image with 4000 pixels for each inch of film. A 35mm film image is 1.5 inches wide by 1 inch high. You end up with a scanned image 6000 pixels wide by 4000 pixels high. The resolution of that image is 4000 ppi, the mechanical/optical limit of your input device, the scanner.

Dots-per-inch and pixels-per-inch do not necessarily mean the same thing but they are often used interchangeably. Let's consider an RGB color image. One pixel may represent a particular color out of millions of possibilities. An 8-bit RGB image consists of 256 possible grayscale levels in each channel — red, green and blue. When combined, these give us a color image that is 256 red levels times 256 green levels times 256 blue levels, which results in around 16.8 million possible colors for any given pixel.

Now let's consider output to an inkjet printer. A photographic quality color inkjet printer typically has 6 to 8 different ink colors. Even the most basic printer will have at least 4 different inks. How do you get 16.8 million colors with just 4 to 8 different ink colors? The printer does not create a single dot for each pixel in your image. Instead, it creates a pattern of individual color ink droplets, laid down side-by-side, to simulate the color of each individual image pixel. This process is known as "dithering". Your printer, therefore, can use more than one dot to represent a given image pixel. In this case, dots are not the same thing as pixels. While it is correct to think of *pixels* as defining an image and *dots* as droplets of ink from a printer or printing press, be aware that dpi is most often used to mean the same thing as ppi.

Size and Resolution

A digital image has no size or resolution. As we discussed above, it is defined only as a number of pixels in two dimensions. When we attempt to *do something* with our image, *then* size and resolution *are* important.

Size and resolution are instructions that we give to our computer graphics card or image-processing program (like Photoshop) to tell them what to do with the pixels in our image; how to display them and how to print them. The size that an image appears on your computer monitor can vary greatly. In Photoshop, the Zoom tool allows you to enlarge or decrease the displayed image. Your computer graphics card can be set to display greater or fewer pixels on the screen, and this will also affect how your image appears. Monitor screen sizes vary. Some software programs automatically scale an image to fit in a window on the screen. But none of these things alter your image. If it is a 2000 x 2000 pixel image, then it remains a 2000 x 2000 pixel image no matter how much you zoom in and out, or otherwise change your monitor settings. The only thing that changes is how you view the image on your screen.

Resolution numbers often create confusion. But there are only three things that should concern us: (1) Input resolution which we have just discussed in the prior section, (2) Computer monitor resolution, and, (3) Output resolution.

Computer Monitor Resolution, including digital projectors

Computer monitors typically display between 72 and 100 pixels-per-inch (ppi). You will hear people say that you should only use 72 to 100 ppi/dpi when preparing image files for the Web or for a PowerPoint presentation, since a computer monitor cannot display any higher resolution. The additional information will not improve the quality of the displayed image. More resolution therefore is a waste, creating an unnecessarily large image file. All of this is true. However, in practice, it is much easier to just think in terms of pixel dimensions, rather than pixels per inch and the size of the computer screen or other digital display. "Inches" means nothing to a computer. It deals only in pixels.

The average computer monitor is usually set to display an Super Video Graphics Array (SVGA) resolution of 800 x 600 pixels or 1024 x 768 pixels (width x height). It is easy to resize your images to fit within these parameters by just changing the pixel dimensions of the images, rather than worrying about specific screen sizes and ppi. So, when preparing images for Web display, or any computer-related display, all we have to concern ourselves with is the image's pixel dimensions and the pixel dimensions of the monitor, which is also known as the screen resolution.

Output Resolution (typically print output)

With normal vision and reading distances humans are generally incapable of resolving detail beyond about 133 to 150 dots per inch. Historically, high quality magazines and books have used a 133 line halftone screen to reproduce photographic images. Recently, with improvements in paper, inks and presses, the 133 line screen is being replaced by a 150 line screen. An image consisting of dots smaller than this visual 133–150 dot threshold appears to us as a continuous tone image. We do not see the individual dots. Instead, we perceive an image consisting of smooth, continuous tonal gradations.

When sizing images for printing, it is important to consider both output size (paper size) and resolution. For maximum quality, it has long been a standard in the printing and graphics trades to use a resolution of 300 dpi (ppi) which is approximately twice the 133 to 150 dpi printing screen. 300 dpi is a conservative setting that will assure print quality. However, there is as a practical matter a fairly large range of settings that is acceptable to various people ranging from 150 to 300 dpi. My advice is to use 300 dpi whenever possible.

It is easy to be confused by printer specifications. Photo quality inkjet printers are listed as having resolutions of 720 dpi, 1440 dpi, 2880 dpi and so on. Once again, there is not a direct relationship between image resolution and printer resolution. Ink dots are not the same thing as pixel dimensions. Digital images sized at 300 dpi (ppi) resolution should appear as sharp, continuous tone photographic images regardless of the printer specifications.

Even here there is disagreement. Some people report that they achieve better results when image pixels are scaled to match the printer's stated resolution. In the case of Epson desktop photo printers, the company literature indicates that they resample any input they receive to 720 dpi (even the printers with 1440 dpi and 2880 dpi stated resolutions). The theory goes that by using an integral multiple or divisor of the "native" printer resolution, fewer "in-between" resampled pixels will be created and a sharper, more accurate print will be the result. In other words, sizing images to 360 dpi would be better than using our standard 300 dpi, since 360 dpi is exactly half the 720 dpi resolution that the printer uses to resample input. Additionally, the resampling method used by the printer (the "Nearest Neighbor" method) is not as good as the one we use in Photoshop (the "Bicubic" method). So, better results accrue by resampling to 360 dpi in Photoshop, rather than letting the printer do it. Some people even maintain that they achieve better prints by resizing or resampling their images to a full 720 dpi when using these printers. Thus the printer will not have to perform any resampling of its own on the image input it receives from your computer. However, it remains unclear to me whether or not this is actually how the printer handles the information it receives from the computer. Even if there are marginal benefits in using a higher resolution, chances are good that for most images any additional benefits will be visible only under close scrutiny (with a loupe) and not at typical viewing distances. Experiment with higher print resolutions and see for yourself!

Other printer features also deserve your attention. First, use the maximum quality settings that yours is capable of delivering. If you have a choice of 720 dpi vs. 1440 dpi, choose 1440 dpi for your photographic work. If the printer can print at 2880 dpi, use either the 1440 dpi or 2880 dpi setting. Likely you would not notice the difference between the 1440 dpi and 2880 dpi settings unless you were printing a monochromatic or black and white image. Second, the printer resolution setting is not the same thing as image resolution (our 300 dpi/ppi standard). You are merely instructing your machine to use its maximum resolution when printing your photograph. Whether that is ink dots or pixels

R. Scott Ireland

does not really matter — you want all the resolution you can get out of the printer. Third, do not be confused by color spaces. Inkjet models work by combining cyan, magenta, yellow and black inks ("CMYK") to create all the colors you see in the final print. However, inkjet printers are not CMYK devices, they are RGB devices. They are designed to receive RGB output from your computer, even though they utilize CMYK inks. Do not change your working color space to CMYK in Photoshop and then wonder why your prints look horrible. Do all your work in the Adobe RGB (1998) color space when printing images, and don't worry about a thing! The printer will handle the rest.

Resizing, Resampling and Interpolation

Resizing and resampling are frequently used interchangeably. I use the term "resizing" to mean changing the output size (print size) of an image and/or its resolution without altering the original image pixels. Resizing may or may not change the pixel dimensions of the image. For instance, as we will see, we may simply increase the canvas size by adding new pixels adjacent to the original image pixels without altering the original ones. Resizing that does not change the pixel dimensions of the image is also referred to as scaling.

Resampling means changing the output size (print size) of an image and/or its resolution by altering the original image pixels to create an image with new pixel dimensions. Resampling uses a software algorithm to *interpolate* pixel values when sizing images up or down. The software creates new pixels and assigns them color values based upon the color values of the original image pixels. In other words, the software makes an "educated guess" at what these "in-between" interpolated pixels are supposed to look like. Interpolated pixels are not true image information. No matter how good the software interpolation algorithm is, and some of them can be excellent, changing the output size by resampling pixel values operates to diminish the image quality if it is used to excess. This is why it is desirable to have the largest number of pixels (larger file sizes) from an input source. To make a high quality print (output), we need 300 dpi/ppi. The more "original" pixels you have the bigger the print you can make before having to resample the image.

Resizing — Photoshop Examples

Sometimes it is possible to just resize an image to meet your output needs, without having to resort to resampling. Resizing is the preferable procedure, as it does not create artificial image information. You should resize, rather than resample, whenever possible. As used in this book, resizing means two things:

- First, it is a way of changing the image size by simply adding new pixels to it. This is done without altering the original image pixels. New ones are simply added around the original pixels' edges. Subtracting pixels from an image is also resizing, but has limited use since it involves discarding some of the original pixels in the image. It is the same as cropping.

- Second, resizing also means changing the resolution of the image (pixels per inch), without altering its original pixels. We are not really doing anything to the image itself. We are simply instructing Photoshop to apply the same image pixels over a larger or smaller area. This resizing is done by changing the resolution as measured by the number of pixels per inch. This process is also known as "scaling."

Let's examine how resizing is done by the first method in Photoshop:

1. From the tutorial disc open the file Jupiter1c.bmp in Photoshop (*File|Open*). This is an image by Tim Khan taken at the 2003 Winter Star Party in the Florida Keys.

2. Open the *Image|Image Size* dialog box (see **Figure 11.1**), and note that this image is 774 pixels by 538 pixels, at a resolution of 72 pixels per inch. The Document Size is 10.75 inches by 7.472 inches. Close the Image Size window by clicking Cancel. Make sure that your Background Color is set to white in the Toolbox.

3. Now open the *Image|Canvas Size* dialog box. Note that the top portion of this dialog box shows the Current Size, Width and Height of the image, and below is shown the New Size, Width and Height. To input your New Width and New Height you manually type the new dimensions into the appropriate boxes. Make sure the units are set to inches.

4. Underneath the New Size, Width and Height boxes is a checkbox called Relative. If you check it, the New Width and Height go to 0. The numbers you enter now will increase the canvas size, so long as you enter positive numbers. Negative numbers will decrease the canvas size. For now,

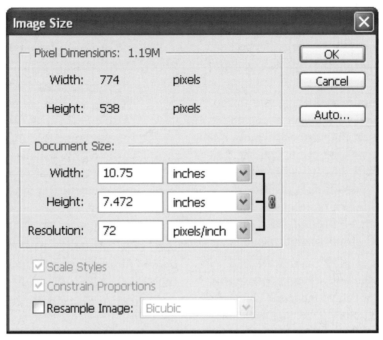

Fig. 11.1 Photoshop's Image Size Dialog Box.

leave the Relative box unchecked. The existing canvas size of 10.75 inches by 7.472 inches will be displayed. Entering numbers into the New Width and Height boxes with the Relative box unchecked means that you are entering numbers representing the total canvas size.

5. Below the Relative checkbox is a graphic display called Anchor. If you click on the different boxes (anchor points), you will quickly see that this changes where new canvas will be added to the image. For now, leave the center box selected, so that canvas will be added in all directions.

6. Enter 12 inches for the New Width and 8.341 inches for the New Height. Again, make sure that the Relative box is unchecked and then click OK. Select *View|Fit on Screen* so that the entire image and canvas is displayed.

7. The image of Jupiter is now surrounded by a white border. If your Background Color had been set to something other than white, the original image would be surrounded by that color. Typically, with planetary images such as this, you would select the Background Color in Photoshop from the sky background values in the image (usually black or very close to black) and thereby use the image background color to seamlessly increase the total image size.

8. Open *Image|Image Size* again. Notice that the dimensions have increased to 864 pixels by 601 pixels, the Document Size has of course increased, and the Resolution remains at 72 pixels per inch. We have increased the total size of the image (resizing), but we have not altered the original pixels (by resampling). We have simply added pixels to an area surrounding the original image.

9. Increasing the canvas size can be useful when trying to create a desired image aspect and print size, particularly with planetary images.

Now let's see how resizing is done by the second method in Photoshop:

1. From the tutorial disc, once again open the file Jupiter1c.bmp (*File|Open*).

2. Next, select *Image|Image Size*. A dialog box appears like the one shown in **Figure 11.1**. This tells us the Pixel Dimensions of the image; in this case it is 774 x 538 pixels, as we have already seen. It also shows us Document Size in terms of Width, Height and Resolution. The drop-down boxes adjacent to these parameters provide various choices of units to display, but we will work with pixels, inches and pixels/inch. Make sure these boxes are set accordingly. At the bottom of the Image Size dialog box, there are two checkboxes, Constrain Proportions and Resample Image. Photoshop CS

and CS2 also display a third checkbox, Scale Styles. Be certain that Constrain Proportions is checked and that Resample Image is unchecked. If you are using Photoshop CS or CS2, check the Scale Styles box.

3. Notice that when you uncheck Resample Image, the Pixel Dimensions are no longer available for change. Also, Constrain Proportions becomes automatically checked, whether or not you checked it in the first place. Click these boxes on and off to see what I mean. Notice too that the Document Size parameters (width, height, resolution) have a lock symbol next to them. Each of these parameters will vary proportionately to any change made in one of the others.

4. With Resample Image unchecked, change the width of the image from 10.75 inches to 12 inches, and look at what happens. The height changes from 7.472 inches to 8.341 inches and the resolution changes from 72 pixels/inch to 64.5. The Pixel Dimensions are unchanged (774 x 538). The image has been "resized" upward, while the proportions of the image have remained unchanged (the long dimension is 1.44 times the short dimension). This has been accomplished by dropping the resolution of the image from 72 pixels/inch to 64.5 pixels/inch. The pixels have not been altered (by resampling). We have merely instructed Photoshop to "spread" the same pixels over a larger area (resizing), which can only be done by reducing the number of pixels per inch (resolution).

5. Now change the Resolution from 64.5 pixels/inch to 300 pixels/inch. The Document Size drops to 2.58 inches by 1.793 inches (still maintaining a 1.44 ratio of width-to-height). Do you see what's happening? Lower Resolution equals a larger Document Size. Higher Resolution equals a smaller Document Size. There is no free lunch. Since we are not altering the pixels in the image, nor are we adding pixels as in the first method, we can only achieve a larger output size (e.g. a larger print) by living with less resolution. Again, this is one of the reasons why you want to create the largest original file size (largest pixel dimensions) that you reasonably can.

6. Here is a handy, time-saving shortcut to check the pixel dimensions, document size and resolution of your image without having to open the Image Size dialog box:

a. Make sure that the Status Bar is displayed at the bottom of the main Photoshop window (*Window|Status Bar*).

b. While holding down the Alt key, left-click and hold in the Doc: section of the Status Bar. A temporary window pops up that shows you the pixel dimensions, document size, number of channels and resolution of your image. In Photoshop CS2, a status bar is displayed at the bottom of each image window. Hold down the Alt key and click in the Doc: section for the same display.

You will check these parameters often while doing image-processing work, particularly when sizing images for printing and Web display. This can be a real time-saver.

You may also quickly bring up the Image Size dialog box by right-clicking once with your mouse cursor placed inside the file name area at the top of the image window (the area with a blue bar at the top). This brings up several selection choices, among which is Image Size.

In both of the above examples, we have not altered the original image pixels. If we were to make a print using each of these resizing methods, we would see that the first method results in a smaller image of Jupiter on paper, even though the total file/image size has been increased. Resolution has remained the same. We have simply added borders to the original image. Using the second method, Jupiter appears larger on paper, but the trade-off is a lower resolution (pixels per inch), which can mean a lower image quality. Is there in fact any way for us to have that free lunch? Can we increase image size and still maintain resolution? Well, maybe. Which brings us to our next topic.

Resampling — Photoshop Examples

On a practical level, resampling an image (up or down) is a process that you will have to perform on many, if not most, of your images. In order to make a print, or to display an image with pleasing proportions on a computer monitor (or on the Web), you will frequently need to change the pixel dimensions of the image up or down, which will usually require resampling.

You can create more pixels and larger file sizes by resampling your original image upward ("upsampling"). But resampling adds artificial "information" to the image. The software uses its interpolation algorithm to determine what all of the new, added pixels are supposed to look like. A larger file created through upward resampling is not nearly as good as a larger original image from your input source. Photoshop, however, is indifferent as to whether the pixels are real or created. They take up the same amount of file space!

Downward resampling of an image ("downsampling") reduces the pixel dimensions by interpolation and is preferable to upward resampling. This is yet another reason why you want to maintain larger original file sizes. Downward resampling is still a manipulation performed by the software algorithm, but working from a larger amount of information to a smaller amount, rather than the converse, will help maintain image quality.

Let's examine how resampling is performed in Photoshop:

1. From the tutorial disc, once again open the file Jupiter1c.bmp (*File|Open*).

2. Select *Image|Image Size*. As we saw from our earlier example the dialog box that appears is like the one shown in **Figure 11.1**. It gives us the Pixel Dimensions and Document Size of the image. Earlier versions of Photoshop labeled output size as Print Size rather than Document Size, which was probably less confusing.

3. Make sure that the Width and Height units chosen in the Document Size drop-down boxes are in inches and that the Resolution is in pixels/inch.

4. Make sure that both the Constrain Proportions and Resample Image selection boxes are checked. Constrain Proportions maintains the current proportions of pixel width to pixel height. Note that leaving the Resample Image selection box checked allows us to alter the Pixel Dimensions. Click it off, and the Pixel Dimensions will be grayed out and cannot be changed (as in **Figure 11.1**). Make sure you click it back on.

5. The drop-down selection box to the right of Resample Image allows us to choose the resampling method Photoshop will use to interpolate pixels. Always set this to Bicubic. Bicubic is the highest quality method available in Photoshop. If you use Photoshop CS or CS2, you may also select two additional Bicubic methods, Bicubic Smoother and Bicubic Sharper. Adobe recommends using Bicubic Smoother for upward resampling, and Bicubic Sharper for downward resampling. We will look at some results using

these methods later in the chapter.

6. Now change the Resolution from 72 ppi to 300 ppi and look at what happens. The Pixel Dimensions went up a lot! — from 774 x 538 to 3225 x 2242. Notice that Photoshop also shows us, at the top of the dialog box, that the new file size will be 20.7 megabytes. The original file size of 1.19 megabytes is shown in parentheses.

7. Compare this to our earlier resizing example using the same image. In our earlier example, we turned off resampling. When we changed the Resolution, the Document Size was simply reduced proportionately. The Pixel Dimensions remained unchanged. With resampling on, Photoshop has left the Document Size (print size) unchanged and has simply increased the pixel dimensions of the image by approximately 4 times to give us a print size of 10.75 inches wide by 7.472 inches high. Resampling allows us to change the print size (Document Size) and resolution independently. It is the number of pixels that changes.

By the way, here is an easy way to get your original settings back. Hold down the Alt key and notice that the Cancel button in the dialog box changes to Reset. If you click on this, the original settings will be restored. This trick works with most other dialog boxes in Photoshop as well.

8. Click OK to accept the new size. You will now have a much larger image on your screen, so select *View|Fit on Screen* (shortcut Ctrl+0) to change the screen size display. The new image looks pretty much like the old one, which is exactly what you want. However, the pixel dimensions of this image are much larger. Photoshop has performed a bicubic interpolation on the original image to fill in all those extra pixels. If you were now to print this image, you would have a 300 dpi print that is 10.75 inches wide by 7.472 inches high. You could have just as easily changed the Document Size as well as the Resolution to make a print of a different size. The Pixel Dimensions will vary accordingly. By the way, remember that 300 dpi is the ideal resolution (most sources agree on this) to use when making prints on your inkjet printer. In most cases, it is also the best resolution to use for material that will be used in books and magazines. It is two times the halftone screen size of 150 lines per inch used in most publications.

R. Scott Ireland

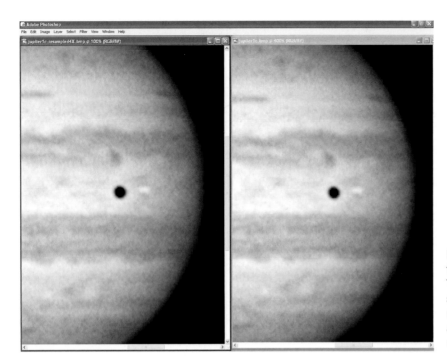

Fig. 11.2 Bicubic interpolation is the method of choice in Photoshop. The image on the left has been up-sampled 4x compared to the original on the right and shows no adverse effects from the enlargement.

9. Open *Image\Image Size* again and you will see the new Pixel Dimensions and file size. **Figure 11.2** shows a side-by-side comparison of the original and resampled images (the resampled image is on the left). It is hard to see much difference between them. In fact, the interpolated image looks better because it contains more pixels. At the screen enlargement shown in the illustration, pixelation (larger, coarser-looking pixels) of the original image is apparent.

10. The image is now resized to make an approximate 8 x 10-inch print. As will be covered in **Chapter 12**, the only thing left to do is to run an unsharp mask on it even if it was sharpened before. Resampling an image softens it and therefore additional sharpening is required. This is why it is best to save images without sharpening them. Sharpening should generally be done after resizing. Choose *Filter\Sharpen\Unsharp Mask* with settings of (160, 3, 0) or other settings that look good to you. Click OK. Then select *Edit\Fade Unsharp Mask*; leave it at 100% Opacity and change the Blending Mode to Luminosity. For ideal inkjet print output, the screen image should appear a little oversharpened.

While not a panacea, Photoshop's bicubic resampling does a remarkably good job of up-sizing images. The resampling algorithm works by determining the weighted average of a 4 x 4 array of surrounding pixels.

This allows the program to evaluate subtle color and luminosity changes when comparing each pixel to its neighbors, so as to arrive at a more precise estimate of how the new pixel array should look. There are limits, however, beyond which upward resampling will result in noticeable quality deterioration and softness.

There are no hard and fast rules about how much upward resampling can be used. It depends on the amount of detail, contrast, colors and other characteristics of a particular image. It should be kept in mind that a large print designed for hanging on the wall will be viewed from an "esthetic distance". When viewed from a reasonable distance, an upsampled image may appear quite sharp, yet look soft under closer scrutiny. Remember that apparent sharpness is subjective. Sometimes even a digital image that has more inherent sharpness than a film-scanned one may appear softer due to smoother tonal gradations and less apparent edge sharpness.

Output from high quality digital cameras and other digital sources may suffer less from upward resampling than film scans. A digitized film image is a second generation image — the process of scanning the film adds a certain amount of noise and softness to the original. Film also contains a grain pattern (noise) that will become more apparent with greater amounts of upsampling. A high quality digital image (e.g. one with a high signal-to-noise ratio) is a first-generation image that does not have any film grain and should have a very low amount of noise. A high signal-to-noise ratio image can withstand more processing (including up-sampling) than a low S/N image can. The tradeoff here is the pixel dimensions that you start with. More pixels also allow for more processing, and frequently the higher quality of a digital original is offset by a smaller chip size (less pixel dimensions).

Recall from our earlier discussion that a computer monitor only displays 72–100 ppi. If you are working in a wider gamut color space (which you should be!) such as Adobe RGB (1998), your image file will contain more information than you can see on your screen. When printed, the image may show more color variation and detail than what appeared on the monitor. Therefore, an upsampled image that may look good on your screen may not produce an acceptable print. Always view your images at a minimum of 100% resolution ("Actual Pixels" setting with the Zoom tool) to make a critical evaluation of quality.

The bottom line here is to experiment. After all, "you got what you got". If you are capturing the full native resolution of your digital input device (scanner, CCD camera, etc.), there is nothing more for you to do on the front end. Divide the native image pixel resolution by 300 to determine how much print size (in inches) you can get from the original set of pixels. For example, a 2200 x 1500 pixel original can produce a top quality 7.33 inch by 5 inch print (2200 divided by 300 and 1500 divided by 300), with no resampling. A relatively modest upsampling to 3300 x 2250 pixels will also produce a very high quality print of 11 x 7.5 inches. Likely a good S/N original image can be resampled up to 11 x 14 inches or even a wall-sized 13 x 19 inches (the largest print size available from most standard photo-quality printers). A very high quality, high S/N ratio original may even enlarge up to an impressive 16 x 20 inches.

Experiment with resampling on your own images by making test prints in various sizes to get a feel for the size, type and quality of image that will enlarge well.

Resizing and Resampling: More Photoshop Examples

Let's look at a few more Photoshop examples to further illustrate these points:

1. From the tutorial disc, open the file Horsehead.tif (*File|Open*). This is a 35mm film image taken by Herm Perez.

2. Before doing anything else, let's duplicate the image so that we can compare the original and resa-

mpled images later. Select *Image|Duplicate* and click OK. You should now have two image windows on your screen, Horsehead and Horsehead Copy.

3. Make sure Horsehead Copy is the active image window and open the Image Size dialog box (*Image|Image Size*). Make sure that the Document Size drop-down boxes are set to display inches and pixels/inch. Notice that the image has a native resolution of 2700 ppi — this is the full resolution of the device Herm used to scan the film image. At 2700 dpi (ppi) the native Document Size is 1.14 x 0.789 inches. The original 35mm film chip was approximately 1.5 x 1-inch. The image was cropped down from its original size to make a more pleasing composition, and to eliminate some stray light at the edges of the frame. Notice too that the Pixel Dimensions of the image are 3077 x 2131 pixels.

4. Now uncheck the Resample Image selection box. The Pixel Dimensions are now grayed-out and will not change no matter how much we change the Document Size and Resolution. Constrain Proportions is also grayed-out and automatically checked. The image proportions must stay the same, since we are not altering the image pixels in any way. Any "resizing" we do simply instructs Photoshop to allocate the existing image pixels over a greater or lesser output (print) area.

5. Change the Resolution from 2700 ppi to 300 ppi. We want to see how big a print we can make without resampling. The Width and Height boxes immediately change to 10.257 x 7.103 inches, respectively. Without any resampling at all, we may make a very high quality print on standard 11 x 8.5-inch inkjet printer photo paper, with some white borders around the edges.

6. Now change the Resolution setting to 240 ppi. The Document Size changes to 12.821 x 8.879 inches. It is possible for us to still make a high quality print of 14 x 11 inches, again without any resampling. The centered image will leave a pleasing border of approximately 0.5 inch on the top and bottom and 1 inch on each side. It can be printed on standard 17 x 11-inch inkjet photo paper and trimmed to fit a 14 x 11-inch frame.

7. So far, so good. But let's say that what we really want is an image size of approximately 17 x 12

inches that can be printed on 19 x 13 inch standard inkjet photo paper (with some white borders) and matted and framed in a standard 20 x 16-inch frame. Just to make sure we are on the same page, click cancel on the Image Size dialog box and re-open it, or hold down the Alt key and click on Reset to restore the original image parameters.

8. Now make sure that both Constrain Proportions and Resample Image (Bicubic method) are checked.

9. Change the Resolution from 2700 ppi to 300 ppi. Notice that the Pixel Dimensions drop-down to a miniscule 342 x 237 pixels. Since we did not yet change the Document Size, Photoshop thinks that we want to downsample the original image to create a Lilliputian print of 1.14 x 0.789 inches at 300 dpi (ppi) Resolution. This only requires 342 x 237 pixels. But we are not finished (unless you're into really itty-bitty prints).

10. Now change the Width to 17 inches and look at what happens. The Height changes to 11.773 inches. So far, so good. This is close enough to the 17 x 12 inch print size that we want. The Pixel Dimensions have increased to 5100 x 3532, and the file size increases substantially from 18.8 megabytes to 51.5 megabytes. We have multiplied the Pixel Dimensions by 1.657 in both Width and Height and the file size has increased by 2.74 times (1.657 times 1.657 equals 2.74).

11. Now click OK. The Horesehead Copy image is re-sampled upward. The image size on the screen gets bigger, since there are now more pixels to display at the display percentage that we were previously using.

12. Select the Zoom Tool (shortcut Z) and click on Actual Pixels at the top of the window. Click on the Zoom Tool again and then hold down the spacebar on your keyboard and move the cursor into the image. A little white-gloved hand appears that allows you to move the image around in the window. Move the image and examine the quality of the details. Our resized image quality looks good.

13. Now let's compare it to the original image. To make room on your screen, press the Tab key to hide all of your Photoshop Palettes. Now select *Window|Documents|Tile* to place the original Horsehead image and the resampled Horsehead Copy image side-by-side. You can move between the image windows by using the Ctrl+Tab keys.

14. For each image, select *View|Actual Pixels* (shortcut Alt+Ctrl+0; another shortcut is to double-click on the Zoom Tool icon in the Toolbox). Each is now displayed at 100% and shows the actual pixels, without any "screen interpolation".

15. Press the letter Z on your keyboard to make sure that you still have the Zoom Tool selected.

16. With the Horsehead (original) image active, click once inside the image window to enlarge the view to 200%. Note that the view percentage is displayed in the file title bar area at the top of the image window. With a 200% view, the original appears closer in scale to our resampled Horsehead Copy image.

17. Now hold down the spacebar, move around in each image, and compare similar areas (**Figure 11.3**). The resampled image looks very good. Its only noticeable difference is a very slight color shift that is most noticeable in the areas with red nebulosity. Don't forget to resharpen your images after resampling by running an unsharp mask filter. Then use *Edit|Fade Unsharp Mask* with the blending mode set to Luminosity to avoid any further color shifts.

Now let's work through another planetary image printing example. We will examine in more detail how to "enlarge" a planetary image with relatively small pixel dimensions:

1. From the tutorial disc, open the file (*File|Open*) Mars Print Example.tif. This is an R(G)B image (the red and blue channels were used to synthesize the green channel) taken by the author and Tim Khan.

2. Open the Image Size dialog box (*Image|Image Size*). The Pixel Dimensions of the image are 900 x 900 pixels. The Document Size is 12.5 x 12.5 inches at a Resolution of 72 pixels per inch. So, one issue we will have to tackle is how we want this square image to appear on rectangular printer paper.

3. Uncheck the Resample Image box. Change the Resolution to 300 ppi. The Document Size Width and Height change to 3 x 3 inches. Now change the Resolution again to 240 dpi. The Document Size increases to 3.75 inches square. So, without any resampling, we can achieve a print size somewhere between 3 inches and 3.75 inches square, in which Mars fills up approximately 50% of the im-

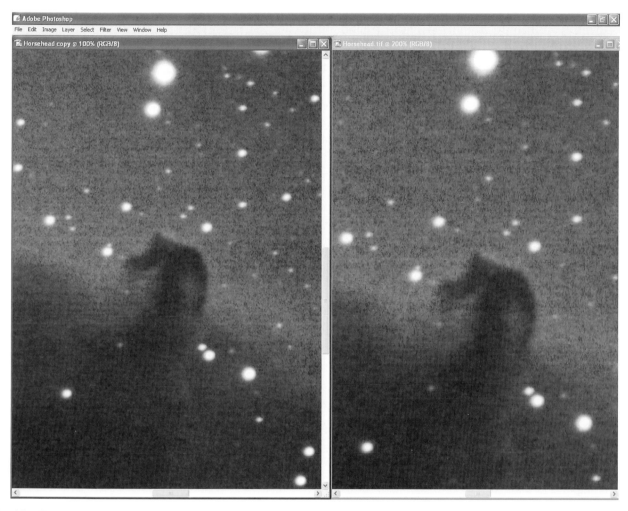

Fig. 11.3 The resampled horsehead.tif image on the left (5100 x 3532 pixels) should make a fine 17 inch by 12 inch print. It compares favorably to the original image file on the right (3077 x 2131 pixels).

age area. But let's say that what we really want to do is end up with a 7 x 5-inch print to fit into a standard picture frame.

4. With Resample Image still unchecked, type 7 inches into either the Width or Height box (the other one will change to 7 inches automatically). Our Resolution drops to an unacceptably low 128.5 pixels per inch. And, we would still need to crop the image or trim the print to fit our 7 x 5-inch frame. Mars would not have enough "space" around it and would not look right.

5. Again change the Resolution to 300 ppi (the Document Size once again changes to 3 inches square) and click OK. Why did we do this? We did not change the pixels at all — the image is still 900 x 900 pixels. Resampling was turned off. We did this for convenience only. The native resolution of

the image was 72 ppi. Changing it to 300 ppi is merely an instruction to Photoshop to consider the image within a context of 300 ppi rather than 72 ppi. Now when we open the Image Size or Canvas Size dialog boxes, our job will be a little easier, since Photoshop will display the Document Size (output size/print size) based upon our standard printing criterion of 300 ppi rather than 72 ppi. Nothing about the image itself has changed, since the pixel dimensions were not altered. Remember, resolution and size mean nothing to the image itself. They are only instructions to Photoshop telling it what to do with the image pixels when making a print (output).

6. So, let's say that we have now settled on resizing (not resampling) our image to a 3.5-inch square output. If we then add 1.5 inches to one side and 3.5 inches to the other, we will have our 7 x 5-inch

R. Scott Ireland

print size. Open *Image|Image Size* again and change the Document Size to 3.5 x 3.5 inches. The Resolution drops to 257.1 ppi, which is still within our acceptable quality parameters, since it is above 240 ppi. Click OK.

7. Now open *Image|Canvas Size*. A dialog box appears, and our 3.5-inch square sizing is reflected in both the Old Size and New Size parameters. What we are going to do is to change the size of our image by adding new pixels to each edge, without altering the original image pixels. The pixel dimensions will ultimately change, but this is accomplished by "padding" the sides of the image rather than altering the original pixels by resampling. What we need to do next is to make sure that the new canvas areas that we create match the sky background in our image. This is usually pretty easy with planetary images, since the "sky background" is usually a featureless black, with RGB values of (0, 0, 0). With some images however, one must take more care to select a proper Background Color that matches the sky background in the image. So, for practice, we will select our Background Color, which will be the color used to fill in the new pixels we are creating with *Image|Canvas Size*, from the image itself, rather than just setting the Background Color to black (although that would work equally well in this case).

8. To change the Background Color in Photoshop, we must first close the Canvas Size dialog box, so click Cancel. Now click on Set Background Color in the Toolbox (the color box on the bottom-right near the bottom of the Toolbox). The Color Picker dialog box appears. Move the cursor into the image window and the Eyedropper icon appears. Make sure that the Info Palette is visible (*Window|Info*) and watch the RGB values as you move the Eyedropper around in the background areas of the image. All of the areas that appear black are in fact black — they all have RGB values of (0, 0, 0). With the Eyedropper on one of these black areas, click once to reset the Background Color. Click OK in the Color Picker window and you have now reset your Photoshop Background Color to the background color of your image.

9. Open the Canvas Size dialog box again (*Image|Canvas Size*). Change the New Size Width to 5 inches and the Height to 7 inches. This

will size the print to display vertically, with the long dimension in Height. Make sure that the anchor point at the bottom of the dialog box is in the middle, so that new canvas will be added uniformly in all directions. Click OK.

10. New black background appears seamlessly around the original image. Type Ctrl + 0 to fit the image onto the screen. The image looks good and should make a nicely proportioned 7 x 5-inch print. Just to see if we like it better with a "landscape" orientation, rather than a "portrait" orientation, let's go back and change it.

11. Make the History Palette visible (*Window|History*). Click-hold and drag the last Canvas Size operation onto the trash can icon at the bottom-right of the History Palette and release the mouse. The image reverts to its history state prior to our Canvas resizing.

12. Open *Image|Canvas Size* again and this time make the Width 7 inches and the Height 5 inches. The Background Color has not changed, so just click OK. Fit the image on the screen with Ctrl+0. Now we again have the image padded with additional background color, but this time it is in a "landscape" orientation.

13. With the History Palette still visible, click back and forth between the last Canvas Size step and the previous step. You see clearly that the original image pixels were not altered — just new "background" canvas was added. The image size has been increased to 1800 x 1286 pixels from the original 900 x 900 pixels, but the new ones were just added alongside. The image is now resized to make a nice, 7 x 5-inch print.

14. It may not be necessary to run a final unsharp mask on an image resized in this manner. Even though the pixel dimensions of the image have been increased, we have not resampled the original image pixels, so they have not lost their original edge contrast. Only run an unsharp mask if your original image was saved without sharpening.

Here's a shortcut method called "Overcropping" that adds canvas without using the Canvas Size dialog box. Although it takes a lot of steps to describe, it is very fast once you get the hang of it:

1. Once again, open the Mars Print Example.tif file (*File|Open*).

2. Maximize the image window to full screen by

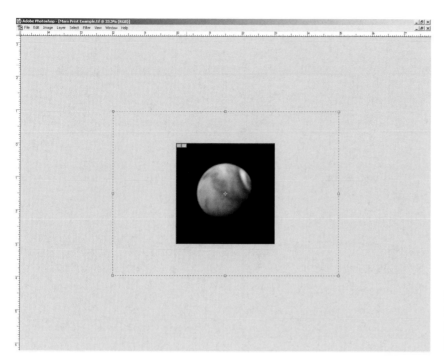

Fig. 11.4 "Overcropping" is a quick resizing method that adds additional canvas and does not resample the original image pixels.

clicking on the Windows Maximize button at the top right side of the image window.

3. Open the Image Size dialog box (*Image|Image Size*); make sure Resample Image is not checked, then change the resolution from 72 ppi to 300 ppi. Click OK.

4. Display Photoshop's Rulers on the screen with *View|Rulers* (shortcut Ctrl+R). Right-click on one of the rulers and select "inches" as the display units.

5. Zoom out (shortcut: Alt+Spacebar) to a 25% or 33.3% image view.

6. Select the Crop Tool (shortcut "C"). Press Clear on the Options Bar (just above the image window) to clear any Crop Tool settings.

7. Turn off Photoshop's Palettes by pressing the Tab key once.

8. Draw a Crop Marquee (bounding box or border) around the entire image. Left-click-hold and drag from outside the image area to surround the image, then release the mouse button. The Crop Marquee will snap to the outside edges of the image and will look like a typical Photoshop "marching ants" selection border. However, in this case, there are adjustment handles (little square boxes) along the border and a little circle in the center of the image.

9. Now let's increase the canvas width of the image to 7 inches, while at the same time keeping it centered. We will use the center adjustment handle on the right side of the image. Hold down the Ctrl+Alt keys and then click-hold and drag the adjustment handle to the right. You'll know when you are "on" the adjustment handle, as the cursor will change into a double-sided arrow. By holding down the Ctrl+Alt keys, the Crop Marquee is enlarged equally on both the left and right sides. Drag until you have added 2 inches to each side of the image (width = 7 inches total).

10. Now similarly drag the top-center adjustment handle to add 1 inch to both the top and bottom of the image (height = 5 inches total).

11. Your screen should now look like **Figure 11.4**. The adjustment handles and marquee remain on the screen and you may make any further adjustments (including rotation) that you wish. Press the Enter key to accept the crop. New border has been added to your image in whatever Background Color you selected. Now let's fix that background.

12. Turn Photoshop's Palettes back on by pressing the Tab key. Select the Eyedropper Tool and make sure that it is set to sample a 3 pixel x 3 pixel area. Click once in the dark area surrounding Mars in the image. This is now your new Foreground Color.

13. Select the Paint Bucket Tool (it may be hidden by

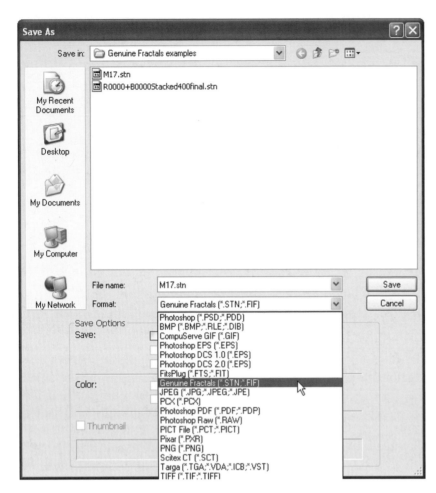

Fig. 11.5 Genuine Fractals is a Photoshop Plug-In that uses a proprietary file format to improve the quality of print enlargements.

the Gradient Tool) from the Toolbox, or press the letter G on your keyboard as a shortcut. Position the cursor over the new canvas area that you added and click once. The new canvas is filled with the sky background from the image. In this case, the background was pure black (0, 0, 0).

14. Open the Image Size dialog box (*Image|Image Size*) to confirm that you now have a 7 inch wide by 5 inch high print at 300 dpi resolution. You may now run an unsharp mask, if the image was not sharpened originally. The dimensions may not be exact, but they should be very close, and this is a quick and easy method to accomplish resizing by adding canvas.

Additional Methods of Resampling Images for Printing

In addition to the Image Size and Canvas Size dialog boxes, there are several other methods available for "upsizing" (upsampling) images in Photoshop. These methods generally require purchasing third-party software "plug-ins" that operate inside of Photoshop.

Tools such as these can be useful when resampling images to make large prints, or when enlarging images that have small pixel dimensions.

There are currently many different third-party plug-ins available, with more appearing on the market all the time. These programs utilize various mathematical algorithms for resampling and interpolation; the goal being to maintain the highest amount of image quality, while at the same time providing significant enlargement of the original pixel dimensions of the image.

The industry standard plug-in is a program called Genuine Fractals (see Appendix), which is widely used by photographers and graphics professionals. Instead of resampling images directly, Genuine Fractals uses a proprietary fractal compression algorithm and a special file format. Images are saved in the Genuine Fractals *.stn compressed format, which appears as a file format option in the Photoshop *File|Save As* dialog box (**Figure 11.5**).

When you re-open a Genuine Fractals image in Photoshop, a special dialog box appears (**Figure 11.6**) that allows you to select sizing and scaling options

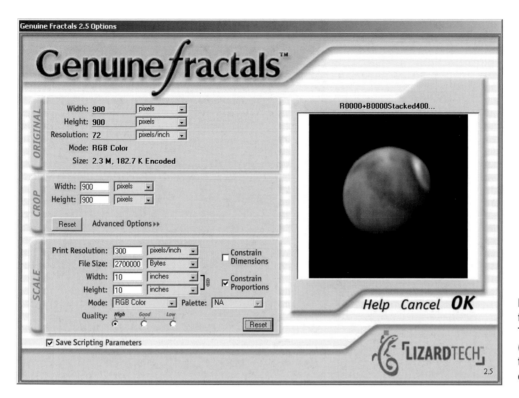

Fig. 11.6 A Genuine Fractals file is "one size fits all". The desired output size (print size) is entered by the user when the file is opened.

(print size options). The image is then sized to whatever dimensions and resolution that you choose. Genuine Fractals claims that their files are resolution-independent images (similar to vector-based images and graphics) and the original relationship between pixels and resolution is eliminated.

Some people swear by Genuine Fractals; some see little difference between it and resampling using the standard Photoshop bicubic method. In truth, a lot depends on the original image size, type of detail present, subject matter and other image characteristics. **Figure 11.7** shows an extreme enlargement of the Mars shot we worked with earlier in the chapter. The original 900 x 900 pixel image was saved in both a standard TIFF format, and also in the Genuine Fractals STN format. The standard TIFF file, shown on the right, was resampled upward in Photoshop to 3000 x 3000 pixels, which would allow for printing a 10 inch by 10 inch image at 300 dpi/ppi. The Genuine Fractals file, shown on the left, was sized for the same dimensions and resolution when the file was opened. Viewed on-screen at 100% (Actual Pixels), the dark surface features on the planet seem to have slightly more contrast and detail in the Genuine Fractals image. However, even with these extremely enlarged images, the differences between the two are subtle.

Figure 11.8 shows a similar comparison using a deep-sky image. This tri-color image of M17 was taken by Tim Khan using a CCD camera with a native resolution of 1092 x 736 pixels. The image on the left was saved in the Genuine Fractals file format; that on the right is a standard TIFF file that was resampled using Photoshop's bicubic interpolation method. Both were sized for a 20 x 14-inch print at 300 dpi/ppi, which resulted in a resampled image size of 6000 x 4044 pixels. The illustration shows an enlarged portion of each image viewed on the screen at 100% (Actual Pixels). In this instance, we can clearly see improvements in the Genuine Fractals enlargement. Stars and nebula features are sharper, with more edge definition and detail. Although the stars appear a little too sharp on-screen, they will look just right when printed.

A word of caution. I strongly recommend saving all of your original files and image-processing work in a standard, lossless file format such as TIFF. Keep all of your original FITS CCD images as well. When working with Genuine Fractals, I simply create an additional file in the Genuine Fractals format. This way, I can always go back to the original image pixels that remain intact in a TIFF or FITS file. I do not use Genuine Fractals to "save" file space, no matter how well it may work with any particular image.

There are a number of other resampling and interpolation plug-ins and programs available. It is beyond

R. Scott Ireland

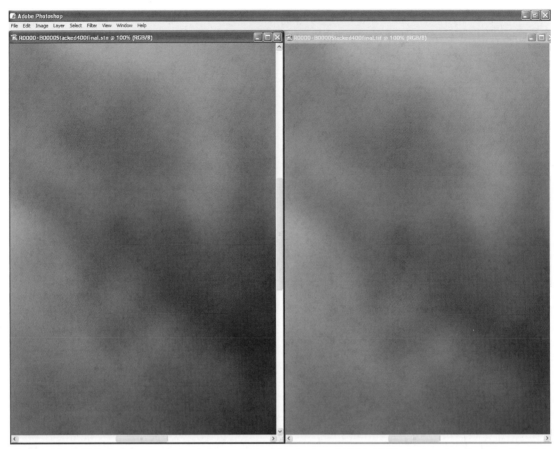

Fig. 11.7 This Mars image was enlarged from 900 x 900 pixels to 3000 x 3000 pixels using Genuine Fractals (left) and Photoshop Bicubic Interpolation (right). The differences are subtle in this case.

the scope of this book to identify or compare them all, but here are some of the options:

- **S-Spline** is a proprietary interpolation package offered by Shortcut Software (see Appendix). Some astrophotographers prefer S-Spline to other methods for enlarging deep-sky images.

- **Lanczos Interpolation** is available in an excellent freeware file browser called Irfanview (see Appendix). **Figure 11.9** shows a side-by-side comparison of the M17 enlargement (20 by 14 inch print at 300 dpi/ppi) that we just looked at. Lanczos resampling was performed in Irfanview. In this particular case, there appears to be no benefit to using Lanczos over Photoshop's bicubic resampling.

- **pxl SmartScale** is a Photoshop plug-in from Extensis (see Appendix), however, as with Genuine Fractals, price may be an issue.

- **Stair Interpolation, also known as Stairstep Interpolation or Bicubic SI** — Stair Interpolation ("SI") is simply resampling in several

small steps, rather than one large step. Using Photoshop's *Image|Image Size* dialog box and the bicubic resampling method, an image is enlarged by small amounts multiple times until the desired size is reached. The theory is that by making small interpolation steps you arrive at a more accurate estimate of the "in-between" interpolated pixels. The result is a sharper and more detailed resampled image.

Stair Interpolation has a strong user base and some even prefer it to expensive plug-in programs such as Genuine Fractals. A rule of thumb when using Stair Interpolation is to move in increments of around 10%. In other words, if you want to enlarge a 500 x 500 pixel image to 800 x 800 pixels, you would do the following:

1. Resample from 500 x 500 pixels to 550 x 550.
2. Then resample from 550 x 550 pixels to 605 x 605.
3. Then resample from 605 x 605 pixels to 665 x 665.
4. Then resample from 665 x 665 pixels to 732 x 732.
5. Then resample from 732 x 732 pixels to 800 x 800.

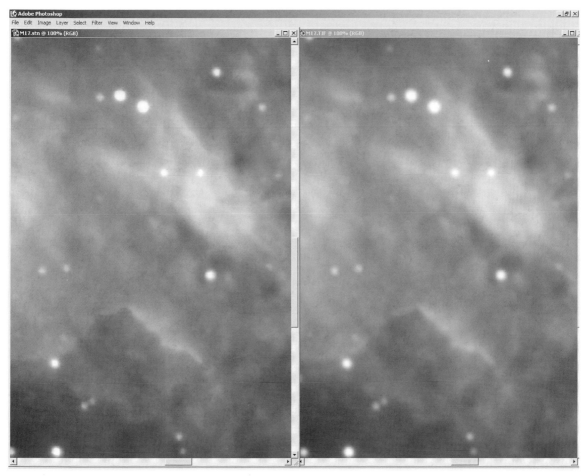

Fig. 11.8 Tim Khan's M17 image was enlarged from 1092 x 736 pixels to 6000 x 4044 pixels to make a 20 inch by 14 inch print at 300 dpi/ppi. The Genuine Fractals enlargement (left) is a clear improvement over Photoshop's Bicubic resampling (right).

So, as you can see, this requires considerably more time than just performing a single upward resampling but the results are usually well worth it. To make the task easier, there are (thankfully!) Photoshop plug-ins available that will automate these steps for you. Hoon Im's Website (see Appendix) has a free Stairstep Image Size download available. Once copied to the Photoshop Plug-Ins directory, it appears under the *File|Automate* Menu as shown in **Figure 11.10**.

Stair Interpolation ("SI") — Photoshop Example

Let's try this method for ourselves with Photoshop. I assume that you have not yet installed an automated utility like Im's Stairstep plug-in, so we will upsize this example step-by-step using nothing more than Photoshop's Image Size dialog box.

1. Open the file M17.tif (*File|Open*). This is Tim Khan's CCD image that we looked at earlier when discussing Genuine Fractals. Let's upsample/up-size this image, using Stair Interpolation, to make a 20 inch by 14 inch print at 300 dpi/ppi. This will require us to resample the image from 1092 x 736 pixels to 6000 x 4044 pixels.

2. Open the Image Size dialog box with *Image|Image Size*. In the Document Size section, make sure that Resample Image is checked and that the method is set to Bicubic. Also make sure that Constrain Proportions is checked and set the units of Width, Height and Resolution to inches and pixels/inch. Make sure that the Resolution indicates 300 pixels per inch. We will be changing the pixel dimensions of the image directly, so by setting the Document Size to our target print resolution of 300 dpi/ppi, we will be able to observe the changing Document Size (print size) as we progressively upsize the image. When we get to around 20 inches by 14 inches at 300 dpi/ppi, we'll be done. In the Pixel Dimensions area, make sure that the Width and Height

R. Scott Ireland

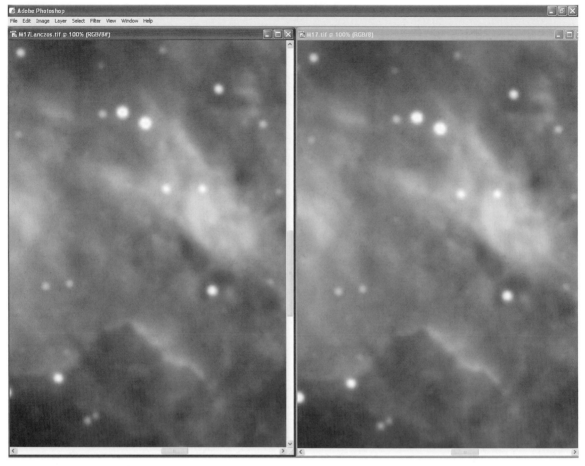

Fig. 11.9 Upsampling using Lanczos Interpolation (left). Lanczos is available in the Freeware program Irfanview. In this case, Photoshop's Bicubic method (right) offers equally good results.

units are set to pixels.

3. Now, in the Pixel Dimensions area, change the image Width from 1092 pixels to 1201 (a 10% increase). Note that since we checked Constrain Proportions, the Height changes automatically from 736 pixels to 809 pixels (also a 10% increase). So, we only have to worry about changing one dimension — the other will be filled in automatically. Click OK.

4. Open *Image|Image Size* again. Now change the Pixel Dimensions Width from 1201 pixels to 1321 (another 10% increase) and click OK.

5. Continue repeating step 4 changing the Pixel Dimensions Width using the following settings:

1. 1453 **2.** 1598 **3.** 1758 **4.** 1934 **5.** 2127
6. 2340 **7.** 2574 **8.** 2831 **9.** 3114 **10.** 3425
11. 3768 **12.** 4144 **13.** 4558 **14.** 5013 **15.** 5514
16. 6000.

Whew! OK, rest your mouse hand for a minute! It took us a total of 18 iterations of *Image|Image Size* to resample the image up to our desired print size of 20 inches by 14 inches at 300 dpi/ppi.

6. Now save this work as a new file (temporarily — it's a big 70 megabyte file with all those new pixels!) with *File|Save As* and give it a different name. Don't close the file though. Let's compare it to a one-step resampling. If you were actually preparing this image for printing, you would likely want to run an unsharp mask on it at this point (*Filter|Sharpen|Unsharp Mask* followed by *Edit|Fade Unsharp Mask* with a Mode setting of Luminosity) as covered in **Chapter 12**.

7. Re-open the original M17.tif file (*File|Open*). Now we will resample the image again, but this time using only one big step.

8. Open *Image|Image Size*. Once again keep Resample Image (Bicubic method) and Constrain Pro-

Fig. 11.10 Hoon Im's Stairstep Image Size Photoshop Plug-In appears in the *File|Automate* submenu. It automates the process of upsampling in small increments to improve image quality.

portions checked. Change the Pixel Dimensions Width from 1092 pixels to 6000 pixels and click OK. This takes us to our 20 inch by 14 inch print size in one step.

9. Press the Tab key once to clear your screen of Photoshop's Palettes (pressing the Tab key again will restore them). This will make it easier to view the two image files side-by-side for comparison.

10. Now select *Window|Arrange|Tile Vertically*. This arranges the two image files side-by-side.

11. Press the letter Z on your keyboard to select the Zoom Tool (this is a shortcut). Enlarge each image to display at 100% (Actual Pixels). You can also do this in one step with *View|Actual Pixels*, or by double-clicking on the Zoom Tool icon in the Toolbox. Hold down your keyboard spacebar to temporarily change the Zoom Tool into the Hand Tool (white glove) and move each image around so that you are looking at the same area.

The Stair Interpolated image looks slightly better (**Figure 11.11**). The stars and nebula are a bit sharper, with more definition. This is particularly noticeable along the edges of objects.

Now Zoom in to 300% (**Figure 11.12**). The improvement in the Stair Interpolated image is now easily perceived. The "one-step" upsized image clearly shows pixelation noise and image details are soft. The SI image is smoother, with less pixelation throughout. It is also sharper; there is more definition in both the stars and nebula.

Figure 11.13 shows our SI image (on the left) compared to the Genuine Fractals enlargement (on the right). Both are shown at a 200% view. In this case, Genuine Fractals produces a superior enlargement. The nebulosity is much more defined and the stars are sharper than the SI image enlargement. However, using Hoon Im's Stairstep Image Size plug-in, set for 5% steps, I created another enlargement shown in **Figure**

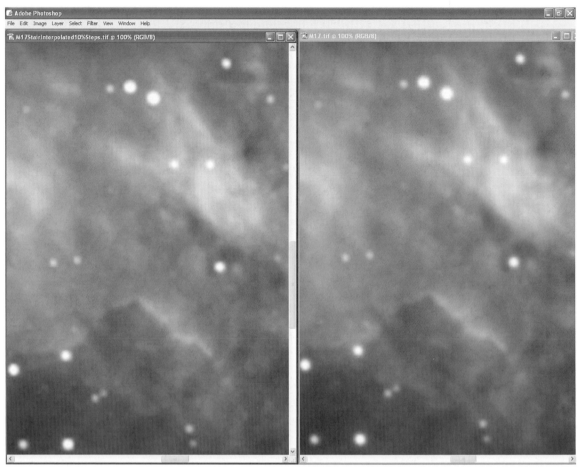

Fig. 11.11 Stair Interpolation using 10% steps (left) results in sharper stars and cleaner edges than to a "one-shot" upsampling (right). Each image is shown at 100% ("Actual Pixels").

11.14. Here we see an SI enlargement that is very close in quality, perhaps even superior to, the one created in Genuine Fractals. The SI image does show some processing artifacts not visible in the Genuine Fractals one, such as dark halos around the brighter stars. However, the fainter nebula details look sharper and more contrasty.

It is difficult to draw any general conclusions about which methods of resampling work best. Too much depends upon the individual image characteristics. Also, personal preferences about how a print should look are an important factor. Ultimately, as with so many things photographic, you must let your own eyes be your guide. Develop your printing workflow and resampling methods based upon your own experimentation and print results.

That said, my recommendation would be to incorporate Stair Interpolation into your workflow as your basic upward resampling method. Use a plug-in such as Im's (another source is Fred Miranda's Website; see

Appendix) to make the process easier. Choose step settings of between 5% and 10%. Using stair interpolation with 16-bit images will provide more tonal scale for all those bicubic interpolation steps, giving a "cleaner" and more accurate final result.

If you make a lot of large prints, consider investing in some additional photoshop plug-ins like Genuine Fractals, or S-Spline. By having different upsampling methods at your disposal, you will be better able to create the print that you want no matter what the size or subject content. As I have said throughout this book, it is best to have as many tools in your processing toolkit as possible. Knowing when to select a given tool and how to use it are the keys to solving image-processing problems and fulfilling your creative intent.

Sizing Images for the Web and Computer Monitor Display

Sizing images for Web display (computer monitor dis-

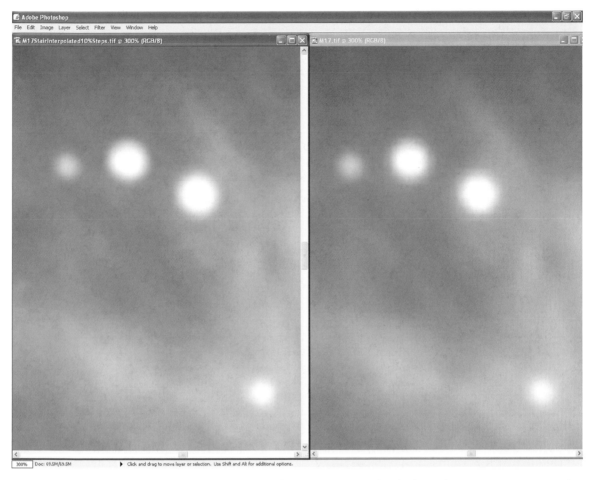

Fig. 11.12 At 300%, the Stair Interpolated image (left) using 10% steps clearly shows improvement over one-step upsampling (right).

play) is fairly straightforward compared to sizing them for print output. Since a typical computer screen normally displays between 72 ppi and 100 ppi, you don't need as much information to make a good-looking screen image as you do for a high-quality print (300 ppi).

There is a one-to-one relationship between a pixel in your image and a pixel on your computer monitor. Each image pixel is represented by one monitor pixel. Unlike printing, there are no halftoning issues, ink dot patterns and ink/paper color issues to worry about. Instead of resampling images upward as we do for printing, we will be resampling images downward ("downsampling or "downsizing"), when preparing them for Web display.

Our goals are as follows:

1. Resample the image and assign an appropriate color profile so that it will display well on most computer monitors.

2. Create a reasonably small-sized image file so that it will load quickly when retrieved from the Web.

3. Retain as much image quality as possible in the displayed image.

Usually there is a tradeoff to be made between items 2 and 3. The smaller the image file size, the lower the image quality and vice versa. File compression using the JPEG format will help us circumvent this problem.

Let's first examine how we want our images to display on a computer monitor. The information that appears on your monitor is displayed in a two-dimensional set of pixels that fills your screen. These pixels can vary in size, since monitors are capable of operating at different screen resolutions. Older VGA monitors were limited to a display 640 pixels wide by 480 pixels high. Today's monitors are capable of higher screen resolutions. SVGA monitors display resolutions of 800 x 600 pixels (the first number is the screen width

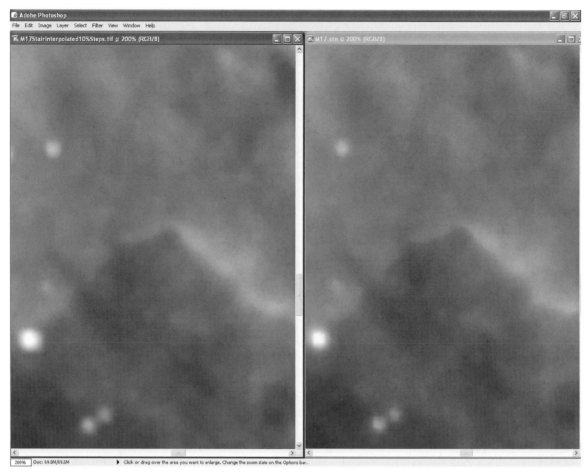

Fig. 11.13 The Genuine Fractals enlargement (right) produces a better result than the Stair Interpolated image (left) when 10% SI steps are used.

and the second number its height), or 1024 x 768 pixels. XGA monitors can display 1280 x 1024, 1400 x 1050 or even 1600 x 1200 pixels. The type of monitor and the video adapter card in use will determine the range of screen resolution settings that are available to the user.

Higher screen resolution settings will make images appear smaller. At a higher resolution setting, the computer monitor's pixels are smaller, and it takes more of them to fill up the screen. Since each image pixel displays as one screen pixel (remember, there is a one-to-one relationship between image pixels and screen pixels) the image will appear smaller on the screen. Conversely, lower screen resolutions display larger pixels and will make an image appear larger. **Figures 11.15**, **11.16** and **11.17** illustrate this point. Using Internet Explorer, I loaded a 792 x 651-pixel solar eclipse image from my Website and set my 21-inch monitor to display in three different screen resolution settings — 800 x 600, 1024 x 768 and 1280 x 1024.

The differences are readily apparent.

If you are using Windows and do not know your screen resolution setting, right-click on a blank area of your desktop, and choose Properties from the pop-up menu. Then click on the Settings tab. The slider labeled Screen Area indicates your monitor's resolution in pixels.

You will recall from our discussion earlier that the way an image appears on your monitor may vary greatly, but this does not affect the underlying image itself. Photoshop, as well as many other programs, allows you to zoom into and out of your image. This is merely a convenience and occurs without any change to your screen resolution. The program is remapping the image pixels to display on the screen either larger or smaller, as you choose. It is analogous to resampling, except that the image pixels themselves are not altered, only the way they are displayed on the screen. This is why it is important to view your image at 100% (Actual Pixels) for critical operations, such as unsharp masking. At

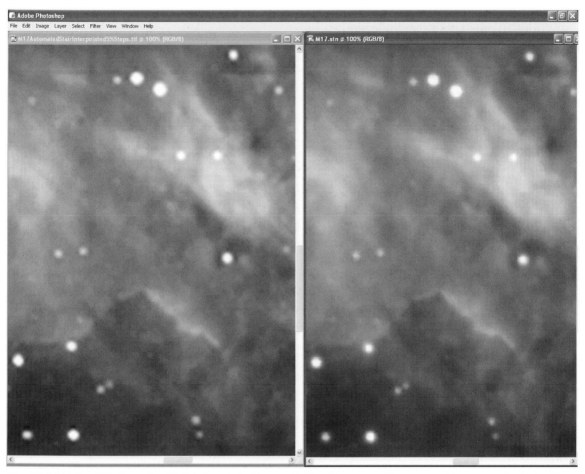

Fig. 11.14 Using 5% steps, the Stair Interpolated image (left) achieves quality comparable or superior to the Genuine Fractals enlargement (right). The SI image is at the limit of acceptability, however. Further processing would exaggerate the image artifacts that are already beginning to appear.

100% each screen pixel represents one image pixel. This is the "one-to-one" relationship between screen and image pixels that we have been talking about.

So, when preparing images for Web display, we must take into consideration that they will be viewed on various types of monitors set to various screen resolutions. If you were to place, say, a 2000 x 2000 pixel image on the Web, someone viewing it on a monitor with a typical screen resolution setting, such as 800 x 600 pixels or 1024 x 768 pixels, would have to scroll around their screen a lot to view it. So, in these circumstances, the image should be resampled downward ("downsampled" or "downsized"), to reduce its pixel dimensions.

We want to size our images destined for the Web so that they will display in a pleasing manner on most "typical" computer monitors. I am currently sizing my Web images to approximately 800 pixels in the long dimension. For most rectangular images, this results in

pixel dimensions of about 800 x 600. My logic in choosing this size is that I want the image to display fully on the screen, without scrolling, on most monitors. 800 x 600 is certainly a typical screen size these days, and many people use even higher screen resolutions. An 800 x 600-pixel image will still look good on a screen set to 1024 x 768 or even 1280 x 1024, so it seems to me to be a safe "middle ground" setting. I make an exception to this rule for special images, such as panoramas and mosaics, in which scrolling seems to be more "correct" in order to portray the image scale and proportions properly.

You will likely also want to create a "thumbnail" image if you are posting on a Web page. Thumbnails are much smaller images that are helpful to the viewer when scanning through many different images on a Website. Rather than having to load each full-sized image file, the viewer can scan through several thumbnails on one page and click on the ones of interest to

R. Scott Ireland

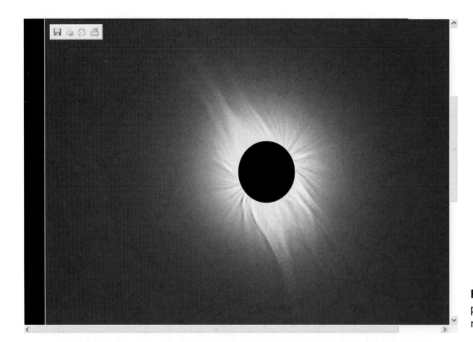

Fig. 11.15 A 792 x 651 pixel image displayed at a computer monitor screen resolution of 800 x 600 pixels.

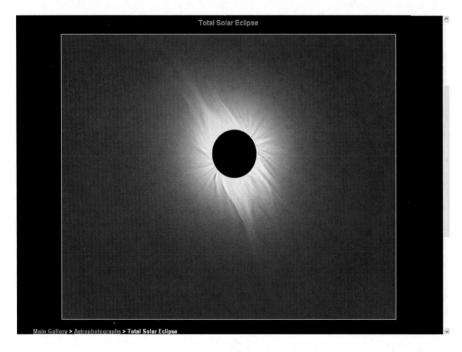

Fig. 11.16 The same image displayed at a computer monitor screen resolution of 1024 x 768 pixels.

load the full-sized image files for display. In my view, the trick to creating good thumbnails is to make them large enough so that the viewer has a good idea of what the image looks like. However, the tradeoff is that you don't want them so large that they take a long time to load, and you also want several of them to fit on one page. I like to size my thumbnails to around 150 to 200 pixels in their long dimension. Some people like to use 100 pixels or so, but I find these a little too small to get a good representation of the image. Using 150 to 200

pixels for the long dimension will give you around 100 to 135 pixels for the short dimension for rectangular images. It is also sometimes desirable to have thumbnails of slightly varying sizes, in order to draw more attention to a particular image, or to create some variability so that the page is visually interesting. **Figure 11.18** shows a thumbnails page from my Website with about 12 images to the page.

Let us now consider file sizes, types and color profiles to use for our Web images and thumbnails. Tradi-

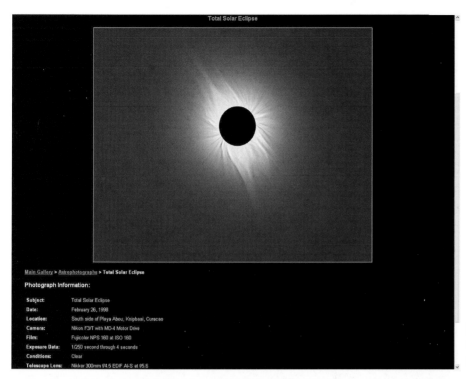

Fig. 11.17 The same image displayed at a screen resolution of 1280 x 1024 pixels.

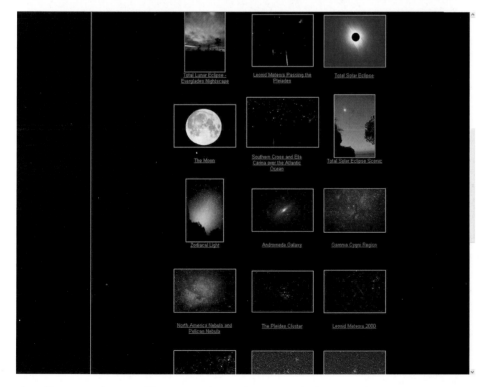

Fig. 11.18 "Thumbnail" images sized between 150 and 200 pixels in the long dimension will give the viewer an excellent preview of the full-sized images.

tionally, two image file types have been used for creating Web pages, JPEG and GIF. The objective is to make the smallest file size possible, so that the Web page will load quickly in the viewer's browser. For displaying photographs on the Web, JPEG is the way to go. GIF files are limited to 256 colors, which is fine for line art, logos and the like, but not for photographs. GIF will posterize photographs due to the lack of sufficient color range. If you want to see what this would look like, just adjust your screen display to show only 256 colors (in Windows, you can make this adjustment in the same screen dialog box described above — just

R. Scott Ireland

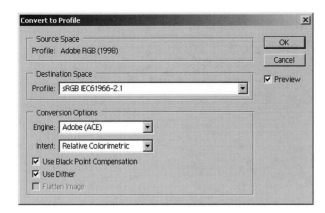

Fig. 11.19 The sRGB color space is preferable for Web images. Photoshop's *Image\Mode\Convert to Profile* (*Edit\Convert to Profile* in CS2) command converts from the Adobe RGB (1998) working color space to sRGB. The color space profile may be embedded and saved along with the image file.

right-click on a blank area of your screen and choose Properties, then Settings and adjust the color quality downward). Newer graphics cards may not even allow for a setting this low, but you may rest assured that if you use GIFs your photographs will look totally weird. Incidentally, while we are on the subject of color range, this would be a good time to make sure that your monitor display is set for True Color or Highest, which will be either 24-bit or 32-bit color.

Sizing an Image for Web Display — Photoshop Example

Let's work through an example to illustrate how to prepare an image for the Web:

1. From the tutorial disc, open the file Solar Eclipse.tif (*File\Open*). This is an image of the 1998 solar eclipse taken by me and my wife Lou in Curaçao.

2. If your Photoshop settings are set to display Extras (in this case, Guides), you may be saying to yourself "what the heck are those blue lines on the screen???" Well, those are registration guides that I used to create the solar eclipse composite. A handy shortcut to toggle the display of these items (which includes color sampler points and the like) on and off is Ctrl+H (on the menu *View\Extras*). If the blue lines are displayed, use Ctrl+H to remove them now.

3. Before we do anything else, let's take a look at the pixel dimensions of the image. Open the Image Size dialog box (*Image\Image Size*). The pixel dimensions are 3918 x 3219. The image is only slightly rectangular. The TIFF image file size is around 36.1 megabytes. We want the Width to be 800 pixels for our Web image. We also want an image that is, say, 170 pixels wide for a thumbnail. So, we need to create two images by resam-

pling the original down in size.

4. In the Image Size dialog box, make sure that both Constrain Proportions and Resample Image are checked, and set the interpolation method to Bicubic.

5. Change the pixel Width from 3918 to 800. The Height changes automatically to 657 pixels. 800 x 657 will be a good size to use for Web display. Notice also that both the new and old file sizes are displayed. Our new, reduced file size will be about 1.5 megabytes. The Document Size settings in the Image Size dialog do not make any difference at all to us. Remember, an image is defined only by its pixel dimensions, and it will be displayed on a computer monitor one for one — one image pixel equals one monitor pixel. Click OK to resample the image downward.

6. The image became much smaller. Type Ctrl+0 (zero), *View\Fit on Screen* or double-click on the Hand Tool Icon in the Toolbox to have Photoshop enlarge the image to fit on the screen (remember this is only for screen display — it does not affect the image pixels themselves).

7. Next, we want to convert the image from our standard working color space — Adobe RGB (1998) — to one that is more suitable for Web display. The color space that we want to use is sRGB. Select *Image\Mode\Convert to Profile* (*Edit\Convert to Profile* in CS2) A dialog box appears similar to the one shown in **Figure 11.19**. The Source Space is Adobe RGB (1998), our standard working space. In the Destination Space area, there is a drop-down selection box that allows us to choose from a variety of color spaces. Choose sRGB (there are also several letters and numbers after "sRGB"; don't worry about those — as long as sRGB is shown at

Fig. 11.20 JPEG is the ideal file type for Web images. It offers significant reduction in file size without a noticeable loss of image quality. A JPEG file should only be created once, when needed, and never re-saved since it is a "lossy" file format.

the beginning, it is the correct color space). Under Conversion Options, make sure that Engine is set to Adobe (ACE); Intent is set to Relative Colorimetric; and both the Use Black Point Compensation and Use Dither checkboxes are checked. Click OK to convert the image to the sRGB color space. You will recall from an earlier chapter that sRGB is a device-dependent color space that has a narrower color gamut (fewer colors) than Adobe RGB (1998). It is designed to make images look their best on an average PC color monitor.

We (almost) always want to work from a wider gamut color space to a narrower one, which is one of the reasons we use Adobe RGB (1998) as our standard working color space. It renders more colors than our monitors can display (sRGB), but this additional color information can be useful when making prints and for other output uses. It does no good to convert an image from a smaller gamut color space to a larger one — such as converting from sRGB to Adobe RGB (1998). Once the additional color information has been discarded, it's gone and cannot be recovered. This is the main reason why we stick with Adobe RGB (1998) as our standard working space and only convert to the narrower gamut sRGB when necessary to create images for the Web.

It is also a good workflow habit to embed color space profiles in your image files, so that you and others will know, when an image file is opened, what color space it was created in. An ICC color profile checkbox is offered by Photoshop when you save the file.

8. Now we will break one of our standard workflow

rules. We will apply some light sharpening to the image, even though we have not yet reached the last processing step. Change to a 100% view (double-click on the Zoom Tool icon in the Toolbox). Run a light unsharp mask with *Filter|Sharpen|Unsharp Mask* and use settings of (100, 1, 3). Then select *Edit|Fade Unsharp Mask* and use the Luminosity Mode (this has the effect of sharpening only the luminosity information in the image, not the color information, the result being fewer processing artifacts). Click OK.

9. So now we have successfully downsampled our image to the correct pixel dimensions for Web display, converted its color space/profile to the appropriate sRGB color space and applied light sharpening to it — but we still have a problem. A 1.5MB file is too big. It would take too long to load into a Web browser. This is where the JPEG file format comes to the rescue. Select *File|Save As*. Under Format, choose JPEG. Make sure that the ICC profile box is checked to embed the sRGB profile in the saved image. Click Save.

10. A JPEG Options dialog box appears like the one in **Figure 11.20**. Notice the Quality settings under Image Options. There is a numerical setting that ranges from 0 to 12. Next to that is a drop-down box with Low, Medium, High and Maximum quality settings. These two settings are interactive — changing one will alter the other. However, it is more convenient to use the Small File — Large File slider located below the quality setting boxes. Make sure that the Preview box is checked and

then drag the slider back and forth and look at the effect on the image. At 0 (low) quality, the image looks pretty bad — there are lots of artifacts in the background areas, and the whole image shows pixelation. You have to move the slider up to around 7 (medium) or higher before the image looks good. Now notice the size information at the bottom of the dialog box. A setting of 7 will result in a 34.85 kilobyte JPEG file. Pretty good considering that we started with a 1.5MB TIFF file. If I were preparing this image for Web display, however, I would choose a setting of 10 (in the "maximum" range), which will result in a file size of around 118KB. I generally try to keep my file sizes at or above 100KB, but below 250KB for full-sized Web images.

Remember that JPEG is a "lossy" file format. The reason that JPEG files are smaller is that the image information is compressed. If you were to re-save a JPEG file, it would be compressed again, resulting in more noise and compression artifacts being introduced into the image. Always work from a "lossless" format like TIFF to a "lossy" format like JPEG. Only save a JPEG file once — never re-save it. This is why we applied sharpening to the image before we converted it to JPEG.

11. Select 8 as the JPEG Quality setting. Check Baseline (Standard) as the format option. Click OK to save the file if you want to take a closer look at the file size and image quality, otherwise click Cancel and close the dialog.

Now let's create the thumbnail image:

1. Re-open the file Solar Eclipse.tif (*File|Open*) and follow the steps through 4 of the previous example.

2. At Step 5, change the pixel Width from 3918 to 170 and click OK. This gives us pixel dimensions of 170 x 140, which will make a nice thumbnail image.

3. Proceed through Step 7 (converting to the sRGB color space), but *do not* run an unsharp mask on the image (Step 9). Unsharp masking is not really necessary for thumbnails. They appear very small on the screen, and applying USM to images with small pixel dimensions quickly creates pixelation and other artifacts. Now view the image at 100% (double-click on the Zoom Tool icon in the Toolbox). This is how it will appear on a page of

thumbnail images.

4. Save the thumbnail as a JPEG file with *File|Save As*. Be sure to use a different file name for your thumbnails so that you do not inadvertently over-write your primary image file. I generally just append the word thumbnail to the end of the file name. Under Format, choose JPEG. Make sure that the ICC profile box is checked to embed the sRGB profile in the saved image. Click Save. In the JPEG Options dialog box, use the Maximum setting of 12 and the Baseline (Standard) format option. This will give a file size of about 19.7K. Click OK to save the thumbnail.

In our discussion of upward resampling, we saw that using the Stair Interpolation method gave us excellent results. Will the same procedure work well for downsampling? Well, not necessarily. **Figure 11.21** shows a comparison using the solar eclipse image that we just worked on. On the left, the image was downsampled to 800 x 657 pixels using Stair Interpolation with 10% steps. On the right, the image was downsampled in one step, just as in the above tutorial. The one-step procedure results in a better image, with sharper highlights, fewer artifacts and less pixelation of the background. Use SI for upsampling, but do your downsampling in one step.

Photoshop CS and CS2 — Additional Resampling Options

Beginning with Photoshop CS, two additional methods of bicubic resampling have been added: Bicubic Smoother and Bicubic Sharper (**Figure 11.22**). Adobe indicates that Bicubic Smoother will produce smoother results (hence the name), with less artifacts than the regular Bicubic interpolation method when enlarging images (upsampling). Bicubic Sharper is supposed to preserve more detail when the pixel dimensions are reduced (downsampling). Some Photoshop users believe that the results are as good as, or even better than, using the Stair Interpolation method.

My tests of Bicubic Smoother and Bicubic Sharper were disappointing. **Figure 11.23** compares images that were upsampled using our previous M17 example (resizing for a 20 inch by 14 inch print). The image on the left was upsampled in one step using Bicubic Smoother. That on the right was upsampled using Stair Interpolation with 5% increments. The Stair Interpolation image is clearly superior in every way. It is sharp-

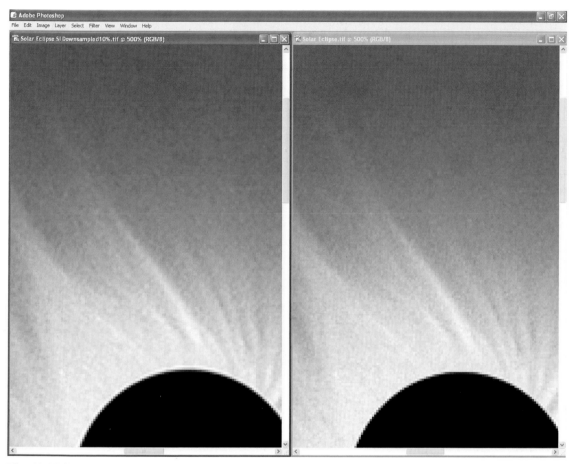

Fig. 11.21 Stair Interpolation is not as effective for downsampling as it is for upsampling. The image on the left, downsampled using SI, shows more pixelation and other processing artifacts. The "one-shot" downsampled image on the right is superior.

er, with more detail, yet it does not suffer from halos, grain or other artifacts. The Bicubic Smoother image looks mushy in comparison.

Figure 11.24 shows the same comparison, but this time the Bicubic Smoother enlargement was made using Stair Interpolation with 5% increments. This made matters worse. The stars have both dark and light halos, and the overall image is less sharp than using Bicubic Smoother in one step.

Figure 11.25 shows the result using the Bicubic Sharper method to downsample the solar eclipse image that we just worked on. The image on the left was downsampled in one step using the Bicubic Sharper method. That on the right was downsampled in one step using the standard Bicubic method. I like the image on the right better. The Bicubic Sharper method

creates too much pixelation. It appears oversharp without bringing out any more image detail. If sharpening is desired, I suspect that better results may be achieved by using the unsharp mask filter on a standard Bicubic downsampled image. This should afford the photographer more control over the final result.

It is possible that Bicubic Smoother and Bicubic Sharper may be useful in certain circumstances, depending upon the particular image. Astrophotographs are very unique in their characteristics, so let me not be too harsh in judging these new interpolation methods. They may prove more useful in upsizing and downsizing standard "daylight" images, for which they were presumably designed. If you use Photoshop CS or CS2, then I encourage you to experiment with them yourself.

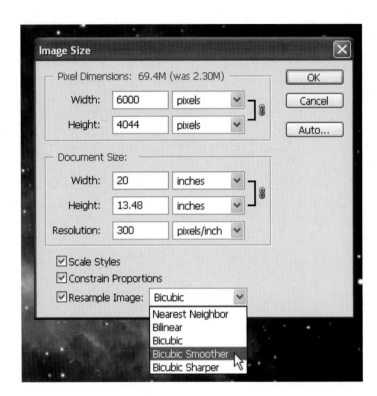

Fig. 11.22 Photoshop CS introduced two additional Bicubic Interpolation methods, Bicubic Smoother and Bicubic Sharper. Bicubic Smoother is supposed to improve upsampled images, while Bicubic Sharper is designed for downsampling.

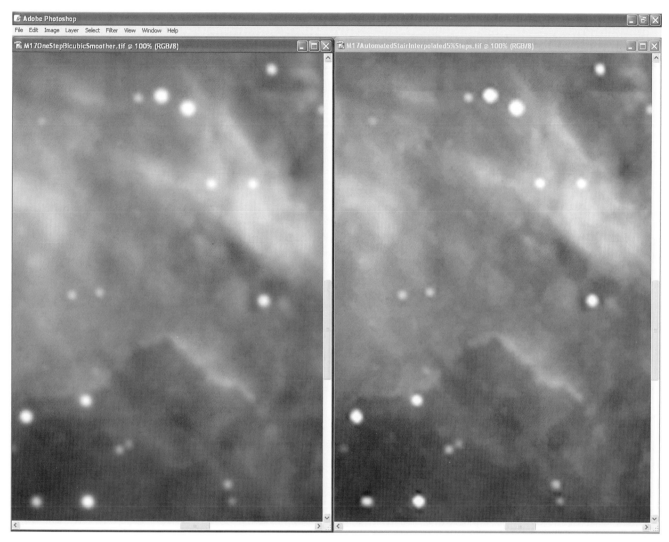

Fig. 11.23 The Bicubic Smoother method was used in one step to upsample the left image. Stair Interpolation, using the standard Bicubic method applied in 5% steps, was used to upsample the image on the right. Stair Interpolation is clearly superior in this instance.

R. Scott Ireland

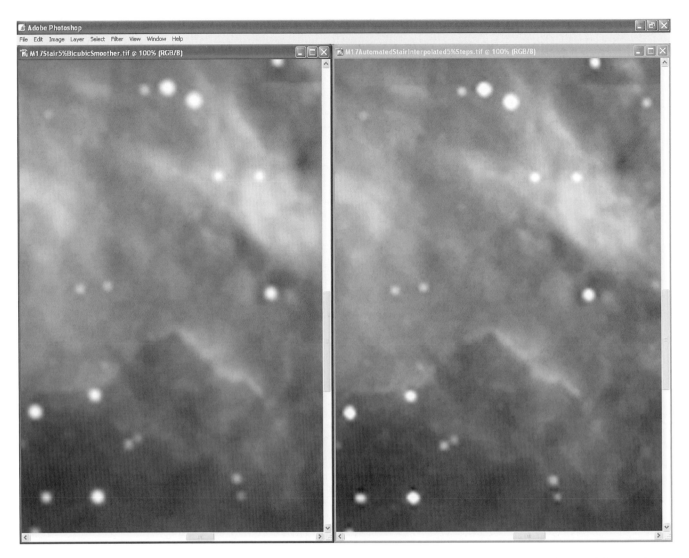

Fig. 11.24 Using Stair Interpolation steps when applying the Bicubic Smoother method (left image) is even less satisfactory than applying Bicubic Smoother in one step. On the right, for comparison, is our standard SI image (5% steps) enlarged using the Bicubic method.

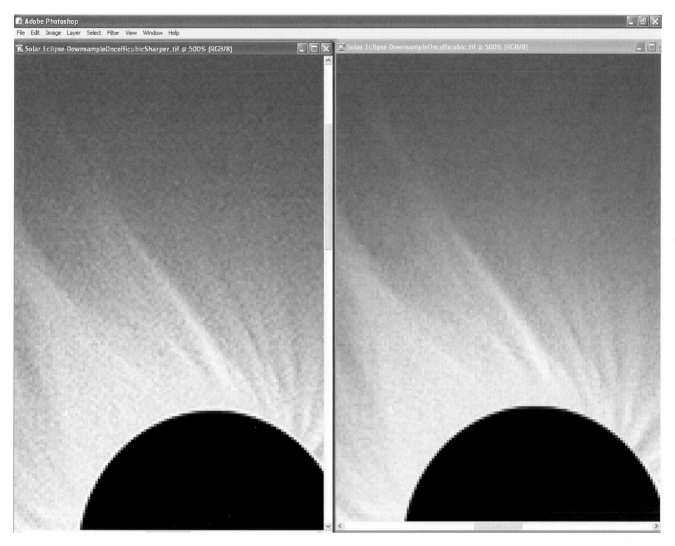

Fig. 11.25 The Bicubic Sharper method was used in one step to downsample the left image. The right image was downsampled in one step using the standard Bicubic method. In this case, the standard Bicubic method gives better results.

R. Scott Ireland

Chapter 12
Sharpening and Unsharp Masking

He was always smoothing and polishing himself, and in the end he became blunt before he was sharp

G. C. Lichtenberg

Unsharp Masking ("USM") is the principal tool that we use to sharpen images in the digital darkroom. The term "unsharp" seems contradictory when describing a sharpening function, and it is a frequent source of confusion among novices. It derives from offset printing practices. A slightly blurred and inverted (negative) film image is registered with the original positive to create a new image on the printing plate. The differences between the softer edges of the "unsharp" version and the sharper edges of the original are exaggerated in the composite. Dark edges become darker and light edges become lighter. This creates an overall impression of increased sharpness.

The two perceptual elements that define "sharpness" are resolution and acutance. Resolution is straightforward. The sharper the optic, the higher the resolution it will deliver and the more detail you will see in the image (for the most part). Acutance describes brightness changes between the edges of objects and the areas surrounding them. When these edge transitions are accentuated (higher acutance), the image appears sharper. An image lacking acutance may appear softer than it really is, for instance, a high-resolution image taken on film with little or no grain, but containing few fine image details, may appear soft. The same effect can be seen in digital camera images, since there is no film grain and backgrounds appear "smoother". Conversely, an image taken with a grainy film may sometimes appear sharper due to the acutance effect relating to the film grains themselves. This is a trick worth remembering for either digital or film captures. Sometimes adding a fine noise pattern to a soft image can create the illusion of higher overall sharpness.

Unsharp Masking increases the apparent sharpness of an image by increasing brightness differences between pixels at the edge of an object and the sur-

rounding pixels. It increases image acutance. Photoshop's Unsharp Mask Filter accomplishes this by examining the contrast between adjacent pixels, and, when the contrast is higher than a user-specified amount (threshold), it increases it some more.

If this sounds like legerdemain, an illusion . . . well, it is. Artists have used this trick for centuries. By painting fine, contrasting dark and light lines around object edges they create definition, direct attention and give the illusion of added dimension. Sharpness is a subjective concept. It depends upon our individual perceptions. Add it to your ever-growing list of examples that prove vision to be an interpretive, and not an absolute, faculty.

Virtually all images benefit from some sharpening. Image softness is introduced by:

1. Translating the continuous tones of the real world into the quantized, discrete pixels of a CCD image.

2. Film scanning, since it is an additional generation removed from the original image and also converts continuous tones into the digital domain.

3. Vibrations, atmospheric turbulence/seeing, haze, water vapor, clouds, atmospheric particulates/transparency and focus.

4. Altering image pixels through image processing. Almost all of the processing steps that we apply operate to soften the image.

5. Resampling an image (up or down). Sharpening must be applied or re-applied after resampling.

6. Printing. Ink droplets "spread out" when applied to paper, softening the image.

Remember, the most information that you will ever have lies in your original image. All image processing decreases this information. Our manipulations do not create details, they re-arrange tonalities to emphasize one thing over another and re-direct the viewer's attention. We are pixel magicians. Done well, our "tricks" can produce amazing results. And Unsharp Masking is one of the best illusions in the repertoire.

Fig. 12.1 Photoshop's Unsharp Mask ("USM") Filter dialog box. Note that the star in the Preview Window is surrounded by a small box in the image window (just below the comet nucleus). It is most effective to gauge the overall effect of USM by viewing the main image at 100% ("Actual Pixels"). Use the USM Preview window to Zoom in and evaluate the dark sharpening halos around bright stars.

"One-Pass" Unsharp Masking

1. From the tutorial disc, open the file Hale-Bopp.tif (*File|Open*). This is a full-resolution 2700 dpi scanned film image of the comet taken by Lester Shalloway and me. No processing has been applied except for a small Levels adjustment.

2. Duplicate the Background Layer with the shortcut Ctrl+J. Select the Zoom Tool from the Toolbox (keyboard shortcut "Z") and Zoom into the image to a 100% view. You may also select "Actual Pixels" from the Tool Options Bar at the top of the Photoshop window or double-click on the Zoom Tool icon in the Toolbox (the little magnifying glass) or use the keyboard shortcut Ctrl+Alt+0. All of these will Zoom the image to a 100% view. Frame the image to place the comet nucleus near the bottom-right of the image window.

3. With the Background copy Layer active ("Layer 1"), choose *Filter|Sharpen|Unsharp Mask*. The Unsharp Mask dialog box appears (**Figure 12.1**). Check the "Preview" box. This will enable you to

preview the effect of your settings in the main image window. As you work with different settings, click this box on and off to judge the USM effect. A small preview window is included in the USM dialog box, but it is much easier to judge the overall effect by looking at the main image window. You can zoom in and out of the image without closing the USM dialog box. In the image window, hold down the Ctrl key and a small magnifying glass with a "+" sign in the middle appears; this allows you to zoom in. Hold down the Alt key and the "+" changes to a "–", allowing you to zoom out.

The USM dialog box has three slider controls — Amount, Radius and Threshold.

a. "Radius" is the first slider we will consider, because it is the most important. This setting determines the width of the sharpening halos (the exaggerated darkening and lightening around edge pixels). A 2-pixel Radius setting does not, however, produce a 2-pixel wide sharpening halo. Instead, it tells Photoshop to "look outward" 2 pixels when comparing brightness differences to evaluate if and how much a pixel should be sharpened. Nevertheless, a higher Radius setting produces broader sharpening halos than a lower setting. The correct Radius is highly dependent upon image content, and it is the key setting for effective use of the USM filter.

b. "Amount" is specified as a percentage. Increasing this value increases the sharpening effect. A narrow Radius setting will require a higher Amount than a wide Radius to achieve a similar amount of sharpening.

c. "Threshold" specifies the amount by which the brightness levels of compared pixels must vary before they are considered edge pixels and sharpening is applied. Increasing this value reduces the sharpening effect, since we are specifying that more variation in pixel brightness is required before the filter is applied. Increasing the Threshold setting increases the "smoothness" of the USM effect, and acts as a sort of noise reduction filter. A setting of "0" sharpens all of the pixels in the image.

4. If you move the cursor into the main image window, you see that it becomes a small box. Center the cursor box over a bright star and click once. The star now appears in the USM Preview window. Zoom the USM Preview window to 300% or 400%.

5. Now set the Amount slider to its maximum setting of 500%; set the Threshold to 0 and adjust the Radius setting to a point where the dark sharpening halos around bright stars are just beginning to be noticeable. Click the cursor on different stars and examine the effect in the USM Preview window as you change settings. Move the cursor into the USM Preview window and left-click the mouse on and off to see the "before and after" effect. Don't worry about how bad the image looks at this point. As is so often the case, it is most helpful to exaggerate effects in Photoshop to find the best path to take, and that is what we are doing here. We must first find the correct Radius setting for this image content, then we will back off the Amount and adjust the Threshold. Move the Radius slider to a high setting (7 pixels or so) and watch the dark sharpening halos around bright stars reduce as you then lower the Radius. My fi-

nal Radius setting was 1.3 pixels. At this setting, I can just detect the dark sharpening halos around the brighter stars. Set the Radius to 1.3 pixels.

6. Adjust the Amount setting to achieve the desired level of sharpening. I backed this setting down to 200%, the point at which the dark sharpening halos around bright stars just disappeared. It is helpful at this point to Zoom the main image window in and out to view the overall effect, and click the Preview checkbox on and off. There are no hard and fast rules to USM. It is much more of an art than a science. The "right" settings will vary considerably from file to file. You must ultimately be the judge. For now, set the Amount at 200%.

7. We have lightly sharpened the image, but we have also sharpened the film grain. The image viewed at 100% (always use 100% — "Actual Pixels" — for critical evaluation) is too gritty. Increase the Threshold to achieve the best balance between reduction of graininess and loss of sharpening effect. My choice for Threshold is a setting of 10. Set the Threshold to 10 and click OK to apply the Unsharp Mask Filter.

8. Immediately select *Edit | Fade Unsharp Mask*. Set "Mode" to "Luminosity", leave the Opacity at 100% and click OK.

Using the *Edit | Fade* command with the Blending Mode set to Luminosity sharpens only the luminance information and not the color information. This helps to reduce noise and graininess and avoid color shifts. Recall from **Chapter 9** on LRGB that we blurred the color information to improve the noise characteristics of the image. Luminance is more important to our perception of detail and sharpness than color. It is better to sharpen only the luminance — sharpening color just increases noise. It can also cause color shifts since USM is applied to each color channel individually. Dark and light sharpening halos are created based upon the grayscale values in each color channel, without regard for what the overall color is supposed to look like. Sharpening luminosity, in effect, sharpens only one combined grayscale image, rather than three separate ones (three channels for RGB; four channels in the case of a CMYK image).

It is also possible to convert an image into the LAB color model (*Image | Mode | Lab Color*) and apply Unsharp Masking to the luminance channel only. However, using the *Edit | Fade Unsharp Mask* command set to Luminosity Mode will generate comparable results,

R. Scott Ireland

Fig. 12.2 Unsharp Masking works by creating light and dark sharpening "halos" where brightness transitions are greatest – presumably the edges of objects in the image. The halos exaggerate these brightness transitions and create an illusion of increased image sharpness.

without the potential for quantization errors introduced by moving the image into and out of the LAB color space (particularly with 8-bit images).

The overall sharpening effect in this example is very subtle. We have merely given the image a touch more definition and clarity. If you'll forgive the simile, Unsharp Masking is like a strong spice, a little goes a long way. Don't overdo it. The best image processing occurs when you cannot tell that the image has been processed at all.

As an independent exercise, I encourage you to try different settings of your own and critically examine the results. Facility with USM improves the more you work with it.

Selective Sharpening using Layer Style Blending Options

Many times you will find that Unsharp Masking applied to an entire image ("one-pass" sharpening) produces desirable results in some areas and undesirable results in others. Sharpening an object of interest may exaggerate background grain and noise, as we saw in our first example. Conversely, there are instances where appropriate sharpening of the background stars may cause a nebula or galaxy to appear oversharpened and harsh.

In such cases, the solution is to apply different amounts of sharpening to different image areas. In the following example, we will employ layer-based sharpening — using the power of Photoshop's three-dimensional layer structure to differentially sharpen an image. We will also explore the use of Layer Style Blending Options as a tool to combine layers based upon specified tonal relationships.

1. From the tutorial disc, open the file M33.tif (*File|Open*). This is an image of M33 taken by Herm Perez.

2. Zoom the image to 100% ("Actual Pixels"). Examine the galaxy, the stars and the sky background. We see that the background is fairly smooth and not very grainy. But the galaxy and surrounding areas show more grain and fine detail. In this case, we will be able to sharpen the stars and sky background more than the galaxy. Now let's look through the individual Channels in search of a mask. We want to separate the galaxy from the stars and background. Open the Channels Palette (*Window|Channels*) and examine the individual color channels. Always look through the individual Channels when considering the use of a mask. Usually you will find that one Channel provides greater contrast between the object of interest and its surroundings, and can be used as the starting point to construct a mask. Remember, whenever possible let the image do your work for you. Here we see that the Blue Channel provides the best contrast and tonal definition of the galaxy (**Figure 12.3**). But in this case, we have a problem. There are too many foreground stars in the same area as the galaxy. We want all of the stars in the image to appear natural, so we need to sharpen them all the same. But it will be difficult to construct a mask that separates the stars from the galaxy. It would require a lot of tedious "hand painting" to mask them out. We need another way to separate the galaxy midtones and three-quarter tones from the star highlights.

3. From the Layers Palette, Duplicate the Background layer with Ctrl+J. First, we will sharpen the stars. With the galaxy centered in the image window, select *Filter|Sharpen|Unsharp Mask*. Determine an appropriate sharpening Radius by setting the Amount to maximum (500%) and the Threshold to 0. Examine the dark sharpening halos around several stars, both near the galaxy's center and in the sky background. Choose a Radius setting where the dark halos are just becoming visible. I ended up with a Radius setting of 0.7 pixels. Now examine the stars and the sky background only, to determine the settings for Amount

and Threshold. Do not be concerned with the oversharpened appearance of the galaxy, we will fix this later. The stars and sky background look good at the maximum Amount setting of 500%. Also, leaving the Threshold at 0 does not produce objectionable background noise. So leave these settings alone. Do not be afraid to use a 500% amount. The key to USM is the Radius, and once we have set that we want to apply as much sharpening as the image will take. Hitting the amount hard is not necessarily a problem if you've carefully regulated the sharpening halos.

For convenience, from this point on I will specify USM settings in this format: (500, 0.7, 0), meaning Amount = 500%; Radius = 0.7 pixels; Threshold = 0.

Enter the USM values (500, 0.7, 0) and click OK to apply the Unsharp Mask. Immediately select *Edit|Fade Unsharp Mask*, set the Mode to Luminosity and click OK. Double-click the "Layer 1" name and change it to "Stars; USM 500, 0.7, 0".

4. Re-center the galaxy at a 100% View. Click on the "Add a layer style" icon at the bottom left of the Layers Palette (it looks like a small "f" surrounded by a black circle). Choose "Blending Options" to open the Layer Style dialog box (**Figure 12.4**). You may also open the Layer Style dialog by double-clicking on the Layer image icon or the area to the right of the Layer Name.

We are interested in the Layer Blending Options, particularly the "Blend If" sliders located near the bottom of the dialog box. These sliders allow us to control which pixel tonalities from both the active Layer, and the underlying Layer Stack, will show through into the final image.

Move the Shadow slider (the left slider) for "This Layer" to the right to a setting of 120. The galaxy and background noise "drop out". We have specified that only pixel values above 120 in all three color Channels (Blend If: Gray) will be added to the Layer Stack. The shadows, three-quarter tones and most of the midtones are excluded. We have eliminated the galaxy and background and applied sharpening only to the bright stars. Click OK to close the Layer Style dialog box.

5. Now we need to sharpen the galaxy. Create another duplicate of the Background Layer and move it to the top of the Layer Stack. The image window now reverts back to the original unsharpened image. Zoom to 100% and center the galaxy in the

R. Scott Ireland

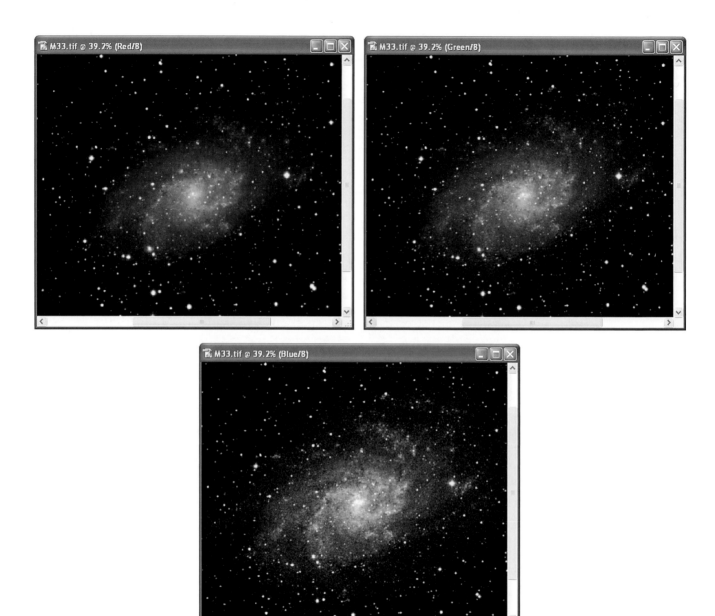

Fig. 12.3 Always examine the individual Color Channels for use as a mask. More often than not, one Channel will provide greater contrast and definition to help separate an object of interest from its surroundings. In this case, the Blue Channel (bottom) would be a good starting point for constructing a mask to separate the galaxy and background.

image window. Select *Filter | Sharpen | Unsharp Mask*, apply settings of (500, 2, 0) and click OK. This looks awful, but we want to exaggerate the USM temporarily to help us determine the best Layer Style settings to use.

6. Open the Background copy Layer Style dialog box and move the shadow and highlight sliders for "This Layer" to drop out the bright stars and background and apply sharpening only to the galaxy. It will be helpful to Zoom in and out of the image while adjusting the sliders to judge the overall effect (hold down the Ctrl key to Zoom in and the Alt key to Zoom out). I used a setting of 50 for the shadow slider and 150 for the highlight slider. Write down or remember the slider settings, then delete the Background copy Layer (drag it to the trash can icon).

7. Make another copy of the Background Layer and place it at the top of the Layer Stack. Zoom to 100%, center the galaxy and select *Filter | Sharpen | Unsharp*

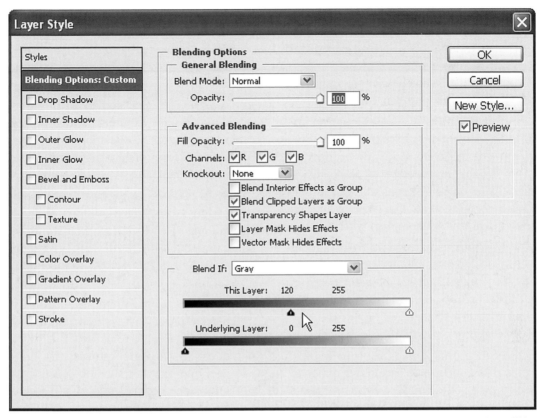

Fig. 12.4 The Layer Style dialog box. Use the "Blend If" sliders to regulate which Layer tonalities will be added into the Layer Stack. In this example, Layer tonal values between 120 and 255 in all three color Channels ("Blend If: Gray") will show through into the Layer Stack. Tones darker than 120 will be excluded.

Mask. Determine the USM settings for the galaxy. I used settings of (350, 1, 5) so enter these and click OK. Immediately select *Edit\Fade Unsharp Mask*, set the Mode to Luminosity and click OK. Open the Layer Style dialog box, move the sliders for "This Layer" to the settings determined in step 6 (50 for the shadow slider; 150 for the highlight slider) and click OK. Now the "Blend If" sliders drop out everything except the midtones and three-quarter tones — only the galaxy and the fainter stars show through. Rename this Layer to "Galaxy; USM 350, 1, 5". Note that you may separate each Blend If slider (although we do not need to for this example) by holding down the Alt key and clicking on it. The outside sliders are the "falloff" sliders; they gradually decrease the blend effect to smooth out tonal transitions.

By using the Layer Style "Blend If" sliders, we were able to target specific tonal ranges for each sharpening layer, effectively separate the galaxy from the brighter stars, and apply different sharpening settings to each. Had we used layer masks, we would not have been able to sharpen the stars in and around the galaxy convincingly. This image is cleaner and will produce a print superior to the original, a "one pass" sharpening technique, or selective sharpening using layer masks.

Sharpening Guidelines and Considerations

1. Under the *Filter\Sharpen* menu, use only the Unsharp Mask filter ("USM") or "Smart Sharpen" in Photoshop CS2. These offer a superior level of control over results. Photoshop's other sharpen filters are far inferior to USM or Smart Sharpen (this does not apply to other filters, such as the High Pass filter, which is a very useful sharpening tool).

2. Virtually all images benefit from some level of sharpening.

3. Sharpening should be performed as the last step in your image-processing workflow (except when sharpening planetary images). Save working files

R. Scott Ireland

unsharpened. After an image is resized or resampled for a particular use, then apply USM as a final step. The appropriate USM settings may differ greatly, for example, between a smaller image sized at 100 dpi for Web display and the same image sized for large print output at 300 dpi.

4. A corollary to #3 — resizing or resampling an image will likely destroy any sharpening halos previously applied, requiring USM to be applied again. This creates unnecessary repetitive USM steps that will degrade image quality. Remember, always use the minimum number of pixel-altering operations necessary to accomplish your task.

5. There are no "standard" USM settings. Proper USM technique depends upon the image pixel dimensions, its content and its intended purpose. Good USM technique requires judgement and is more of an art than a science.

6. As a general rule, larger files (larger pixel dimensions) require more sharpening than smaller files. Larger files also require more care and attention to USM techniques and settings. Lower sharpness settings used on a small file will achieve a similar apparent sharpness to higher settings used on a larger file. This is one of the reasons why sharpening should not be applied until the output size is determined.

7. The key to USM is the Radius setting, which controls the size of the dark and light sharpening halos. Determine the Radius setting first, then set the Amount and Threshold. The correct Radius will depend upon image content. A large Radius has more of an affect on broad (low frequency) details, while a small Radius has more affect on fine (high frequency) details.

8. Sharpen only Luminosity to avoid color shifts. Use the *Edit| Fade Unsharp Mask* command set to Luminosity Mode immediately after each USM operation, or set a sharpening layer to the Luminosity Layer Blending Mode. An exception to this rule occurs with multi-pass sharpening of planetary images. You may also convert an image to the LAB color model (*Image|Mode|Lab Color*) and sharpen only the Luminance channel. This also allows for blurring the "a" and "b" color channels to reduce noise.

9. Be careful to avoid obvious "haloing". Exaggerate USM by setting the Amount to 500% and Threshold to 0 when determining halo size (Radius). Independently adjust dark and light sharpening halos for more control.

10. Sharpen Web images and images to be displayed on computer monitors until they look good on screen. This also applies to images that will be output to any continuous-tone device, such as a film recorder or dye-sublimation printer. Images destined for normal print output should be slightly oversharpened.

11. With predominantly fine detail (high-frequency) images, experiment with "wide radius — low amount" USM settings. Sometimes this produces a more pleasing result, with less background noise than the typical "narrow radius — high amount" settings.

12. Don't be afraid to blur an image in order to gain more sharpness. It is often helpful to apply a light Gaussian Blur between each USM step in a sequential sharpening process. Or, convert the image into the LAB color space to sharpen the luminance channel and blur the color channels. Or, create a luminance layer in RGB and blur the underlying color information. These steps remove some of the harshness and "edginess" of USM and allow for a greater amount of overall sharpening. I alluded to this with the aphorism quoted at the head of this Chapter. You may be surprised to discover how often blurring can be used to create more effectively sharpened images. The larger lesson here is to think broadly and apply seemingly opposite concepts. As in life, the shortest path may not always be a straight line, you must frequently move in a direction opposite your goal. Blur to sharpen, add noise to sharpen, blur color in LRGB, use a contrasting complementary color to emphasize its opposite, reduce saturation to direct emphasis elsewhere, select stars to get a clean background selection, and so on.

13. Use USM carefully, but apply the maximum amount of sharpening that the image will allow. This requires finding the right balance. The best sharpening occurs when the image does not look like it was sharpened. Always strive for natural-looking results.

Layer-Based Selective Sharpening Using Layer Masks

Some images require extensive processing to achieve a desired level of sharpness. This is often true with planetary and solar images, particularly webcam and digital camera image stacks. It is more realistic to perform sharpening prior to resizing these images. Repeating a complex series of masks and sharpening layers every time you resize is just not practical. In these cases, sharpening becomes an integral part of creating the basic image, rather than a subtle touch applied at the end of the process.

A disadvantage of Photoshop's Unsharp Mask filter is that it is a destructive edit. When you click "OK", sharpening is applied to the pixels in the Background layer, and there is no way to go back and change the settings later. You could use the History Palette to delete the sharpening step, but then you would lose subsequent processing steps. Furthermore, USM is applied to all of the pixels. If the image contains both large-scale features and fine details, a "one-pass" application of USM will be a compromise, and will produce a less than optimum result.

In the M33 selective sharpening tutorial, we utilized "Layer-Based Sharpening" combined with Layer Style Blending Options to apply differential sharpening based upon tonal range. In the following example, we will use layer masking to apply different sharpening settings to both large- and small-scale features in an image.

1. From the tutorial disc, open the file Jupiter 400 Stack.tif (*File|Open*). This is an image taken by Tim Khan and the Author. It is an unprocessed stack of 400 video frames from a Philips ToUCam webcam. The frames were stacked using K3CCDTools.

2. First, we will bring up the brightness level of the image. Create a Levels Adjustment Layer (click on the "Create new fill or adjustment layer" icon in the Layers Palette) and drag the Levels highlight slider (the right slider) in the RGB Channel to the beginning of highlight data shown in the Histogram. This will result in a highlight Input Level of around 185. There is a bit of prismatic dispersion in the image. If you wish, you may re-align the color channels using the technique described on **page 176**.

3. Duplicate the Background layer twice (with the Background layer active, press Ctrl+J two times). Make sure that the Levels Adjustment Layer remains at the top of the Layer Stack.

4. Change the Layer Blending Mode of both Background copy Layers from "Normal" to "Luminosity". These will be our USM sharpening layers, and we want to apply sharpening only to the luminance information. Double-click on the Zoom Tool icon in the Toolbox to display the image at 100% ("Actual Pixels").

5. Make "Background copy" the active Layer (click on it once — it will then be highlighted in blue) and turn off the visibility of the "Background copy 2" Layer (click off the little "eyeball" icon at the left of the Layer in the Layers Palette).

6. Select *Filter|Sharpen|Unsharp Mask*. Set the Amount to 500% (maximum setting) and Threshold to 0 (minimum setting). Now adjust the Radius to bring out the larger-scale details in the equatorial cloud bands. Don't worry about losing fine detail. In this layer, we want to maximize detail in the broader, darker features, which will require a wider Radius setting. Use the keyboard arrow keys to move the Radius setting in small increments as you fine-tune your result. Increase the Radius as long as details improve and stop when they start to "break-down". The Radius you choose will likely be between 6 and 10 pixels. For now, use my settings. Enter (500, 7.0, 0) and click OK. Change this layer name (double-click on the Layer name to change it) to "Coarse USM (500, 7.0, 0)".

7. Now make the Background copy 2 Layer active and select *Filter|Sharpen|Unsharp Mask*. Again set the Amount to 500% and the Threshold to 0, but this time adjust the Radius to bring out the finest details. A Radius of 2.1 to 2.4 pixels brings out the fine details. Enter (500, 2.4, 0) and click OK. Change this layer name to "Fine USM (500, 2.4, 0)".

Now we are faced with the problem of how best to blend these USM layers together. The details we need from the Coarse USM Layer lie principally in features between quarter-tones and midtones. We could try combining these layers using the Layer Style Blending Options sliders, as we did with M33, but there are just too many small, overlapping areas and the tonal variation is narrow. It would also be quite difficult to control

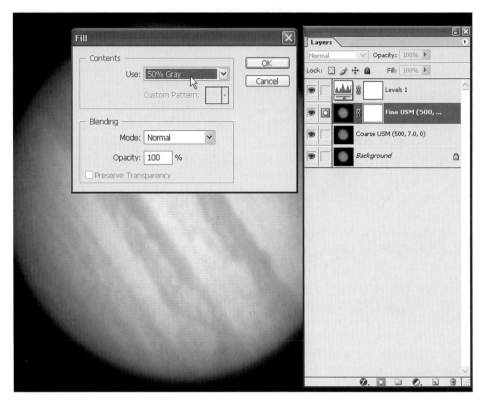

Fig. 12.5 *Edit | Fill* is used to fill the Fine USM Layer Mask with a neutral 50% Gray. Gray tones are used in a mask to selectively vary layer opacity. The Coarse and Fine USM Layers are now "blended" 50%/50%. Darker and lighter shades of Gray painted into this Mask will add or remove more of the underlying Layer.

the sharpening halos. We need something that allows us more direct control for making subtle adjustments. We will use a Layer Mask.

8. Add a "Reveal All" (filled with White) Layer Mask to the Fine USM Layer by holding down the Shift key while clicking on the "Add layer mask" icon in the Layers Palette. Note that this shortcut also works when you want to add a "Hide All" Layer Mask — just hold down the Alt key instead of the Shift key. Click on the Layer Mask window icon in the USM Fine Layer to activate the Mask. Note that the mask icon — a small white circle inside a shaded square — appears just to the right of the visibility ("eyeball") icon, indicating that you are working on the Mask. If you click on the image window icon a paintbrush appears, indicating that you are working on the image itself. (These indicators have been deleted in Photoshop CS2.)

9. Select *Edit | Fill*; in the Contents area select "Use: 50% Gray"; leave the Blending Mode set to Normal, the Opacity at 100% and click OK (**Figure 12.5**). Your Layer Mask is now filled with a neu-

tral, 50% Gray (RGB values of 128, 128, 128). Remember that Gray tones in a mask vary the transparency between White (revealing everything in the layer) and Black (hiding everything in the layer). Gray tones are used in a mask to selectively vary layer opacity.

We have now "blended" the Fine USM Layer 50%/50% with the Layer Stack below it (effectively the Coarse USM Layer). The same result could be achieved by setting the Fine USM Layer Opacity to 50%, with one important exception. We may now paint the Mask with White, Black or any shade of Gray to carefully control where, and how much, of the Coarse USM Layer we want in our final image. Painting with tones darker than middle-gray will reveal more of the Coarse USM Layer (we are "hiding" more of the Fine USM Layer), while tones lighter than middle-gray will hide more of the Coarse USM (we are "revealing" more of the Fine USM Layer).

10. Hold down the Shift key and click in the Layer Mask window icon to turn the Mask on and off. A red "X" appears when the Mask is de-activated.

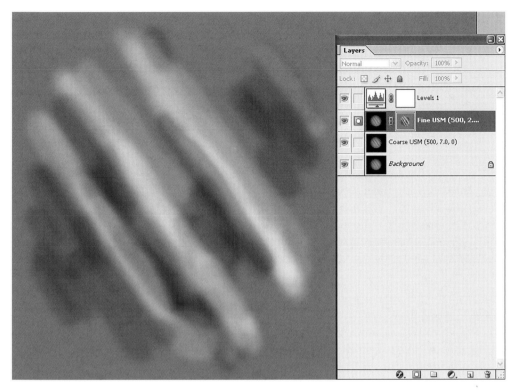

Fig. 12.6 A monochromatic finger-painting exercise? No, this is the Layer Mask I created for the Fine USM Layer. It is possible to combine image elements with great precision using Gray tones in a Layer Mask.

Turn the Layer Mask on and select a soft-edged Brush (shortcut "B") of around 40 pixels. Use the keyboard bracket keys to vary the Brush size. Hold down the Shift key and use the bracket keys to vary Brush softness. In the Tool Options, leave the Brush Mode set to Normal, the Flow set to 100%, but set the Brush Opacity at 20%.

11. Make the Foreground Color White and paint the Mask to apply more of the Fine USM Layer. Paint the areas where the light sharpening halos from the Coarse USM layer are visible at the edges of the equatorial bands. Apply lightening to any other areas where you wish to accentuate more of the Fine USM Layer. You will want to repeatedly turn the Mask and Layer visibility on and off to carefully examine where to alter the Mask. It may also be useful to create an on-screen duplicate of the image (*Image | Duplicate*) and set the duplicate to display only the Coarse USM or Fine USM Layer to guide your efforts in painting the Mask.

12. Paint the Mask with Black to apply more of the Coarse USM Layer. Use the keyboard "X" key to quickly toggle the Foreground Color between Black and White. Since we are using a fairly low Opacity Brush, we are in reality painting the mask with darker and lighter Gray tones. Paint with Black to bring areas of detail from the Coarse USM Layer into the image. One advantage of working with Layer Masks is that you can go back and forth between dark and light tones as much as you like to refine the Mask. If you make a mistake, just paint with the opposite color to correct it. Paint until you are satisfied with your sharpening composite. My final mask is shown in **Figure 12.6**.

13. You may want to increase the color saturation, since we used two luminance layers for sharpening (an LLRGB). Add a Hue/Saturation Adjustment Layer and place it directly above the Background Layer. Add Saturation as desired. You may also want to build some additional image contrast. Add a Curves Adjustment Layer and place it at the top of the Layer Stack. Adjust contrast in the RGB Channel as desired.

14. There is one thing left to do. Perhaps you noticed a fine pattern of "mottling" which has appeared in the image. If you check the Histogram, you will see that our image processing has created "gapping".

R. Scott Ireland

The image has been posterized. Make certain the visibility of all Layers is on and press Shift+Ctrl+Alt+N+E. This creates a new pixel Layer that combines all of the other visible Layers. In essence, it "flattens" the image into a new Layer and still retains all of the other Layers intact, unlike a standard flattening. Move the combined Layer ("Layer 1") to the top of the Layer Stack (click-hold and drag it). Open *Filter|Blur|Gaussian Blur*, set the Radius to 1 pixel and click OK. The Histogram gapping has been eliminated, with only a modest reduction in sharpness. Rename Layer 1 to "CAB; GB 1 pxl" (meaning "Combine All Below; Gaussian Blur 1 pixel"). The before and after images, along with my final Layers Palette, are shown in **Figure 12.7**.

You may use as many different sharpening layers as you wish. Blend them together using Layer Masks, working upward through the Layer Stack to gradually build up the final sharpened result. In our next example, we will look at a completely different approach to applying differential sharpening.

Sequential, or "Multi-Pass" Sharpening using Photoshop Actions

This technique involves application of the Unsharp Mask filter to an image several times in sequence, using a different Radius setting for each pass, and a reduced Amount. By applying less sharpening on each pass, and varying the Radius over a wide range, we gradually sharpen both small- and large-scale features in the image. Frequently, this results in more visible detail without introducing artifacts that appear when "one-pass" sharpening is used with a higher Amount setting.

The difficulty with this approach is that it is tedious. Manually applying the USM filter over and over, only to find that you have over-sharpened and must begin again, is a daunting task. But Photoshop allows us to automate repetitive keystrokes using the Actions Palette. In this way, we can record a set of Photoshop Actions that allow us to apply various USM settings with a single mouse-click. Experimentation is easy, giving us the tools we need to find the best sharpening sequence with a minimum amount of effort.

1. On the tutorial disc, you will find a set of Photoshop Actions called "Unsharp Mask Actions.atn". Copy this file to the "Photoshop Actions" folder on your computer, which is found in the "Presets" directory (example: C:\Program Files\Adobe\Photoshop CS\Presets\Photoshop Actions).

2. Restart Photoshop, and then form the tutorial disc, open the file Mars Webcam Stack.tif (*File | Open*). This is a webcam stack of Mars taken by Don Parker. The file has not been processed, other than re-alignment of the color channels to correct prismatic dispersion. Zoom the image to 100% ("Actual Pixels").

3. Open Photoshop's Actions Palette (*Window|Actions*). Access the Palette Options by clicking on the small, right-facing arrow at the top-right of the Actions Palette, choose "Load Actions", and select "Unsharp Mask Actions.atn". See **Figure 12.8**.

Action Sets are saved with the file extension *.atn and may be loaded and unloaded from the Actions Palette whenever desired. To record an Action, you must first create a Set (or save the new Action in an existing set) and then create the new Action. The buttons at the bottom of the Palette operate like a tape recorder. Click on the circle icon to begin recording keystrokes (it turns red while recording) and press the square icon to stop. The right-arrow icon "plays" the highlighted Action, applying the recorded steps to the current image. Actions are easily edited, since all of the steps are listed in a nested structure that expands and collapses (click on the arrows at the left of the Action Set to expand/collapse). Just double-click on a step to access and modify it. Actions or steps may be turned on and off by clicking on the "check" mark at the left side of the Action. The area to the right of this is the dialog box toggle — if activated, the Action will stop and allow you to enter values directly into the dialog box.

4. Notice that there are two basic groups of Actions in this set. The top group applies USM at various Radius settings with a 50% Amount. The bottom group uses a 100% Amount. A Gaussian Blur is applied after each pass (with the exception of Radius = 1 pixel USM). For this image, we will begin with the 50% Amount USM Actions.

5. Duplicate the Background Layer with Ctrl+J. Change the Layer Blending Mode to "Luminosity". Highlight the "USM 50, 10, 0; Blur 1" Action and click the "Play selection" button (a right-facing arrow icon) at the bottom of the Actions Palette once. The image is sharpened and blurred almost instantaneously using the saved Action settings. Go to the History Palette and you will see

Fig. 12.7 The image before (left) and after (below) Layer-Based Selective Sharpening.

both an Unsharp Mask and a Gaussian Blur History State.

6. Move to the next Action down in the list ("USM 50, 7, 0; Blur 1") and apply it to the image once. Do the same for the remaining three "USM 50" Actions. Rename this Layer to "Amount 50% One Run". The image looks pretty good, but we will

have to do some touching up to reduce excessive sharpening halos in certain places. First, let's see if we can do better.

7. Make another copy of the Background layer with Ctrl+J and place this new Layer at the top of the Layer Stack. Change the Layer Blending Mode to "Luminosity" and rename the Layer to "Amount

R. Scott Ireland

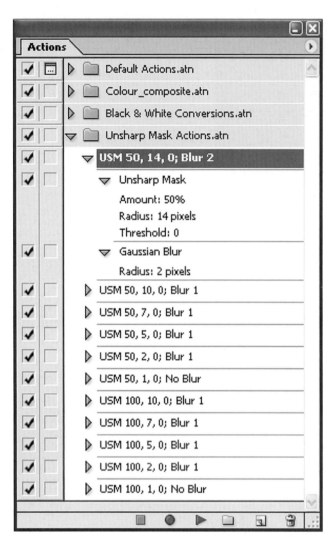

Fig. 12.8 Photoshop Actions are used to automate repetitive tasks. Here several Unsharp Mask / Gaussian Blur sequences have been recorded to simplify and speed up sequential sharpening. Action Sets may be saved (file extension *.atn), re-loaded and shared among different computers. This set is included on the tutorial disc.

100% One Run". Turn off visibility of the "Amount 50% One Run" Layer (click the "eyeball" icon off). Now apply the five "USM 100" Actions, one time each, starting with "USM 100, 10, 0; Blur 1". This result looks pretty harsh and over-sharpened. Reduce the Layer Opacity to 60%. Now it looks much better. I like this version better than one run at 50%. But what if we tried two applications of the 50% Actions? I will leave it to you to try this exercise. I found that two applications of 50% did not produce anything better than one application at 100%. But I did find something else that improved the image.

8. Make another copy of the Background layer with Ctrl+J and place this new Layer at the top of the Layer Stack. Change the Layer Blending Mode to "Luminosity" and rename the Layer to "100% Fine Detail". Turn off visibility of the other USM Layers but leave the Background Layer visibility on. Now apply the "USM 100" 10, 7 and 5 Radius Actions once each, apply the 2 Radius Action twice and the 1 Radius Action three times. Reduce the Layer Opacity to 60%. To my eye, hitting the fine details harder has improved the image somewhat over the one run 100% version.

Isn't this easy? Just think how hard it would be to experiment with various sequential passes without using Photoshop Actions. When comparing different sequences, it is extremely helpful to create an on-screen duplicate of the image (*Image|Duplicate*) and compare each new trial to the best version previously obtained.

Do not "get married" to the canned set of Actions that I provided. Create your own and try different settings. USM is all about squeezing every drop of sharpening that you can out of an image (without making it look unnatural). See if you can come up with something better.

9. Now we need to put the finishing touches on the image. There are excessive dark and light sharpening halos that we must fix. But we should be careful not to eliminate the blue cloud features in the process. Create a Layer Mask for the "100% Fine Detail" Layer (*Layer|Add Layer Mask|Reveal All*). Activate the Layer Mask and select a soft-edged 20 pixel Brush (keyboard "B"). Lower the Brush Opacity to 20%. Paint the Mask with Black to mitigate the excessive light and dark sharpening halos. Vary Brush size and Opacity as needed. If you wish, add Curves and Hue/Saturation Adjustment Layers. I felt that the image looked fine with no further adjustments. **See Figures 12.9**, **12.10** and **12.11**.

Separating Dark and Light Sharpening Halos

The cardinal sin of Unsharp Masking is oversharpening. Yet for most images, we want to apply as much sharpening as possible, without making the image look harsh or unnatural. Finding the thin line between "just right" and "too much" can be quite a challenge. The more control we have over the process, the better.

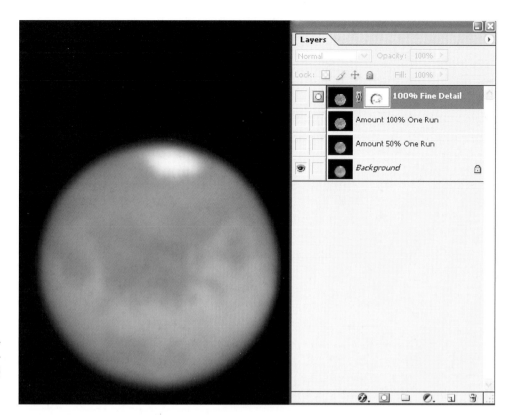

Fig. 12.9 Don Parker's original Mars image before applying Sequential (Multi-Pass) Sharpening.

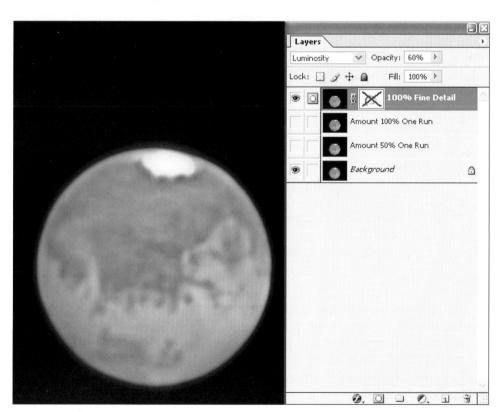

Fig. 12.10 Eight passes of Unsharp Masking using various Radii have been applied to the image. Objectionable dark and light sharpening halos are clearly evident. Note that the Layer Mask is turned off.

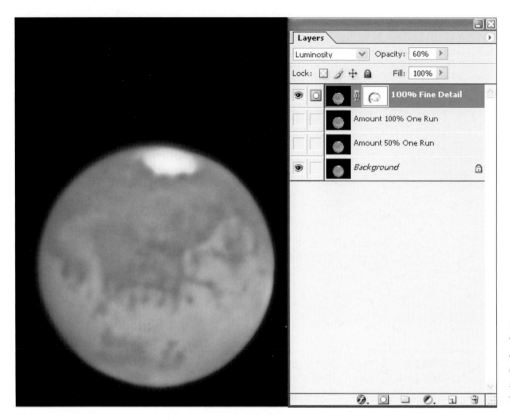

Fig. 12.11 The final, Sequentially sharpened image. A Layer Mask is used to reduce excessive dark and light sharpening halos. Compare this to **Figure 12.10**.

In the following example we will use Photoshop's Layer Blending Modes to isolate and separately adjust the dark and light sharpening halos created by the USM filter. This additional level of control gives us a powerful new tool to add to our sharpening workflow.

1. From the tutorial disc, open the file Jupiter 400 Stack.tif (*File | Open*). This is the same image we worked on earlier, taken by Tim Khan and me.

2. From the Layers Palette, Make two copies of the Background Layer by pressing Ctrl+J twice. Re-name the first layer above the Background "Unsharpened Luminance" (double-click on the Layer name to change it) and change its Layer Blending Mode (accessed from the drop-down selection box at the top-left of the Layers Palette) from "Normal" to "Luminosity".

3. Activate the second copy located at the top of the Layer Stack ("Layer 1 copy"). We will apply a sequential sharpening run to this layer. Open the Actions Palette (*Window | Actions*). If you do not have the Unsharp Mask Actions from the tutorial disc loaded, refer to step 1 in the previous example and load them now. Apply the following Unsharp Mask Actions in sequence:

   1. "USM 100, 10, 0; Blur 1" — 1 pass
   2. "USM 100, 7, 0; Blur 1" — 1 pass
   3. "USM 100, 5, 0; Blur 1" — 1 pass
   4. "USM 100, 2, 0; Blur 1" — 3 passes
   5. "USM 100, 1, 0; No Blur" — 2 passes.

   Re-name this sharpened Layer to "Lighten".

4. Make a copy of the Lighten Layer (Ctrl+J) and re-name this copy to "Darken". You now have two copies of the same sharpened layer ("Lighten" and "Darken") located above the "Unsharpened Luminance" Layer in the Layer Stack. Hold down the Alt key, move the cursor to the Layer boundary between "Unsharpened Luminance" and "Lighten" until the cursor changes into a half white/half black circle, then click once. Do the same for the "Darken" Layer. We now have Clipping Masks that link the two sharpened layers to the luminance layer (See **Figure 12.12**). This will allow us to use the Darken and Lighten Layer Blending Modes for the sharpening layers while still sharpening only the luminance information. They are linked to the "Unsharpened Luminance" Layer where we have set the Layer Blending Mode to "Luminosity".

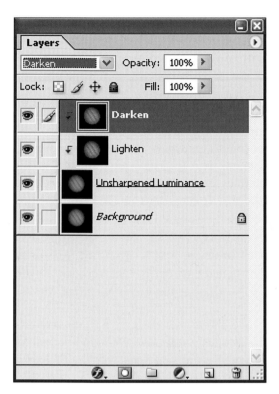

Fig. 12.12 Sharpening has been applied to the Lighten Layer, which is then copied to create the Darken Layer. By using "Lighten" and "Darken" as the Layer Blending Modes, we gain separate control over the light and dark USM sharpening halos. Converting these Layers to Clipping Masks allows us to sharpen only the luminance information by setting the underlying Layer Blending Mode to "Luminosity".

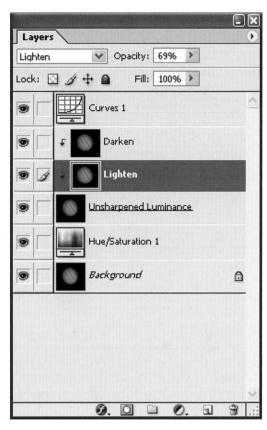

Fig. 12.13 Vary the Opacity of the Lighten Layer to adjust the light USM sharpening halos; vary the Opacity of the Darken Layer to adjust the dark halos. Use Layer Masks to further refine how the light and dark halos will appear.

5. Change the Layer Blending Modes of the Lighten Layer to "Lighten" and the Darken Layer to "Darken". Now, varying the Opacity of these Layers will adjust either the light or dark USM sharpening halos.

6. Add a Curves Adjustment Layer at the top of the Layer Stack (*Layer|New Adjustment Layer|Curves*). We will use an "S" Curve to build some image contrast. In the RGB Channel, leave the black and white points unchanged, but place two more adjustment points (click once on the Curve) with Input/Output values of (33, 15) and (198, 231). Type these values in. Don't try to move the Curve this precisely with the mouse.

7. We also need to boost the color saturation of our LRGB. Create a Hue/Saturation Adjustment Layer and place it directly above the Background Layer (click-hold and drag in the Layers Palette to move Layers). Increase the Master Saturation to +40. Your Layers Palette should now look like **Figure 12.13**.

8. Adjust the Opacity of the Lighten Layer to vary the light USM sharpening halos. Adjust the Opacity of the Darken Layer to adjust the dark ones. Work back and forth between to two to create the best overall effect. I used an Opacity setting of 87% for the Lighten Layer and 58% for the Darken Layer. I then touched-up the light halos with a Layer Mask. If desired, create Layer Masks for the Lighten and/or Darken Layers to apply any final touches to the sharpening halos.

9. Make sure that the visibility ("Eyeball" icon) of all Layers is on and press Shift+Ctrl+Alt+N+E to combine them into a new pixel layer. Place this Layer at the top of the Layer Stack. Select *Filter|Blur|Gaussian Blur*, enter a Radius of 0.7 pixels and click OK. This removes gaps/spikes from the Histogram and avoids posterization. If you use Photoshop CS or later, you can observe

R. Scott Ireland

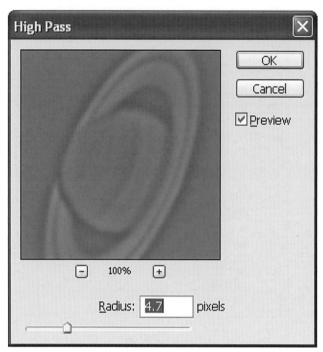

Fig. 12.14 Photoshop's High Pass Filter (*Filter|Other|High Pass*) emphasizes edge details in an image within a specified pixel Radius. The remainder of the image is suppressed by rendering it a neutral gray.

the Histogram change (you must keep refreshing the cache) as you change the pixel Radius in the Gaussian Blur dialog box. You can watch as the gapping/spiking gradually disappears, and "dial-in" just enough blurring to do the job.

Sharpening with the High-Pass Filter

One of the themes repeated throughout this book is the value of mastering multiple techniques to accomplish a particular image-processing task. Each image presents its own unique challenges, so having a broad repertoire of skills will serve you well. This philosophy is particularly important when sharpening images to extract hidden details.

In addition to the Unsharp Mask Filter, Photoshop provides another filter that is highly useful for sharpening images — the High Pass Filter (*Filter|Other|High Pass*). This filter emphasizes edge details where strong tonal transitions occur within a specified Radius. All other image elements are suppressed by rendering them as a neutral, middle-toned gray (**Figure 12.14**). This filter characteristic offers us the opportunity to use one of Photoshop's contrast Layer Blending Modes (Overlay; Soft Light; Hard Light; Vivid Light; Linear

Light or Pin Light), where neutral gray tones have no affect on the underlying layer. Only the dark and light edge information created by the High Pass filter will modify the image, producing more apparent detail and sharpness.

1. From the tutorial disc, open the file Saturn Video Stack.tif. This is an image taken by Lester Shalloway and Tim Khan using a mini-DV digital video camera. The Registax program was used on 3 minutes of this video file to parse and stack the best 400 frames. This image is the result of that stack before any further processing.

2. Zoom the image to a 200% view using the Zoom Tool (keyboard "Z"). From the Layers Palette, Create a copy of the Background Layer with Ctrl+J. Change the Layer Blending Mode of the new layer from "Normal" to "Overlay". Don't worry about how the image looks. By selecting the Overlay mode now, you will have a direct image preview as you apply the High Pass Filter in the next step.

3. Select *Filter|Other|High Pass*. Adjust the Radius setting to bring out detail in the dark bands on Saturn's surface. We are going to create multiple layers and use 2 different Radius settings in this example. For this first pass, we want the largest Radius setting that continues to improve surface detail and does not just exaggerate the sharpening halos. For now, just use the setting that I selected. Enter a Radius of 4.1 pixels and click OK. Rename this Layer (double-click on the Layer name to change it) to "High Pass; 4.1 pixels".

4. Make another copy of the "High Pass; 4.1 pixels" Layer by pressing Ctrl+J. Note that the "Overlay" Blending Mode is duplicated also. We now have two iterations, or "passes", of High Pass sharpening at a Radius of 4.1 pixels.

5. Create another duplicate of the Background Layer (make sure it is highlighted and press Ctrl+J). Place this Background copy Layer at the top of the Layer Stack (from the Layers Palette, click-hold and drag it there) and change the Layer Blending Mode to "Overlay".

6. With the Background copy Layer active, select *Filter|Other|High Pass*, enter a Radius of 2.5 pixels and click OK. Change the Layer name to "High Pass; 2.5 pixels".

7. Make another copy of the "High Pass; 2.5 pixels"

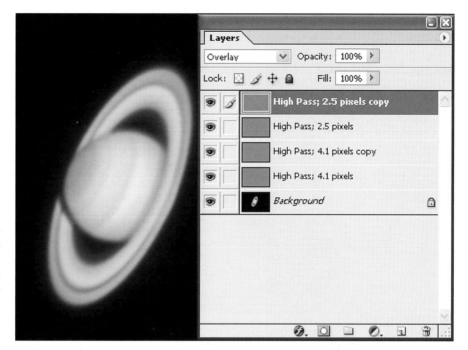

Fig. 12.15 By using one of the Contrast Layer Blending Modes, the neutral gray areas created by the High Pass Filter drop out — they have no affect on the underlying image. Only the edge details lighten and darken the underlying image to create a sharpening effect.

Layer by pressing Ctrl+J. Now we have two additional applications of the High Pass filter at the narrower Radius setting (See **Figure 12.15**). We will finish up the image by building more contrast and making a color adjustment.

8. Create a Curves Adjustment Layer at the top of the Layer Stack (*Layer|New Adjustment Layer|Curves*). In the RGB Channel, create a new point with Input/Output values of (86, 70) and click OK to close the dialog. Change the Layer Blending Mode of the Curves Layer to "Multiply". Layer Blending Modes may be used with Adjustment Layers too.

9. Create a Hue/Saturation Adjustment Layer at the top of the Layer Stack, set the Master Saturation to –30 (minus 30) and click OK.

10. Create another Curves Adjustment Layer at the top of the Layer Stack. In the RGB Channel, create a new point with Input/Output values of (92, 116) and click OK.

11. Make sure that all layers are visible (the little "eyeball" icons are all on) and create a new "combine all" pixel layer at the top of the Layer Stack with Shift+Ctrl+Alt+N+E. Select *Filter|Blur|Gaussian Blur*, enter a Radius of 0.7 pixels and click OK. Rename this Layer to "CAB; GB 0.7 pxls" ("combine all below; Gaussian Blur 0.7 pixels"). This light blur fixes the slight Histogram gapping without any material affect on image details. The final image and

Layers Palette are shown in **Figure 12.16**.

Using the High Pass Filter for this example allowed us to bring out detail and contrast, yet still retain a very natural-looking image. Because the image was so soft to begin with, most Unsharp Masking procedures would have rendered it in a harsh and artificial manner. Sometimes, less is more.

"Wide Radius-Low Amount" Sharpening

There are times when you will be pulling your hair out trying to find USM settings that work. Photographs containing fine details typically require a fairly narrow Radius setting. But sometimes these images break down when we apply a reasonably high Amount. Background noise and grain become too harsh. If we lower the Amount or adjust the Threshold setting to compensate, the sharpening effect disappears.

We may, of course, create complex selections and masks to separate the sky background from the stars and subject, and apply differential sharpening. But before wheeling out the big guns, try the "wide radius — low amount" sharpening technique.

This method is simple. Use a very large USM Radius (start with 50 pixels) and a very low Amount (start with 20%). Threshold is generally 0 or quite low. That's all there is to it! Let's give it a try.

1. From the tutorial disc, open the file Hale-Bopp.tif

R. Scott Ireland

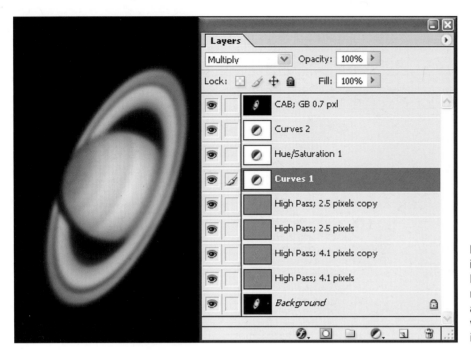

Fig. 12.16 The original of this image is quite soft. Sharpening with the High Pass filter retains a smoother, more natural look than would almost any application of Unsharp Masking, which would create an overly harsh image.

(*File|Open*). This is the image used in our first example.

2. Duplicate the Background Layer (click-hold and drag it to the "Create a new layer" icon in the Layers Palette, then release the mouse). Set the screen view to 100% using the Zoom Tool.

3. With the Background copy Layer active, select *Filter|Sharpen|Unsharp Mask*. Set the Radius to 50 pixels and the Threshold to 0.

4. Start with an Amount of 20% and work up from there, adjusting to your desired level of sharpening. I chose an Amount setting of 35%. For now, enter my settings of (35, 50, 0) and click OK.

5. Immediately select *Edit|Fade Unsharp Mask*, set the Mode to "Luminosity" and click OK.

6. Rename the Background copy Layer to "USM (35, 50, 0); Fade Lum". This reminds us of the USM settings used and also indicates that we "faded to luminosity".

7. Create another duplicate of the Background Layer. This time, we will apply the settings we used in our first example ("One Pass" Unsharp Masking on **page 238**). Select *Filter|Sharpen|Unsharp Mask*, enter the settings (200, 1.3, 10) and click OK. Immediately apply *Edit|Fade Unsharp Mask*, with the Mode set to Luminosity. Rename this Layer "USM (200, 1.3, 10); Fade Lum".

8. Now we want to Zoom well into the image to compare the stars and backgrounds of these two sharpening layers. Select the Zoom Tool (keyboard "Z"). In the image window, click-hold and drag out a small square or rectangular Zoom area, then release the mouse. The area you outlined now fills the window. Make sure you are at a Zoom ratio of between 150% to 200%.

9. Toggle the visibility of each of the sharpening layers on and off and compare results. Zoom out to a full screen view and compare the overall appearance also. It is clear to me that the "wide radius — low amount" version looks better on all counts. The narrow radius version sharpens all of the background noise along with the image details, and there is no Threshold or Amount combination that satisfactorily reduces this noise without losing too much of the sharpening effect.

By choosing a wide Radius for this "fine detail" image, we have, in actuality, enhanced the local contrast. Look carefully and you will see that the original "one pass" sharpening (200, 1.3, 10) is actually crisper and more defined (albeit the noise is crisper also!). The "wide radius — low amount" version (35, 50, 0) boosted the contrast and provided the illusion of more sharpness. A Curves adjustment to enhance contrast would not have worked as well (try it for yourself and see). This method is more targeted and produces a result similar to building a contrast mask. But it is a lot easier!

Edge Masking

Processing planetary stacks frequently evolves (de-volves, really) into a "siege of sharpening" blindness. After spending the better part of an evening trying to tweak out the last bit of detail in an image, you load it the next day and gasp at the appalling visage on your monitor. You wonder, "What in the world was I think-ing!?! Am I blind?".

In a certain sense, you were blind. This is our old friend, the eye/brain adaptive visual system, at work again. Our "eyes" gradually become acclimated to the ever-increasing sharpness and contrast as we work on an image. We become more and more focused on small-scale changes in detail, and miss the big picture. Don't feel bad. This happens to all of us.

If you try to make a print of one of these hyper-sharp wonders, chances are you will be disappointed. As we have seen in the High Pass Filter example, it is possible to bring out detail yet still retain a smooth and natural appearance. In the following tutorial, we will examine another useful technique to create the illusion of sharpness, while retaining a smooth overall image structure.

1. From the tutorial disc, open the file Jupiter 400 Stack.tif (*File | Open*). This is the webcam stack that we have already worked on twice before.

2. Open the Layers Palette (*Window | Layers*) and duplicate the Background Layer (click-hold and drag it to the "Create a new layer" icon at the bot-tom of the Layers Palette, then release the mouse). Set the screen view to 100% using the Zoom Tool.

3. Create a Levels Adjustment Layer (*Layer | New Adjustment Layer | Levels*) at the top of the Layer Stack. Move the White Point slider (the white slider at the right of the histogram) to an Input val-ue of 186 (or type it in) and click OK. For good or-der's sake, you may wish to delete the automatically-created layer mask, since we won't need it. Just click-hold and drag it to the trash can icon at the bottom-right of the Layers Palette.

4. Create a Curves Adjustment Layer (*Layer | New Adjustment Layer | Curves*) at the top of the Layer Stack. In the RGB Channel, enter a new adjust-ment point with Input/Output values of (110, 82) and click OK. Delete the layer mask for this layer.

Now that we have adjusted brightness and contrast, we are going to build our edge mask. This technique is re-ally just a sharpening layer (or multiple layers) with a layer mask that applies sharpening only to the principal edges within the image. The trick is to come up with a good mask.

The first step in creating any mask is to think about how to use the image itself to create it. The next step is to examine the individual color channels to see if one will work better than the others for the task at hand.

5. Open the Channels Palette (*Window | Channels*) and examine the individual color channels. We want to create a mask that applies sharpening only to the principal edges within the image. So we need a channel (or a Channel Mixer combination) that provides the broadest overall contrast. The Red Channel contains a good bit of detail, but not much contrast. The Green Channel looks pretty good, but the Blue Channel looks better (**Figure 12.17**).

The Blue Channel will be the starting point. But it is too soft to make a good mask. Somewhat ironically, we need to sharpen it first!

6. Turn on all Color Channels (click on the RGB Channel), open the Layers Palette and make the Background copy Layer active. Open the Actions Palette (*Window | Actions*) and access the Unsharp Mask Actions. If you do not have the Unsharp Mask Actions from the tutorial disc loaded, refer to step 1 in the Sequential Sharpening example on **page 248** and load them now. Apply the following Unsharp Mask Actions in sequence to the Back-ground copy Layer:

   1. "USM 100, 10, 0; Blur 1" —1 pass
   2. "USM 100, 7, 0; Blur 1" —1 pass
   3. "USM 100, 5, 0; Blur 1" —1 pass
   4. "USM 100, 2, 0; Blur 1" —1 pass
   5. "USM 100, 1, 0; No Blur" —1 pass.

   Re-name this sharpened Layer to "USM 100 Se-quence for Mask".

7. Open the Channels Palette and create a copy of the Blue Channel by click-holding and dragging it to the "Create new channel" icon (overlapping squares) at the bottom of the Channels Palette, then release the mouse. A "Blue copy" Channel appears.

8. With the Blue copy Channel active, select *Filter | Stylize | Find Edges*. Next, select *Fil-

Fig. 12.17 From left to right, the Red, Green and Blue Channels of Jupiter 400 Stack.tif. To create an edge mask, we want to start with the channel containing the most overall contrast, in this case, the Blue Channel.

ter|Other|Maximum, set the Radius to 1 pixel and click OK. Finally, select *Filter|Noise|Median*, set the Radius to 2 pixels and click OK. See **Figure 12.18**.

We now have a white image with dark edge "traces". Applying the Maximum Filter and the Median Filter helps to eliminate extraneous details and stray pixels. At the end of this process, we want a high-contrast mask containing only a black background with white

edges.

9. Invert the mask (the Blue copy Channel) with Ctrl+A (*Select|All*) and Ctrl+I (*Image|Adjustments|Invert*). Select *Image|Adjustments|Levels*, move the White Point slider to an Input value of 20 and click OK. Again select *Image|Adjustments|Levels*, move the Black Point slider to an Input value of 175, move the Midtone (Gamma) slider to an Input value of 1.24, move the White Point slider to an Input value of 200

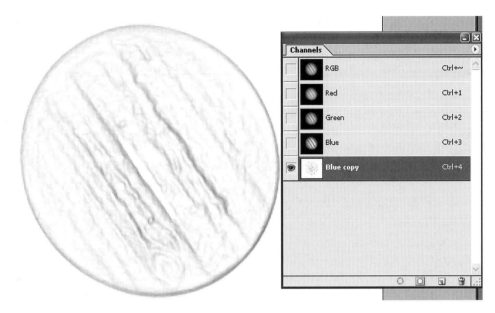

Fig. 12.18 A copy of the Blue Channel has been transformed into a white image with dark edges using *Filter\ Stylize\ Find Edges*. A narrow radius application of the Maximum Filter (*Filter\ Other\ Maximum*) and the Median Filter (*Filter\ Noise\ Median*) helps clean up stray details.

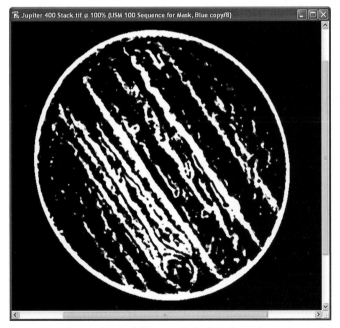

Fig. 12.19 The white Edge Mask of **Figure 12.18** has been inverted and two Levels adjustments have been applied to "drive" the tonal values to black and white. A light Gaussian Blur will complete the Edge Mask.

and click OK. Your mask should now look like **Figure 12.19**.

We inverted the mask because we need the edges to be white, not black. When we add this mask to a sharpening layer, we only want the edges sharpened ("white reveals"). The two rather severe Levels adjustments were needed to "drive" the tonal values to black and white.

10. With the Blue copy Channel still active, select *Filter\ Blur\ Gaussian Blur*, enter a Radius of 3

R. Scott Ireland

pixels and click OK. This smoothes and feathers the mask, so that harsh edges will be avoided when we sharpen. But it has also reduced the tonal values of the white areas.

11. Once again, select *Image|Adjustments|Levels*, move the White Point slider to an Input value of 163, move the Black Point slider to an Input value of 24 and click OK. This restores our black and white values while still retaining smoothness in the mask.

12. Copy the mask to the clipboard with Ctrl+A (*Select|All*) and Ctrl+C (*Edit|Copy*).

13. Open the Layers Palette (*Window|Layers*) and make another copy of the Background Layer. Place this copy just below the Levels Adjustment Layer (above the "USM 100 Sequence for Mask" Layer). Add a Layer Mask to the Background copy Layer with *Layer|Add Layer Mask|Reveal All*. Activate this mask by holding down the Alt key and clicking on the Layer Mask thumbnail. The main image window is now all white, since the mask contains no other data. Paste the mask into the main image window with Ctrl+V (*Edit|Paste*). Click on the image thumbnail to re-activate the main image.

14. Either turn off the visibility of the "USM 100 Sequence for Mask" Layer (click off the "eyeball" icon in the Layers Palette), or discard it. We no longer need it. (You may want to retain it if you are going to experiment with a different edge mask later. Save the file as a *.psd to retain the layers and alpha channels.)

15. Make sure that you still have a 100% view ("Actual Pixels") and that the Background copy Layer is active. Select *Filter|Sharpen|Unsharp Mask*, enter values of (200, 5, 0) and click OK. Rename this Layer to "USM (200, 5, 0)". You may prefer different USM settings. I find that a Radius between 4.5 and 6.5 pixels, and an Amount between 150% and 200% seem to work best. At this point, you may also want to fine-tune your edge mask or adjust the Layer Opacity.

16. Make sure that all layers except "USM 100 Sequence for Mask" are visible (the little "eyeball" icons are on) and create a new "combine all" pixel layer at the top of the Layer Stack with Shift+Ctrl+Alt+N+E. Select *Filter|Blur|Gaussian Blur*, enter a Radius of 0.7 pixels and click

OK. Rename this Layer to "CAB; GB 0.7 pxls" ("combine all below; Gaussian Blur 0.7 pixels"). This light blur fixes the slight Histogram gapping without any material affect on the edge sharpening. The final image and Layers Palette are shown in **Figure 12.20**.

Edge masking produces a subtle but important sharpening effect. It creates the illusion of sharpness, even when a majority of the image is not sharpened at all. Sometimes, this is just what the doctor ordered as a remedy for all of those harsh, oversharpened images. By now, it should be apparent that edges are the name of the game, no matter what sharpening technique you use.

Difference Masking — Working with Layer Sets (Layer Groups)

At the beginning of this Chapter, I discussed the origin of the term "unsharp masking". Recall that a blurred version of an image is inverted (turned into a negative), "sandwiched" together with the positive original, and then printed. The difference between the unsharp negative and the original produces greater edge enhancements (e.g. greater apparent sharpness) in the composite. The soft negative contributes the contrasting dark and light sharpening halos. By now, this concept should sound familiar to you.

In our final example, we will see how to achieve a similar effect with Photoshop, using a technique I have dubbed difference masking.

1. From the tutorial disc, open the file Hale-Bopp.tif (*File|Open*) we have already worked with twice before in this Chapter.

2. Open the Layers Palette (*Window|Layers*) and make two duplicates of the Background Layer (click-hold and drag it to the "Create a new layer" icon at the bottom of the Layers Palette, then release the mouse).

3. Access the Layers Palette menu by clicking on the small, right-facing triangle in the upper-right corner of the Layers Palette. From this menu, click "New Layer Set" ("New Group" in CS2). The New Layer Set dialog box appears (**Figure 12.21**). Type in the Name "Difference Mask" and click OK.

Layer Sets/Groups is a powerful tool. It enhances Photoshop's "3-D" power by providing a hierarchical Lay-

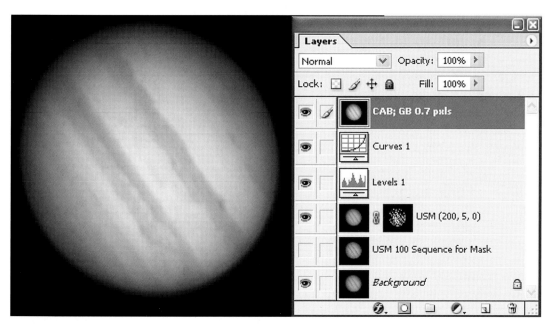

Fig. 12.20 Edge Masking produces a subtle but important sharpening effect. It creates the illusion of sharpness, even when most of the image is not sharpened at all. As with any sharpening technique, edges are the name of the game.

Fig. 12.21 Layer Sets (Layer Groups in CS2) may be used to organize and manage complex Layer Stacks. They enhance Photoshop's "3-D" power by providing a hierarchical Layer structure. Attributes and masks may be applied to multiple Layers simultaneously. Layer Sets may even be included within other Layer Sets.

er structure. Attributes and masks may be applied to multiple Layers simultaneously, allowing complex processing tasks to be separately performed and then merged into the Layer Stack as a single unit. Layer Sets may even be nested within other Layer Sets to provide virtually unlimited image-processing control.

4. In the Layers Palette, move the two Background copy Layers into the Difference Mask Layer Set by click-holding and dragging them "over" the Layer Set and then releasing the mouse. Your Layers Palette should now resemble **Figure 12.22**.

5. Activate the Background copy Layer (click on it) that is "above" the other Background copy Layer

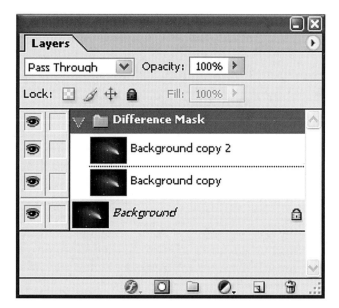

Fig. 12.22 Two copies of the Background Layer have been placed into the Difference Mask Layer Set. Clicking on the triangle at the left of a Layer Set alternately expands or contracts display of the Layer names in the Set. Note that this is not the same thing as visibility of a Layer in the Layer Stack, which is controlled by clicking the "Eyeball" icons on and off.

in the Layer Set ("Background copy 2" in **Figure 12.22**). Select *Filter | Blur | Gaussian Blur*, enter a Radius of 50 pixels and click OK. Immediately select *Edit | Fade Gaussian Blur*, set the Mode to

"Luminosity" and click OK. Rename this Layer to "GB 50 pxls; Fade Lum".

This Layer is now our "unsharp mask". Rather than invert and overlay it, we will achieve the same benefit by subtracting it from the underlying Layer in the Set (a copy of the original image) to create our difference mask. I used a very wide blur Radius (50 pixels) to get a strong sharpening effect, since we are going to selectively modify it later. A smaller Radius, such as 2 or 3 pixels, would produce a finer, subtler sharpening effect.

6. Change the Layer Blending Mode of the "GB 50 pxls; Fade Lum" Layer from "Normal" to "Difference".

7. The image is pretty dark! We will bring the image back up by darkening the difference mask and lowering its contrast. Create a Curves Adjustment Layer (*Layer|New Adjustment Layer|Curves*) above the GB 50 pxls; Fade Lum Layer. Move the White Point such that the Input/Output values are (255, 130) and click OK. Hold down the Alt key and move the cursor between the Curves 1 Layer and the GB 50 pxls; Fade Lum Layer in the Layers Palette until the cursor changes to two overlapping circles, then click the mouse. We have created a Clipping Mask linking the Curves 1 Adjustment Layer to the GB 50 pxls; Fade Lum Layer. The Curve is only applied to the mask.

8. Create a Levels Adjustment Layer (*Layer|New Adjustment Layer|Levels*) above the Curves 1 Layer. Move the White Point slider to an Input level of 132 and click OK. This brings up the brightness of the entire Difference Mask Layer Set. You may discard the empty Layer Masks in the Curves and Levels Layers (click-hold and drag them to the trash can icon), since we won't need them. Your Layers Palette should now look like **Figure 12.23**.

Step back and take a look at what we have accomplished so far. We have built a Layer structure that contains three different processing hierarchies. First we created a blurred layer and adjusted it independently with Curves. This result was subtracted from a copy of the Background Layer (the original image), and that result was further adjusted with Levels. The combined effect of these steps is applied to the original Background Layer through the Difference Mask Layer Set. At this point, only the Difference Mask result shows

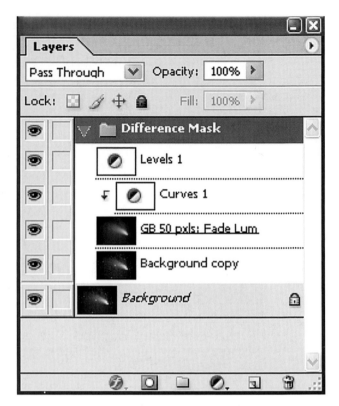

Fig. 12.23 Three processing hierarchies have been created using a Layer Set. 1. The blur layer ("GB 50 pxls; Fade Lum") was created and separately adjusted with Curves (by creating a Clipping Mask), 2. The adjusted blur layer was subtracted from the original (Background copy Layer) and that result adjusted with Levels, 3. The combined results of 1 and 2 were applied to the original image (Background Layer).

through the Layer Stack. It merely obscures the Background Layer, but we will change that in our next steps.

9. Activate the Difference Mask Layer Set by clicking on it once (it will be highlighted in blue). Change the Blending Mode from "Pass Through" to "Luminosity". Our difference mask sharpening set is now applied only to the luminance data in the original image.

10. You may now preview the entire sharpening effect by clicking the visibility of the Difference Mask Layer Set on and off (click on the "eyeball" icon adjacent to the Layer Set). The sharpening is still too harsh, and we need to restore color saturation. With the Difference Mask Layer Set active, choose *Layer|Add Layer Mask|Reveal All*. Load this blank mask into the main image window by holding down the Alt key and clicking on the mask thumbnail. Select *Edit|Fill*, set Use: to 50% Gray (in the drop-down selection box) and click OK.

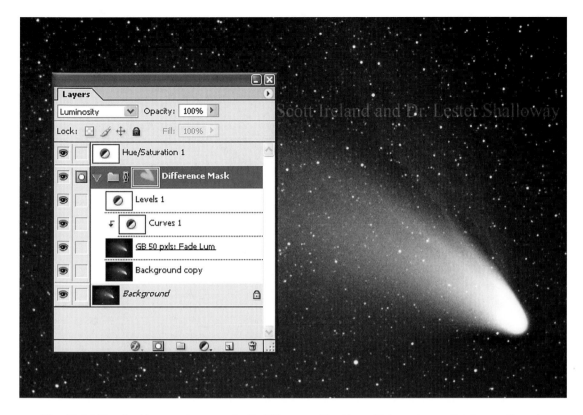

Fig. 12.24 The final image sharpened with Difference Masking utilizing a Layer Set (Layer Group).

We have created a Layer Mask for the entire Difference Mask Layer Set and filled it with a middle-toned neutral gray. This produces the same result as setting the Opacity of the Layer Set to 50%. Everything within the Layer Set is blended into the Background Layer at a 50% Opacity. Now we will refine the mask further.

11. Restore the image by clicking on the Background Layer. Now activate the Difference Mask Set Layer Mask by clicking on its thumbnail once. Choose a wide (400 pixels), soft-edged brush from the Toolbox (keyboard shortcut "B"; use the bracket keys to change Brush size; use Shift+bracket to change Brush softness) and set the Brush Opacity to 20% (in the Tool Options at the top of the Photoshop Window). Zoom the image to "Fit on Screen", set the Foreground Color in the Toolbox to white and paint the mask with white to add back sharpness to the Comet.

We have utilized our third level of processing by changing the blending mode of the Layer Set and adding a Layer Mask to it. We have applied 50% of the sharpening set to the background and stars, and then added back more of the sharpening to the Comet by gradually lightening the mask. We could further refine the sharpening effect by varying the Opacity of the Difference Mask Set.

12. Add a Hue/Saturation Adjustment Layer above the Difference Mask Layer Set (*Layer│New Adjustment Layer│Hue/Saturation*), set the Master Saturation to +20 and click OK. The final Layers Palette is shown in **Figure 12.24**.

There are several other sharpening techniques that may be used advantageously with astronomical images, such as deconvolution and wavelets processing. Inasmuch as these algorithms are unavailable in Photoshop, I have omitted a discussion of them here. It should be noted, though, that the concept of wavelets sharpening is similar to the sequential unsharp masking techniques that we examined in this Chapter. Sharpening with both wide and narrow Radii USM settings is analogous to wavelets sharpening of low and high frequency domain information.

Appendix — Suppliers and Other Resources

Third-party scanner software
Silverfast, www.silverfast.com
VueScan, www.hamrick.com

Archival photographic storage supplies
Light Impressions, www.lightimpressionsdirect.com

File browsers and viewers
IrfanView, www.irfanview.com
ThumbsPlus, www.cerious.com
ACDSee, www.acdsystems.com

Image management (cataloging) software
IMatch, www.photools.com

FITS file format Photoshop plug-in
FITS Liberator, www.spacetelescope.org/projects/fits liberator/

Online resources for printer/paper/ink profiles
Inkjet Art Solutions, www.inkjetart.com
Digital Dog, www.digitaldog.net
Chromix, www.chromix.com

Specialized stacking software
Registar, www.aurigaimaging.com
RegiStax, http://registax.astronomy.net
Ray Gralak's Sigma program, www.gralak.com

Specialized grain and noise reduction programs
SGBNR, Pleiades Astrophoto, www.pleiades-astro-photo.com
Grain Surgery, Visual Infinity, www.visinf.com
Noise Ninja, Picture Code, www.picturecode.com
Neat Image, www.neatimage.com

Photoshop plug-ins for resampling images
Genuine Fractals, LizardTech, Inc., www.lizard-tech.com
S-Spline (Photozoom), Shortcut Software, www.short-cut.nl
Irfanview (contains Lanczos interpolation algorithm), www.irfanview.com
Pxl Smart Scale by Extensis, www.extensis.com

Stair Interpolation Photoshop plug-ins
Stairstep Image Size (freeware), Hoon Im, www.im-photography.com
SI Pro, by Fred Miranda, www.fredmiranda.com

Index